The Voice
of Misery

SUNY series in Contemporary Continental Philosophy

Dennis J. Schmidt, editor

The Voice of Misery

A Continental Philosophy of Testimony

Gert-Jan van der Heiden

Published by State University of New York Press, Albany

© 2019 State University of New York Press

All rights reserved

No part of this book may be used or reproduced in any manner whatsoever without written permission. No part of this book may be stored in a retrieval system or transmitted in any form or by any means including electronic, electrostatic, magnetic tape, mechanical, photocopying, recording, or otherwise without the prior permission in writing of the publisher.

For information, contact State University of New York Press, Albany, NY
www.sunypress.edu

Library of Congress Cataloging-in-Publication Data

Names: Heiden, Gerrit Jan van der, 1976– author.
Title: The voice of misery : a continental philosophy of testimony / Gert-Jan van der Heiden.
Description: Albany : State University of New York, 2020. | Series: SUNY series in contemporary Continental philosophy | Includes bibliographical references and index.
Identifiers: LCCN 2019011267 | ISBN 9781438477619 (hardcover : alk. paper) | ISBN 9781438477602 (pbk. : alk. paper) | ISBN 9781438477626 (ebook)
Subjects: LCSH: Testimony (Theory of knowledge) | Continental philosophy.
Classification: LCC BD238.T47 H45 2020 | DDC 121/.3—dc23
LC record available at https://lccn.loc.gov/2019011267

10 9 8 7 6 5 4 3 2 1

Why have you left the light of the sun and come here to behold the dead and the place where there is no joy?

—Homer, *The Odyssey* XI.93–94

I'd prefer to be at the threshold . . .

—*Book of Psalms* 84:10

Contents

Acknowledgments ix

Introduction xi

Part I.
To Give a Voice: Six Literary Experiments

1. Letters for the Soul 3

2. Experiment I. Socrates, the Interpreter 15

3. Experiment II. Alice, the Secretarious 33

4. Experiment III. Helena, the Poetess 53

5. Experiment IV. Johannes, the Poet 69

6. Experiment V. Bartleby, the Scrivener 87

7. Experiment VI. Er, the Messenger 107

Part II.
A Distinctive Sense of Testimony

8. Elements of Testimony 125

9. An Exceptional Attestation 151

10. A Typology of the Witness 177

Part III.
On the Threshold of Being and Language

11. An Ontology of Testimony	203
12. The Truth and Untruth of Testimony	221
13. Subject and Commitment	239
14. In Lieu of a Conclusion: Celan's Poetics of Testimony	257
Notes	271
Works Cited	303
Index	317

Acknowledgments

I would like to express my gratitude to the Freiburg Institute for Advanced Studies (FRIAS) for its hospitality that allowed me to work on parts of this study in Spring 2015. Especially, I would like to thank Günter Figal for supporting my stay there. I'm grateful for my home department, the Faculty of Philosophy, Theology and Religious Studies of Radboud University, for offering me the opportunity to continue working on this study in Fall 2016.

I would like to thank Dennis Schmidt for supporting the publication of this book in the SUNY series in Contemporary Continental Philosophy. I would like to thank Andrew Kenyon from SUNY for his advice in the process of publication and in fine-tuning the manuscript to its current form.

An earlier version of chapter 4 was published as "To Speak for the Speechless: On Erwin Mortier's *While the Gods Were Sleeping*," *International Yearbook of Hermeneutics* 17 (2018): 84–94.

Introduction

> And what else is left to resist with but the debt which each soul has contracted with the miserable and admirable indetermination from which it was born and does not cease to be born? [. . .] This debt to infancy is one which we never pay off. [. . .] It is the task of writing, thinking, literature, arts, to venture to bear witness to it.[1]
>
> —Lyotard, *L'inhumain*, 15/7

Philosophy did not begin to reflect on the meaning of bare existence with the present-day concept of *la nuda vita*, bare life. In fact, this idea has a long history. If one were interested in writing this history, one could, for instance, start with Plato and his use of the adjective *gumnos*. If one followed the political philosophical reverberation of bare life as addressed today, one could begin with a reference to *Laws*, which describes how perpetrators of a crime in a temple, if they are slaves or foreigners, are to "be cast out naked beyond the borders of the country."[2]

Yet Plato uses *gumnos* also beyond the confines of political philosophy. In the *Sophist*, for instance, the word is used to describe what is set apart or stripped bare—*apērēmōmenon*—from other beings.[3] Here, *gumnos* describes a state of being exiled or banned from the sphere to which something or someone belongs. In the *Gorgias* and the *Cratylus*, this meaning of *gumnos* is taken up in a metaphysical context when Plato describes the bare soul, that is, the soul stripped bare (*gumnoō*) from the body and from all its living conditions.[4] Thus, that which in the history of philosophy has been interpreted as the immortality of the soul in fact concerns, in these particular passages of Plato's dialogues, the soul's bare existence set apart from all that is normally attached to it. It is what survives and remains of the souls when everything else is mortified, whether it be their body, their wealth, their moral guidance by the *polis* in which they live, and so on. Rather than offering a spectacle of the soul's very own and immortal wealth, the stories on the bare soul, such as the myth of Er at the end of the *Republic*, tell the tale of the soul left to its own misery. The myth of Er bears witness to this uncanny realm of bare existence and makes it perfectly clear that this realm has nothing paradisiac or heavenly. Rather, it offers a dismal and ridiculous scene of souls in their utter formlessness, misery, and poverty, as I discuss in more detail in Part I of this study. Only in this realm, when the soul is stripped bare from all "leafage [. . .] by which he can conceal his misery," the soul can truly be judged because—as most of the examples offered by Er suggest—without this protection of what covers it, it plainly displays its own disorientation.[5] When addressing the bare soul, the interlocutors in the *Gorgias* or the *Republic* do not offer a *logos*, an argument or statement concerning, for instance, a dualism of *psuchē* and *sōma*. Rather, the bare soul can apparently only be borne witness to in an exceptional testimony, which is offered by the *muthoi* because the bare soul, the poor ending and miserable provenance of all life, is only encountered in the land of the dead, which is inaccessible to the living.

With this sense of the bare soul, we are approaching the sense of bare existence that motivates this study on testimony. It is motivated by the following question: how to experience or bear witness to the soul deprived of body and all living conditions? It is not a coincidence that in the *Gorgias*, the bare soul is only addressed in a myth; and a description of the soul's ultimate trial over the past life and pivotal choice for the life to come is offered to us at the end of the *Republic* in the soldier Er's testimony of the realm in which the dead, bare souls are gathered. This testimony, this mythical attestation articulates in the discourse of the living that which cannot be experienced by the living themselves, but which is nevertheless attested to be the experience of the bare souls—as well as up to a certain point, as I explain, the experience of the soldier and guard who is positioned at the threshold of life and death. Apparently, the notion of bareness refers to an ontological depth in Plato's thought that requires a distinctive form of testimony to be made known.

Another Platonic myth that uses the adjective *gumnos* does not locate bare existence on the other side of human life but rather at its very inception, that is, at the event of the birth of humankind. Nevertheless, the sense of *gumnos* of that which remains after human life is stripped bare of its basic living conditions is retained. The myth of this event, narrated by Protagoras in the dialogue with the same name, marks the birth of humankind by a specific lack. Whereas all other animals, the *aloga*, are provided with the natural capacities to survive and take care of their existence by nature, humankind is not. The human is thus, at the event of their birth, the animal that is offered only a bare or mere existence, without the capacities needed to provide and support it without its living conditions. Thanks to the work of Stiegler, this myth retrieved a significant place at the center of the reflection on the human's intrinsic connectedness to technics and technology. Yet by these inquiries into technology one might easily lose sight of the specific presupposition of this analysis, namely that humankind is, by its very nature, bare existence.[6] As Protagoras narrates, the human "was naked, unshod, unbedded, unarmed."[7] Hence, to be naked means in this context to be stripped bare of the basic powers to maintain and support existence. In particular, at the moment of its birth, humankind is deprived of what the ancients determined as its defining characteristic: *logos*. Originally, the human is thus a creature whose mode of existence is *infancy*, non-speaking-ness. According to the myth, this bare human life of the infant, *zōē*, only becomes a life that has language, *zōon logon echon*, when Prometheus steals the arts and fire from the gods. With this gift of *logos* and the other *technai*, the human receives the capacities to take care of themselves, that is, to preserve their existence in line with the sense of awe, *aidōs*, and justice, *dikē*, that Hermes delivers to humankind.[8] Yet it also means that the human is the creature who is always indebted to the miserable state of its infancy and that the gifts of *logos* and the other *technai* are first and foremost given as response and attestation to the bare existence from which human life unfolds.

Thus, according to this myth, *logos* is only a supplement to the human's natural condition of infancy and bare existence, the "miserable [. . .] indetermination from which it was born," as Lyotard suggests. When he writes in the passage that I used as an epigraph to this introduction that it is the task of thinking and literature to bear witness to this bare existence, which withdraws itself from the self-experience of the humans who understand themselves as always already having language and the arts, it makes sense to read the *Protagoras*, the *Gorgias*, and the *Republic* as offering such testimonies in the exceptional form of *muthoi*. These testimonies are of crucial importance because they reflect a dimension of bare existence at the heart of human life, which is forgotten and erased from human memory and experience as soon as the gift of *logos* is received or, in the case of the bare soul as depicted in the myth of Er, the soul's new turn of life has started. Only in these testimonies is this dimension of existence preserved and guarded, announced and made known.

What if—thus are the stakes of this study—we begin to understand testimony proceeding from the task to bear witness to the bare existence at the heart of human life? What if this dimension of existence were set apart from our common human experience and from our common human discourse or *logos* because the latter is somehow denied access to the realm of bare existence?[9] Would this not assign to testimony a distinctive, exceptional sense on the threshold of *logos* and bare existence? Yet perhaps testimony has always already been marked by such an exceptional sense throughout the history of its philosophical and theological usage, and perhaps the contemporary "normalization" of testimony in the epistemological approaches to this theme is the mark of the forgetfulness of this particular exceptional provenance of testimony.[10]

The stakes of such an inquiry into testimony are to (1) characterize the contemporary continental philosophical interest in bearing witness and (2) offer possibilities for a new theory of testimony. Concerning (1), there are, in fact, good reasons to claim that continental philosophy's account of testimony privileges the bearing witness to bare existence. This is not only the case in the reflections on testimony in Agamben's *Quel che resta di Auschwitz*, in which the witness bears witness to the *Muselmann*, the figure of *nuda vita*, bare life, but also in Lyotard's attention to testimony as the bearing witness to infancy. Moreover, it is already the case in Heidegger's account of attestation in *Sein und Zeit*. The call that marks attestation calls from the mode of being disclosed by the basic attunement of anxiety. Heidegger describes this mode of being as *das nackte Dasein*, "bare existence," which he also paraphrases as "the naked 'that it is and has to be,'" and "the naked 'that' in the nothingness of the world."[11] In each of these cases, the question of bearing witness is raised with respect to this exceptional phenomenon of bare existence. Leibniz, perhaps, has offered the most striking description of this realm when he speaks of the "monads that are wholly bare," *les Monades toutes nues*, which are the monads that exist at a level of perception marked by a "continual state of stupor" and that do not arrive at the capacity of *logos* and discourse.[12] Concerning (2), this means in more general terms, for a theory of testimony, that the reflection on testimony is never simply an epistemological issue but finds its motivation in the ontological question of how to acknowledge and articulate this particular realm of being. In the examples mentioned above, bearing witness is not simply a mode of speech among others, but it is a mode of speech that takes place on the threshold of bare existence, which excludes human speech, and human speech; on the threshold of the mere voice and meaningful discourse; on the threshold of *alogos* and *logos*.

This first orientation of what the stakes of a continental philosophy of testimony are suffices for this introduction. Part I as a whole offers a further orientation. Following the basic insight of Derrida as explored in *Demeure* that testimony has to be thought in relation to literature and Agamben's suggestion that literature offers experiments that allow us to experience and be oriented in a certain domain of being, this study on a continental philosophy of testimony does not set out with a definition of testimony but begins with an attempt to gain an appropriate sense of bearing witness in its reflection on some literary examples and experiments. Part I offers the report of these experiments and the accompanying reflection. Thus, a first sense of bearing witness is taking shape that guides the more theoretical reflections in Part II and Part III, in which the different elements of testimony are discussed and the specific ontological sense of testimony is developed. Therefore, let us turn without further ado to (some of) the literary texts that give to think and give to understand what bearing witness is.

Part I

To Give a Voice:
Six Literary Experiments

Chapter 1

Letters for the Soul

> But this imperative of self-knowledge is not first felt or dictated by any transparent immediacy of self-presence. It is not perceived. Only interpreted, read, deciphered. A hermeneutics assigns intuition.[1]
>
> —Derrida, *La dissémination*, 77/69

"Thus Socrates begins by sending myths off."[2] Perhaps more than any other sentence, this quote from Derrida's essay on Plato's *Phaedrus* in *La dissémination* captures the well-known, almost cliché-ridden point of departure of philosophy. Philosophy, so the story goes, is born as the interruption of myths and stories. Some, such as Badiou, embrace this initial gesture of philosophy.[3] Others, such as Derrida, problematize it and ask whether philosophy succeeds in holding myths, poems, and stories at bay. Nevertheless, both agree that Socrates bids farewell to stories *"in the name of truth."*[4] Yet is this true? Does philosophy begin thusly?

To begin, as I do, a philosophical study on the notions of witness and bearing witness by turning to six literary creations—myths, novels, and stories—is no obvious choice. What does it mean to consider these particular stories as literary experiments that help us gain an initial sense of bearing witness? A testimony makes something known to an audience not present at the testified events or not firsthandedly perceiving the testified phenomena. If we depend on stories to get a first sense and experience of bearing witness, this means that we approach these stories as bearing witness to bearing witness; and this means that the truth and the meaning of bearing witness as explored in this study somehow depend on or at least begin with, find their *archē* in a *literary* testimony. Does this not sound as an oxymoron—"a literary testimony"? Is testimony, insofar as it is concerned with the truth of the events it bears witness to or the phenomena of which it speaks, not called upon, not *sworn* to stay away from any suggestion of fiction, illusion, or perjury? In this sense, there seems to be a certain kinship between the initial gesture of philosophy and that of testimony. Philosophy and testimony share a dependence and insistence on truth over fiction and over the literary. Should we not say of both philosophy and testimony that *either* they are "*in the name of truth*," sworn to truth, sending off the stories . . . *or* they are not?

Moreover, this first delineation of philosophy (as well as testimony) gets blurred as soon as one, for instance, considers the context in which "Socrates begins by sending myths off." Not only are there at least two more myths that appear later in the *Phaedrus*, but there are also different kinds of letters at work in this dialogue, such as a text that Phaedrus hides under his cloak and a Delphic inscription of which Socrates speaks. They, apparently, are not sent off. In fact, they rather seem to determine the course of the dialogue, as Derrida has argued. Thus, different experiments of letters are found at the heart of this dialogue, this "gardens of letters," grown with different aims and to different effects.[5] Yet these letters seem to share one characteristic. They impose themselves when philosophy is incapable of simply speaking in the name of truth, when truth is not present, not there in its immediacy or transparency. A philosopher can only speak in the name of truth when knowing the truth. Yet a philosopher, if we follow the Socratic rather than the Aristotelian intuition, is the one who lacks knowledge of the truth and knows of this, their own miserable condition. Similarly, one might suggest that a witness can only speak truthfully, be sworn to the truth, when knowing the truth. Yet we do not know whether a witness knows the truth or is even concerned with such a knowledge. We only know they claim to bear witness to the truth, but what this exactly involves is unclear. Moreover, even the witnesses themselves do not know this, separated as they are from the original event of which they testify by the distance of time and the possible distortions of memory.

To bear witness, perhaps, is not so much to speak "*in the name of truth*" or to live truth, but rather and in the first place to give a voice to this particular poverty in human life. Below I show how this can be traced in the *Phaedrus*. In the literary experiments that follow in Part I, this is the main concern: not how to live truthfully but how to give a voice to a certain misery in and of human life, to what is exempt from paradigmatic and exemplary lives, to what is kept in reserve and can only be arrived at by fostering a certain mode of reservedness and restraint with respect to paradigms and examples, with respect to particular forms that are imposed or supposed. It is the wager of Part I that some stories, novels, and myths offer experiments of such a bearing witness. In this sense, when it comes to bearing witness, I propose to speak in the register of Lyotard who speaks of *misère de la philosophie*, the misery and poverty of philosophy. As he so often argues, the letter, both philosophical and literary, is called to bear witness to this misery.[6]

Literary Experiments on Truth

An important explication of the idea of a literary experiment can be found in Agamben's reading of Melville's *Bartleby, the Scrivener*—and this story itself is discussed in the fifth experiment. Agamben suggests that literary experiments are in a fundamental way different from scientific ones. Linking, in a more or less Heideggerian fashion, thinking to poetry, he argues that both "poetry and thinking conduct experiments," and he continues:

> These experiments do not simply concern the truth or falsity of hypotheses, the occurrence or nonoccurrence of something, as in scientific experiments; rather, they call into question Being itself, before or beyond its determination as true or false. These experiments are without truth, for truth is what is at issue in them.[7]

Thus, literary experiments are "without truth, for truth is what is at issue in them." We now discern a tension between what is done "*in the name of truth*" and what is experimented "without truth." The literary experiment is not concerned with establishing the truth of what happened and does not presuppose truth. Rather, it is without truth because truth itself is the issue that needs to be addressed. Therefore, this experiment cannot be done "in the name of truth." After all, whatever is done "in the name of X" presupposes X as background and horizon. Rather than truth, the stakes seem to be a particular mode of life because such an experiment "jeopardizes" one's "very mode of existence." As Agamben writes in full:

> Whoever submits himself to these experiments jeopardizes not so much the truth of his own statements as the very mode of his existence; he undergoes an anthropological change that is just as decisive in the context of the individual's natural history as the liberation of the hand by the erect position was for the primate or as was, for the reptile, the transformation of limbs that changed it into a bird.[8]

The scientific experiment is concerned with judging the truth of one's statements or of the existence of a particular object. The literary experiment is concerned with something else. Perhaps the best term to capture what the stakes of this latter experiment are is the term "bearing witness." The literary experiment bears witness to forms of life and modes of existence that were absent from readers' lives before but are now intuited by them through the intuition this experiment assigns to them and by following the experience the experiment offers.[9] By this testimony, literature is no longer simply *poiēsis* but becomes a form of *ēthopoiēsis*, the making of a new mode of life.[10] Thus, the literary experiment exposes the reader to a real peril because existence itself is at stake. This existence is apparently not simply "there" to be described by statements and theories, nor is there a paradigm available that it can simply follow to exist properly. Literature, some literature, offers experiments that bear witness to these modes of existence that form an exception to the paradigms that were being followed.[11] The experiments I interpret not only bear witness to such exceptions but also speak of bearing witness itself and of the witness that bears witness to such exceptions.

Letters in the Phaedrus

These considerations lead us back to the initial gesture of philosophy. Would it not be possible that philosophy, rather than speaking in the name of truth, is concerned with an attestation that is found in *one* of the letters of the *Phaedrus*? "Thus Socrates begins by sending myths off."[12] Indeed? Is this true and is this done "*in the name of truth*"? Does the notion of truth explain why Socrates dismisses the myths, and why he turns to the question of self-knowledge, in accordance with the imperative that is written in the *Delphikon gramma*, as the opening scene of the *Phaedrus* tells us?[13] Although the opening scene does contain the adjective "true" (*alēthes*), this adjective is not used by Socrates and is not used in relation to self-knowledge. Rather, Phaedrus uses it when asking Socrates whether he thinks that the legend on Boreas, the God of the northern wind, whose story is situated at the place where Socrates and Phaedrus are at that moment, is actually true: "But tell me, Socrates, in the name of Zeus, do you really believe that that legend is true?"[14]

To grasp the importance of Socrates's response to Phaedrus's question, it might be enlightening to hear it in the key of Aristotle's famous description of the activity of first philosophy. For Aristotle, first philosophy is only possible if we have leisure, *scholē*, a particular mode of time that is only at our disposal if we do not have to worry about our basic needs in life but are free to reflect disinterestedly on whatever theoretical problem we deem worthwhile.[15] Only in this way can we aspire to attain the highest, divine knowledge, which serves no goal outside itself. Whereas the philosopher, as Aristotle claims, shares with the lover of myth (*philomuthos*) a sense of wonder, the philosopher transcends this wonder and is capable of truly knowing.[16] In Aristotle's *Metaphysics*, myth is genuinely interrupted and sent off because it is of no avail to the philosopher. Unlike the *philomuthos*, the *philosophos* is a friend of truth more than of wonder and stories.

When hearing Derrida's reading of the opening scene of the *Phaedrus* in this key, it seems as if he transfers this Aristotelian account of truth and philosophy to the *Phaedrus* so that it can orient his interpretation of Socrates's words. Yet Socrates's response wanders off in another direction.[17] Consider what he says on the myths on Boreas: "Anyone who does not believe in them, who wants to explain them away and make them plausible by means of some sort of rough ingenuity [*sophia*], will need a great deal of time [*scholēs*]. But I have no time for such things."[18] After this comment, Socrates uses the verb *chairein*. What he bids farewell to are not myths, the realm of stories or literature as such, but rather the inquiry into the question of whether the myths are true. It is to those who do not believe the myths and who therefore engage themselves in offering a more "scientific" explanation of the phenomena the legend tries to explain mythically that Socrates says: "This is of no avail to me." He insists: "I do not have enough leisure to engage in a disinterested inquiry into the truth of *whatsoever*, that is, into the truth of facts, phenomena and circumstances that do not *urgently demand* to be addressed." Socrates refuses to get involved in these matters. Instead, to save time, he simply accepts "what is generally believed" about them.[19] Thus, he anticipates Agamben's distinction between two types of experiment: not the inquiry of nature by scientific means, but the questioning of the modes of human existence—"Know thyself!"—receives philosophical primacy.[20]

For Socrates, compared to the question that does occupy his mind and soul, the attempt to attain a truthful, scientific account of the legend of Boreas is a ludicrous enterprise. For him, rather than inquiring into the truth of the myths of Boreas, he is guided by the demand of the Delphic inscription, "and it really seems to me ridiculous [*geloion*] to look into other things before I have understood that."²¹ Hence, rather than distinguishing truth from myth, Socrates is involved in distinguishing literature from literature, the letter of Delphi from the letter of the legend of Boreas.

Yet by which mark, by which exceptional letter can such a distinction be made? Moreover, when insisting on such a distinction, do we not run the risk of repeating the Platonic gesture that has given rise to Derrida's hesitation over the distinction between, for instance, good and bad writing?²² A distinction in the realm of writing, of the letter, and of literature is indeed at stake here, but it is not a distinction in the name of truth, certain knowledge, or fixed determinations. Rather, it is one that derives from a sense of distress and urgency found in the uncanniness that one is to oneself. This distress goes hand in hand with its "opposite," the ludicrous spectacle offered by those who do not recognize the distress and urgency of which Socrates speaks here. To anticipate the sixth experiment, let me note that the reference to an absurd or ludicrous spectacle is not limited to the *Phaedrus*. The same word, *geloios*, appears in the myth of Er where it is used to describe the absurd and pitiful (*eleeinēn*) spectacle of the souls in the afterlife who have to choose a new life for themselves and who lack the capacity to "distinguish the good life from the bad."²³ There is a fundamental kinship between the Delphic inscription and the spectacle offered by the myth of Er. Neither of them is a *description* of the self, which one subsequently might judge to be true or false. Rather, they articulate and bear witness to a particular demand or imperative. The Delphic inscription demands, but does not grant self-knowledge; and the myth of Er demands, but does not grant righteousness.²⁴

When Derrida writes that Socrates's bidding farewell to myths "will be twice interrupted in order to welcome" two other, Platonic myths in the course of the *Phaedrus*, he seems still too much indebted to the distinction between *muthos* and *logos*, to reading the *Phaedrus* in light of the value of truth. *Muthos* intervenes in the argumentative course of the dialogue when something needs to be said that exceeds the argumentative discourse of *logos*.²⁵ Indeed, as Derrida keenly observes, when the myth returns in the *Phaedrus*, it is done so "in the name of writing."²⁶ Yet Plato's dialogues do not use *whatever* story, and the myths do not return in the name of *whatever* writing. In the *Phaedrus*, Socrates bids farewell to the pursuit of indifferent truths, because another, urgent task demands all the time he has at his disposal. As Derrida also acknowledges, the true Socratic discovery is not the truth but the "*imperative* of self-knowledge" that speaks from the Delphic letter.²⁷ With this letter, Derrida in fact marks the difference between imperative and truth: offered only as a written command, the truth of self-knowledge "is not perceived. Only interpreted, read, deciphered. A hermeneutics *assigns* intuition."

This quote leads us to a crucial question. What kind of hermeneutics are we dealing with here? What is a hermeneutics that can *assign* an intuition? And how is it related to the letter? To capture the radical dimension of Derrida's proposal in this formulation, one should be aware that, in its more classical sense, hermeneutics presupposes a horizon of meaning that orients the interpreter, thus offering him an a priori intuition or a pre-understanding, as Heidegger and Gadamer might put it. According to Derrida, however, the hermeneutics we are dealing with here somehow springs from the letter. It is a *hermeneutics of the letter*. Yet this "of" in the expression "hermeneutics of the letter" wavers between its objective and subjective genitive sense. This wavering captures the stakes of the differentiation that Socrates introduces, and it corresponds to a difference between two letters in the *Phaedrus* that accompany its composition until the end.

On the one hand, on the side of the objective genitive, we have the book that Phaedrus carries under his cloak. This book seduces Socrates to leave the city and his natural habitat.[28] This hidden *logos* represents the signifier that opens up an endless play of referral, signification, and truths. Here, as a signifier, the letter has no natural or original meaning to disclose. Only by reading, interpreting, or deciphering, as Derrida writes, only by a hermeneutics of the letter, an intuition or orientation is assigned to it. The reading of the letter thus opens up the very horizon of meaning in which the reader subsequently orients themselves. Consequently, to conceive of the letter as what naturally comes equipped with intuition and orientation is to confuse hermeneutic cause and effect. Yet the letter is, in this sense of the genitive, what offers itself as what welcomes truth and meaning to be assigned to it. This duality between the letter that invites interpretations and the letter that is the very sign of their incompleteness and inadequacy asking for other interpretations is strikingly captured by Derrida's account of dissemination.

Yet, on the other hand, in the composition of the *Phaedrus*, the value of dissemination seems not applicable to the *Delphikon gramma*. This other letter does not hide or conceal anything in particular. It has no truth or meaning in store for us that it promises to disclose when we attempt to interpret it. It also does not inaugurate an endless play of signification and truths. Rather, it is simply the articulation of a demand;

this letter bears witness to the uncanniness of human existence and calls (back) the human to this uncanniness. This suggests a second sense of the hermeneutics of the letter in which the letter is the *subject*. The letter and the literary are interpreters that articulate a demand that stems from a certain uncanniness of the self. In this letter, Socrates does not perceive an answer to the question "Who am I?" but he rather hears the articulation of an agony of doubt: "Am I a beast more complicated and savage than Typhon, or am I a tamer, simpler animal with a share in a divine and gentle nature?"[29] If the divine and gentle nature of the human refers to the truly human capacity to speak and reason, to have *logos*, then the image of Typhon, with its many heads and "with all the tongues of all his throats," does not simply refer to the category of the animal within which the human would occupy a special place, but rather to the monstrous, mythical creature that challenges Zeus, that challenges any divine order.[30] In this case, the hermeneutics of the letter also "*assigns* intuition," not by being deciphered but by bearing witness to the uncanniness of human existence that demands humans to take care of their soul. Only by the letter that gives to experience this urgent demand does one become capable of discerning among the many letters and myths, the ones to which to pay heed.

When Socrates at the end of the *Phaedrus* distinguishes good from bad writing, as Derrida so keenly points out, distinguishes the writing of dissemination from the writing in the soul, it is not done simply "*in the name of truth*." It is not a distinction between a writing that lacks and one that provides truth. To interpret the value of fertility solely in terms of truth and to replace it by the fertility of the sowing of meaning runs the risk of missing the specific Socratic concern.[31] By interpreting the fertility of writing in the soul along these lines, one suggests that Socrates has already solved or successfully followed the Delphic inscription. Yet there is another motive at stake in the introduction of the idea of writing in the soul. By writing in the soul, the letter that is written becomes *empsuchos*. Perhaps one should offer a translation of *empsuchos* that marks the similarity to the English word "embodied," and translate *empsuchos* as "ensouled." The *logos* that is subsequently spoken is a *logos empsuchos*.[32] Yet this writing in the soul is not necessarily the writing of truth. In its most favorable version, it ensouls the demand of the Delphic letter. In its most harmful version, it "ensouls" the ridiculousness of those people who live in the conceit and illusion of wisdom, in *doxosophia*. This illusion is, however, no less written in the soul, as Socrates makes clear to Hippocrates in the *Protagoras* when Hippocrates is about to consult the famous sophist. Socrates points out that Hippocrates does not see the true stakes and the genuine peril of "writing in the soul."[33] The sophist's writing in the soul is not less effective or fertile than the writing in the soul of the Delphic letter. Thus, the *Phaedrus* is part of the Socratic strategy of retrieving among the different kind of letters, those that write in the soul in order to capture the true strength and danger of writing. The letter does not only open up a play of signification, truths, and referral, but the letter can also write in the soul—the Delphic demand *as well as* what places the soul "among the ridiculous in rank and nature"—and assign an intuition. The philosopher, for Socrates, is thus never the one who has or possesses truth and knowledge. To claim to have or to possess knowledge is rather a sign of *doxosophia*, of the conceit of wisdom. The philosopher is rather the one who ensouls one particular letter—or some particular letters—namely the demand of the Delphic letter, that is, the letter that recalls the claims to truth in both speech and writing and calls them back to the demand of human life and soul at the core of human language. One could also say that it is not the primordial task of human language to express truths and knowledge but rather to bear witness to this demand stemming from the uncanniness of human life, which is an uncanniness that cannot be separated from the risk of writing in the soul—be it may what helps or what injures. To this demand, in turn, corresponds a promise of language that it is not limited to the endless play of signification, truth, and referral but that it can indeed write the letters that succor the soul.

Articulating the Voice of Misery

Thus, the opening scene of the *Phaedrus* is important because this attestation of human misery is not borne witness to by the human voice itself. In the *Phaedrus*, a letter is the interpreter that bears this message. In the *Republic*, it is an *apologos* or story that bears witness to this human misery. This suggests that one aspect of this misery is not accessible by (and not capable of) an immediate or direct self-attestation. With respect to this claim, as I do in Part II, I will have to engage with Heidegger's account of *Selbstbezeugung* from which a different intuition seems to speak. The Socratic-Platonic take on this problem is as follows. There is something in human language that suppresses the human voice that would immediately express its misery and distress. In this sense, the detour along the letter and along literature suggests a more primordial absence of a direct attestation of this misery by the human itself. The letter and literature or, rather, some letters and some stories, can succor the human and be heard to attest to this absence of attestation. Yet the letter itself is marked by a double hermeneutics; therefore, it has the nature of a double, ambiguous interpreter: limited to the realm of semiotics, it is a signifier opening up an endless play of signification, truths, referral, and deferral; yet it may, sometimes, perhaps, give way to a voice in distress, offer a refuge to the misery in human life.

Given this indecisiveness or undecidability of the letter, the stakes of the six literary experiments that follow in this first part of the study are easily explained: they run the risk that the letter is nothing but a signifier in a play of endless signification, truth, and referral, and they run the risk that the letter injures and disables the soul, but they do so in light of the chance that the letter of literature, perhaps, articulates voices of misery and thus bears witness to the demand of these voices. This is also why they are called experiments. Etymologically, experiments comprise peril. There is a risk and danger in turning to literature for one's orientations and intuitions; the literary also misleads, confuses, fictionalizes, and conceals; it can create the sense or effect of reality where there is none, a mere signifier in the guise of meaning and truth. Yet without running this risk, we lack the chance, the promise, and the demand of a testimony of literature, of letters that are sometimes, perhaps, on the side of what lacks form and voice.

Finally, as for the choice of the six literary examples that follow, I can only say that these texts rather than others offered the opportunity to experience the problems of witness and bearing witness. Also in the chronological order of this study, they were the first sources of inspiration and intuition. Because these literary experiments offer their specific directions in interpreting and approaching the topics of testimony and giving a voice, and because the orientations they offer have also directed my course through the texts of present-day philosophers with whom I engage in the other chapters of this book, it only seemed accurate to analyze these experiments here to explicate the questions and orientations they offer. The first experiment is conducted in a part of Plato's dialogue *Theaetetus*; the second in the novel *The Little Girl Who Was Too Fond of Matches* by the Francophone Canadian novelist Gaétan Soucy; the third in the novel *While the Gods Were Sleeping* by the Dutch-speaking Belgian novelist Erwin Mortier; the fourth in Søren Kierkegaard's *Fear and Trem-*

bling; the fifth in Herman Melville's *Bartleby, the Scrivener*; and the sixth in the myth of Er that closes Plato's *Republic*. Each of these experiments introduces a witness who gives voice to something that cannot speak for itself or someone who cannot speak for themselves. In each case, I analyze what these fictional witnesses are doing when they bear witness and give a voice to whom or what cannot speak for itself. Each of these experiments is therefore named after the witness it introduces, except for the fifth one, as I explain below: Socrates, the Interpreter. Alice, the Secretarious. Helena, the born Poetess. Johannes, the Poet. Bartleby, the Scrivener. Er, the Messenger.

Chapter 2

Experiment I

Socrates, the Interpreter

I shall be the interpreter (*hermēneusō*) of what he would say if he were alive and able to speak to you now.[1]

—Plato, *Eighth Letter* 355a

Living speech, as Heidegger argues in his reflections on Plato's dialogues, forms the very core of the ancient Greek experience of truth and language. According to him, this would be the reason for Plato to write dialogues so that, "before the end of Greek thought [. . .] once more," this thought "wanted to speak about itself and attest to [*bezeugt*] the essential rank [*Wesensrank*] the word enjoys" in the human relation to *alētheia*.[2] Hence, according to Heidegger, in addition to the different topics that the dialogues discuss, the very form Plato adopted for his writings is a testimony attesting to the essential role of speech and *logos* in Greek thought. In line with Heidegger's remarks, Nancy notes: "the object of the *Meno*, the *Theaetetus*, the *Sophist*, the *Symposium*, in order only to cite them, is it not always likewise the dialogue or the dialogicity [*dialogicité*] as such?"[3] Plato's dialogues not only treat or discuss a particular topic, but also attest to the type of *logos* at stake in the dialogue.

Both Nancy and Heidegger relate this particular attestation to *logos* to a primordial sense of hermeneutics they find in Plato's dialogue *Ion*. Before referring to the art of the explication of meaning, the Greek verb *hermēneuō* and the noun *hermēneus* mean "to interpret" and "interpreter" in another sense. Heidegger's remarks on this matter are rather concise and limited to the comment that in the *Ion*, the *hermēneus* or interpreter is in the first place the messenger of the gods for Plato.[4] The interpreter thus is not in the first place the one who explicates meaning but the one who hands down meaning and opens up the horizon of the mortals by a message from the realm of the divine. Nancy elaborates Heidegger's hints and suggests that for Plato, one of the basic constituents of a dialogue is sharing voices.[5]

One might be inclined to interpret this idea of the sharing of voices as follows. In a dialogue, more than one voice speaks, and these voices share in one dialogue. The participants respond to and question each other, but their voices remain distinct and do not melt into one voice. A dialogue always speaks with (at least) two voices, and if there is a form of *Einstimmigkeit* at stake in a dialogue, as for instance Gadamer argues, it will always be the end of dialogue.

Yet for Nancy, the sharing of voices also concerns something else. In Plato's *Ion*, this sharing is illustrated by the famous image of a chain of iron rings that transmits a magnetic force. This image depicts how a divine power inspires the voices of poets and rhapsodes and is communicated to an audience.[6] This image needs to be understood in the right way, according to Nancy. It does not claim that there is a preceding, original voice of the gods. The words of a god are not spoken with the voice of this god itself, but rather *first* spoken and handed down by the voice of the poet and subsequently that of the rhapsode, who both are intermediaries that deliver the words of the gods to an audience. The poet does not simply translate divine words into human language, but rather gives a first linguistic expression to a divine power: the poetic voice allows the divine power to appear in and as *logos*. Hence, there is no first, original divine voice. Normally, the ones who bring messages or tidings are a mere supplement to an original speaker whose words they transmit. Yet the poet is not a supplement to an original voice; the interpreter's voice is rather an original supplement, a shared voice: the god speaks *only* through the voice of the poet. Plato calls this original supplement *hermēneus*, an interpreter, who as a proper heir of Hermes carries over from the divine into the mortal realm.[7]

For Nancy, these considerations are supposed to say something on dialogue itself. Yet the particular structure of mediation, interpreting, and messaging he finds in the figure of the poet and the rhapsode does not concern a dialogue in the strict sense of the word. This is the case for at least two reasons. First, the poetic song sung to an audience is not an example of a dialogue at all because there is no play of question and answer going on. There is a unilateral communication from the divine through the interpreter to the mortals. Therefore, it is not immediately clear in which sense the model of the poetic song can help us to understand dialogue itself. Yet it might help us to rethink what we mean by the interpreter, *hermēneus*, and how the hermeneutic activity brings something from the outside, from another, divine realm into the realm of discursiveness to which dialogues belong. Second, because the gods speak only *through* the poets, divine speech is never spoken with the living, speaking, and present voice of the gods. Instead, the poet or rhapsode *gives a voice*—or is forced to lend a voice—to the gods so that the latter may be heard in the first place. In this sense, the authentic voice of the gods is absent: the voice of the gods is only present for mortals as and in the poetic or rhapsodic voice.

What these two considerations show is that Nancy's account of the sharing of voices dis- or replaces our attention from the living, speaking, and present voices in a dialogue to the particular nature of the voice of the interpreter who lends their voice to someone or something that cannot speak (for) itself at a specific instance or event of speech. Living speech, the basic ingredient on which dialogue depends, is thus haunted by absent voices. The poetic song is not a dialogue and does not have the discursiveness of dialogue—in fact, this is a theme in the *Ion* itself because the dialogue on the rhapsode is not a rhapsodic activity itself. Nevertheless, the structure of the interpreter that Nancy discerns in Plato's *Ion* still affects the nature of dialogue because one of the partners in conversation may always be an interpreter who lets the dialogue be haunted by what cannot speak at this very moment, thus opening up the dialogue to a realm beyond its own taking place. More precisely, the interpreter, by speaking for someone else, introduces a voice in the dialogue that is not their own. In these cases, the interpreter speaks with a double voice; the first voice speaks to allow the second, absent voice to come to speech. The interpreter bears witness to this other voice in the dialogue by interpreting it.

Plato's dialogues offer many examples of this particular structure and are populated by interpreters speaking for gods, for people who cannot speak because they are withdrawn from the dialogue, for people who are dead and can no longer speak, and for people who do not speak up for themselves. The interpreter thus interrupts and transforms the basic condition of living speech. The epigraph of this first experiment offers an instantiation of this form of interpreting in Plato's texts in which the speaker does not speak on his own behalf, but rather lends his voice to another speech. In fact, this is clearly visible from the context of this epigraph: a direct form of speech follows it as if the voice of the other is speaking here and now, among the living. The epigraph itself reminds the ones who are addressed by direct speech that follows that they do not hear the voice of the speaker, but rather of the forefathers or an absent speaker, of someone who is withdrawn from the argument or conversation.

The Contours of a "Proper" Dialogue

These introductory remarks indicate how, out of Heidegger's and Nancy's interest in the sense of living speech and the sense of the hermeneutical, a theme emerges at the horizon of their reflections that they do not directly address themselves, namely the theme of the interpreter's double voice and the interpreter's bearing witness to another voice. In this first experiment, I explore this theme by discussing a striking example of such an interpreter from Plato's *Theaetetus*. In this dialogue, (at least) one of the speakers gives a voice to someone who can no longer speak and thus allows the others to share in the voice of this absent, dead speaker. A "proper" dialogue is limited to a conversation between speakers who are present at the conversation; this limit applies to a dialogue because in it, speakers aim to arrive at understanding, and this particular aim requires that the opinions that are expressed can be examined and interrogated so that the speakers can arrive at a mutual understanding of the truth of the expressed opinions. Yet we often are confronted with opinions or claims inherited from people who are not present at the dialogue. How can a discussion involving these opinions or claims take place if there is not someone who is willing, for the sake of argument, to adopt the role of the "owner" of this opinion or claim? Because the first part of Plato's *Theaetetus* stages exactly this situation, it allows me to examine how and in which sense it is imperative for a dialogue not to limit itself to the voices of the present speakers but to be able to give a voice to those who are absent as well.

The *Theaetetus* introduces three speakers: Socrates, a young Theaetetus, and Theodorus, the teacher of Theaetetus; and it is important to know from the outset that, at first, Theodorus refuses to participate in the conversation. To understand the meaning and function of this refusal is the basic question that guides my inquiry here. To introduce this inquiry, let me start with the following long quote in which Socrates seems to confirm the aforementioned, self-evident conception of a "proper" dialogue:

> Only I beg that you will observe this condition: do not be unjust in your questions. It is the height of unreasonableness [*pollē alogia*] that a person who professes to care [*epimeleisthai*] for moral goodness should be consistently unjust in discussion. I mean by injustice, in this connection, the behavior of a man who does not take care to keep controversy [*diatribas*] distinct from discussion [*dialegomenos*]; a man who forgets that in controversy he may play about and trip up [*sphallē*] his opponent as often as he can, but that in discussion he must be serious, he must keep on helping his opponent to his feet again, and point out to him only those of his slips [*sphalmata*] which are due to himself or to the intellectual society which he has previously frequented. If you observe this distinction, those who associate with you will blame themselves for their confusion and their difficulties, not you. They will seek your company, and think of you as their friend [*philēsousin*]; but they will loathe themselves, and seek refuge from themselves in philosophy, in the hope that they may thereby become different people and be rid forever of the men that they once were. [. . .]
> So, if you take my advice, as I said before, you will sit down with us without ill will or hostility, in a kindly spirit [*ileō tē dianoia*]. You will genuinely try to find out [*hōs alēthōs skepsē*] what our meaning is when we maintain (a) that [. . .].[8]

There are many issues that demand our attention in this quote. I limit myself to three.

(1) First, Socrates introduces a (famous) distinction between a mere controversy or debate and a true philosophical dialogue. Whereas a speaker in the former is focused on tripping up the other, a speaker in the latter is trying to help the other back on their feet whenever they slip so that they may stand (and be) upright again. The usage of the verb *sphallō*, to trip up, and the noun *sphalma*, to trip or stumble, refers back to an earlier moment in the dialogue in which Theodorus uses the same verb when he is asked by Socrates to engage in the dialogue. Theodorus refuses to do so *because* he fears that Socrates's arguments will make him fall.[9] We

discuss below what is at stake in this refusal. For now, it is enough to note that by using the same verbs, Socrates directly responds to Theodorus's fear by saying that only in a debate is someone tripped up, whereas in a proper dialogue nobody needs to fear being tripped up. Hence, Socrates implicitly says: "Whatever the reason for your refusal, Theodorus, it is not valid in a discussion with me because I only engage in proper dialogues." Consequently, the distinction between debate and dialogue is not simply a matter of defining dialogue; rather, it has a strategic role in the composition of this dialogue: Socrates introduces this distinction to counter and overcome Theodorus's refusal to participate in a dialogue.

(2) Second, the distinction between debate and dialogue is understood in terms of unjust versus just, unreasonable versus reasonable, and ill will or hostility versus a kindly spirit. For dialogue to be possible, the speakers need to be of a certain character and need to display a particular comportment. They are required to be just to the questions that are posed to them; they should be reasonable, that is, a harmony should exist between the care for virtue and the just approach to the questions that are raised; and they are supposed to have a kindly spirit toward what is said in order to truly capture the point that is being put forward by the other speaker. One might say that for Socrates, the care for virtue or excellence, which is the way in which one cares for the self, is the very presupposition of philosophical dialogue: this care needs to be affirmed or professed because otherwise one will not understand why another attitude than the kindly spirit to the other's questions and remarks is unreasonable and unjust.

(3) Third, the care for moral goodness is not only the presupposition of a philosophical dialogue but also the goal of such a dialogue. Socrates introduces a hierarchy in this dialogue: those who are tripped up need to be helped, and those who help put the first ones straight. Putting the others straight so that they stand upright is the goal of the dialogical inquiries: once people have their slips pointed out to them in philosophical dialogue, they will seek "refuge from themselves in philosophy." We see here that the care of the self, as Foucault has pointed out, is not a care about the self in its present state, but rather a care that aims at a transformation of the self so that the self is prepared to receive the truth: the fallen ones seek refuge in philosophy because philosophy may transform them.[10] They hide in philosophy in the hope of becoming "different people and be rid forever of the men that they once were." It is in this sense that philosophical dialogue is concerned with *parrēsia*, a speech that consists in frankly telling the truth: the philosopher is the

one who tells the truth about the fallen state of the ones with whom he speaks, and because of this, the ones who learn about their true state will consider this philosopher as their true friend.

Yet, for our purposes, it is important to note that this reference to friendship and to taking refuge in philosophy to be saved is *also* part of the strategy Socrates develops in this part of the *Theaetetus* to make Theodorus speak and engage in the dialogue. This second dimension of Socrates's comments—his engagement with Theodorus's refusal to participate in this dialogue—does not lie within the confines of a *proper* dialogue; it rather belongs to its threshold. This is not only the case because Theodorus is not yet properly participating in the conversation and stating his points of view, but also and more importantly because, at this stage of the dialogue, Socrates is mainly concerned with seducing Theodorus to *enter* the dialogue. In the above long quote from the *Theaetetus*, philosophy and dialogue are portrayed as something desirable in which one has to participate if one truly cares for virtue and for one's self. Socrates urges Theodorus to affirm dialogue—an affirmation that only happens when he actually participates. In this sense, one would misunderstand Socrates if one would only find a description, definition, or delimitation of dialogue here. Rather, Socrates's words attest to the stakes of philosophy and are to be understood as a call, *euchē*, to those, such as Theodorus, who have not yet affirmed these stakes by sharing in dialogue.

To fully understand what happens in this call and attestation, it is necessary to consider more carefully what and why Theodorus exactly refuses. The reading I offer here might go against the grain of what one tends to read in Plato, but it seems to me that the composition of this part of the *Theaetetus* does invite such a reading. Therefore, let us highlight some crucial passages to understand Theodorus's refusal.

Socrates Speaking Directly

The prologue of the dialogue sheds an interesting light on Heidegger's comments that Plato's dialogues remember and mimic living speech. The prologue, which precedes the proper dialogue but which nevertheless belongs to the text that we know as the *Theaetetus*, is important because it situates the dialogue and its questions and thus attunes us to its content in a particular way. With respect to the questions we are raising here—what is the role of the interpreter and how do they affect the dialogue's living speech—the prologue offers some important hints and insights. Three characters appear: Euclides, Terpsion, and Euclides's anonymous slave. Euclides tells Terpsion that he went to the harbor, where he met Theaetetus, who had just returned from battle. Terpsion asks how he found him: "Alive or dead?" Euclides responds: "Alive; but that's about all one could say."[11] Theaetetus is barely alive; he wavers in between life and death. Because the proper dialogue that is about to be presented took place years ago, when Theaetetus was still young, we may assume that both Socrates and Theodorus are dead—the death of Socrates is actually mentioned. In honor of Theaetetus, who is on the verge of dying, Euclides proposes to read the text of the conversation the young Theaetetus once had with Socrates and his teacher Theodorus. In fact, as Euclides informs Terpsion, Socrates told him the story, and after writing the text, he checked with Socrates about whether his rendering of the story was correct, thus establishing the trustworthiness of the account. Yet, as Euclides adds, the style in which he wrote it down was different from the one Socrates used to narrate it to him. Rather than adopting the indirect mode—"As Socrates told me . . ."—he wrote the dialogue in a direct mode, mimicking a proper dialogue and a living speech, thus making Socrates talk directly to Theaetetus and Theodorus, as Euclides also says: "I have made him talk directly to them."[12]

The effect of this style becomes clear when Euclides orders his slave to read it. When the slave reads, because of the direct mode of the text, he thus *lends* his voice to Socrates, Theaetetus, and Theodorus. The fact that the slave is anonymous thus carries an additional significance: his reading voice is completely at the disposal of the voices of the dead and the dying and adds nothing of itself—no name, that is, no character, no opinion, and no form of itself. This implies that writing has a very specific character here. It is neither only a supplement, as Derrida argues, nor only that of which the meaning is to be understood. Rather, the structure of supplement is doubled: the written text as the supplement of the living voice is itself supplemented with another voice that is at the disposal of the written words and allows them to come to speech again. Without someone lending their voice, the words and voices of the dead and those who are about to die will not be heard. Writing is not conceived as what merely *lacks* the original voice of the father, but rather as what *demands* a voice that will be lent to it so that it can speak again, can address and affect. The living voice is thus not so much the origin or foundation of meaning but rather the supplement of writing granting it the capacity to speak and communicate.

The voice of Euclides's slave is not the original voice, and it does not possess or master itself. Rather, this other voice attests to a doubled structure in which the words of Socrates are spoken again, and the conversation of Socrates, Theodorus, and Theaetetus takes place again and is heard as taking place, as a repetition of an unrepeatable event of speech. Whether or not the slave understands what he reads is not the heart of the matter. Perhaps the slave can enact the voices of the three participants in the conversation better if he has an understanding of the text; yet this understanding is not what is at stake in this interpretive work. The slave is rather like an actor who brings characters alive on stage and shows them as alive. Consequently, what we encounter here is not a representation of the conversation; in one sense, it would even be misguided to call the slave a mediator because his voice is Socrates's voice (and Theaetetus's voice and Theodorus's voice). Rather, the conversation is presented and performed as in a play or a musical performance, which is not a representation but the only true presentation. Moreover, it is through the slave's voice that we hear Socrates speaking directly. Hence, Socrates's speech is not rendered in another medium, such as writing, but is present in the speaking voice of the slave. In this sense, the voice of the slave is truly a slave's voice, that is, a voice that does not speak for itself and does not belong to itself but speaks for another and is used to make this other, died-out voice be heard.[13] The slave lends his voice to another so that this other voice takes over his voice and addresses and affects the listeners directly and without mediation.[14]

The phenomenon of giving a voice is thus inscribed in the prologue of the *Theaetetus*, and it may well offer one of the answers to the question of why Plato writes dialogues. When someone takes on the role of the interpreter of the dead or the barely living—and we come across this particular dimension of the barely living again when discussing Agamben's conception of testimony in Part II and Part III—these voices are heard again as if speaking to us immediately. It is thus a form of mediation that aims to become diaphanous or transparent: the interpreter is supposed to disappear fully in the voices to which they give a voice. The anonymity of the slave is a clear indication of this. In this sense, to let a nameless slave read the text is not only customary in Plato's ancient culture, but also befits the particular form of a mediation *that is not heard*: Euclides and Terpsio only hear the words of Socrates and the others, directly addressing and affecting them, but they do so thanks to a voice that is lent to Socrates and the others.

For now, let me draw only one conclusion from these considerations: the form of dialogue is—at least in the *Theaetetus*—less concerned with the immediate human relationship to *alētheia*, as Heidegger argues, but rather with the problem of making the voices of the dead and the barely living be heard again. If indeed this is one of the concerns that explains why Plato chose the form of dialogue for this text and if, consequently, by giving a voice to the dead and the dying, Plato raises the question of dialogue itself in the *Theaetetus*, it might be worthwhile to pay attention to those moments in this dialogue in which the phenomenon of giving a voice imposes itself on the speakers.

Theodorus Remaining Silent

Given Plato's talent for composition, it will not surprise us that there is indeed at least one dead voice in the actual dialogue that somehow insists on being heard and whose voice is indeed given a voice. In fact, he is given at least three voices. In the actual dialogue, Socrates, Theodorus, and Theaetetus interrogate the nature of knowledge, and Theaetetus's first attempt to answer the question of what knowledge is is not his answer but turns out to coincide with "what Protagoras used to maintain."[15] With Protagoras, another dead voice enters the scene of this dialogue. Because he is no longer among the living, he cannot defend his own teachings.

First, Theaetetus adopts the task of defending Protagoras's teachings. Although there does not seem to be any explicit mentioning of Theaetetus's role as an interpreter of Protagoras up to approximately 162a, after this point in the text, the question of interpreting, speaking on behalf of, and giving a voice to the dead becomes a prominent theme. This theme is announced for the first time when Theodorus refuses to be interrogated by Socrates. At a certain moment, almost in passing, Socrates starts addressing Theodorus with his questions.[16] By emphasizing that Protagoras used to be Theodorus's friend, Socrates suggests that Theodorus rather than Theaetetus should be the one to defend the teachings of the deceased. Yet, in his response, Theodorus argues that it is exactly *because* Protagoras was his friend that he refuses to participate in the conversation: "Protagoras was my friend [*philos*] [. . .]. I could not consent to have him refuted through my admissions; and yet I should not be prepared to resist you against my own judgment."[17] In his response, Theodorus mentions two obligations that he fears exclude each other: the obligation of friendship and the obligation of reason (or perhaps rather rhetoric persuasion). Looking back to the long quotation on the difference between debate and dialogue, we now see that not only the reference to tripping up someone but also that to friendship responds to Theodorus's initial refusal to participate in the dialogue.

It is important to see what happens between the above and the long quote and to the double conception of friendship they introduce. For Socrates, friendship is dependent on truth and therefore can never be at odds with reason. Only those who contribute to our self-understanding and self-care deserve to be considered as true friends. Therefore, if the interrogation of Socrates should lead to a refutation of Protagoras's teachings, this only means that he would prove to be Theodorus's true friend because he would be saving him from self-deception. Theodorus, on the other hand, allows for a tension between his friendship with Protagoras and his incapacity to be a real match for Socrates's argumentative skills. Therefore, Theodorus considers it his task to remain silent and avoid choosing between friendship and reason. As a response to Theodorus's refusal, Socrates insists on the importance of speaking for Protagoras's teachings and insists that someone should take on the task of defending his teachings. He says, "For Protagoras, or anyone speaking on his behalf, will answer us like this," thus suggesting that Protagoras's voice needs to be present in the dialogue and if need be by someone who lends Protagoras his voice.[18] By remaining silent, Theodorus does not take on this task.

Yet it remains to be seen whether he does not, at this moment of the dialogue, offer his own way of interpreting Protagoras's absent voice exactly by not speaking: does he not, as a participant in the dialogue that remains silent, *bears witness to the very silence of Protagoras's voice*? What is at stake here is the following: can any actual interpretation, any actual speaking for Protagoras do justice to what he might have wanted to object to Socrates? Protagoras's absent voice is also the realm of potential objections, arguments, twists and turns of the dialogue that may never be thought of by any of his interpreters. Thus, the following question arises. *Should there not be, in addition to the interpreters who speak, a silent voice, present but refusing to participate in the argument in order to manifest this very potentiality to say and speak in unforeseen and unthought-of different ways*? Indeed, Socrates phrases a concern with respect to the question of whether the interpreters in this dialogue can do justice to Protagoras. Who among the interpreters, if any, can be trusted to be an adequate interpreter of Protagoras? This trust is perhaps less a matter of any good will than it is one of capacity. Who can come close enough to the intellectual capacities of the old and wise Protagoras?

This singular moment in the dialogue in which Socrates demands Theodorus to speak and in which Theodorus remains silent may be analyzed in terms of Agamben's comments on the dialogue's demand on everyone who can speak to actually speak. Referring back to the works of Apel and Aristotle, Agamben notes that this demand goes back to the following claim: "Whoever declares himself not wanting to communicate contradicts himself, for he has already communicated his will not to communicate."[19] One might be inclined to say that this claim applies to Theodorus's position as well. Does he not communicate his will not to communicate? Indeed, he refuses to participate. Yet his *will* (not to communicate) is not the reason or ground for this refusal: he prefers not to participate because he fears he cannot do justice to his friend's teachings when interrogated by Socrates. Hence, his refusal rather communicates his *incapacity* to defend Protagoras's teachings in such a way that it meets the demands of both friendship and reason. His refusal points to a residue or a reserve of what is and can be said in this dialogue: the absent voice of Protagoras refers to a potentiality to speak and to say that exceeds what is and can be said by the present speakers—and, paradoxically, this potential can only be present in the dialogue in the form of a maintained silence.[20]

Hence, Theodorus's refusal suggests that to interpret the voice of those who can no longer be heard requires more than one voice: not only one that actually speaks and defends the teachings in the dialogue but also one that refuses to speak and positions itself outside the realm of refutations, thus attesting to a residue of and a void in the dialogue, to a potential or an absence of attestation that demands to be attested to. By keeping silent, Theodorus guards and keeps the irreplaceable loss of Protagoras's voice. To see in which sense this is also a fundamental concern in the dialogue itself, and in particular for Socrates, who insists that someone has to speak on behalf of Protagoras, let us consider some of the subsequent passages of the *Theaetetus*.

Interpreting Protagoras

When, after Theodorus's refusal, Socrates continues to interrogate Theaetetus, it does not take long before he completely refutes Protagoras's teachings as well as the version Theaetetus puts forward in his answers. After some arguments, Socrates finds himself in the position to conclude: "And so the tale [*muthos*] of Protagoras comes to an untimely end; yours too, your tale about the identity of knowledge and perception."[21] Yet, and this is very important, Socrates does not claim this conclusion as a victory over Protagoras. Rather, he points out that the first interpreter of Protagoras's voice is not skilled enough to be a match for him, Socrates. In fact, exactly because of that lack of skill, Theaetetus disqualifies as interpreter of Protagoras. As Socrates notes:

> But I don't think this [refutation] would have happened, my friend, if the father of the other tale were alive. He would find plenty of means of defending it. As things are, it is an orphan we are trampling in the mud. Not even the people Protagoras appointed its guardians are prepared to come to its rescue; for instance, Theodorus here. In the interests of justice, it seems that we shall have to come to the rescue ourselves.[22]

This quote brings three important elements together.

(1) First, the reference to trampling in the mud seems to be a variation of the tripping up and the slips of which we spoke above, but this time it concerns the injustice done to a teaching of which the father is no longer there. This means that whatever the strategic function of this reference to tripping up, slips, and trampling in the mud might be for Socrates, he is not aiming at an easy victory over Protagoras. Rather, because Theodorus, an appointed guardian of the heritage of Protagoras, also refuses to assist the latter's orphans, Socrates is confronted with the task of trying to rescue and assist Protagoras himself. This particular problem is explored in the interplay of the *Theaetetus*, between Theodorus's refusal and Socrates's lending his voice to Protagoras: who is an heir to and a guardian of the argument? And how to deal with this heritage?[23]

(2) Second, Theodorus is not only once more addressed as the one who should speak because he is the guardian of Protagoras, but also Socrates is from now on engaged in giving a voice to Protagoras, as we see

in the passages that follow, beginning with Socrates saying: "But perhaps you'll ask, what argument would Protagoras himself bring to the help of his offspring. Shall we try to state it?"[24] By saying "I imagine him saying," Socrates starts a long impersonation of the voice of Protagoras.[25] Note that only Socrates *directly* gives a voice to Protagoras. He abstains from stating his own words, but fully lends his voice to Protagoras. The stakes of this impersonation are twofold: to do justice to Protagoras and to get Theodorus to participate in the dialogue.[26]

(3) Third, the reference to Protagoras's teachings as an orphan cannot but direct us to Derrida's interpretation of the same figure as it appears in the *Phaedrus*. In "La pharmacie de Platon," Derrida mentions the reference of the orphan in the *Theaetetus* only in a footnote, and for him, this reference indicates that for Plato, the orphan is always the one who is persecuted and in need of assistance.[27] Yet he does not notice in which sense the orphan seems to play an additional role in Plato. In his reading of the *Phaedrus*, Derrida argues that Socrates emphasizes the risks and weakness of writing because the father is absent to defend it. Yet in the *Theaetetus*, the need and demand for assistance is not understood in terms of the absent father alone, and the reference to the origin, which Derrida so strongly emphasizes throughout "La pharmacie de Platon," is much more complicated in the *Theaetetus*. In fact, the whole composition of the *Theaetetus* indicates that the orphan does not so much require the actual father—this, after all, is impossible—but rather is in need of *interpreters* who are willing to assist the orphan and are willing *to give a voice* to their father. In the form of the interpreter, the value of the substitute and the supplement forms the very basis of the assistance that is given here: not writing as supplement, but rather a supplement to writing so that the written words may speak again. Moreover, the lack of the father's voice gives rise to a new, positive phenomenon, namely that *all* speakers present become responsible for the opinions that are trampled upon. This is the very ethos of philosophical dialogue.[28] Whereas Derrida seems to interpret the figure of the orphan to mean that writing is for Plato merely the decay of speech, the usage of this figure in the *Theaetetus* suggests a much more "Derridean" usage of this figure by Plato himself. Indeed, the orphan is in danger and under threat to be trampled upon. Therefore, it is in need of protection, but if the speakers are willing to lend their voice to the orphan, it is also given the chance to speak anew. We need to insist that the Derridean ambiguity of risk and chance belongs to Plato's dialogue itself and is explicitly thematized there—it is not the effect

of a deconstructive reading. The chance to speak again is no guarantee that the orphan will not be trampled upon. Theodorus's refusal to speak articulates this risk. He fears that when he speaks, his friend's heritage will soon be discarded and rejected.

Thus, we see that there are two types of interpreter appearing here. Theodorus insists that Protagoras's voice must be kept, guarded, and protected as a lost voice for which no other voice can compensate. His silence in the dialogue enacts this guardianship. Socrates, on the other hand, insists that another justice demands that someone speak up for Protagoras and take the risk of misrepresenting him because otherwise his teachings will be done injustice. It seems to me that in this singular moment in the *Theaetetus* in which both interpreters are present, the dialogue reaches an unstable equilibrium that shows that Protagoras is *in need of two interpreters and of two voices at the same time*: one who preserves his silence and one who makes him speak. By this double voice, the speakers in the *Theaetetus* come to the rescue of Protagoras's orphan—and in what follows in this study, we shall see how often this double voice is at the heart of the phenomenon of bearing witness.

Yet this equilibrium is an unstable one. In fact, at this very point of the dialogue, we finally start to see the contours of the composition in which the long quote on the distinction between a debate and a dialogue is taken up. Although it is Socrates who speaks in this long quote, these words are uttered when he is the interpreter of Protagoras! Thus, the distinction is presented as belonging to Protagoras rather than to Socrates. Consequently, when by these words, by the reference to tripping up and slips, Theodorus is once more invited to reconsider his refusal to participate in the dialogue, *it is not Socrates but Protagoras who is speaking*—at least according to Socrates. In this passage, Theodorus is thus called on by his friend Protagoras and not simply by Socrates. Although not thematized explicitly, the reader cannot help but noticing the fundamental ambiguity at stake here in Socrates's impersonation of Protagoras. On the one hand, the words he speaks are concerned with doing justice to Protagoras and coming to the rescue of his offspring. On the other hand, Protagoras also seems to become the mouthpiece of Socrates in these pages because he says exactly those things that Socrates needs, first to make Theodorus speak and subsequently to refute Protagoras's teachings—destroying the equilibrium of Protagoras's double voice.

We encounter here the fundamental ambiguity of the mode of speech by which people (claim to) lend their voice to someone else: does their voice *let* the other speak or does it *make* the other speak? It is from this ambiguity that the necessity arises to raise, in relation to the listeners to such an attestation, impersonation, or interpretation, the question of trust and distrust. Can Socrates be trusted here, or is his impersonation a means to another end: not to let Protagoras's voice revive, but to smother his descendants? Does Protagoras speak through Socrates, or is this Protagoras merely another Socrates? It is exactly with regard to those questions that Theodorus's silence gains its full significance: it marks the risk of trusting Socrates and stands for the absent voice of Protagoras despite all that is being said in his name.

If Socrates is indeed truly aiming to voice Protagoras's arguments and ideas, he will not know the answer to the above questions. He only knows that he will never be able to do full justice to Protagoras, as he notes when concluding his interpretation of Protagoras: "Well, Theodorus, here is my contribution to the rescue of your friend—the best I can do, with my resources, and little enough that is."[29] Thus, confronted with such an undecidable mode of speech, it is Theodorus who has to decide: does he believe this interpreter of Protagoras, and will he participate in the dialogue? Does he trust this interpreter, this bearing witness to the voice and the heritage of Protagoras? Although aware that he is confronting Socrates and his ingenuity of argument and style, he nevertheless seems to be convinced that Socrates indeed let Protagoras speak. Therefore, he finally abandons his refusal to participate: "Socrates, it is not easy for a man who has sat down beside you to refuse to talk."[30]

When assessing Socrates's insistence that Theodorus must speak, we should keep in mind that we cannot understand it in terms of the discussion between Agamben and Apel. For Apel, we must speak because we are always already communicating: even when we refuse to communicate, we have communicated our will not to communicate. Yet Socrates's insistence that Theodorus must speak is not founded in such an "always already" of communication. Rather, he complains that Theodorus does not take his guardianship seriously. That is to say, it is not a matter of a presupposed communication. Rather, Theodorus neglects the *appeal* by the offspring of Protagoras and by Protagoras himself to speak for them. In fact, not even this appeal on Theodorus is presupposed. Rather, it is Socrates who has to *begin* with Protagoras's voice and address Theodorus with this appeal. This is what happens: Socrates becomes both the messenger and the initiator of a call on Theodorus. One might say that in the transition from Apel's insistence that one must speak to Socrates's, the meaning of the word *archē* has changed: the former's insistence concerns indeed the very principle that is always already presupposed as and in the beginning, ruling all communication; the latter's insistence can only be understood from the actual beginning he enacts when giving a voice to Protagoras. In this sense, the lost voice of the father is not to be understood as a lost origin, but rather as an imperative for speakers to become the orphan's foster parents; that is to say, to give a voice to the father so that this voice resounds in and through the interpreter. It is by adopting this task that Socrates voices Protagoras's call on Theodorus to interpret him and defend his offspring.

Yet Socrates's interpretation of Protagoras retains its ambiguous character, as the aftermath of Theodorus's change of mind shows. When Socrates starts examining Theodorus, what Theodorus feared most is exactly what happens: Protagoras's teachings are quickly and effectively refuted. Once more he tries to defend his friend by exclaiming: "Socrates, we are running my friend too hard." This time Socrates is less inclined to ask for other interpreters, as he did when Theaetetus's defense of Protagoras turned out to be too weak, but rather he invokes the image of the ghost of Protagoras that speaks to them once more and then disappears permanently:

> But it is not at all clear, my dear Theodorus, that we are running off the right track. Hence it is likely that Protagoras, being older than we are, really is wiser as well; and if he were to stick up his head from below as far as the neck just here where we are, he would in all likelihood convict me twenty times over of talking nonsense, and show you up too for agreeing with me, before he ducked down to rush off again. But we have got to take ourselves as we are, I suppose, and go on saying the things which seem to us to be.[31]

This quote deserves to be read from many angles, but I limit myself to a few remarks. One may wonder whether Socrates's claim that Protagoras is really wiser because he is older is not one of the famous examples of Socratic irony. Would he really believe that Protagoras is capable of proving abundantly that he is talking nonsense? Moreover, the sentence that concludes the previous quote, "but we have got to [. . .] go on saying the things which seem to us to be," insists on the necessity of speaking. It is as if, after Theodorus's hesitations to participate and Socrates's subsequent successful impersonation of Protagoras, Socrates wants to go back to business as usual and focus on a dialogue as the mode of speech in which the speakers state their opinions on a subject matter, as if the strange interruption of the normal functioning of dialogue by the attempts to give a voice to Protagoras and his offspring has finally come to an end. What exactly is Socrates trying to expel when he evokes the ghost of Protagoras? Could it not be that he is trying to expel the silent voice? And would thus Socrates's Protagoras indeed only be a mouthpiece of Socrates? Or should we say that at this point Socrates only affirms what he had Protagoras saying in the long quote on the difference between a debate and a dialogue, namely that the philosopher's primary task is to attest to the truth and, above anything else, to give voice to the truth and the truth alone?

We are not in a position to answer these questions, but they do help us understand how the *Theaetetus* takes on the issue of interpreting in the sense of giving a voice to the dead. We have encountered three basic instantiations of this form of interpreting.

First, the anonymous slave who reads a text and thus interprets Socrates and the others as directly speaking so that they speak again and address and affect the listeners, Euclides and Terpsion. In this way, the slave lends his voice to them—and his own voice is nothing but a voice in the service of voices that no longer speak. The voice that is heard is therefore doubled: Socrates speaks with the slave's voice and can be heard only insofar as he shares in the slave's voice.

Second, during the time that he refuses to speak, Theodorus is not an interpreter who speaks up for Protagoras's offspring, but his silence and his refusal to participate attest to the absence of Protagoras's voice. As a speaker who remains silent, he transgresses the demands of the dialogue, yet in this way he also introduces a reserve and a residue into the dialogue. The silence of Theodorus's voice represents and guards the irreplaceable loss of Protagoras's voice.

Finally, Socrates, the interpreter, belongs to the same genus as the witness. In the dialogue between the living and the dead voice of Protagoras, Socrates takes on the task of speaking for Protagoras by giving him a voice and addressing Theodorus with an appeal to speak for his old friend. Socrates adopts this task out of his sense of justice. As I have suggested, Socrates and Theodorus together form the true witness and interpreter of Protagoras: to speak for him and to keep silent for him—to attest to his appeal on the listeners and to guard the loss of his voice. It is this sense of a double voice that will guide the conception of bearing witness that is developed in the rest of this study.

Chapter 3

Experiment II

Alice, the Secretarious

> One could call it *mute* if one remembers that the root *mu* connotes the shut lips which signal that one stays silent or emits a mute sound. From this root come *murmur*, *moo*, *mystery* and the low Latin *muttum* which has, in French, given us the word, *mot*.[1]
>
> —Lyotard, "La phrase-affect," 51/238

Articulate and Inarticulate Voices

Our conception of the voice is marked by an important distinction derived from Aristotle. To anticipate discussions in Part II and Part III, let me already announce here that this distinction will be complicated by another Aristotelian distinction. In the *Politics*, Aristotle defines the human being as a "political animal" because the human has "the gift of speech" (*logos*) in distinction to other animals in which one only finds a "mere voice (*phōnē*) [which] is but an indication of pleasure or pain."[2] As Aristotle adds, the human capacity to utter meaningful voices goes hand in hand with the human capacity to recognize what is beneficial and harmful and "therefore also the right and the wrong."[3] Whereas the mere voice simply cries out the very disposition, *pathos*, of the animal (or the human), without offering any sense of the justness of this disposition, human speech offers the possibility to bring into play the questions of *dikē* and *dikaiosunē*, what is fitting and justice.

Aristotle's distinction between *phōnē* and *logos* led in the works of Aristotle as well as those of the ancient grammarians to the notion of the *phōnē enarthros*, the articulated voice: in distinction to the mere animal voice, an articulated voice is a voice that is composed of recognizable elements, letters, that intends to signify and that, therefore, can be understood. For Aristotle, this articulate voice is the properly *human* voice, which speaks in meaningful phrases.[4] In one sense, this Aristotelian distinction seems unproblematic. When someone cries of pain, everybody will hear this voice as the (animal) voice expressing and signaling nothing but this pain. Nobody will mistake a meaningful sentence for an animal voice because, as soon as we hear a meaningful sentence, spoken in our language, we will hear and understand the meaning of the sentence—and if we do not hear or immediately understand this meaning, we will inquire into its meaning. Therefore, Aristotle adopts this distinction in *On Interpretation* to delimit the scope of what he calls interpretation (*hermēneia*) to names (or nouns) and sentences. For Aristotle, a name is "a spoken sound significant by convention." In distinction to a name, which signifies something, the inarticulate noise (*agrammatoi psophoi*) of the animals does not signify something but only reveals a *pathos* such as pain or pleasure. Consequently, the inarticulate, animal voice is not a name and hence not part of *logos*; it lacks meaning and an intention to signify. Although this distinction is rather straightforward and limits the question of interpretation to the articulate voice, it does have a rather peculiar implication for the human voice. According to the ancient definition of the human as *zōon logon echon*, the living being that has language, the human belongs to that category of animals that has an inarticulate voice to express and indicate its pain and pleasure but, in addition, by the gift of speech—which is *taught* to the human being although the human has from their birth onward a propensity or capacity to speak, which it can lose—it has another, articulate voice. Apparently, the human voice is *divided* or doubled in itself in an articulate and an inarticulate voice. Yet how are these two are related?

In "La phrase-affect," a short essay supplementing his much more well-known *Le différend*, Lyotard recapitulates this Aristotelian distinction between the articulate phrase and the inarticulate or phrase-affect. There is no translation or transition possible between these two types because the phrase-affect is by definition banned from meaningful, signifying discourse: "[*Phōnē*] is banished from human language."[5] Apparently, there is something of the human animal that is removed from human language, and this ban runs from Aristotle to Apel. This means that *phōnē* constitutes a remainder or reserve of human language that has no entrance to language. Yet, because the human being still has this animal voice, this voice does affect and may even interrupt human language. This is the reason why the inarticulate voice and the affects it expresses "are testimonies, but testimonies that represent nothing to anyone."⁶ They render the order of *logos* or discourse inoperative and confront us with something that cannot be expressed in this order.

In order to capture what is at stake here, let me pause here for a moment and ask what exactly happened in the course of the last paragraph. In one sense, Aristotle's distinction seems obvious: if some (human) animal is in pain and attests to this by their inarticulate voice, no one will mistake this for an attempt to formulate a meaningful sentence. Hence, it cannot be the duality as such that constitutes a problem, not even in the human being. When Lyotard calls these affects testimonies, the question is to whom they testify and of what they testify. The problem is not so much that the human might have two voices, but rather that these two voices *cannot* be separated in any strict sense. Somehow, the theoretical division of the articulate and inarticulate voice cannot do justice to the human reality that the inarticulate voice *speaks in* the articulate voice. More than Lyotard's insistence on Aristotle's conceptuality that maintains the dichotomy of affect and meaning, Heidegger's concept of *Stimmung*, mood or attunement, might be better equipped to capture what is at stake when we say that these two voices cannot be separated. When the human speaks about the world with their articulate voice and in meaningful language, this speaking is not indifferent or detached, but always speaks in an attuned way. Using the etymological relation of *Stimmung*, which also translates the Greek *pathos*, and *Stimme*, voice, we might perhaps say that this attunement is as an inarticulate voice that speaks in the articulate voice. For instance, if we express our concerns for the state of affairs in institutions such as the university in which we invest our energy, time, and life, the articulate voice that speaks about these institutions does not speak alone. When it speaks, another voice speaks in it, the inarticulate voice that may express "the pain of supporting" these institutions or "the temptation to escape them," as Lyotard writes elsewhere.⁷

To do justice to this complex relation of inarticulate and articulate voice, Lyotard—as well as Agamben—does not refer to this inarticulate voice in the human simply as an animal voice. Rather, he refers to it as *enfance*, infancy, to capture the dimension of non-speaking-ness in this other voice. *In-fans* or non-speaking should be understood as not-speaking-meaningfully or, better still, as *alogos*, meaning both without reason or language and in want of reason and language. This infancy is marked by what Lyotard calls *misère*, that is, by an initial poverty to speak that marks the human (and, by extension, by an initial poverty to be able to participate in the different institutions in which we find ourselves). Yet it is exactly this initial poverty that corresponds to a particular *demand*: this poverty demands to be said and is in need of language. This is, at least, how I would interpret Lyotard's reference in "La phrase-affect" to the categories of *dommage*, *tort*, and *différend* from *Le différend* that actually deepens the type of wrong that is being committed, when it concerns the differend of articulated phrase and phrase-affect, when he writes: "From their differend results a wrong," which he characterizes as "radical."[8] What else can this wrong, more radical than the one thematized in *Le différend*, demand than that the inarticulate voice is being attested to, by a witness who bears witness to this wrong and thus speaks up for the inarticulate voice for the tribunal of human language?[9] (In the French, to speak up for someone can also be expressed as *témoigner en faveur de quelqu'un*, literally: to testify in favor of someone.) The sense of the demand also mirrors a basic interest in Agamben's notion of *esigenza*, which will become more and more important in the course of this study. In turn, what else can this *demand* hope for than a *promise* chiming at the heart of the language to offer the witness the capacity to attest to the inarticulate voice's absence of articulation and attestation? Lyotard's reflections culminate in the motto to this second experiment:

> One could call [the inarticulate voice] *mute* if one remembers that the root *mu* connotes the shut lips which signal that one stays silent or emits a mute sound. From this root come *murmur*, *moo*, *mystery* and the low Latin *muttum* which has, in French, given us the word, *mot* [*qui a donné en français le* mot].[10]

Apparently the inarticulate voice plays the role of the silent, mute voice, much like the voice that Theodorus gives to the dead Protagoras in the previous experiment. Moreover, it refers to a mystery, to a secret that the spoken language holds in reserve. This mystery, if we follow the etymological connections offered by Lyotard, concerns nothing less than the very gift of the word—at least in French. It seems to me that for Lyotard the notions of misery and the particular muteness of the inarticulate voice have to be taken together. In the French, *misère* also means poverty, referring to the inarticulate voice being poor in language; and in the Dutch, my own mother tongue, misery can be expressed by the word *ellende*, which one could translate literally as "outlandish" but in which one should especially hear the sense of being in exile, being away from the land in which one is at home. The notion of misery, as it appears in the title of this book, should be understood in the first place in this semantic field, referring to what is poor in language or what cannot enter language or cannot be said because it is exiled, banned, and removed from it, but which nevertheless concerns the very heart of human existence. These connections are brought to life, to a macabre, miserable life, in the novel that forms the point of departure for the second literary experiment.

Keeper of the Secret

The intriguing novel *La petite fille qui aimait trop les allumettes* (*The Little Girl Who Was Too Fond of Matches*) written by the Canadian author Gaétan Soucy, a literary master of suspense, offers us a proper testimony.[11] The witness we encounter in this story is a young woman who first introduces herself as a man, and who narrates the ghastly and ghostly story of her life and her family. Although the one who firsthandedly experienced the narrated events is usually seen as the most reliable witness, the first uncovered falsity in the story—she presents herself as a boy although she is, in fact, a pregnant woman—ignites a certain doubt in the reader concerning the trustworthiness of this witness and his or her testimony. Can someone who either does not know who she is or desperately tries to hide it be the one whom we can rely on to tell us what happened to her and to her family on their estate? And, yet, hers is the only account we have at our disposal. If we reject her testimony because we don't consider it to be trustworthy, we will never know what happened. And if we apply the legal principle that one witness is no witness, we are without any hope of getting the slightest sense of what happened. At the same time, beyond our cares for legal principles and trustworthiness, language will do what it does and will effectively—even if we worry it to be composed of lies, fictions, or perjuries—find its way in our perception of the events that have taken place on the family's estate.

It is actually quite clear that this testimony demands the reader's suspicion rather than their immediate or unequivocal trust. The chain of deeply traumatic experiences disclosed to us are unfolding one disaster after another. One might therefore be tempted to conclude that we may only learn the truth of this family *despite* the witness herself. Indeed, her bearing witness does not simply disclose, but discloses only through a whole array of distortions, disguises, concealments, and cover-ups. This complicated form of disclosure does explain, though, why Alice, the witness and narrator in *La petite fille qui aimait trop les allumettes*, refers to herself as "secretarious," from the Latin *secretarius*, from which also our common word "secretary" is derived and which originally means confidant or keeper of a secret. (And let us not forget that *muein*, the Greek verb on which the motto to this experiment depends, also means "to initiate in mysteries," as a particular way to tell and keep the mystery or the secret at the same time.[12]) Which secret does she keep and guard, and of whom or what is she a confidant? And, more importantly for our immediate purposes, how is this related to the distinction between the inarticulate and the articulate voice with which I introduced this experiment? The answer to these questions will have to wait, because first we need to follow the story and confront the order in which the story itself says what it has to say. We know only one thing for sure. Lyotard's etymology of the root *mu* from mute to murmuring to mystery will have to be followed in a reverse order, starting with the mystery and the secret that is kept by our witness to find a murmuring and muteness at its core, which is the ultimate object of this testimony.

The testimony of Soucy's novel has a similar point of departure as the demand for an interpreter we encountered in the *Theaetetus*. It opens with the scene in which Alice and her brother learn that they have become orphans because their father committed suicide. The children were raised in complete isolation from the outside world. Therefore, their father was to them a characteristic patriarch, a godlike figure who established, maintained, and was the order of their world. For them, he was the ground that kept the world a habitable place in which they could dwell. With his death, their existence and world loses its structure, its meaning, and its inhabitability. It is not difficult to see, in the opening pages of the novel and in the description of the role of the father, a literary version of onto-theology and its nihilistic ending in Nietzsche: the order created, maintained, and founded in God is wiped out by the latter's death. For the children, the world turns into a sheer wasteland.

In the very first paragraph of the book, Alice bears witness to this experience: "Without papa we didn't know how to do anything. On our own we could scarcely hesitate, exist, fear, suffer."[13] What we encounter in this experience cannot be explicated fully along the lines Heidegger proposes in *Sein und Zeit*. There, the disappearance of a meaningful world leads to the basic mood (*Grundstimmung*) of anxiety and opens up the basic dimension of one's being as care. Here, however, it seems that even the very ground that the moods or the attunements provide in the human relation to the world, namely a ground for a most basic openness to world, seems to be swept away. It is as if, with the disappearance of the father, the whole arrangement of human care and concern itself is suspended: "We could scarcely hesitate, exist, fear, suffer." The same experience is attested to much later in the book when Alice writes:

> When father existed on this side of things, at least the life of the world had a meaning, twisted and bumpy though it may have been, that's the point I'm trying to make. [. . .] Now that he was defunct, it was as if a gigantic gust of wind had swept the earth with just one blast and had left nothing standing.[14]

The deactivation of the principle that grounded the horizon of meaning in which they lived has made the earth fully desolate.[15] If one tries to capture the experience that Alice articulates here, it is less the experience of an abyss, that is, of a dizziness or vertigo inspiring a sense of the absence of any ground (*Abgrund*), than it is an experience of the absence of *phusis*, of an earth that is no longer covered by what naturally grows and what discloses itself out of itself. Thus, Alice narrates an experience of a basic concealment, an absence of *phusis* that inscribes itself into the tradition of the plain of forgetfulness or the field of concealment (*to tēs Lēthēs pedion*) introduced in Plato's myth of Er, to which I turn in the sixth experiment. When addressing this field, Heidegger notes that Plato describes this plain as the "counter-essence" (*Gegenwesen*) of *phusis*. He writes: "This field of concealment is opposed to all *phusis*. *Lēthē* does not admit any *phuein*, any emerging [*Aufgehen*] and coming forth [*Hervorkommen*]."[16] That is to say, nothing can grow or emerge in this field that is the very counter-essence of *phusis*; therefore, it is a field in which humans cannot dwell or care for their own existence. It is a desert in which nothing is left standing. Or, as the myth tells us: "they travelled to the Plain of Forgetfulness in burning, choking, terrible heat, for it was empty of trees and earthly vegetation."[17] Indeed, "as if a gigantic gust of wind had swept the earth with just one blast and had left nothing standing." All circumstances that would allow for life to grow and contribute to the place's livability are absent in this plain. In a similar way, Alice and her brother experience their world as a desolate place in which they cannot dwell; they experience their earth as a place in which nothing grows to provide for a living.

This remarkable beginning on the uninhabitability of the world and its connection to the special task Alice awards to herself, to be a keeper of a secret, suggests that it might be fruitful to consider Soucy's novel in light of the chain of words that, in the German, Heidegger explores, which all vary on the word for home (*Heim*), bringing together the secret (*Geheimnis*), secretive (*heimlich*), uncanny (*unheimlich*), not being at home or being out of place where one is (*unheimisch*), native (*heimisch*), and, eventually, the return home (*Heimkehr*).[18] Let me emphasize that considering the novel in light of this chain is not meant to suggest that the novel follows this chain. In fact, Soucy's "secretarious" might be located at the limit of Heidegger's enterprise and, thus, on the threshold toward another. This limit can be traced best by focusing on Alice's singular relation to language. For Heidegger, language is the house of being.[19] Therefore, language is the very place where truth happens and thus where a world and an inhabitable place emerge and come forth. To be at home in one's own language therefore is one of the basic tasks for the poet and the thinker. Even the encounter with the foreign (*das Fremde*)—a foreign world, truth, and language—ultimately is not to be understood as a possible crumbling down of language as the locus of truth, but is rather, as he suggests in his reading of Hölderlin, part of a return home (*Heimkehr*), that is, of a process in which one gets essentially acquainted with one's language and truly comes home in one's own language. Hence, even the confrontation with the foreign and the strange is part of a process that establishes the intrinsic connection between language and dwelling more profoundly. However, this connection needs to be rethought and complicated when the task is assigned to language to bear witness to what is, in Heidegger's words, the counter-essence of *phusis*, that is, a realm of the uninhabitable.

If we confront these Heideggerian reflections with the sense of language that appears in the activities and considerations of Alice, we discern the following striking contrast. For Alice, language is not the house of being, but rather the house of horror. Language is the medium in which she is compelled to think and to tell the macabre reality of her existence. Language does not offer a dwelling place, but rather is the means to relate to what is outlandish in her existence, how she is exiled from the world as an inhabitable place. At the same time—and this explains the continuous ambiguity of Alice's narrative—language is a hiding place. Because the world itself is uninhabitable, language is the only place for her to be and in which she does not need to confront her deepest secrets directly. In this sense, language retains in one regard its function as a dwelling place, although it is no longer the dwelling place of being. It is rather the place to hide from existence—and it hides only as long as it is capable of keeping the misery of existence outside. In the words of Johannes de Silentio, one of Kierkegaard's pseudonyms to whom we turn in the fourth experiment, the poet is the one "who, to a person overwhelmed by life's sorrows and left behind naked, reaches out the words, the leafage of language by which he can conceal his misery."[20] Language thus covers the human being's initial *misère*, the poverty and misery that is the human condition. In line with this sense of language, we may understand how Alice adopts the words from the books she reads, such as the bible, romances of chivalry, Spinoza's *Ethics*, and, especially, the memoirs of the Duc de Saint-Simon, in which he describes life at the court of the French King Louis XIV.[21] Their words are like a barrier between her desolate, miserable existence and her articulation of this existence. Thus, she can rightfully claim that words are all she has left in this abandoned and forsaken world.[22] These words are in the first place the ones she inherited from these books, as she notes: "if I've learned anything at all as secretarious I owe it to the duc, to his thunderous language and his extraordinary stories, to his sentence which shoots up to its summit like farts from a burning log."[23]

In a world that is at odds with what these books tell her, such words, however, are marked by a fundamental fragility and finitude and are not the proper means to comprehend the world. Both of these aspects are attested to by Alice, whose narration is also an exploration of her relation to language and of her task to bear witness beyond the protecting confines of the language of the books she loves. Concerning the finitude of these words, it is striking that, immediately after her praise of Saint-Simon, she notes how "the rain that is welling up from the ground" is corrupting the books in their library—these books and their words "are dying a natural death like all the rest."[24] They are already being eaten away by the reality at the threshold of her hiding place. To capture the fragility of the words she has at her disposal, she refers to them as her "dolls of ash" (below, I look into two of the passages in which she uses this term). Concerning the inadequacy of these words to offer a house of being, it is striking that when Alice uses these words to describe and register the world and the horrors it brought her, these words do not truly help her to understand anything. She notes that it is her "duty" as a secretarious to give "a name to things" because "we are bereft of everything we know not how to name."[25] Yet, although this may seem to approach Heidegger's account of language as the house of being, this naming does not offer a dwelling place. In fact, her words strike those who hear her speak as well as the narrator herself with either incomprehension or disbelief. As she notes, this interpreter and witness is only "reporting" and not understanding: "But I'm just reporting what was said to me, I'm not trying to understand."[26] And describing how people respond to what she tells them: "He didn't seem to find what I told him very clear but I can't help that, when I say things I always say them the way they are and if they seem strange it's not the fault of my bonnet, blame the things themselves."[27] Reality imposes itself on her words, but this does not help her in any way but rather shows the weakness of her words to both ward off and comprehend reality. Yet, despite her sense of this fragility, she insists on her task as secretarious and does not let herself be deprived of her "dolls of ash," not only because they are all she has—she has "already been disarmed enough by life," as she notes—but also for another reason.

Despite their fragility and weakness, words can be trusted and are capable of doing something remarkable, and one might interpret this remarkable capacity of the words as a deepening of their ability to let something appear: language is continuously marked by the promise to overcome its own weakness at some specific moments. In two highly intriguing quotes, our secretarious attests to this. In the first quote, she says:

> but I trust words, in the end they always say what they have to say. Turn around five times with your eyes shut, and before you open them you will know that a stone you've thrown, which has taken off in you know not what direction, has finally landed on earth. So it is with words. In the end they always settle down somewhere, no matter what, which is all that counts. I don't mean that the secretarious lets herself write any old way. I mean that when she writes she lets herself go by forging ahead, which isn't the same thing.[28]

When reading these words, one might at first think of the Derridean notions of writing and dissemination. Is language not marked by a fundamental form of disorientation that Derrida captures with these two notions? Rather than having a specific sense or direction—in the French, *sens* means both sense and direction—words can go in any direction. The striking image Alice offers us here, of turning five times with your eyes shut while throwing a stone, captures the sense of disorientation or lack of orientation that Derrida describes with the term "dissemination."

It does so in at least one sense: a writer lets words go as a child who plays this turning game, and, therefore, words are not destined for any particular place or addressee, but can go in all directions. Yet, when sense and direction are not the right terms to describe how the author moves the words, this does not mean, as Alice adds, that words do not have a certain gravity. Although they are not destined by an author or speaker to go into a certain direction, they do land and "always settle down somewhere" and, more importantly, "always say what they have to say." The words speak and say what they have to say despite the author. This is the fundamental promise that, for Alice, constitutes the essence of language and the very reason why she does not give up on her dolls of ash. In the last two sentences of the above quote, the secretarious speaks of this particular relation between writer and word: the writer does not simply write arbitrarily—"in any old way"—but is also not the owner, the origin, or the director of what the words have to say; the writer forges ahead, but is always overtaken by the gravity of words, which allows them to say what they have to say.

In the second quote, the gravity of the words that allows them to say what they have to say is depicted by yet another figure. Once more affirming the fragility and uselessness of her authorship, Alice goes on to describe the power of words in the following way:

> For what is there to do in this life but write for nothing? I know, I know, I said, "words: dolls of ash," but that too is misleading because some of them, when they're well ranked into sentences, give you a genuine shock when you come in contact with them, as if you were laying your palm on a cloud swollen with thunder at the very moment when it's about to let go. That's the only thing that helps me.[29]

Sometimes, when words are brought together by the grace of language, they are charged with an astonishing power of expression giving "you a shock when you come into contact with them." This power of expression is what Alice finds in her "dolls of ash." Ultimately, despite all fragility and inadequacy, and as opposed to language's capacity to ward off and protect from the misery of existence, the words of Alice, the secretarious, are taken over by this power of expression in which the promise of language is fulfilled, as slowly becomes clear in the course of her testimony: the gravity and weight of her words cannot but deeply and genuinely shock those who hear them. Rather than protecting Alice and warding off the family's fate, language guards and keeps its secret. The words "that always say what they have to say" ultimately tell the story of Alice being raped by her brother; of her subsequent pregnancy; of the suicide of her father, probably driven by the pure despair over the incest of brother and sister; of a horrid burning of her mother whose embalmed body has been placed on a bier for many years. Finally, these words speak of Alice's twin sister, Ariane, who caused their mother's death because the little girl was too fond of matches. Although Ariane is still alive, she is the true misery of the family tragedy. She has lost all her humanity. The severe burns she suffered in the same accident that killed her mother deprived her of the capacity to speak and required her to be swaddled, like a second mummy kept in the same space as her dead mother. In between life and death, she is, as Agamben would say, *nuda vita*, bare or naked life—or, as her father suggested, she is the "Fair Punishment."

A Faint Lament

In this story, writing—that is, allowing the words their power of expression—is not concerned with aesthetic enjoyment and ultimately also not with a flight from the horrid, uninhabitable world in which Alice lives; it is rather a way of approaching the traumatic secrets that haunt and determine her life. The words of which her narrative is composed do not transform this world into an inhabitable place, but they bear witness to the secret, that is, to the heart of her desolate, abandoned existence that is marked by something deeply uncanny (*unheimlich*). If the writer is carried away by her words, it is not as if by gods that inspire her, but rather by a true misery that torments her, by which she is affected in her innermost self and which she somehow *takes on* in her narration. This, I would argue, is the basic sense of bearing witness that speaks from this story: Alice's struggle with the words is to let her deepest fear and secret appear, not in order to domesticate them or to become familiar with them, but to give a voice to them so that her dolls of ash can indeed give their genuine shock and say what they have to say.

With the introduction of the "Fair Punishment," Alice's twin sister, Ariane, we encounter the uncanniness and the true misery of the family. Being a twin sister, Ariane is the double of Alice. In this sense, the uncanniness and misery indeed belong to the core of her own existence: this is the very secret she keeps in herself and in her testimony. Confronted with this duplication of Alice in her sister, it becomes clear that we are dealing here not simply with one, but with two witnesses who are bound together as twin. The first is secretarious, engaged with words. To capture what the second, Ariane, represents, let us consider how she is described—and with this last piece of the novel's mystery, we finally arrive at the sense of the mute voice and of the murmuring that we kept in reserve so long and encounter the distinction between *phōnē* and *logos* with which we opened this experiment.

Ariane, in Agamben's vocabulary, represents bare life. Ariane is the one who has gone through the full experience of what has happened: she is soaked up in the event and although, strictly speaking, she survived what happened, she did so only to the extent that she is alive. As Alice tells us: "but that's about all one could say."[30] Ariane is not capable of speaking about it. Ariane is, in this sense, the one who saw the Gorgon and who therefore cannot speak about it.[31] She is human, but she is also banned from *logos*—or, strictly speaking, we find her on the threshold of language because sometimes, with some gestures, she seems to be capable of indicating something.

Thus, Alice's double cannot speak. She can only utter soft murmurs. As Alice writes: "a very faint lament comes from the throat of the Fair."[32] This inarticulate, mute voice of Ariane can only be heard in "a huge silence," as Alice explains, and she adds: "She doesn't have the gift of speech, you have to understand her, so she closes her left eye like that when she wants to say no, it's only human."[33] On the threshold of language, we are also on the threshold of humanity and yet, just as the narrator in *Bartleby, the Scrivener* will do, to whom I turn in the fifth experiment, Alice insists that her twin sister is human.[34] Thus, by her testimony, Alice proclaims the humanity of a figure that is on the threshold of humanity, on the verge of life, in between life and death. Alice takes it upon herself to insist on the humanity of what appears to be hardly human, what appears to be mere life that has lost any previous humanity. Without her twin's testimony, the Fair Punishment would be bereft of it: the inarticulate voice, the soft *phōnē* that faintly laments, is borne witness to as a *human* voice in the *logos* of Alice's testimony.

This mute voice is not only important because Alice bears witness to it, but also because it plays a constitutive role in Alice's capacity to speak and to bear witness. This is a crucial point in the novel because it clarifies why it is necessary that Ariane and Alice are twins, why Ariane is the double of Alice: Ariane is not simply someone else, but she also forms a split unity with Alice; Ariane is the inarticulate voice of this split unity, separated off from the articulated voice that is Alice's. Alice insists a number of times that Ariane's lack of the power of speech is not a mere privation, but rather is the very source of Alice's own ability to speak. According to Alice, Ariane has "taken all the silence on herself to free us from it and enable us to speak." The Christian overtones of this quote—they seem to refer directly to a certain interpretation of Christ as the one who has taken all sins upon himself to free the believers from their sins—are difficult to miss. Yet in this Christian vocabulary, Alice articulates what human misery means in relation to the human capacity to speak, thus connecting the inarticulate and the articulate voice, which have been disconnected in the philosophical tradition. Let me provide the full quote:

> Without [the Fair Punishment], I wonder if we'd even be able to use words. That came to me once when I was thinking about it. Perhaps all the silence that fills the life of the Fair allows my brother and me to be on first-name terms with speech, especially me. I mean, it's as if the Fair had taken all the silence on herself to free us from it and enable us to speak, and what would I be without words, I ask you. Hurray for the Fair, that was a fine piece of work. Can you see? You could say this is suffering in the purest state, all wrapped up in a single package. She's like pain that doesn't belong to anyone.[35]

This quote brings a number of elements together. The reference to a Christian discourse is even more strikingly present here, including, of course, the macabre and hilarious "Hurray for the Fair, that was a fine piece of work." The last sentence of the quote refers immediately to the quote from Wittgenstein on pain that Soucy has chosen as a motto for the book, thus suggesting that this sentence and this passage is indeed of crucial importance for the stakes of this novel. Ariane represents a certain anonymity: the pain she has taken upon herself is not only hers, but also is the pain of the horrors that happened on the family estate, thus stretching out to Alice and her brother as well. This pain is so overwhelming that it robs Ariane of her identity and takes on the misery of Alice as well. Everybody who is exposed directly to this pain cannot but lose their sense of speech. Therefore, as Alice suggests, it is only by concentrating the family's misery in Ariane's mute, murmuring voice that the others received (or retained) the gift of speech and of words. The contraction of a misery that is so vast that it could swallow everybody into the first half of Ariane-Alice grants the other half the space and the capacity to speak.[36]

The power of speech and the power of the word thus have a silent origin. Looking back on the etymological development of the root *mu* to which Lyotard points in the epigraph to this chapter offers an apt description: mystery, muteness, and murmuring concern the provenance of *le mot*, the word. Yet this relation also points to a particular task and duty on the part of the one, or the half, that can speak. The capacity to speak and the gift of words are born as a *demand* from a mute voice. Ariane as the silent and uncanny misery, in her faint lamenting, is a voice that cannot speak but that by this incapacity demands speech, demands humanity. The gift of words and the capacity to speak are born from this demand as the task to bear witness to this demand. As testimony of this demand, the articulate voice of Alice belongs to and is one with the inarticulate voice of Ariane so that the *logos* of the former creates a locus in *logos* in which that which is banned from *logos* can nevertheless be attested to. We see here a similar duality of a silent and a speaking voice, as we saw in the case of the *Theaetetus*: together these voices are the constituents of testimony. This duality of a silent and a speaking voice, an inarticulate and articulate voice is at stake in the witness, who is not simply Alice, but rather Ariane-Alice: on the one hand, the touching of the sheer experience of misery and its demand to speak and, on the other hand, the speaking that bears witness to this demand and effectuates the promise of language to speak beyond its own boundaries, to speak of its reserve so that, in Agamben's words, the language of testimony "advances into what is without language."[37] Only now we see why Alice's dolls of ash are not merely futile and fragile but keep in reserve this highest of promises: "some of them, when they're well ranked into sentences, give you a genuine shock when you come in contact with them"—a contact in which language is affected by the mute experience, in which the articulate voice is born from the inarticulate one, bearing witness to it.

Hurbinek's Demand to Speak

As no other, Agamben can be trusted to complicate the distinctions we thought were clear and well conceived, and point to a third term, in between the two poles of the distinction, in order to capture where to locate exactly the point of transition, or the threshold, between the two distinguished terms. In the case of Aristotle's distinction between *phōnē* and *logos*, this third term is the *gramma*, the letter. According to Lyotard, as we noted above, this Aristotelian distinction was taken up by the ancient grammarians as the distinction between the articulate and the inarticulate voice. Lyotard also offers us the means to see why such an interpretation of Aristotle's distinction is already prepared by the Greek philosopher himself: in *On Interpretation*, Aristotle's version of the same distinction introduces the inarticulate noise (*agrammatoi psophoi*) as a synonym of the inarticulate voice. The reference to the letter, *gramma*, in this expression indicates that the inarticulate voice is in the first place the voice that cannot be written (and not so much the voice without meaning; the "without meaning" rather seems to be an effect of its incapacity to be written). The articulate voice, then, is the voice that can be written because the letter is its "constitutive element" (*stoicheion tes phōnēs*).[38] According to Agamben, this particular understanding of the articulate and inarticulate voice goes back to Aristotle's account of the voice in *On Interpretation* in which "he is not merely speaking of the *phōnē*, but uses the expression *ta en tē phōnē*, what is in the voice. [. . .] the voice articulates *grammata*, letters."[39] This means, as Agamben points out, that grammar as the study of language "begins by distinguishing the 'confused voice' of animals (*phone agrammatos*; the Latins translate this as *vox illiterata, quae litteris comprehendi non potest*, [. . .]) from the human voice, which can be written (*engrammatos*) and articulated."[40] The letter, therefore, has never been understood as the (external or arbitrary) representation of the voice alone, but always also, at least from Aristotle onward, as the basic element (*stoicheion*) of the human voice. In this sense, as Agamben notes, Derrida's "grammatology," in which the primacy of the letter over the voice is ascertained against the idea of the letter as the mere, external, and arbitrary supplement and representation of the voice, is correct when considered from an Aristotelian point of view and goes back to this old conception of the relation of *gramma* and *phōnē*. Yet this emphasis on the letter and its constitutive role for language also shows the specific limitations of this account of language, which are due to the specific point of departure, or presupposition, of this account.[41] By departing from the letter, a reflection on human language may offer a convincing account of the articulated voice and show how the realm of meaning always presupposes the realm of the meaningless letter or sign.

That is to say, how semantics presupposes semiotics. Yet it will necessarily also *affirm* the abandonment or the banishment of the inarticulate voice in a grammatical or grammatological account of language because this voice is excluded by the letter, and thus also by any understanding of language that finds in the letter its ultimate presupposition.

Interestingly enough—and I am mentioning this here to prepare some of the examinations in Part II of this study and to point to one shared motive at work in some of the experiments offered in this part—Agamben attempts to capture the exact status of the letter and of the semiotic realm. What is presupposed when the letter is presupposed? In both *Categorie Italiane* and *Il linguaggio e la morte*, Agamben argues that the letter is the index of an intention to signify: as soon as we read letters or recognize marks as letters, we read them as indices and signs of meaning. It is this intention to signify presupposed in the articulate voice that marks the difference with the inarticulate voice that is pure self-expression of, for instance, pain and pleasure. That is, it is pure self-expression of the living being. Agamben discusses a number of examples in which this domain of the intention to signify, between *phōnē* and *logos*—no longer *phōnē* or animal voice and not yet *logos* or meaningful language—appears in itself: in Paul's *1 Corinthians*, he points to the phenomenon of glossolalia, which we encounter in the fourth and the fifth experiment; in Augustine's *On Trinity*, he examines the experience of the dead word (*vocabulum emortuum*); and in Dionysius Thrace's *Technē Grammatikē*, he notes the "imitations of irrational animals, like *brekekeks* and *koi*," of which Dionysius writes: "these voices are inarticulate, since we do not know what they mean, but they are *engrammatoi*, since they can be written."[42] As Agamben comments on this third example, by introducing the animal voice into language, the voice "shows itself in letters as a pure intention to signify whose signification is unknown." That is to say, it does not show itself as the voice of a living being, but rather as the intention to signify, as part of the presupposition of human language, banning the inarticulate voice itself from this language. Therefore, Agamben can conclude the essay in which he refers to this example with the remark that "human language is therefore always 'language that no longer sounds on the lips of the living' in the double sense that it is necessarily a dead language or a dead voice, and it is never the living voice of man or the speech of any living creature."[43] Although Agamben attributes this conception of language to the Italian poet Pascoli, it seems to resonate with his own concerns regarding the limitations of human language, which by the presupposition of the "dead letter" is never understood as the voice of "any living creature."

Yet this seems to be a negative conclusion and does not indicate how, in language, the voice of a living creature may resound. Thus, Agamben's delimitation of the problem of language, the articulate voice, and the letter shows exactly why, in *Quel che resta di Auschwitz*, he has to return to this problem and, in fact, finds in the figure of the witness a possible positive response to the problem of the dead letter. Primo Levi, the witness at the center of Agamben's argument, introduces and describes the figure of Hurbinek, who is a version of Ariane become real:

> Hurbinek was a nobody, a child of death, a child of Auschwitz. He looked about three years old, no one knew anything of him, he could not speak and had no name [. . .]. He was paralyzed from the waist down, with atrophied legs, as thin as sticks; but his eyes, lost in his triangular and wasted face, flashed terribly alive, full of demand, assertion, of the will to break loose, to shatter the tomb of his dumbness.[44]

Although Hurbinek is banned from human language and does not even have a name, the voice he utters is "full of demand," which is a demand to speak, "to shatter the tomb of his dumbness."[45] Although Hurbinek cannot speak himself, this demand of his voice is attested to by Levi. He does so by bearing witness to the single sound that Hurbinek repeats, which does not seem to refer to a specific word or a particular meaning: articulated in language, reads like "*m-a-s-s-k-l-o, m-a-t-i-s-k-l-o*."[46] When reading this in light of the example from Dionysius Thrace, one could wonder why this articulation deserves to be called a form of bearing witness. Is it not simply a way of transforming Hurbinek's voice into letters and hence into "a pure intention to signify"? Although Agamben does not refer back to this example in *Quel che resta di Auschwitz*, his comments indicate that he has exactly this problem in mind when he writes: "To bear witness, it is therefore not enough to bring language to its own non-sense, to the pure undecidability of letters (*m-a-s-s-k-l-o, m-a-t-i-s-k-l-o*)." Such a procedure would, after all, simply describe what the ancient grammarian already described: as non-sense, the letters are the semiotic presupposition of the semantic. Yet this also means that these letters exclude the inarticulate voice and offer nothing but the dead letter. Nevertheless, what makes Levi's recollection and articulation of his word—of rendering Hurbinek's inarticulate voice articulate—a genuine form of bearing witness is the following: "It is necessary that this senseless sound be, in turn, the voice of something or someone that, for entirely different reasons, cannot bear witness." To bear witness thus is exactly to give a voice to these letters. In this way, the language of the witness "advances into what is without language," that is, into what lies beyond the mere presupposition of the letter. Only if language harbors the promise of such a transgression of its own presupposition—if it is capable of giving a voice to what it articulates—it is affected by and meets the demand of the human misery that cannot speak.

At the end of this experiment, we thus encounter a particular way of understanding the stakes of bearing witness. Bearing witness is only possible if the articulation of a voice does not simply transform the voice into letters, the *phōnē* into the *gramma* and its intention to signify, but rather promises to give, preserve and guard this voice in its articulation—here and only here, the human truly begins to speak. This is the secret that language is supposed to keep as it keeps a promise: that letters begin to bear witness to an inarticulate voice. In line with the story that Alice, the secretarious, tells us, we can now conclude that if there is a secret to language or a secret that needs to be kept in and by language, it does not so much concern what mystically has to remain silent, but rather concerns the promise of language to bear witness to a silent and silenced voice and articulate its demand to speak in language, to give it a voice. To keep this secret as one keeps a promise is the sole duty that "a secretarious, a real one never shrinks from"—nor do any of the witnesses akin to her.[47]

Chapter 4

Experiment III

Helena, the Poetess

What the lost demand is not to be remembered and commemorated but rather to remain in us and with us as forgotten and, only in this way, remain unforgettable.[1]

—Agamben, *Il tempo che resta*, 43/40

Hermes, the Interpreter

If the muses are the gods of the poets inspiring them to sing, Hermes must be the god of the interpreters. Hermes, as Socrates notes in the *Cratylus*, "is an interpreter, a messenger."[2] He brings and voices tidings and messages of the gods to the mortals. He addresses the latter on behalf of the former. Thus, he belongs at the threshold, traveling between the gods and the mortals, and traversing the gap that separates realms. Therefore, he does not respect limits and boundaries but rather transgresses them. Consequently, he is also the god of merchants, travelers, and thieves.

These different traits also characterize Hermes's relation to language, as Socrates explains: "Well, the name 'Hermes' seems to have something to do with speech: he is an interpreter (*hermēneus*), a messenger, a thief and a deceiver in words, a wheeler-dealer—and all these activities involve the power of speech."[3] To explain further what this means for human language, Socrates adds an account of the meaning of the name of Pan, the son of Hermes, who is "double-natured": human-like from the top and goat-like (*tragikon*) from the bottom. *Logos*, Hermes's invention, has the characteristics of his son; it is double-faced or double-tongued, true and false, conveying upon human language its tragic nature: "for it is here, in the tragic (*tragikon*) life, that one finds the vast majority of myths and falsehoods."[4] The power of speech is thus ambiguous. On the one hand, it can be divine and speak the truth; on the other hand, it can be goatish and tragic and distort and confuse the human perspective on reality. It is important to see that the ambiguity of language is not simply a negative phenomenon, but truly an ambiguous one. Language and speech have the capacity to deceive. Therefore, language is a risky business in human affairs. Yet this risk results from the fact that language needs to be able to transgress borders, limits, and boundaries: there is no communal language between humans and gods; the divine language cannot simply be spoken in a human tongue. The change from divine to human language involves a risk: perhaps, when the divine word is spoken in such a way that it remains too close to its divine tongue, it turns out to be incomprehensible to humans; or, perhaps, the attempt to render the divine word in human language twists and distorts the original message to such an extent that it remains mute. Yet Hermes is to adopt this risk if he wants to retain the chance of conveying the divine message: he needs to traverse the threshold and bear witness to the divine in the human realm.

Thus, bearing witness risks being caught up in the fraudulent side of language, of distortion and deception. This Derridean concern needs to be added to the framework of language and bearing witness that we encountered in the previous experiment in line with Lyotard's and Agamben's work. Agamben has a striking critique of Derrida's emphasis on the primacy of the letter. Moreover, he is capable of showing how a demand on language is made beyond the presupposition of the letter. In this way, he is capable of understanding language as the promise to bear witness to the voice that transcends the letter as the presupposition of language. Yet this linguistic transgression of the boundary of language is itself a characteristic theme in Derrida's oeuvre, and he will insist on the *différance* of the traversal of thresholds between, for instance, languages or genres. This traversal harbors the chance of transforming a language, but it is never clear from the outset how this transformation will affect this language and what it discloses and conceals, what it says and what it distorts. The English expression "out of joint" perhaps describes best what is required to let the divine, other language speak in a human language: the latter language needs to be deactivated, twisted "out of joint," that is, rendered inarticulate. Yet what exactly starts to speak or is given a voice in this process remains undecidable, caught between a risk and a chance. Thus, when bearing witness, the interpreter has to take into account both the smooth and the rough, goatish, and tragic side of language.

Helena, Hermes's Heir

This third experiment does not follow or imitate the characteristic scene of Hermes precisely. After all, as the title of the novel *Godenslaap* by the Belgian author Erwin Mortier indicates, whatever is borne witness to, it took place *While the Gods Were Sleeping*. They have nothing to say or communicate. They have turned their attention away from the human realm and scenes to which the Helena, the protagonist and narrator of *Godenslaap*, bears witness. She has come to the end of her life and looks back on it. In particular, she recalls the period of the First World War. She is thus an eyewitness, but she does not only speak on her own account. She also speaks for those who are no longer among the living to bear witness to their experiences. Like Alice, the narrator in Soucy's novel, Helena has a remarkable relation to language. Yet their relation to language is different. The language Mortier lends to his protagonist is breathtakingly beautiful and marked by a refined poetic style. It is almost as if the language used by Helena is the very opposite of the gruesome, horrific reality of the Great War that occupies most of her narration. It is also clear from the outset that she perceives herself as a descendant of Hermes commuting and communicating between the dead and the living. Being the sole survivor amid her family and friends, she is the only one who can tell not only her own but also their story, and grant them a voice.

In this reading, I focus mainly on the first part of the novel, which is not so much concerned with the details of the story of the Great War itself but rather with the questions of Helena's relation to language and of what kind of narrator-witness she is. It is remarkable to see that the first reception of the book, which was hailed in the Dutch and Belgian press as Mortier's truly important novel and which won many prizes and has been translated into several languages, did not pay due attention to this first part of the book, as if it were not really understood. This is odd because it discloses Helena's relation to language, to the past, and to the deceased, and it informs us about her sense of duty to the dead, which she experiences as the need to give the dead a voice in the present. Therefore, the questions this part raises are: How to give a voice to the dead? How to allow them to be present among the living? How to speak on and for them?

On several occasions, Helena argues that to keep silent about the dead implies forgetting them. They disappear if we don't tell and recall their stories. Following this logic, one might be inclined to argue that giving a voice to the dead or telling their stories is a mode of remembering them. Moreover, because we tell their stories based on our memories, it seems that these stories are made possible by memories that, in turn, are preserved by these stories. According to Helena, however, this logic does not apply here. The interplay of remembering and forgetting alone does not truly capture what the stakes are for her. For her, the true question is of how the past and the deceased remain with us—and for Mortier, the task is to explain how the past and the deceased remain with us in the form of fiction.

One might be on the right track to suspect here an affinity with what Agamben calls "the unforgettable." The unforgettable, as he explains, should not be understood as what cannot be forgotten because we remember it, but rather as what cannot be forgotten because we did not remember it in the first place. When considering the devastating destruction encountered in the Great War, we only need to turn our eyes to the many graveyards they leave behind filled with anonymous soldiers, drowned in the trenches, to understand what Agamben means with the category of the unforgettable. We cannot forget these soldiers because when they were killed we did not even have the chance to remember their lives or simply record their names. In light of such a disaster, Agamben's explanation of the category of the unforgettable is utterly clear: "In every instant, the measure of forgetting and ruin, the ontological squandering that we bear within ourselves far exceeds the piety of our memories and consciences."[5] He adds that the unforgettable comes with a particular "exigency" or demand (*esigenza*), namely "to remain with us."

The limitations of the "piety" of our memories are also Helena's concern. Memories are not the simple antidote to forgetting but are part and parcel of the process of forgetting that, in fact, causes the ones we want to remember to disappear. As Helena notes: "We have memories to tame the dead until they hang as still in our neurons as foetuses strangled by the umbilical cord. [. . .] Their true resurrection is elsewhere."[6] By taming and domesticating the dead, memories don't keep them alive, but stabilize them, rendering them as motionless as they are in their graves. The image that is chosen here is striking: the uterus, the place of a new life, is the image for the second graveyard of the dead in which they are finally completely dealt with. Above all, their motionlessness, their hanging still, means that the memories of the dead no longer move us, as the living do. In such a desperate situation, it is imperative to find another way than the interplay of memory and forgetting to respond to the demand of the deceased to remain unforgettable. Therefore, Helena says: "Their true resurrection is elsewhere."

To understand the shortcomings of memories, Helena's lifelong dispute with her mother concerning the proper human relation to the dead provides important clues:

> For [mother] the most unforgivable thing a living person could inflict on the dead was to make them speak; they can't defend themselves against what you put in their mouths. In her eyes the coin that the Ancient Greeks put under the tongue of their dead, as the fare for the ferryman who was to transport them to the far bank of the Styx, had a different purpose: it was hush money. If the dead had started chattering, they would immediately have choked on the coin [*muntstuk*]. They have no right to speak, she said, which is why no one must be their mouthpiece [*mondstuk*].
>
> I myself have my doubts, still. [. . .] everything that is dead keeps its vanished opportunities to exist [*mogelijkheden tot bestaan*] shut up in itself like a hidden shame.[7]

This quote, in the opening scene of the novel, captures one of the basic stakes of *Godenslaap*. From childhood onward, Helena doubts whether the dead indeed have no right to speak and whether the dead should not be given a voice. In fact, in relation to them, Helena senses a strong demand to be their "mouthpiece." Her mother, however, strongly opposes the propensity in her daughter to speak for the dead. In her argument, she proves herself to be as good a poet as her daughter: the mouthpiece, in Dutch *mondstuk*, is poetically contrasted with the coin, *muntstuk*, which the mother interprets as "hush money" to deprive the dead of their voices permanently.

The mother's objections seem quite reasonable. Is she not right when she claims that the dead cannot defend themselves against what we put in their mouths? Does she not demonstrate a keen awareness of the distorting dimension of the activity of Hermes and his descendants? Not the frozen, solidified memory of the dead but rather the words the living put in their mouths do injustice to their memory. Yet, as she adds, as opposed to a *mondstuk*, they should receive a *muntstuk*, to be put in their mouths so that they will choke in case they attempt to speak. Thus, the mother not only describes a state of affairs—the dead simply cannot speak—and states that the attempt to let them speaks trespasses the laws of nature, but she also affirms this natural state of affairs by referring to a particular (lack of) right on the part of the dead. They had their chance to speak when they were alive, but they no longer have any *right* to speak. This right is the expression of a more basic law, formulated by the mother at the end of the novel: "everything that is dead must be silent."[8] This "must" wavers between the necessity of nature and the obligation of the law, between what is their natural state and what we impose on them. She insists that the survivors have to observe this law in their relation to the dead. In later stages of the novel, it is noticed that the mother is fond of exclamation marks as well as tautological expressions. In light of these habits, one might perhaps phrase her objection to her daughter's attempts to give a voice to the dead in the tautology: "Dead is dead!" Helena's mother is only interested in determining and fixing the truths of her statements, affirming them by repetition and exclamation mark, thus opposing the "unforgivably provisional" language used by poets.[9] To her great dissatisfaction, however, her daughter turns out to be one of them, "a born poetess."[10]

In an intriguing quote, to exemplify her attitude to language, the born poetess compares books with children, gods, and the dead. What the last three share, among others, is that they are deprived of the capacity to speak themselves, but require a voice or a spirit to (re)inspire them and to let them speak again:

> I still believe that books, like gods and children, inhabit a limbo in existence, a dimension in which effects can lead to causes and yesterdays crawl forth from tomorrows. It is impossible to make final judgments there: who deserves heaven and who hell. Everything is yet to happen and everything is already over; that is the essence of paradise.
>
> As a child I regarded books as a kind of dead people, and actually I still do. Anyone who writes is organizing his own spirit realm. Books were filled with the same stillness as the stiff limbs of relatives on their deathbeds. True, they had more to say for themselves, but seemed like the dead to be yearning for a living spirit to linger in.[11]

Books, gods, children, and by definition some of the dead have a remarkable dwelling place: they are not at home in the world—in the *real* world, as perhaps Helena's mother might have emphasized—but they are to be found in what is described here as "a limbo in existence" (*het voorgeborchte van het bestaan*), that is, a realm in which things are not yet fixed or determined. This is the realm of the provisional itself, one might say. Provisional to such an extent that even the basic principles, the *archai* of our reality, such as that of cause and effect, can be put upside down so that effects lead to causes and yesterdays follow tomorrows. This dimension of being is addressed not in the language of tautology, in the language in which things are fixed and stabilized so that they can no longer move, but only in the language of poets, as Helena's mother attests: " 'For goodness's sake stop turning words on their heads, Hélène. Soon you'll be taking the world off its hinges and the poles will change places . . .' "[12] In this realm, even the basic principles can be otherwise and are thus provisional and contingent—in the poetic language of her daughter, the order of things is truly out of joint. One is therefore tempted to connect the idea of a limbo of contingency with what Helena said in a previous quote: "everything that is dead keeps its vanished opportunities to exist [*mogelijkheden tot bestaan*] shut up in itself." This limbo is characterized by possibilities of existence that are withdrawn from reality because their existence is terminated in reality. The living live their lives in light of their possibilities, actualizing them. The dead, on the other hand, represent possibilities that can no longer actualize themselves among the living. These possibilities exemplify par excellence the ontological squandering of which Agamben speaks to which I referred above: the possibilities or potentialities-of-being of those lives that have come to their untimely end will never be lived, actualized, or enacted; they are simply wasted with their death.

Yet this realm in which books, children, gods, and the dead dwell alike is a place where basic principles no longer apply, but can be revoked or put upside down. Therefore, this limbo is a limbo of possibilities because it *preserves* these possibilities; it is the realm in which these possibilities are returned to the dead—or, rather, still belong to the dead. Another passage of Agamben comes to mind in this context when he writes that redemption is to "restore possibility to the past"; and he goes on to explain: "making what happened incomplete and completing what never was."[13] Of what it means to restore possibility to the past, *Godenslaap* offers us a literary articulation: "Everything is yet to happen and everything is already over." Redemption, the "essence of paradise," is therefore only to be found in a realm in which the possibilities of existence are preserved even after their actualization has become utterly impossible.

In the logic of Helena, the dead demand these possibilities to be given back to them. Therefore, the giving back of these possibilities is the counter figure of the memories that kill the dead for a second time. Moreover, now it becomes clear in which sense the mother's "dead is dead" is more than a tautology. If memories can kill the dead, the dead can die a second death, which is brought upon them by the survivors.[14] The tautology "dead is dead" commits the murder causing this second death, by choking them with umbilical cords or with a coin put in their mouth. It is only by restoring these possibilities to them that they do not die *again*. Poetry can do this by bearing witness to the dimension of being that Mortier calls "limbo" in which the death of the dead is not confirmed but rather suspended in such a way that the dead remain with us—and this is nothing less than a condition of the poetess's existence: "I could not live without the dead, believe me [. . .]. I would feel empty if I could not fill their goblets with my funereal gifts: words that I put in their mouths, which I pour as libations over their altars."[15] As the gods and the children, also the dead and their nonactualized possibilities belong to the limbo of existence, which has no place in our everyday existence and therefore is prone to being silenced. To bear witness to the dead is to invite this limbo into the full light of existence and language: their demand to exist and to speak is borne witness to when the dead are given a voice. Once they are granted the chance to speak, the voices of the dead "burst out endlessly as if they are still alive."[16]

A Place to Be

Helena's testimony is not so much concerned with reconstructing what exactly happened, but rather with offering the dead a place they can inhabit. In our discussion of Soucy's novel, we noted how Alice bears witness to a world that has become desolate and purely uninhabitable. Also for Helena, bearing witness is concerned with the transformation of a dwelling place, but in a different sense. The dead have their own refuge in a limbo in existence, but this particular realm also means that they no longer have a dwelling place in the world itself, and one of Helena's concerns therefore is continuously: how can the dead remain with us? At one point in the novel, this problem is directly addressed. When calling to mind her aunt, Tatante, Helena notes that her aunt no longer has any place in this world. All the places where she used to be are destroyed, and all the spatial traces she left behind are thus erased. "Where else could she be? None of the places where I spent my childhood still exists."[17] One might have hoped that the living memory of the dead who were close to us, would be summoned by the places where they once dwelt. Yet Helena points out that, once these commemorative places have disappeared, only the survivors can be the dwelling place of the deceased—and in particular the language, words, and voices the survivors place at their disposal. In fact, even when these commemorative places would still exist, the dead could not dispense with the voices of the survivors because what is lost with the death of humans is their voice, their words, their gestures, their characteristic way of doing things, and their characteristic use of language, as Helena notes:

> As time goes on I miss such ostensibly insignificant details of those who are no longer there. [. . .] Usually I only notice them when they have died away for ever and leave me with the feeling that a whole language has been struck dumb, the complete vocabulary with which a person closes a book or arranges a dinner service like no one before or after them.[18]

Therefore, it must be the task of Helena's words to create a place and a space in this world where Tatante can be. Yet Helena is aware of the possibility that her words might result in the exact opposite of what they aim to do. Could they not, instead of creating a space for her aunt to inhabit, fully banish her aunt from the world? Helena doubts: "Am I capturing [Tatante] in these syllables, or are the words, which are never simply ours, making a place free in the great throng of things, a well-circumscribed empty space, in which she can here and now take up residence?"[19] As a true heir of Hermes, Helena worries about the ambiguity of inviting into one's own language what comes from elsewhere and what belongs to a different dimension of existence. She is the messenger of a limbo in existence, but what happens when she tries to convey her message in language? To capture Tatante would mean to make her motionless and dead in the words that are used for her. Hence, rather than inviting her to dwell in the language of the living, Helena fears that it might become her second death, fixed in the language of another. Yet, because language is "never simply ours," the words Helena uses for Tatante are not simply hers and are not controlled by her. This overflowing capacity of language, due to the fact that language is never owned, is the condition of possibility to provide a place for the dead in language so that they can remain with us.[20] This transgression of what the author masters is the very chance of language to speak for the other: when the poet speaks, they do not only hear their own words and voices but invite the dead in, allowing them to dwell in their words. Because the world no longer offers this opportunity, and because, to put it in Celan's famous words, "the world is gone," the poet hears the demand and responds: "I have to carry you."[21] Only in this way does poetic language offer the possibility to touch and encounter the other. Both Soucy's and Mortier's novels, insofar that each in its own way addresses the question of dwelling in a world that has become uninhabitable, follow the imperative that speaks so strongly from Celan's famous phrase "The world is gone, I have to carry you."

At the same time, the dwelling place that language offers can never be ascertained. The poetic attempt to let the dead speak is marked by the inseparability of chance and risk, of promising and withholding. The risk to fix and capture Tatante cannot be separated from the only chance that, perhaps, a place is made free for her to dwell in. Here, one might say, we discern the very meaning of the ambiguity of language in relation to bearing witness. In its most basic sense, the truth and falsity of language does not concern the question of whether language does or does not represent the world correctly. Rather, truth and falsity mean that language may or may not keep its promise, may or may not be trustworthy in creating a dwelling place for the dead and attesting to their demand to speak. It is against all the evidence of the contrary, as we shall see below, that language has to regain its trustworthiness, that language has to show that it is more than a collection of dolls of ash.

Thus, like Soucy's novel, *Godenslaap* complicates the relation between language and dwelling; it introduces the witness, poetess, and interpreter as the ones who have to build a dwelling place in language for the world that is lost and for the language that "has been struck dumb." Language is the house of being, but not in the sense that in and through language, being gives itself as a meaningful and inhabitable world. Poetic, testimonial language becomes the locus in which a limbo of existence, a dumbness of language, and the faint lament of a voice are offered a space to resound, not in order to become meaningful and comprehensible but to remain with us as unforgettable.

How (Not) to Trust Language

In addition to the inseparability of risk and chance that characterizes Helena's attempt to let and make the dead speak, her bearing witness is in yet another way concerned with the vulnerability, weakness, or incapacity of language. Testimony is not a way of overcoming this vulnerability, but rather speaks out of it and is born from it in three senses, as *Godenslaap* suggests: the misguidance of language, the incapacity of language to express what longs and demands to be expressed, and the immensity of untold stories.

Helena mentions the first two in direct reference to the Great War, which, like all wars, had a huge impact on the human relation to language and gave rise to a double suspicion of language, disavowing the capacity of language to keep its promise. On the one hand, language is the vehicle of propaganda and swollen rhetoric, guiding people to a war that only brought utter despair. On the other hand, language attested to its deep incapacity to offer the victims and soldiers who fought at the frontiers the means to bear witness to their experiences. Both elements are brought forward by Helena in the following striking quotation:

> We all mistrusted words. A combination of suspicion and bewilderment after years of ambiguous communiqués, lying newspapers, swollen propaganda and the inability of those who came back from the fronts to force what they have been through into an appropriate form, a vocabulary that would not distort, belittle, falsify their experience.[22]

This twofold mistrust is grounded in the capacity of language to distort and to be ambiguous, to lie and to falsify, to exaggerate and to belittle, but also in its utter incapacity to meet the demands of those who want to express their deepest experiences. If language is indeed the house of being in the sense intended by Heidegger, namely that it orients us and shapes a meaningful world, this distorting quality of language leaves this house in ruins: when we distrust the place that we used to call home, we are no longer at home there.

Whereas the war situation brings out this deceptive quality of language in all its poignant consequences, it is characteristic for human language as such. If language indeed has to be thought as the dwelling place of the human being, it is a dwelling place that is marked by this particular secret—its deception and incapacity to truly speak to the demands of the victims and the dead—that needs to be silenced if one is to trust this dwelling place, but that can nevertheless always rear its ugly head and hurl the human being out of its trusted home. What then happens, in the words of Helena confronted with the horrors of the Great War, is reminiscent of Heidegger's description of anxiety in *Sein und Zeit* in which all things lose their meaning. It is as if the meaning of all beings and the language in which it is articulated is merely a garment or a leafage that one can take off in order to show everything in its sheer nakedness. As we will also see in the next experiment on Kierkegaard's *Fear and Trembling*, language is a leafage to cover up the human's deepest secret, their nakedness. Helena extends this to all things:

> I wait until death dawns in objects, the naked hour when things lose their leaves and all becomes leggy and dumb, not able to clothe themselves with the habits or meanings in which we usually drape them—as if a short moment of symbolic weightlessness occurs in which the world forgets its coherence and God Himself washes his hands of creation so that everything shudders, eye to eye with itself.[23]

This loss of meaning is also the loss of (a trust in) language. It does not only affect the human being, and does not only describe the nakedness of the living voice without the leafage of language, but also affects being as such and confronts being with itself in its pure nakedness and meaninglessness, without any reference to a higher order. This encounter with being itself is, as in my account of Soucy's novel, a destitution of the world; the world loses its coherence; it is out of joint, which also means that it loses its basic principles, which are the very foundations on which language as the house of meaning is built.

The question—or, rather, the need and urgency—of testimony stems from the confrontation with this deception and incapacity intrinsic to language. Testimony is born from the inability of language to guide and orient humans as well as from its inability to express the experience of the world becoming desolate and incoherent. There is a striking passage in *Godenslaap* in which one of the characters, Etienne Leboeuf, is introduced as someone who carries the horrid experiences of the Great War in the movements of his flesh but is incapable of expressing them in language: "the flesh that weeps and trembles before the word, but the word that cannot deal with that quaking fear."[24] Etienne's flesh demands to speak, but language is incapable of letting him speak. Confronted with this incapacity, the urgency of testimony is born from this gap between language and experience, and between language and being. Bearing witness consists not so much in speaking *instead of* this flesh but in *articulating the demand* of this flesh.[25]

When writing that testimony is born from this incapacity, I do not mean that testimony simply overcomes this incapacity and finds a way to express these experiences after all. It rather means—and we will see in Part II how this motif returns in the accounts of Blanchot, Derrida, and Agamben of testimony—that testimony is in the first place a paradoxical mode of speech that bears witness to the absence of testimony. It is at this point that we return to Agamben's motif of the unforgettable, which we might rephrase in terms of the novel as the motif of the *untold* stories. Ricoeur strikingly captures these untold stories under the heading of the "more deeply concealed forms of suffering," which he explicates as "the incapacity to tell a story, the refusal to recount, the insistence of the untellable."[26] Agamben's unforgettable as well as Ricoeur's "more deeply concealed forms of suffering" concern a dimension of human experience that is not borne witness to, that does not or cannot find expression. At the threshold of the experiences that are expressed in testimonies and stories, there are experiences that are never attested to. Helena attests to a similar problem when she expresses her concerns with the task of poetic testimony. Although she is writing her story of the Great War, she emphasizes that this attempt to bear witness is surrounded by a universe of untold stories, some almost reaching the surface and almost solidified in writing, some never even reaching the mind of any poet: "Some stories brush past the still-liquid surface, drawing at most a light trail in the sky, but most things come and go unseen, and are pulverized silently. There is so much that will never be forgotten, because no one will ever have known that it existed."[27] One cannot hope for a clearer expression of the unforgettable and of the meaning of the untold story. As Helena's mother responds, insisting on the futility of such untold stories: " 'Then it's of no importance, child. If we don't know what we don't know, it doesn't exist!' " The repetition of "we don't know" plus the exclamation mark aim at expelling the ghost of the dead and their demand to speak. In this sense, Helena's mother is like Socrates, who concludes his interpretation of the dead Protagoras in the *Theaetetus* by expelling his ghost so that he may never speak again. Yet the unforgettable remains with us and gives Helena's testimony its specific depth. As a *fictional* account of what happened during the Great War, *Godenslaap* stands (in) for these untold stories: because a fictional account implies the suspension of its claim for truth, it liberates itself to stand for and to exemplify the stories of the dead that will never be told.[28] Understood in this sense, fiction offers indeed the possibility to put being into question. Rather than arguing, as the mother does, for the nonexistence of these untold stories, novels such as *Godenslaap* employ the testimonial potential of fiction to bear witness to the absence of testimony by telling a (fictional) story that invites and continuously refers to what has not been told and what remains hidden and, as such, unforgettable. Understood in this way, fiction is—or, rather, some novels are—one of the modes in which the unforgettable remains with us.

Any understanding of Mortier's novel along the lines of the unforgettable and untold stories resonates strongly with the motif of anonymity, which appears in at least three crucial moments. First, Helena argues that books and in particular her stories should appear without the name of an author.[29] The story is anonymous and thus tells the story of no one in particular, but for exactly this reason it can stand for all these anonymous histories that have never been told and for all these people whose stories will never be told. Second, Helena suggests that there should be "memorials for anonymous lumps of flesh, missing in action," emphasizing the importance of the anonymity of what is lost—the naked lumps of flesh that become utterly meaningless when detached from the body—and of what will never be told.[30] Third, when reflecting on what makes the human being speak, Helena refers to an anonymity in the human being itself that the human flees away from: "as we get older, everything [. . .] is drowned out [*overstemmen*] even more loudly by the breath of that alert sleep in us, which we try in vain to tuck in with words, but which also drives our words."[31] The question is what this void of speech is, from which we speak and which can drown us out. The Dutch *overstemmen* offers a clear indication: it contains the Dutch word for voice, *stem*. In this breath, we find a voice that speaks louder in us than all our speech and actions. This suggests that what sleeps in our speaking and acting is an inarticulate voice, a breath, that demands our words and that we can never fully capture with our words. The mute, inarticulate voice and the incapacity to speak is found within every human being, both speaking and non-speaking. Lyotard and Agamben call this anonymous voice "infancy," relating it to the beginning of human life. Mortier, on the other hand, relates it to the other end of human existence, old age. Both infancy and old age, in which speech and action crumble down, concern an inarticulate voice, a breath and spirit, in the human being that demands to speak, that demands our words and to which our words respond by acknowledging their incapacity to do justice to it. In this sense, the human being as a speaking being does not simply have an articulate voice, but also a breath, a faint lament, an inarticulate voice that demands to speak.[32] Here, the descendants of Hermes are located: between the living and the dead, between language and non-language, between promise and demand. Their task is to bear witness in the "unforgivably provisional" language they have at their disposal.[33]

Chapter 5

Experiment IV

Johannes, the Poet

> Only if language is not always already communication, only if language bears witness to something to which it is impossible to bear witness, can a speaking being experience something like a demand [*esigenza*] to speak.[1]
>
> —Agamben, *Quel che resta di Auschwitz*, 59/65

Experimenting Existence

Sometimes philosophers adopt the role of the poet themselves and compose a dialogue or narrative as *methodos*, as a way to do philosophy.[2] Plato's dialogues are exemplary in this respect, as are many of the works of Kierkegaard. For the latter, as the subtitle of his *Repetition* suggests, these poetic inventions are experiments.[3] Hong and Hong note that Kierkegaard uses the verb "to experiment" transitively; hence, his poetic constructions do not experiment *on* a human existence, but each of them experiments an existence, allowing the reader to experience this existence and to sense the peril at the heart of it.[4] Despite the existentialist thrust of his oeuvre, Kierkegaard does not portray his own actual psychology or existence in his poetic constructions. Rather, by adopting the position of the poet, "he puts [brackets] around his own personality" in order to experiment and experience not so much his own life but rather human existence in its imaginative variations.[5] This suspension of the writer's own existence implies that there is a source that remains silent in the poet's productions but that is nevertheless the source of the poet's power of language: "for with his little secret that he cannot divulge the poet buys this power of the word to tell everybody else's dark secrets."[6] There is always a remainder, a reserve that remains mute in poetic language, namely the secret of the poets themselves. Yet, by keeping their own secrets in reserve, poets can bear witness to the secrets of others. At this point, we discern a similarity with Alice, the secretarious. The source of her capacity to speak is the speechlessness of her twin sister, who embodies and carries the traumatic experience of their family. Trauma and voice are thus separated and assigned to two different bodies, Ariane and Alice, which nevertheless belong together in the unity of their twinhood. This indicates that this experience does not have one (articulate) voice of its own to express itself in language. It only enters language through a mediation, which is made possible by a doubling of language and experience. Kierkegaard's conception of the poet is marked by a similar duality. The actual experiences poets undergo in their existence cannot be part of their experiments. Nevertheless, this experience that precedes the articulate, poetic voice is the very source of the poet's capacity and compels them to write.

In *Fear and Trembling*, Kierkegaard directly addresses this duality of experience and poetic voice. Or, rather, it is Johannes de Silentio, who introduces himself as the poet who composed *Fear and Trembling*, who addresses this duality. What it means to be a poet becomes clear when Johannes, referring to Shakespeare, writes: "Thanks, once again thanks, to a man who, to a person overwhelmed by life's sorrows and left behind naked, reaches out the words, the leafage of language by which he can conceal his misery."[7] Language does not express human experience, but rather conceals the basic misery of human life. Language is depicted as the leafage by which humans may cover their nakedness, that is, their vulnerability, poverty, hardship, and need. In its most desolate forms, this misery might be identified with the human capacity to experience more than humans can bear, that is, to be traumatized, to encounter the very limit of their humanity, and to be brought to the very threshold of their human life.[8] In relation to the human capacity to speak, to transgress a limit also means that one can be robbed of this capacity or that one can experience something that cannot be said or spoken of. Here language and experience drift apart.

Fear and Trembling famously experiments the faith of the patriarch Abraham. This experiment imagines faith not simply as *a* possibility of human existence, but rather as its "highest" possibility; this means that it is a limit of human existence, which cannot be expressed or spoken of, and which has all the characteristics of a traumatic experience—or of an event in Badiou's sense of the word. Abraham's trauma concerns the order to slaughter one's child and to conceive of this act as a divine sacrifice. In relation to such an experience, poetry can only be a supplement, an addition that covers over this basic misery.⁹ In this way, poetry protects humans from a direct contact with their misery and, in *Fear and Trembling*, with Abraham's faith. Therefore, this secondary status of poetry with respect to experience and (actual) existence has one important positive dimension: the poet offers a leafage of language in which the basic experience can clothe itself and become presentable in public, and protect, guard, and keep in reserve this basic experience and peril of human existence.

Let me contrast this account of the poet with the account of *Fear and Trembling* Derrida provides in chapter 4 of *Donner la mort*. There, Derrida emphasizes the importance of seeing and of the divine, and especially of divine seeing. Departing from a marginal quote from the gospels in Kierkegaard's "novel"—"for [God] sees in secret"—Derrida suggests that the Dane remains too attached to the sense of sight in his account of Abraham's secret. If Derrida's insistence on the importance of sight indeed strikes a basic chord in *Fear and Trembling*, we would have to conclude, following an important line of thought in Derrida's oeuvre as a whole, that this positions Kierkegaard in the proximity of all those authors who remain caught up in the metaphysical affirmation of the primacy of light and sight. Yet Derrida's argumentation for this suggestion is rather complicated and perhaps too much of a detour. It does not deal directly with Kierkegaard's text (except for the reference to the sentence "for he sees in secret"). It rather follows an indirect path along Kierkegaard's adherence to Christianity, to the sermon of the mount from the *Gospel of Matthew*, in particular, toward the Latinized version of the hidden God, the *deus absconditus*. The Latin expression, much more than its Greek counterparts, privileges a sense of secret marked by sight: secretive is what is hidden from sight, as Derrida emphasizes. Moreover, Derrida interprets the phrase "for he sees in secret" in terms of the other who sees in me, and this means in the context of the Gospel of Matthew, God who sees in me. Applying this to the story of Abraham, Derrida notes that God apparently did not (fore)see what Abraham would decide, whether he would or would not actually sacrifice his son, but that he does immediately see Abraham's decision, and at the moment that Abraham raises his knife to strike his son, he intervenes.¹⁰ With respect to the story, these points seem somewhat one-sided and even far-fetched. They, in turn, give rise to the concern of whether Derrida did not see that in *Fear and Trembling*, the issues of seeing in the other and seeing the secret of the other are not so much raised in relation to God, but first and foremost in relation to the poet, as the above citations from *Fear and Trembling* indicate. Moreover, the poet is not said to *see* the secret of the other. God may be seeing in secret according to Matthew, but the poet only *tells* the secret of the other, according to Johannes de Silentio. Secret, thus, is not concerned in the first place with sight, but rather with speaking, hearing, telling, and poeticizing. By his own definition of the poet, Johannes promises to tell the "dark secrets" of Abraham. Because poets do not narrate or experiment their own experiences, we may conclude that faith is neither Johannes's mystery nor his misery.

To Tell a Secret

What does it mean to tell a secret? According to general theories in hermeneutics, we tell stories because they allow us to understand the meaning of what happens around us and to us. Narratives are tools for the understanding of our world and ourselves. This is, at first sight, also at stake in *Fear and Trembling*: Johannes de Silentio is a poet who tells a story to understand something of human existence.[11] Or, perhaps, it would be better to say that he retells the story of *Genesis* 22. Yet why is it necessary or beneficial to tell another, supplementary story in addition to the one we find in *Genesis* 22?

In *The Genesis of Secrecy*, Kermode argues that the successive gospels of Mark, Matthew, Luke, and John offer different versions of the same story, in which every consecutive version explicates the previous one by rendering intelligible what remained mysterious and unclear in the previous version.[12] Hence, by retelling a story, one offers an interpretation of its older version(s), by which it becomes more intelligible. Such a conception of consecutive storytelling would fit nicely with the general understanding of what interpretation is. Interpretation aims to render more intelligible what at first is unclear, ambiguous, or mysterious. A story can be expanded by adding details by which the course of a story becomes more comprehensible. By determining what in the previous version is un- or underdetermined, the connection between the different situations, actions, remarks, and characters in the story becomes more transparent in the unity of a more elaborate plot. Moreover, retelling the story not only involves adding new details, but also may consist of removing or substituting details and elements that obstruct the route toward a more integrated plot. In this case, we are guided by the hermeneutic principle that "we omit what we do not understand."[13] In sum, to tell and retell a story leads to a chain of consecutive interpretations, marked by a process of sorting and (re)arranging: the story is supplemented; parts of the story are substituted, omitted, or rearranged.

It is not difficult to see also that Johannes's retelling carries the traces of this process. To provide only one example, the language of the poet's narration is marked by that of German Idealism. The different categories that are introduced—such as the ethical, the religious, faith, the paradox, and the absurd—are all explained in the vocabulary of this school of thought. In this sense, many aspects of the story of Abraham are translated and rendered in the philosophical and cultural language of Kierkegaard's day and age.

Yet, in one important respect, Johannes's narrative puts the hermeneutic process of sorting and arranging upside down. The poet Johannes is without a doubt an interpreter, but his interpretation is of a different kind. It is not guided by the goal of offering an *understanding* of Abraham and his faith, as is repeated again and again, from the very first pages of the story onward: "'No one was as great as Abraham. Who is able to understand him?'"[14] Thus, we see that by adding the secret in the poet's task of telling a story, the type of interpretation Kierkegaard's Johannes offers does not remain within the confines of the sense of interpretation used by Kermode and De Man alike, in which the aim of the practice of interpretation is meaning and understanding, often at the cost of forgetting incomprehensible elements. For Johannes, to tell a secret is not to disclose it, but rather to keep it. Therefore, we have to ask again: what does telling and interpreting mean for Kierkegaard's poet?

In the opening sections of *Fear and Trembling*, Johannes questions the Hegelian conviction that faith can be grasped conceptually and that such an understanding, because it captures the very truth of faith, goes beyond faith itself. Johannes doubts the idea that the concept of faith is higher than faith. *Fear and Trembling* aims to show that faith—or at least Abraham's faith—lies beyond the capacities of the concept and its understanding:[15]

> I am constantly aware of the prodigious paradox that is the content of Abraham's life, I am constantly repelled, and, despite all its passion, my thought cannot penetrate it, cannot get ahead by a hairsbreadth. I stretch every muscle to get a perspective, and at the very same instant I become paralyzed.[16]

This is an intriguing quote because it shows that it is only by the utmost attempt to approach Abraham that the conceptual grasp is paralyzed and rendered inoperative. We find here a characteristically skeptic experience in Kierkegaard: the quest for understanding runs aground and therefore needs to be suspended. This is what *telling* the secret apparently is. By deactivating the conceptual grasp intrinsic to language—because language is the medium of understanding—the secret is not penetrated, understood, captured, or explained. The secret is not exposed, but it is *kept*, exactly in this unstable equilibrium of a poetic language that deactivates language as the medium of conceptual understanding, thus allowing an additional capacity of language to be brought into play. As a poet's creation (*poiēsis*), *Fear and Trembling* is at a basic level concerned with the question of language: in language, the very medium of clarification, a secret need not be silenced or excluded or exposed, but can be kept. To tell a secret is, thus, for Johannes de Silentio, to keep this secret, in the double sense of this expression. To tell a secret is, first, *not* to tell the secret, that is, not to give it away in such a way that it can be understood and is fully available for the conceptual grasp. And to tell a secret is, second, to preserve the secret, that is, not to silence, forget, or banish it from language as if it is nothing.

To get a better sense of the poetic strategy at work in this paralysis of the conceptual grasp as well as of the rhetoric by which it can keep the secret, let me analyze some other passages from *Fear and Trembling*. When Johannes mentions his incapacity to capture Abraham's secret, he also introduces the figure of the tragic hero. The tragic hero can be comprehended, although it belongs to the limit of comprehension. Johannes uses this figure, as well as the knight of resignation, to approach Abraham; and he does so throughout *Fear and Trembling*. At first sight, one might, once more, suspect that he follows a well-known hermeneutic principle: we approach what we do not understand in light of what we do understand, and if we see similarities between the two—for instance, between the knight of resignation and the knight of faith—we acquire access to the foreign phenomenon of the knight of faith by our comprehension of the knight of resignation. Yet this is not the strategic or rhetoric function of the figures of the tragic hero and the knight of resignation. Although they come close to Abraham, their proximity does not disclose similarities. Rather, they imply the closure and downfall of this hermeneutic principle:

> I *think* myself *into* the hero; I cannot think myself into Abraham; when I reach that eminence, I sink down, for what is

offered me is a paradox. [. . .] Philosophy cannot and must not give faith, but it must understand itself and know what it offers and take nothing away, least of all trick men out of something by pretending that it is nothing.[17]

The hermeneutic quest for similarities runs aground on the experienced dichotomy of "I *think* myself *into* the hero" and "I cannot think myself into Abraham," exemplifying the sheer impossibility of entering faith conceptually.[18] Yet this conceptual impenetrability does not mean "that it is nothing." For Kierkegaard's poet, faith is a member of the set of those categories that have always baffled philosophy because they appear as nothing or as not-being in the language of philosophy, although they are not simply nothing. In this sense, it is not so strange that Kierkegaard has chosen to portray faith in such a way that it continuously appears as the other of philosophy, as what is different from philosophy, as if reminding the reader of Plato's (and the Stranger's) concerns in the *Sophist* to commit patricide on Parmenides—as Kierkegaard perhaps aims to do on Hegel— to understand the particular mode of being of forms of non-being that lead him to introduce the "kind" of otherness. When the poet's language succeeds in paralyzing "philosophy," what remains is not nothing, but Abraham's secret. With this notion of paralysis—in the historical orbit of which also Heidegger's *Destruktion*; Derrida's *déconstruction*; and Blanchot, Nancy, and Agamben's *désoeuvrement* and *epochē* belong—we approach the true calling of poetic language in *Fear and Trembling*. This novel or "dialectical lyric" is only successful if it forces philosophy to acknowledge that something remains beyond its grasp *and* that the poetic creation responds to this reserve's demand to be said.

In *Fear and Trembling*, this is in the first place a battle with Hegel's dialectics. Therefore, we have to be careful and note that it is not enough that philosophy recognizes its other because in the dialectical process this recognition and the accompanying negation is the very *dunamis* of thought's movement. Rather, philosophy should be confronted by an otherness it cannot recognize or negate so that its machinery is truly deactivated by it. Kierkegaard's poet thus is engaged in the same enterprise that, more than two centuries later, Derrida describes as follows:

Philosophy has always insisted upon this: thinking its other. Its other: that which limits it, and from which it derives its essence, its definition, its production. To think its other: does this amount solely to *relever* (*aufheben*) that from which it derives, to head the procession of its method only by passing the limit? Or indeed does the limit, obliquely, by surprise, always reserve one more blow for philosophical knowledge?[19]

All depends on the question of whether this "other," which Kierkegaard calls the secret, has one more blow in reserve. How could this be? If the knight of resignation and the tragic hero are close to the knight of faith, but if this proximity is not a source of the similarities that make the application of the aforementioned hermeneutic principle possible, what then is their relation? Perhaps they are doubles. They are much alike. Yet, exactly at the point at which they do not coincide, an abyss opens up between them so that the double becomes the realm of uncanniness for the first, familiar figure. This seems to be affirmed toward the end of *Fear and Trembling*, when Johannes discusses some more examples of the tragic hero and the knight of resignation. There, he actually notes that he took a detour along these figures to approach Abraham, yet

> not as if Abraham could thereby become more comprehensible, but in order that the incomprehensibility could become more salient, for, as I said before, I cannot understand Abraham—I can only admire him. [. . .] they were explained, while being demonstrated each within its own sphere, only in order that in their moment of deviation they could, as it were, indicate the boundary of the unknown territory.[20]

Hence, indeed, the introduction of the tragic hero and the knight of resignation does not lead to the disclosure of similarities allowing one to slyly slide into "the unknown territory" of Abraham's existence in order to grasp it. Rather, these examples are so close to the knight of faith that the point at which they differ—"their moment of deviation"—turns into a *no pasarán*, an aporia, a non-access for thought to enter Abraham's secret. To approach an unknown territory by exploring its boundaries might best be understood as an approach of the very promise of a secret, but this promise does not give to the understanding what it promises: it (with) holds the secret in reserve as a blow to reason.

Johannes develops this strategy not only in his reading of these examples, but also in his appropriation of the dialectical opposition between the universal and the singular. For him, the universal corresponds to the ethical. Ethically, Abraham is a murderer, willing to murder his son, to whom he actually has the highest ethical obligation to protect. This judgment on Abraham's behavior is universal in the sense that it can be understood, communicated, and shared by all. The singular, on the other hand, is what confronts or resists the universal. For Hegel, such a confrontation is a moment in a further development of the universal. Yet, in the case of Abraham, this resistance is not the mark of a lack in development, of the obstruction of the next dialectical move that elevates the singular and reconciles it with the universal. Rather, we encounter here a singularity that interrupts the very movement of inclusion in the universal. It is a singularity *beyond* the universal. This singularity is an exception, as discussed in Kierkegaard's *Repetition*, engaged in a "dialectical battle [. . .] in which the exception battles his way through and affirms himself as justified." He continues: "On the one side stands the exception, on the other the universal, and the struggle itself is a strange conflict between the rage and impatience of the universal over the disturbance the exception causes and its infatuated partiality for the exception."[21] The resistance of the exception to the universal implies, in negative terms, that the singularity of Abraham's secret can only be approached as what cannot be shared, cannot be understood, and cannot be spoken of in a meaningful way, that is, as the negation of the universal. This is the very reason why, in Hegel's thought, the concept of faith holds the truth of faith, because in the concept faith has become shareable and understandable to all. Yet, for Kierkegaard, this fails to recognize how this singularity is beyond the universal. In positive terms, it turns out that the universal is not the medium in which everything eventually will be taken up, but that there is an exception to it. Moreover, according to Kierkegaard, the universal has an "infatuated partiality" for this exception. Hence, it is not the universal or the ethical that represents the ultimate *telos* of the dialectical battle, but it is rather the exception that is the real goal of this battle that aims to move beyond the universal.[22] In a formal sense, Kierkegaard's perversion of Hegel's dialectics provides the very (formal) meaning of the phenomenon of faith: the "paradox that the single individual is higher than the universal."[23]

The Communicable and the Incommunicable

By allowing the secret to enter into a battle with the universal, the secret becomes incommunicable and incommensurable, without a common measure or a common sense. This is reflected in Johannes's repeated statement that he does not understand Abraham. Yet this is not all he says. Often, if not always, he accompanies the statement that he does not understand Abraham with the confession that he nevertheless admires him. Apparently Johannes is attuned in a particular way to Abraham, and this attunement or mood, as in the sense of Heidegger's *Stimmung*, is reflected in the voice or *Stimme* with which he tells Abraham's secret. This voice is not the voice of reason or understanding, but the voice of admiration.

It is important to capture this mood by which the poet is attuned to his subject. To admire faith is not to have faith. To admire faith is not to understand faith. To admire faith is not even to condone faith or the actions with which it goes hand in hand. In fact, sometimes, when Johannes speaks of his admiration, he also says that he is appalled by Abraham. The ethical condemnation of Abraham's behavior thus is never bypassed by the poet.[24] To admire faith thus is to be outside of faith but nevertheless drawn to it, not in order to become one who has faith, but rather to favor faith, albeit in a particular way. Moreover, one should not forget that the English terms "to admire," "admiration," as well as the Danish terms *beundre* and *beundring*, which are close to the German *bewundern* and *Bewunderung*, have a specific philosophical impact. Aquinas translates Aristotle's notion of to wonder, *thaumazein*, as the noun *admiratio*; and in Hegel's German it is rendered as *Verwunderung*.[25] To admire thus is also to be in the particular attunement of the perplexity and astonishment that initiates philosophy; it is an encounter with a phenomenon that resists understanding, that withdraws from reason's grasp, and that is experienced in this particular withdrawal. By this admiration, which experiences its own ignorance of the confronted phenomenon, the poet does not simply "repeat" the other's existence, but he creates his story, that is, gives a voice to the exception in the realm of the communicable, which by nature excludes the exception. Yet he does not speak with the voice of reason but with the voice of admiration. To get a better sense of what this means and what type of language this voice speaks, we need to inquire more carefully into the different senses of language that play a role in *Fear and Trembling*.

Language as the medium of commensurability and understanding denies Abraham the chance and the possibility to speak. As Johannes states: "Abraham [. . .] cannot speak. As soon as I speak, I express the universal, and if I do not do so, no one can understand me."[26] These remarks do not mean that Abraham does not say anything at all. Although he does not say much and mainly keeps his silence on the three-day journey to

Mount Moriah, the place where the sacrifice takes place, he does say something. However, these words cannot be understood, and thus do not belong to language as the medium of reason and understanding. Yet, because Abraham does say something, one cannot help but wonder what type of linguistic competence is left to the patriarch.[27]

Abraham's experience of the divine demand to sacrifice his son is so traumatic and singular that he cannot share it. He cannot express it. It renders him mute: "Abraham remains silent—but he *cannot* speak. Therein lies the distress and anxiety. [. . .] The relief provided by speaking is that it translates me into the universal."[28] Thus, it is Abraham's singular experience that robs him of his capacity to speak on this issue and to disclose it to others because as soon as he would start to speak, he would stop being Abraham and betray the very singularity that constitutes his existence.[29]

Yet, if this is the case, how are we to understand the words that he speaks to his son? To what mode of speech does the following verse attest? "And Abraham said: God himself will provide the lamb for the burnt offering, my son."[30] As masters of irony, Kierkegaard and his poet discern the ironic sense of this saying. It is not untrue what Abraham says—if Isaac is sacrificed, it will have been on God's demand, but if God selects another lamb than Isaac ("because by virtue of the absurd it is indeed possible that God could do something entirely different"[31]), it will also be true. Yet at the same time, this response does not respond to Isaac, who wonders, when seeing the fire and the wood, where the lamb for the sacrifice is.[32] As Johannes interprets this response: "His response to Isaac is in the form of irony, for it is always irony when I say something and still do not say anything."[33] Although Abraham says something, he does not say anything that can be understood and that directly responds to Isaac's question.[34] Thus, by speaking, Abraham does not respond, but he only offers a "response without response," as Derrida puts it. Perhaps we can say that this "response without response" takes on the task of paralyzing language as medium of the universal. For instance, it frustrates and interrupts the normal dialogical order of question and answer in which the answer not only addresses the question but also offers a response that, in the act of answering, is communicated to the questioner. An ironic response does not respond, but paralyzes and suspends the communicability of language. One could perhaps also say that in the medium of language, Abraham withdraws from language. Yet he does so *in* language and thus imprints a mark or trace on the body of the language he uses to keep his secret in reserve.

The Divine Language

In one sense, the previous sentences are profoundly misleading: I've put Abraham in the position of the subject in these sentences. Kierkegaard's poet emphatically denies that Abraham, even when speaking, displays a capacity to speak. Rather, the language he speaks and that we hear through his mouth does not belong to human tongues. Johannes says this in two different quotes in which Abraham's "response without response" is interpreted as a form of glossolalia, as a speaking in tongues: "Speak he cannot; he speaks no human language. And even if he understood all the languages of the world, even if those he loved also understood them, he still could not speak—he speaks in a divine language, he speaks in tongues."[35] The phenomenon of speaking in tongues refers back to 1 *Corinthians* 14:1–20. In this part of 1 *Corinthians*, the apostle Paul argues that speaking in tongues is not upbuilding for the community because without an interpreter, nobody can understand the one who speaks. Those who speak in tongues therefore remain "children" in their "thinking" or understanding.[36] Yet, in another sense, speaking in tongues is also considered worthwhile for the individual because their spirit is then in a direct or absolute relation to God, no longer mediated by the community, and in this way these individuals "build up themselves."[37]

Agamben notes that the last part of 1 *Corinthians* 14:11 is translated in a strange way in, for instance, the Vulgate and the King James Bible. According to the latter translation, Paul says about the one who speaks in tongues: "he that speaketh shall be a barbarian unto me." Yet, as Agamben points out, the Greek expression that is used here, *ho lalon en emoi*, does not mean "he that speaketh *unto* me," but rather "he that speaketh *in* me." He continues:

> if I utter words whose meaning I do not understand, he who speaks in me, the voice that utters them, the very principle of speech in me, will be something barbarous, something that does not know how to speak and that does not know what it says. To-speak-in-gloss is thus to experience in oneself barbarian speech, speech that one does not know; it is to experience an "infantile" speech ("Brethren, be not children in understanding") in which understanding is "unfruitful."[38]

With this explanation, Agamben offers an illuminating background against which we can read Johannes's reference to speaking in tongues. It is not simply Abraham who speaks, but his secret speaks in him. While this secret is the very origin of his existence, it is not his property or possession; he does not master it or understand it, but is rather the effect of it. This secret consists in faith, that is, Abraham's absolute relation to the universal, and this description also refers to the Pauline passage on glossolalia. Thus, the voice of this absolute relation speaks in Abraham. He experiences and expresses this "barbarous" dimension that does not belong to "normal" adult language that can be understood.

Following Paul's suggestion, Agamben writes that to speak in tongues is "to experience an 'infantile' speech." Here, "infantile" does not simply mean "childish" in the pejorative sense of the word, but rather refers to the etymological meaning of *in-fans*, non-speaking. This experience is a primitive, primordial one that precedes language and that cannot be expressed in the language of understanding, but it does leave its traces on and in language, and is in this way "communicated" to the ones who hear this speech: those who hear this speech do not understand, but are affected by it.[39]

Hence, no one knows what to make of it when hearing this divine tongue "unless someone interprets [*diermēneuō*]," as Paul adds.[40] Agamben does not discuss this addition; in fact, he interprets glossolalia as an example of the pure intention to signify, and the interpreter would, in this case, simply be the one who manages to find some meaning in the gibberish of the glossolalist.[41] Yet when he interprets glossolalia in this way—grammatologically, if you like—he seems to forget that the reference to the infant in this letter suggests that we are dealing here with an inarticulate voice that does not need to be accounted for in terms of meaning but that can be recognized as the voice of a singular existence. Paul's addition of "unless someone interprets" plays a significant role in the composition of *Fear and Trembling*. The language and the voice of reason have nothing in common with the divine language of glossolalia and its inarticulate voice, *unless* there is a third voice that speaks for the glossolalist, an interpreter or a poet.

Three Languages, Three Voices

Abraham is the true witness, as Johannes de Silentio writes, of his singular existence and the singular, absolute relation to God, that is, the absolute relation to an instance for which "all things are possible," as Johannes writes; he continues: "The absurd does not belong to the differences that lie within the proper domain of the understanding. It is not identical with the improbable, the unexpected, the unforeseen."[42] Thus, Abraham finds himself in a state of exception; he finds himself in a situation in which the universal as the ethical is suspended. Here, the sovereign God can ask everything of him—and he does ask everything—but Abraham relates to this God as a knight of faith, that is, in the faith that God will return his dead son to him, and thus he relates to a God for whom all things, even the impossible resurrection of the dead, must be possible. This Kierkegaardian state of exception is marked by the structure of the promise to which faith adheres at the very moment that the promise not only withholds what it promises—God has not yet given anything back when Abraham is asked to believe—but even seems to result in the opposite of what it promises, namely the death of his son. In fact, it is the promise that marks the realm of the singular. If the promise would be reasonable or foreseeable, faith would not be required because the mediation by the language of understanding would suffice. Yet, in the encounter with this particular promise—a posterity is promised to the man who is supposed to butcher his only son—there seems to be no reason except for the divine demand: "You have to have faith in me!" Of this exceptional promise, Abraham is the witness by his faith and existence.

Yet, as Derrida's perceptively writes, Abraham can only be called a witness in a particular way:

> [H]e doesn't witness to it in the sense that to witness means to show, teach, illustrate, manifest to others the truth that one can precisely attest to. Abraham is a witness of the absolute faith that cannot and must not witness before men. He must keep his secret. [. . .] Can one witness in silence? By silence?[43]

Before addressing the questions Derrida raises on witnessing in silence, we should note that indeed, for Johannes, Abraham is "never the teacher," but a witness in a particular sense, namely that of *martyr*: he bears witness to this promise by his very existence, by his way of life and the faith it expresses. In exactly this sense, the martyr does not teach or speak; he is a mute witness who endures "the martyrdom of misunderstanding."[44] This misunderstanding is the effect of the "secrecy and exclusivity [*non-partage*]"[45] that mark the promise and the faith that constitute the absolute relation of Abraham and God. As Johannes writes: "He who desires only to be a witness confesses thereby that no man, not even the most unimportant man, needs another's participation."⁴⁶ A witness is usually the one who experiences something and bears witness to his experiences. Abraham is only half of this witness: he is the one who truly experiences, but he does not tell his experiences.

These latter remarks bring us back to Derrida's questions. Indeed, how does one "witness in silence" or "by silence"? What is a witness who does not make anything known? The problem we are dealing with can be formulated in terms of the two languages and the two voices we have encountered so far. The common language and the divine language are mutually exclusive. The voice of reason cannot speak in this divine language, and the barbarous voice cannot speak in the common language. This is why Lyotard calls the speech of Abraham "idiolect" and adds that a third party, beyond God and Abraham, has access to neither the addresser, Abraham, nor the phrase, that which Abraham says.⁴⁷ Yet this is only the point of departure for the figure of the witness and the task of bearing witness. To witness the divine language and to express it by speaking in tongues does not amount to a bearing witness that simply speaks the language of its tribunal, which after all is the *common* tongue.

Yet, on the threshold between these two languages, a third voice speaks. This third voice speaks to the tribunal for whom Abraham cannot speak, and this third voice speaks for Abraham, gives him a voice in the common language. This is the voice of the poet. Johannes is the messenger of a "residual incommensurability" in human existence.⁴⁸ To tell a secret is exactly this: to be the messenger of a mute and silent dimension of human existence—this is why Johannes is *de Silentio*, of the silence. He is the messenger of a human existence of which the singularity can only be expressed by an inarticulate voice. Johannes is the poet, the messenger of this silence, and the one who *speaks for* this silence and gives it an articulate voice.

This can be traced in Johannes's description of his own poethood. He calls himself "a supplementary clerk."⁴⁹ This means that he has a secondary role: he is not the hero or protagonist of the story; he does not speak of his own experiences but is rather the scribe who writes the story because, apparently, the hero and the protagonist do not—and, in the case of Abraham, cannot—speak for themselves:

> The poet or orator can do nothing that the hero does; he can only admire, love, and delight in him. [. . .] He is recollection's genius. He can do nothing but bring to mind what has been

done, can do nothing but admire what has been done; he takes nothing of his own but is zealous for what has been entrusted.⁵⁰

In the terminology of Aristotle, with which Kierkegaard was familiar, the poet is the one whose task it is not to act (*prattein*) and experience, but to create (*poiein*) the remembrance of action and existence. To emphasize that indeed the poet does not take any initiative himself for true action, Johannes writes that the poet "can do nothing but admire what has been done." Yet exactly this distance from any true initiative opens the poet to the possibility of admiration, to the reverence for something sacred that attracts the poet and repels him—and with which he will therefore never identify himself. This admiration, the proper attunement or *Stimmung* of the poet grants him the specific power to be "zealous for what has been entrusted." Thus, he offers his voice or *Stimme* to the hero and sings the song and story that belongs to someone else, starting every story with the epigraph "not mine the tale."⁵¹ Nevertheless, it is the poet who takes care of this story, who creates it, and who makes it known to others.

Johannes the poet is thus another heir of Hermes who delivers messages from the gods to the mortals: Johannes is a *hermēneus* who speaks for an existence that can no longer speak, not only because Abraham no longer lives but also because this existence cannot speak for itself in the common tongue. There is one thing that Abraham, if he were confronted with the necessity to account for himself, could never respond: "I will let my actions speak for themselves." When these actions speak for themselves, they will only say in the common tongue: "Murderer, murderer!" Johannes, on the other hand, keeps Abraham's secret by his admiration and remembrance. He does so by speaking in a comprehensible way to an audience that understands the common language. Does this not mean that he, after all, betrays Abraham's secret? Perhaps. The poet always runs this risk of not keeping the secret. By speaking, the poet adopts this risk, but he adopts it in light of the chance to come to the aid of the true witness, Abraham. As a pseudo-witness, the poet offers Abraham a voice so that his experience will not remain merely mute, forgotten, and inarticulate, excluded by language. In its most minimal sense, to adopt a formulation explored by authors such as Blanchot, Derrida, and Agamben, the poet can attest to the absence of attestation, that is, to the absence of a voice or reason in an inarticulate possibility of existence, which nevertheless is not nothing. Such an attestation already supplements language with an attestation that common language would be tempted to exclude as superfluous. In a less minimal sense, and this might be the basic task of all poetic language, the poet may do something *to* language. As a "supplementary clerk," the poet supplements not only the mute existence for which he speaks—adding a comprehensible word to that of the glossolalist; interpreting it for the community that is dazzled by what it thinks is nothing but the gibberish of a madman—but he also supplements the common language by creating a new idiom in this language that carries all the marks of the singularity it bears witness to. What Derrida writes on the translator-poets—and what else is Johannes if not a translator-poet, a poet who strives to write the divine language in the common tongue—applies *mutatis mutandis* to the work of Johannes: "It is their task to explain, to teach, that one can cultivate and invent an idiom, because it is not a matter cultivating a given idiom but of producing the idiom."[52] Only in such a way, by creating a new idiom in a common language—for instance, by perverting the dialectical relation between the universal and the singular, by admiring rather than understanding, by invoking the impossible as a possibility for God, and so on—may Kierkegaard's poet hope to supplement the real witness's idiolect. Here, to bear witness means to speak with this double vocabulary of idiolect and invented idiom. Johannes thus belongs in the gap between language and experience, between the common voice and the divine, infantile voice, between common language and idiolect. On this threshold, he speaks as a witness for the one who is prosecuted as a madman and a murderer in the realm of the universal. Before the tribunal of common sense and common reason, Kierkegaard's poet bears witness to a secret to keep the secret.

Chapter 6

Experiment V

Bartleby, the Scrivener

So true it is, and so terrible too, that up to a certain point the thought or sight of misery enlists our best affections; but, in certain special cases, beyond that point it does not.[1]

—Melville, *Bartleby, the Scrivener*, 19

Although the title of this fifth experiment resembles that of the others, it is nevertheless oddly out of place among them. Each of the other ones consists of the name of the narrator or interpreter. This experiment, however, carries the title of the one who is silent and cannot be understood. The reason why I nevertheless have chosen this title is simple. Although there is a narrator in Herman Melville's *Bartleby, the Scrivener: A Story of Wall Street*, he remains anonymous. Yet this experiment also will zoom in on the narrator's work. Thus, perhaps, a more suitable title would have been "X, the Narrator" or "Anonymous, the Witness." It is as if, stronger than in the other stories—but perhaps similar to the slave in the *Theaetetus*—the narrator has remained nameless for the sake of the object of his testimony to speak as clearly as possible to us.

Deleuze's Bartleby

The passage from the fourth to the fifth literary experiment, from *Fear and Trembling* to *Bartleby, the Scrivener*, might best be described as an intensification of the issues encountered in the analysis of the poet's task to tell a secret.[2] Derrida already surmises that a relation might exist between Bartleby and Abraham. Like Abraham, Bartleby's famous "I would prefer not to" seems glossolalist: "Is it not as if Bartleby were also speaking 'in tongues'?"³

Perhaps this kinship explains why there is a proximity between Derrida's reading of *Fear and Trembling* and Deleuze's reading of *Bartleby, the Scrivener*. Not only are both texts written in the same period—Deleuze's text was first conceived in 1989, and Derrida's stems from 1992—but we also see a remarkable consonance on the theme of the in- or non-human language expressed in Abraham's and Bartleby's response. Perhaps the most significant difference between Derrida and Deleuze, and between their different choices in texts in which this inhuman language is traced, is that Deleuze is less preoccupied than Derrida to determine this sense of language as or in relation to the figure of the secret. Yet to be less preoccupied with these figures does not mean to avoid them altogether. In fact, Deleuze does employ this figure: "All referents are lost, and the formation [*formation*] of man gives way to a new, unknown element, to the mystery [*mystère*] of a formless [*informe*], nonhuman life, a *Squid*."⁴ This sentence is exemplary for the way in which Deleuze conceives of mystery: with this term, Deleuze does not refer to another, hidden *form*, kept away from sight in secret, but rather to a "new, unknown element," which is *formless*. From the context in which this quote appears, it becomes clear that this formlessness is something that slowly manifests itself in Melville's story. Whereas *Bartleby, the Scrivener* first offers a clear portrait of the different protagonists in the opening pages of the story—of the attorney who tells the story and his employees Turkey, Nippers and Ginger-Nut—these forms are transformed or, rather, deformed by "the advent of Bartleby."⁵ While the term "transformation" suggests that the characters take on a different form in this process, Deleuze argues that they are rather de-formed, that is, they are affected by the formlessness of Bartleby.

This theme of the formless occupies a fundamental place in Deleuze's reflections on Bartleby. When he classifies the narrator-attorney under the category of "Witnesses, narrators, interpreters" in Melville's oeuvre, he does so because the attorney bears witness to the "formless, nonhuman life" of Bartleby, but he can only do this because he is losing his own, well-defined form because he is affected by Bartleby's formlessness. Hence, for Deleuze, the witness is truly in between the language of clearly delineated forms and the (divine) language of formlessness that Bartleby represents. This reference to divine language is echoed when Deleuze mentions that, for Melville, such witnesses are not psychologists who dissect the mind of the characters they encounter, but rather prophets who announce something that is not of this world.⁶ In fact, as Deleuze writes: "The role of the prophets, who are not originals, is to be the only ones who can recognize the wake that originals leave in the world."⁷ Despite the fact that Deleuze is obviously much more interested in the "originals"—the Bartlebys and Ahabs in Melville's literary universe—to which the witnesses and narrators bear witness, he also acknowledges the indispensable role played by Hermes's heirs in Melville's oeuvre: like Johannes, the poet, who is the only one who recognizes what Abraham is beyond a murderer, the anonymous attorney is the only one who recognizes Bartleby. Abraham and Bartleby do not speak for themselves, nor do their actions (if they say: "Let my actions speak for themselves," they will be misunderstood and misjudged as murderer or "forger"⁸). Therefore, they need an intermediate, an interpreter who bears witness to the truth of their existence, which for Deleuze consists in their formlessness.

This Deleuzean account of Melville's story offers a clear indication of why the anonymous attorney who tells the story of Bartleby indeed deserves a position among the interpreters who are discussed in the first part of this study. Moreover, Deleuze brings into play the important category of the formless. The distinction between form and formless seems structurally akin to the distinction between *logos* and *phōnē*, at least if we render this latter distinction as the one between the articulate and the inarticulate voice. The form of the letters that clearly mark and form the meaningful sounds that are spoken by the articulate voice are distinguished from the voice that utters sounds that do not have such a clear grammatical form.

If indeed it makes sense to follow these connections, Deleuze's account of literature as proposed in *Critique and Clinique*, which includes the essay on Bartleby, becomes all the more interesting. After all, the letter has also given rise to literature and, hence, the letter seems to be the very condition of possibility, or the very presupposition of a literary experiment. What a literary experiment can achieve, one might be inclined to say, cannot transgress the letter. Yet one should immediately ask whether it is not conceivable that writing is capable of transgressing its own presupposition. For Deleuze, the category of the formless imposes itself if one wants to take this latter question seriously. Literature may be understood as a form of bearing witness of which the object indeed transgresses the presupposition of the letter and its form. At least, these are the stakes of Deleuze's reflections on literature in *Critique et clinique*: "To write is certainly not to impose a form (of expression) on the matter of lived experience. *Literature rather is on the side of the formless.*"⁹ Literature is not a way of imposing a form on a certain matter, or lived experience. Literature can only be defined as the poetic enterprise that aims at bearing witness to the formless. In exactly this sense, it sides with the formless. Thus, we may also say that literature experiments and experiences the formlessness that precedes all forms, of which all forms are an index and to which all forms need to grant access in bearing witness.

In relation to both Abraham and Bartleby, this dimension of what is without form appears in the form of language as a strange or foreign language; as Deleuze notes, literature "opens up a kind of foreign language within language, which is neither another language nor a rediscovered patois, but a becoming-other of language, a minorization of this major language, a delirium that takes it off."[10] For Derrida, the task of the translator-poets is to "cultivate and invent an idiom." The resemblance to the above quote is striking. Literature is neither creating another language nor rediscovering a forgotten or extinguished dialect, but rather is inventing a new idiom in a given language. Deleuze calls this the "minorization" of a major language. If, indeed, literature is engaged in such a minorization, it is concerned with giving a voice to what has no (articulate) voice, a minority, in a major language. Minority does not refer to a particular form that is not (yet) expressible in an existing language, but rather to the formless itself that precedes all forms that have taken shape in a language and to which all forms return in the literary process.

For Deleuze, this formlessness concerns the "people who are missing," such as Abraham and Bartleby, who are not offered a place in the order of the common tongue and in the humanity that is founded by this common tongue. To write, as Deleuze remarks, is "to write for this people who are missing [. . .]('for' means less 'in the place of' than 'for the benefit of')."[11] Note that the French expression *à l'intention de*, which is translated here as "for the benefit of," can also mean "in honor of." Both senses are meant here. The narration of the anonymous attorney does not replace Bartleby, as the narration of Johannes de Silentio does not replace Abraham. Rather, these narrators speak out of admiration and awe for what is silent or silenced. Therefore, they do not replace them, but rather bear witness to them. This is what literature should do, "to take up the experiment once again, to find [. . .] a pure sound and unknown chords in language itself."[12] "A pure sound" may be interpreted as Deleuze's version of the *phōnē*—or the *agrammatoi psophoi*—and this sound may be connected to the "psychotic breath" and "the wind of madness"—that is, a *pneuma* or spirit that is at odds with a common *logos*—that Bartleby introduces into language. It is this voice and breath of Bartleby that the narrator bears witness to and introduces into language as its foreign element. Let us therefore turn to Melville's experiment to see how this is done.

Stretching the Limits of Understanding

If Deleuze's suggestions make sense and *Bartleby, the Scrivener* concerns the type of literary becoming that is "on the side of the formless," the following question arises. What does it mean to *understand* a novel or a story of which the experiment aims to have us experience "a formless, nonhuman life"? What does it mean to bear witness to this "formless, nonhuman life," and how to perform this act? In the general framework of philosophical hermeneutics, to understand a life means to tell the story of a person's life, to write this person's biography. Yet can we say the same about the "formless, nonhuman life" that is the subject of Melville's story?

In the opening paragraph of *Bartleby, the Scrivener*, the narrator offers a first take on these questions. He begins by telling that he had the privilege of meeting many scriveners in his lifetime, but none like Bartleby, the scrivener. Interestingly, the gap that separates Bartleby from the other scriveners is first of all described in terms of the impossibility of telling the story of Bartleby's life: "While of other law-copyists I might write the complete life, of Bartleby nothing of that sort can be done." He goes on to contrast "the biographies of all the other scriveners" with "a few passages in the life of Bartleby."[13] Thus, what we will hear from him are only fragments, but not from different sources or different witnesses. Except for a small gossip on Bartleby's former employment in the "Dead Letter Office" of which the narrator informs us in the epilogue to the story, the fragments are restricted to the narrator's own observations: "What my own astonished eyes saw of Bartleby, *that* is all I know of him, except, indeed, one vague report which will appear in the sequel."[14] This attorney, as Dieter Meindl notes, who has never pleaded in court, now pleads for Bartleby, speaks as a witness for the accused.[15]

If we follow this suggestion to approach the narrator as a witness, we are immediately confronted with a basic problem at the heart of this testimony. According to the ancient legal principle from the Code of Justinian *testis unus, testis nullus*—one witness is no witness—a testimony, not corroborated by other witnesses, is not valid in court.[16] So what to make of this testimony that does not seem to respect the limits of testimony?

In fact, these limits are stretched in more than one sense in this story. A testimony aims to make something known of, in this case, a human life, to an audience or tribunal who has no other access to this life than through this testimony. For such a testimony to be fruitful, it is imperative that the audience can indeed understand what is said, and that they can recognize it as truthful and probable. This means, as Ricoeur notes, that the effectiveness of testimony—effective in addressing and convincing an audience—depends on the question of whether this testimony is marked by what he calls "human resemblance." The "comprehension" of such a testimony, as he writes, "is built on the basis of a sense of human resemblance at the level of situations, feelings, thoughts, and actions."[17] Let me emphasize both words in the expression that attracts our attention in this quote: *human* and *resemblance*. An effective testimony also offers an understanding, which is only possible on the basis of a recognized commonality *between* the lives and the world experiences of the addressees *and* the singular life and world the testimony makes known to these addressees. Simply put, we only understand what is a *variation* of our own lives. In a classical hermeneutic framework, the range of this variation seems to have no intrinsic limit.[18] This is the very *archē* or principle of all hermeneutics: there is no (human or worldly) phenomenon that cannot give rise to an event of meaning, that is, become meaningful for those who encounter it. Yet, despite this confidence of the hermeneutic tradition in its capacity to understand and interpret everything human, it is more precise to say, as Ricoeur does, that the space opened up by this variation is the space of human resemblance. It remains unclear whether this sense of resemblance then demarcates the space of humanity or whether the sense of humanity itself makes sure that this range of resemblance is wide enough. One might and ought to worry, as Ricoeur also does, that this demarcation is a true demarcation line aiming to separate the human from the non-human. It is in this context that the story of Bartleby introduces a testimony that problematizes these separations.

The space of human resemblance also includes the space of stories and testimonies to be considered trustworthy. The core question concerning all testimony is implied in the moment of understanding: Is the offered testimony trustworthy? Does it offer a believable account of what happened? How important commonality or resemblance is in this respect can, perhaps, best be seen from its contrast. If we encounter a testimony that tells us something that is completely beyond our expectations, our first response will not be one of belief but rather one of disbelief, expressed by exclamations such as "This is impossible!"; "This cannot have happened!"; or "This is nonsense!" Such testimonies that are approached with initial disbelief rather than initial belief are quite important from the perspective of hermeneutic theory because it means that testimony is different from what is usually termed "understanding" in one crucial respect: whereas understanding only takes place as variation of our life and world experience, and is thus always confined to the limits of human resemblance, testimony *can* transgress these limits and can say something to which the audience cannot relate—likely at the cost of not being believed.

It was suggested before that Bartleby's singularity intensifies that of Abraham. This seems to make sense from the perspective of the issues just raised. Abraham's existence is read in light of the phenomenon of faith. This phenomenon is never fully banished from the space of understanding of any audience because we may always find it, or versions of it, around us. Bartleby, however, offers no such phenomenon to which we can relate. He indeed seems to exemplify formlessness at its very core. This also means that the narrator's testimony will be met with initial disbelief rather than belief. Let me emphasize once more that, in Ricoeur's expression, the word "resemblance" is preceded by the adjective "human." What is at stake here is the understanding of a *human* world and a *human* life and what, by the audience, is recognized as a believable story and thus acknowledged to be a believably *human* life. Consequently, what lies beyond the limits of this human resemblance not only does not resemble our particular world and does not meet our expectations of a world, but also does not belong to what is human. It is rather understood as non-human, inhuman, barbarous, and so on—and we will see how this theme will return in the story the anonymous attorney has in store for us.

This, then, is how we begin to read the story of Bartleby's life. The testimony it offers is not complete, but fragmentary. Because we know how one can manipulate the original meaning of quotes when integrating them in another, foreign context, we also know that fragments of a life are never conclusive for a true, trustworthy, stable account of this life. A different ordering of these fragments may give rise to a fully different story. Moreover, the testimony it offers is not based on multiple witnesses but on only one. Finally—although we still have to prove this point in our reading of the story—the offered testimony cannot fulfill the demand of commonality, resemblance, or common sense, and it even seems to exceed the realm of the properly human. What if "the experience to be transmitted is that of an inhumanity with no common measure with the experience of the average person"?[19] Here, the possibility (and reality) is raised of a testimony that bears witness to an experience marked by "inhumanity" and a lack of "common measure"—or "incommensurability," as Johannes de Silentio might have called it. How can such a testimony, held in reserve in the margins and limits of common testimony, be heard, trusted, accepted, or understood?

To bring these questions even closer to our attorney, let us add the following complicating questions, which also offer resources to address the previous questions. What if this incommensurability concerns not only the audience and the discourse in which the witness has to testify, but also the witness themselves? What if the witness is in the close proximity of something that baffles them just as much? How, even when the limitations of discourse and addressee are bracketed, can such a witness bear witness to the foreign life they encounter? How can this testimony speak for or give to understand such a life?

To (Bear) Witness (to) Bartleby

Bartleby, the Scrivener tells us a story through the eyes of an attorney who manages a law office on Wall Street. It tells how the attorney hires Bartleby, a pallid-looking scrivener who at first works like a machine but soon develops a passive resistance to his employer's request—a resistance expressed by the often quoted and commented phrase "I would prefer not to." The story depicts this encounter between the attorney and the scrivener and how it affects their lives. Or, more precisely, we learn of the imprint Bartleby's formlessness leaves behind on the anonymous narrator's moods, character, and existence.

Bartleby's mysterious character has given rise to many different interpretations. Some see him as an exemplification of Christ because he suffers without objecting. Others suggest that he might be a *mort vivant*, a living dead, "who [. . .] in some unimaginable way experiences death," because he is associated with a lack of life.[20] Without simply affirming or dismissing either of these interpretations, one might suggest, following the narrator, a less distinct or direct account of what Bartleby would stand for. After all, as soon as he turns into an example of something, a kind of an emblematic personage, one might run the risk of losing his singularity and formlessness. Perhaps one should rather start from a more formal understanding of Bartleby and trace a term in which the formlessness, which interests us here, resonates. One option for such a term might be "an austere reserve," which is a term the narrator uses to articulate his experience with Bartleby: "And more than all, I remembered [. . .] an austere reserve about him, which had positively awed me into my tame compliance with his eccentricities."[21] This remark is found in the midst of the story, at which point already many events have taken place in the attorney's office, so we need to head back to the beginning of the story in a second, but let us first pay attention to two words that stand out in this quote: "reserve," which even deserves to be called "austere" according to our witness, and "awe." What actually shines forth in the confrontation with the pallid scrivener is not the person of Bartleby and not what is present(ed) of him, of what phenomenally is there for the witness. Rather, what imposes itself is what or *that* Bartleby holds back from appearing and speaking. He is reserved; he withholds himself from speaking in public and with his employer. He does not give himself fully as what or who he is in what appears of him. Because this reserve inspires reverence and awe in the attorney, the suggestion is that this reserve corresponds to what cannot be said in a tongue that the narrator could understand or would be able to capture. After all, awe is inspired by the sacred, that is, that which is separated.

Nevertheless, although this reserve is not a phenomenon in the common sense of the word, because it does not appear, it does offer itself as what can be borne witness to, as the narrator does. It would be perfectly accurate, at least formally, to interpret this reserve as the formlessness of which Deleuze speaks: because everything that appears has its form (otherwise there would be nothing to perceive or understand) and because everything that is comprehensible has its meaning, that which is held back is without form and without meaning. In the philosophical heritage of Neo-Platonism and Plotinus's *Enneads* in particular, the absence of form is not necessarily identical to matter as what *lacks* form, but may also be a formlessness that is the very provenance of all form and meaning and therefore corresponds to a reserve that invokes awe. Here, the ambiguity of formlessness—is it a lack or a provenance of form?—is importantly similar to what Kierkegaard discusses in terms of inwardness and its demonic and divine side. In both cases, one is confronted with a certain withdrawal but, only in one case, this reserve and this reservedness is fruitful. Yet in the realm of the public, the exterior, or the forms, this ambiguity cannot be decided. In exactly this sense, one—that is, one who is in the realm of the public, the exterior, and the forms—relies on those ghostly appearances of inwardness and austere reserve because only in their existence—Abraham, Bartleby—this ambiguity is dissolved.

Let us consider more closely, with this key term of the reserve in the back of our mind, how the anonymous attorney depicts Bartleby and how he responds to the scrivener. We can already understand why these responses are so important. They are not the responses of a man with a strong will or identity—he does not even have a name—that would stamp these responses with his own signature. Rather, they are evoked in and by the encounter with Bartleby. They express the resonances in the narrator of the encounter with Bartleby. These resonances are made possible by the empty, open space that is called here Bartleby's "austere reserve." In these responses, the narrator's pale imitation of the reserve vibrates. To capture these responses and resonances, we need to read some passages of this story more closely.

The Advent of Bartleby

The singular, nonhuman, incommunicable character of Bartleby is present from the outset, even before Bartleby displays his passive resistance. Consider, for instance, how the narrator describes his very first encounter with Bartleby. Because he was looking for another clerk to help him with his work, he put an advertisement in the newspapers, and soon after the following happens: "In answer to my advertisement, a motionless young man one morning, stood upon my office threshold, the door being open, for it was summer. I can see that figure now—pallidly neat, pitiably respectable, incurably forlorn! It was Bartleby."[22] The narrator assumes that Bartleby is there "in answer" to the advertisement, but this is not affirmed by anything the scrivener says or does. In fact, their first encounter happens in a rather strange constellation. Bartleby is found on the "office threshold." Yet there is no mentioning of him saying or doing anything, such as knocking, calling, or ringing, to make his presence be noticed. He is only noticed because the door is already open because of the warm summer weather. Despite the narrator's conviction that Bartleby is there because he wants this job, it is utterly unclear what Bartleby wants. In fact, would it not be in complete agreement with the rest of the story that he stay on the threshold of the office, on this place in between, on the very space of nonpreference, wanting to be neither here nor there because, as he often says, "I am not particular"?[23] What happens here is that the gesture or behavior of Bartleby is not understood as it is, but rather is transcribed and interpreted by the narrator as a response to his own question: "Why are you here?"[24] By rationalizing Bartleby's appearance, the narrator, thus, might fully miss what Bartleby is actually doing on his doorstep. He articulates the behavior of Bartleby and transforms the gesture, which according to Lyotard belongs to the field of the *phōnē*, into the letter, into an articulation that is characterized by an intention to signify—he wants to have a job.[25] By this transfer of the gesture into articulated, meaningful discourse, the gesture itself may very well be missed. We thus see here a similar structure as the one we discussed in terms of *phōnē* and *gramma* in the second experiment. As in this experiment, we are confronted with the crucial, all-determining question of whether articulation can only be of the order of this transfer or whether another sense of articulation is possible—one that bears witness to gesture and voice. As Lyotard argues, in close proximity with Deleuze and Derrida: "It is the task of writing, thinking, literature, arts to venture to bear witness to it."[26] These authors thus conceive the literary experiment to be experimenting the promise of language to bear witness to voice and gesture. Everything depends on the question of whether literature can fulfill this promise.

The motionlessness of Bartleby, which the narrator immediately notes at their first encounter, indicates that the above considerations are more than mere suggestions. If Bartleby is indeed motionless, he is not about to enter the office space. He is simply standing still, not on his way to any place in particular. Later in the story, when the narrator once more mentions Bartleby's "long-continued motionlessness," he adds that "he must be standing in one of those dead-wall reveries of his."[27] What if Bartleby was in the same state of mind when he was on the threshold of the attorney's office—not responding to a job advertisement, as the attorney transcribes his behavior, but rather caught up in what seems to be a reverie? In the literature on Bartleby, this motionlessness is often interpreted as a mark of his lack of life. However, in a philosophical setting, the combination of standing motionless in a porch while being taken away by thoughts and reveries evokes another, ancient scene, from Plato's *Symposium*, when Socrates suddenly begins "to think about something." Losing "himself in thought," he goes off "to the neighbor's porch," simply "standing there." When Agathon suggests fetching him, Aristodemus comments: "Leave him alone. It's one of his habits: every now and then he just goes off like that and stands motionless, wherever he happens to be."[28] If this comparison with Socrates makes sense, Bartleby is not on his way to this office at all, but simply "lost in thought," in a reverie, in an arbitrary moment, standing on an arbitrary threshold, not on his way toward any place at all.[29] Perhaps the best the attorney could have done for him would have been to leave him in peace. Don't force Bartleby in the space of a common office; he and his reveries are out of place there—just as thinking is always out of place, as Arendt beautifully suggests when she writes that we are nowhere when we think.[30] Forcing Bartleby in will lead to unexpected incidents and accidents, for him as well as for those around him.

Inhumanity and Incomprehensibility

Yet Bartleby is invited or forced in, and he starts working in the office. From the very first moment, he is marked by a certain inhumanity. During his first days in the office, he works as a writing machine: "he did an extraordinary quantity of writing, . . . day and night . . . copying by sunlight and by candle-light, . . . he wrote on silently, palely, mechanically."[31] It is almost as if Bartleby fully coincides with his work. In this sense, he is truly opposed to the other clerks, Turkey and Nippers, who only do their work properly during a part of the day: their relation to their work and their devotion to the machinery of the law one of negotiation—partly offered and partly withdrawn, a characteristically human behavior in order to keep their work bearable. Bartleby, on the other hand, appears as the automatism of a copying machine, affirming the law by multiplying it.

Yet this form of inhumanity does not persist. In a number of stages, Bartleby changes from a perfectly operating cog in the machine into the one who deactivates the machine and renders it inoperative. Although the narrator was struck by Bartleby's zealous work and recognized the inhumanity in it, he did not worry too much about it. It did not bother him because it contributed to the work that needed to be done. Yet on the first occasion when the scrivener actually speaks—at least according to the narrator's testimony—he displays a passive resistance to the machinery. Upon the lawyer's quite reasonable and common request to examine some of the copied work, Bartleby replies: "I would prefer not to"—and he repeats it three times.[32] It is as if Bartleby returns to a certain form of humanity: he makes his voice heard; and it is indeed the first time that the story records Bartleby's voice—if it is not really the first time that the scrivener speaks, it is the first time that his voice is noticed by and affects his witness.

Yet it is not with a human voice that he speaks—at least not if by "human" we mean a voice that speaks in comprehensible terms. He no longer identifies with the machinery of the law, but he also does not develop the common human strategy to negotiate and comply with this machinery, as Nippers and Turkey do. Bartleby's voice rather expresses an absolute and austere reserve with respect to this machinery, as if saying to it: "let me be." In this sense, Bartleby's characteristic formula of "I would prefer not to" has no common measure with the all too human negotiations with the work that needs to be done for the law displayed by the others in the office. In fact, the formula deactivates all forms of commonality, common sense, and common measure. As a seismograph, the narrator registers this in his own moods and responses, and there are some striking quotes that attest to this. After his request to check some of the copied work is rejected by the scrivener, the narrator experiences an utter breakdown of communication:

> I sat awhile in perfect silence, rallying my stunned faculties. Immediately it occurred to me that my ears had deceived me, or Bartleby had entirely misunderstood my meaning. I repeated my request in the clearest tone I could assume. But in quite as clear a one came the previous reply, "I would prefer not to."[33]

We see here to which extent Ricoeur is right that the comprehensibility of a word spoken to us depends on the question of whether it resembles the type of expression we expect. In this case, the response is utterly unexpected: the narrator registers a linguistic event of pure contingency, a confrontation with a pure formlessness that shares in no way in the forms of the discourse in and with which he addresses Bartleby. Therefore, his primitive, initial response is one of utter disbelief: This cannot be true; this cannot really be happening! In fact, and this is important for a narrator who introduces himself as the only witness of Bartleby's life, this event shakes him so deeply that does not even trust his senses. His ears must be betraying him. This raises a question for the readers whom he addresses: How to trust a witness, a single witness, who does not even dare to rely on his own senses?

The second time Bartleby repeats his "I would prefer not to" does not cause the same shock to the narrator. Yet his mood still signals that all common boundaries are transgressed in this event. He gets angry and shouts: "'Prefer not to,' echoed I, rising in high excitement, and crossing the room with a stride. 'What do you mean? Are you moon-struck?'"[34] The narrator still does not understand the response—"What do you mean?"—and perceives that Bartleby's response does not belong to the discursive order in which he thought they were both speaking.[35] Although the words "I would prefer not to" have nothing enigmatic about them, except for, perhaps, a certain peculiarity of wording, they turn into words as meaningless as an empty signifier for the narrator, leaving him in a full lack of understanding. Confronted with such an empty signifier, a decision needs to be made: does this signifier simply manifest nonsense—thus still belonging to the presupposition of the intention to signify—or does it bear witness to a voice? For the narrator, the only solution is to place the source of his incomprehensibility in Bartleby, positioning him on the other side of what is mentally sound, on the side of nonsense. Bartleby must be mad, "moon-struck." Yet if there is someone who is suffering from mood swings in the story, caused by the moon or otherwise, it is the narrator and not Bartleby whose even-temperedness is interpreted as a mark of his inhumanity:

> Not a wrinkle of agitation rippled him. Had there been the least uneasiness, anger, impatience or impertinence in his manner; in other words, *had there been any thing ordinarily human about him*, doubtless I should have violently dismissed him from the premises.[36]

The confrontation with this inhumanity and formlessness of Bartleby's resistance—"not a wrinkle of agitation rippled him"—paralyzes the narrator. Confronted with anger or impertinence, he would have known what to do, namely to throw the inflexible employee out of his office. Now, however, he becomes utterly passive and paralyzed—and he is no longer capable of the most basic hermeneutic gesture, namely to assume, when hearing the words of another, that the other says and does something meaningful, that they might be right.

This is how the encounter with Bartleby takes place, and this is how the testimony of the narrator is made possible. The narrator does not understand what happens to him, but he registers what happens to him. He registers the impact of Bartleby on him and how it dismantles his horizon of meaning. The anonymous attorney bears witness in this mediated way. His own body and, especially, his own mind—rather than his senses—are the organs for this witness. He testifies with the afflictions on his body and on his mind and with the sentiment that grows in him when encountering the reserve of Bartleby. He is not addressed but affected by Bartleby.[37]

Perverted Language, Perverted Communication

There are many ways in which this latter description of the narrator's mode of bearing witness may be illustrated. Let me, to deepen this encounter in terms of the reference to a sickness, that is, an affliction of Bartleby's body and mind, continue to show how Bartleby's "sickness" affects the narrator. Although it seems as if there is no communication possible, that is, no meaningful exchange of words, another communication is taking place.[38] (I develop this particular theme of the type and mode of communication that is at stake here in my discussion of authors such as Agamben and Nancy in Part II of this study.) We have already seen how Bartleby's meaningless words affect the narrator. During another dispute with Bartleby, the narrator's response slightly alters. Although he still considers Bartleby utterly unreasonable, the uncompromising nature of this unreasonableness thwarts the narrator's convictions on his own sense of reasonableness:

> It is not seldom the case that when a man is browbeaten in some unprecedented and violently unreasonable way, he begins to stagger in his own plainest faith. He begins, as it were, vaguely to surmise that, wonderful as it may be, all the justice and all the reason is on the other side. Accordingly, if any disinterested persons are present, he turns to them for some reinforcement for his own faltering mind.[39]

The encounter with Bartleby's uncompromising reserve starts to tear down those basic convictions that are grounded in common sense and common usage or, to put it in the narrator's terms, that are merely *assumed*. The phrase "I would prefer not to" discloses that Bartleby does not share these assumptions. His "preference not to" opposes the logic of assumptions that underlies any commonality and habitualness. It is therefore only fair that the narrator concludes much later in the story that Bartleby's preference has nothing in common with the assumptions on which he bases his convictions: Bartleby "was more a man of preferences than assumptions."[40]

The consequence of this tearing down of basic assumptions and convictions is that the attorney "begins [. . .] vaguely to surmise that [. . .] all the justice and all the reason is on the other side." This vague surmising of a foreign truth out of the common—vaguely surmised, that is, not articulated, not understood, not founded but somehow experienced—is a tear in the common horizon of understanding. It is indeed a moment in which the narrator is in touch with the reserve of this common horizon. Yet, in response, he shies away and turns to his other clerks to find in their convictions and opinions a new ground for his own reasonableness and Bartleby's unreasonableness. The narrator thus hesitates and wavers between Bartleby's singularity and common opinion. This in-between is exactly the position of the true witness who does not properly belong to either realm but who can only be what they are if they waver, hesitate, mix up and betray both sides.

The attorney's employees confirm their boss's request without hesitation: "With submission, sir." In this way, his response to the encounter with a reserve that shakes all his assumptions and convictions is to patch up the horizon of understanding that has just been torn down: although he refers to his clerks as "disinterested persons," they are not disinterested because they, together with him, constitute the common sense in the office; together they form the fabric of the horizon of understanding that Bartleby cuts down. Nevertheless, a communication does take place here, and the narrator's initial response, to start doubting his own convictions, attests that he *did* communicate with Bartleby, but on such a basic level that it was not a communication within the boundaries of a presupposed and shared language. The narrator was not addressed but affected by Bartleby.

This other communication does not stay outside language. Although the narrator may have thought that his attempt to neutralize the encounter with Bartleby worked out quite well, not only his moods and convictions but also his involuntary choice of words attests to how much the encounter with Bartleby affected him. Although Bartleby does not say much, the only direct expression of the reserve that he is—"I would prefer not to"—is transferred to all in the office. First, the narrator notices it in his own articulations when he addresses his clerk, Nippers, by saying, "I'd prefer that you would withdraw for the present." He comments:

> Somehow, of late I had got into the way of involuntarily using this word "prefer" upon all sorts of not exactly suitable occasions. And I trembled to think that my contact with the scrivener had already and seriously affected me in a mental way. And what further and deeper aberration might it not yet produce?[41]

It is not only the narrator who is adopting the language of Bartleby. He also notices it in the responses of the clerks, who are not even aware that they use the word, even when he points it out to them: "It was plain that it involuntarily rolled from his tongue. I thought to myself, surely I must get rid of a demented man, who already has in some degree turned the tongues, if not the heads of myself and clerks."[42] If, indeed, Bartleby speaks in tongues when he says, "I'd prefer not to," as Derrida suggests, then the foreign power that speaks in him also speaks in the others now: the encounter with Bartleby has "turned the tongues." His language has contaminated theirs, much to the narrator's concern: although he is drawn to Bartleby, he also shies away from him in awe, as if confronting something holy and mad, divine and demonic. If it is true that the expression "I'd prefer not to" is like an empty signifier, the attorney's own language, by adopting such a signifier, is losing its sense(s); and his own humanity is no longer heterogeneous to the inhuman or nonhuman life of Bartleby because he now carries this heterogeneity also in himself to such an extent that it starts to speak in his own language—in that which defines him as a human being. Thus, the people in the office start carrying the voice of Bartleby in themselves. The narrator is an involuntary witness who gives a voice to Bartleby's reserve by his encounter with him and by registering both the conscious and unconscious effects he has on him. Whatever it is that Bartleby experiences to the full, it affects and finds its way into the narrator and his language. This might be the basic reason why the narrator has no name: He speaks with two voices in two languages and no longer has an identity of his own. Exactly by having become such a double-tongued, ambiguous creature, he can be a witness "who can recognize the wake that originals leave in the world," as Deleuze writes.[43]

What this other communication suggests is that Bartleby is not so much a message or meaning but rather a force that affects and *partly* takes over the narrator. It is not a brute force, but rather a mild one, as the narrator suggests, although no less effective:

> Indeed, it was his wonderful mildness chiefly, which not only disarmed me, but unmanned me, as it were. For I consider that one, for the time, is a sort of unmanned when he tranquilly permits his hired clerk to dictate to him and order him away from his own premises.[44]

The imagery of being unmanned is also the image of the reversal or the perversion of roles that takes place here. Whereas it is the task of a clerk to write down what the attorney dictates to him, it is now the clerk who dictates to the attorney. It is indeed the clerk's words that speak in the words of the attorney; it is the clerk whose story is being told. It is only because the clerk has this influence on the narrator that the latter tells the former's story. Because the narrator has no direct access to the clerk, he attests to the former's austere reserve by telling how it affected him, how Bartleby begins to speak in him, so to speak, how he takes over his voice, his behavior, and his premises. Thus, the narrator more and more loses his form and becomes the embodiment of ambiguity, of form and formlessness. He adopts the clerk's language but also maintains his own. He senses a deep affinity with Bartleby and melancholically experiences a "bond of a common humanity," but he also knows that in these moments he is on the brink of madness and inhumanity—"chimeras, doubtless, of a sick and silly brain."[45]

Moreover, when the emotions of "pure melancholy and sincerest pity" intensify by an ever-deepening sense of the abyssal reserve Bartleby represents, and when he has to confront Bartleby's sheer "hopelessness" and misery, his melancholy and pity transform into "repulsion," as the attorney sighs: "So true it is, and so terrible too, that up to a certain point the thought or sight of misery enlists our best affections; but, in certain special cases, beyond that point it does not."[46] Only up to a point can the narrator attune to Bartleby's misery.

Yet it is the very ambiguity and limitedness of the narrator that make him the only suitable witness of this misery. If he were able to go down into Bartleby's experiences as Bartleby himself did, he would go under and not be able to tell the story of the scrivener, as the scrivener cannot be the witness of his own life. As witness, he is allowed only on the threshold of this reserve. If, on the other hand, he were fully unaffected by Bartleby, if he retained his identity and sound language, he would not be able to tell Bartleby's story. Thus, this witness is only possible thanks to his limited "charity," and in this sense Melville's story shows the limits of Levinas's outraged statement that "there is no greater hypocrisy than that which invented well tempered charity."[47] More precisely, the witness is a hypocrite, but only if we use this term in the specific sense of the Greek *hupokritēs* that Plato uses in the *Timaeus* to describe the "interpreters of the mysterious voice and apparition."[48] This "hypocrite" is the one who offers the stage to another voice, but always on the stage of a shared language. As witness, the narrator is only allowed on the threshold of the common language. Here, in between the realms of language and misery, on the threshold separating them, he can give a voice to Bartleby and tell some fragments of his life. Although this witness is the only witness and has no one to corroborate what he tells us, and although he testifies what his own eyes have only seen *in disbelief* and what his own ears have heard *without comprehension*, his encounter with Bartleby has affected his moods, his words, his behavior, his office, his language, and his voice—and, therefore, only he can speak for Bartleby, his misery, and his austere reserve.

The story famously ends with the exclamation "Ah Bartleby! Ah humanity!"[49] Among the many interpretations one can offer for this exclamation, one might be that this is the formula of the witness who is on the threshold of the singularity of Bartleby and the commonality of humanity, who stands in their separation, holding them together, demanding the latter not shut its ears to the silence, the misery, and the meaningless utterances of the former.

Chapter 7

Experiment VI

Er, the Messenger

> What sort of stranger is there within the philosopher, with his look of returning from the land of the dead?[1]
>
> —Deleuze and Guattari, *Qu'est-ce que la philosophie?*, 67/69

Philosophers in Exile

In their discussion of the conceptual personae of Plato in *Qu'est-ce que la philosophie?*, Deleuze and Guattari describe the philosopher as someone who is longing for a "Fatherland or Homeland," but who is also banished from it:

> Philosophy is inseparable from a Homeland to which the a priori, the innate, or the memory equally attest. But why is this fatherland unknown, lost, or forgotten, turning the thinker into an Exile? What will restore an equivalent of territory, valid as a home? What will be philosophical ritornellos? What is thought's relationship with the earth? Socrates the Athenian, who does not like to travel, is guided by Parmenides of Elea when he is young, who is replaced by the Stranger when he is old, *as if Platonism needed at least two conceptual personae*. What sort of stranger is there within the philosopher, with his look of returning from the land of the dead?[2]

If one asks what the philosopher's homeland exactly is, Deleuze and Guattari offer some markers in this quote that immediately complicate the sense of homeland. It is a realm preceding and surpassing our actual lives but in such a way that it harbors the very heart and soul of our existence. This homeland is not well-known; one is not familiar with it but is always in need of discovering it. In fact, the realm to which the above quote refers as "Homeland" does not share the characteristics of what we would call a "home" or what we consider to be *heimlich*, but rather of what is *unheimlich*, uncanny; it does not refer to the ordinary but rather to the extraordinary, to what is *ungeheuer*. This description of the philosopher as banished from this homeland complements the Platonic description of the philosopher as the one who chooses or is forced to be exiled from the *polis* and the community in which we all live because they do not feel at home there, because they sense that this is not their homeland. The Platonic understanding of exile and banishment explains why the homeland of the philosopher is a marker of strangeness and foreignness, which the philosopher adopts and cultivates. That such an interpretation also makes sense for Deleuze and Guattari can be seen along the following lines of thought.

First, Deleuze and Guattari note that the conceptual persona of Socrates, the man who is at home in the polis and who does not like to leave the city, as he notes in the *Phaedrus*, is supplemented by the conceptual persona of the Stranger, the one who does travel and who comes from elsewhere. Apparently, Plato needs *two* personae for his project. The first indicates that the basic position of the philosopher's home territory is the *polis* rather than a faraway homeland. Yet this first position does not suffice for Plato and needs the second as its supplement. This second persona exemplifies the philosopher as being out of place in the city and as coming from elsewhere. The philosopher thus belongs to two realms, and perhaps the philosopher's proper position is therefore at the threshold in between the *polis* and the homeland.

Second, for Deleuze and Guattari, the Stranger is not someone coming from another *polis*. Therefore, when asking for the "language" of the Stranger, they do not point to another language than Greek or another Greek dialectic, but rather to the principle of the barbaric in language itself. The barbaric is not simply a non-Greek language, but rather what is *alogos* in language. Anticipating the answer to the questions they ask in the previous quote, they introduce the term "philosophical ritornellos." The term "ritornello" also appears in Deleuze's reading of *Bartleby, the Scrivener* to describe the type of language that characters such as Bartleby employ:

> What remains is precisely their "originality," that is, a sound that each one produces, like a ritornello at the limit of language,

but that it *produces* only when it takes to the open road (or to the open sea) with its body, when it leads its life without seeking salvation, when it embarks upon its incarnate voyage, without any particular aim, and then encounters other voyagers, whom it recognizes by their sound.[3]

A ritornello is thus what *remains*, and I return to this remainder or reserve in the last pages of this experiment. Yet what is a ritornello? In the French, the verb translated as "to produce" is *rendre*, which is the same verb Deleuze uses to describe how, in an ordinary language, an unknown language is rendered or produced: "Psychosis characteristically brings into play a procedure that treats an ordinary language, a standard language, in a manner that makes it 'render' an original and unknown language, which would perhaps be a projection of God's language."[4] Hence, a ritornello does not refer to another language but should rather be interpreted as the characteristic voice or sound of Bartleby's "unknown language," his glossolalia. Similarly, in *Qu'est-ce que la philosophie*, the philosopher's ritornello refers to a characteristic deformation or deactivation of the Greek *logos* by the persona of the Stranger; there, it is the voice of the life that deserves to be called philosophical.

For Deleuze, literature is to bear witness to an unknown, uncanny language in a given language. This understanding is mirrored in Deleuze and Guattari's description of the philosopher's look: "What sort of stranger is there within the philosopher, with his look [*air*] of returning from the land of the dead?" There is an alien dimension within the philosopher, which is so strong that it determines the philosopher's "look." It is important to note that the French *air* does not mean only look or appearance but also attitude and way of behaving and living. The philosopher's ethos, their form of life *attests* to this stranger in them.

If we follow this line of thought, we might even feel compelled to make a small correction to the above quote from *Qu'est-ce que la philosophie*. Rather than emphasizing the value of the homeland or the fatherland, it might make more sense to see in Plato's philosophical enterprise, exemplified by the doubling of the conceptual persona into Socrates and Stranger, one belonging to the city and one not-belonging to the city, a particular strategy of exile. In his recent *L'uso dei corpi*, Agamben lends some important credence to this suggestion when referring to Plato's *Theaetetus*. In this dialogue, Socrates notes: "That is why a man should make all haste to escape [*pheugein*] from earth to heaven; and escape [*phugē*] means becoming as like God as possible; and a man becomes like God when he becomes just [*dikaion*] and pious, with understanding."[5] Agamben comments that in Greek, the term *phugē* does not only mean escape or flight, but is also a technical term for exile; therefore, he translates part of this quote as "the assimilation of God is virtually an exile."[6] He connects this to Plato's use of the metaphor *apodēmia* in the *Phaedo*. This word means emigration, or going or being abroad, but is "literally the abandonment of the *demos*," according to Agamben. He argues that Plato uses it here to "define the separation of the soul from the body."[7] *Apodēmia*, being outside the community and the polis of body and soul, thus describes a journey abroad—and abroad means in the *Phaedo* a journey beyond the grave.[8] The philosopher is engaged in this exile from the city, from the community of the living and in the accompanying separation of soul and body. What is the value of such an ethos to go beyond the community and the grave? What does the philosopher find there? And is it worthwhile if it gives the philosopher the look of "returning from the land of the dead"?

In the context of Agamben's project on the ban, as developed in the *Homo Sacer*-series, it is understandable that he emphasizes especially the political-juridical value of terms such as *apodēmia* and *phugē* to describe the philosopher's tendency to move toward a realm beyond the political order in which we live. Hence, for him, these terms do not simply reflect a metaphysical dualism of body and soul, this world and afterworld, and so on. By their very nature, they have important political repercussions offering a space beyond the *polis* in which the philosopher can take up their abode to criticize the order of the *polis*. Yet if one was forced to phrase in one term what the stakes are for Plato to refer to these figures of ban, exile, and separation, could one not also and more basically refer to the term *dikaion*, just, as the *Theaetetus* suggests, and to the term *dikaiosunē*, righteousness, which are of crucial importance to politics but also beyond the political realm for every form of care for the self, the other, and the world? Is this not at stake in the exile and separation of Plato?

Moreover, in the context of my own project and in light of my introductory remarks on Deleuze and Guattari, another line of thought imposes itself. Both *apodēmia* and *phugē* describe the philosopher's attitude (*air*) to the earth and to life on earth in terms of exile, flight, or moving away from. Yet the philosopher does not simply stay in exile. The philosopher returns, as Deleuze and Guattari note, but they return as if from the land of the dead. The terms *apodēmia* and *phugē* are used in the same way, as a flight to what lies beyond this life for the sake of rendering possible a particular form of life. If this is true, the philosopher might be another heir of Hermes, traveling between the land of the dead and the land of the living, between the *topos daimonios* and the earth, between the exile of the Stranger and the belonging to the city of Socrates. If, indeed, the philosopher returned from the land of the dead, what did he see and experience there? What did he learn about justice and righteousness in this gloomy region that Plato identifies as a demonic, extraordinary place, a *topos daimonios*?

Called to Bearing Witness

In this constellation of questions, there is one obvious passage from Plato's dialogues to consider. At the end of the *Republic*, Socrates tells the story of the soldier Er who died in battle but whose body did not decay on the battlefield.[9] When his body is found and is about to be burned, Er suddenly returns from the land of the dead.[10]

Let me briefly recall the context in which the myth of Er makes its appearance. It is the final piece of one of the main lines of argument that runs throughout the *Republic*, which is an argument or *logos* on righteousness, *dikaiosunē*.[11] Its concluding piece, however, is not a *logos*, but rather an *apologos*, a story. Following Thrasymachus's fierce and furious arguments in Book I, and the subtle way in which Plato's brother Glaucon deepens Thrasymachus's objections to the just and righteous life in Book II, Plato's second brother, Adimantus, asks Socrates whether it is not better to appear to be righteous to the society to which one belongs while not being so than the other way around.[12] Adimantus points out that a society honors those who appear to be righteous irrespective of whether they actually are so. Moreover, as he adds, everyone who strives for this honor is already lacking righteousness because to be truly just implies that one does not care for how people or the gods award one for one's righteousness. By arguing in this way, Adimantus brings out the difference and tension between appearance and being in its most radical way. In each of its appearances, justice risks being contaminated by the desire for honor, wealth, and women. Although Adimantus does not draw this conclusion, his argument implies that justice is best served when done in concealment.[13] This conclusion, which in a way is reiterated in the conclusion of the *Republic* as a whole in the stages leading up to the myth of Er, implies that the rift between appearance and being cannot simply be understood as a metaphysical rift but should also and rather be understood out of Plato's basic concern for the question of *dikaiosunē*, justice or righteousness. The metaphysical distinction between appearing and being concerns not only the metaphysical realm but also goes at the soul of human existence and the human mode of living. Yet, if one insists on the fundamental withdrawal of righteousness and justice from the realm of appearance, the question is how one may have access to justice or touch it in one's existence. Clearly, as Plato's reflections on the law, *nomos*, show, he is not of the opinion that the withdrawal of justice implies that the realm of appearance is a pure lack of justice. He does seem to argue, though, that there is a certain necessity for the withdrawal of justice to safeguard that justice is never essentially contaminated by the risks of its appearance in the public sphere *because* justice is not of the order of appearing, *because* it always exceeds any of the forms or constructions in and by which it is manifested in the realm of appearance.

In Book X of the *Republic*, Socrates returns to this problem. There, he first argues that the just may hope for prosperity even in this life because the gods will grant them prosperity.[14] Thus, he tries to solve the rift between appearing and being by invoking the gods because for them the problem of mere and false appearance does not exist. Glaucon agrees with this conclusion. Yet, against the background of his brother's arguments in Book II, this consent can only be called superficial. Socrates, however, perhaps reminiscent of Adimantus's keen arguments, does not seem to be satisfied himself. At any rate, for him the argument is not complete, and therefore he goes on to tell a story because, apparently, his arguments are no longer strong enough to give any additional support or credence to his plea for justice. One might therefore argue that we encounter a true literary experiment in the myth of Er. Socrates requires an experience to which the *logoi* offer no access. As Agamben writes on the relation of *muthos* and *logos*: "the myth is a complex figure, which seeks to explain something that the *logos* by itself cannot clarify and that therefore demands in its turn an uncommon hermeneutic capacity."[15] This uncommon hermeneutic capacity is demanded from the one who is supposed to tell a story that grants us access to the realm of the afterlife.

The reason why such a story on the afterlife is necessary follows from the line of argument in the *Republic* itself. First, it might be only wishful thinking that humans indeed will receive the prosperity they deserve in life from the gods. Second, the hope for this prosperity contaminates the righteousness of the just. Third, this contamination of justice is inextricably bound up with justice in human life. In Derrida's terminology, one could also say that every appearance of justice in human life is deconstructible. After all, how will we ever know for certain that so-called just acts are not motivated by the promised prosperity in this sublunary life? Yet this does not mean that there is no justice, but it is only as withdrawn, as what remains beyond and before its formation and formulation in systems of justice. This means that justice, in its withdrawal, is first as *demand* and second as *promise*. Even Derrida seems to affirm this. In *Force de loi*, without mentioning Plato, he attests to his own indebtedness to this Platonic structure of justice and the necessity of its basic withdrawal when he writes that justice cannot be deconstructed and that, in fact, "the undeconstructibility of justice also makes deconstruction possible, indeed is inseparable from it."[16] He can say this because justice is the demand for deconstruction, for the deforming of those forms that contaminate justice, and deconstruction is thus also the promise of justice, that is, the promise to disclose in which sense the given embodiments of justice in legal structures are unjust.

Yet such an argument requires one to displace the scene of justice and to experience a realm that cannot be experienced because it is withdrawn, but that is still concerned with the basic question of Plato's thought, the care for one's soul or, in terms of the *Republic*, the polity of oneself (*tēs en autōi politeias*).[17] To this end, it is apparently necessary to place the soul beyond the reach of human life and experience, beyond the reach of human *logos*, in a realm that can only be disclosed in and through a story (*apologos*) on the threshold that separates the land of the living from the land of the dead.

This story is presented as a testimony given by the Pamphylian warrior Er, the son of Armenias, who is thus granted, as Schmidt writes, "the chance to witness the actions of the dead."[18] This witness dies on the battlefield, but on the twelfth day returns to life and tells the bystanders "what he had seen in the world beyond," a world that he describes as a *topos daimonios*, a mysterious place in which the souls of the deceased are gathered together and where their lives are judged.[19] Er, however, is not one of the gathered souls. By his death, he is banned from the land of the living. Yet, when joining the line of souls who are about to be judged, and coming to the front of the line, the judges set him apart. They suspend their judgment on him and his life: "When Er himself came forward, they told him that he was to be a messenger to human beings about the things that were there, and that he was to listen to and look at everything in the place."[20]

This is the first of three suspensions by which Er is excluded from sharing in the experiences the other souls undergo in this mysterious, uncanny place. This first suspension indicates that Er is excluded from the company and community of the living as well as the community of the souls in their afterlife. Thus, by belonging nowhere, Er belongs in the gap between these two communities on their threshold so that he can become a medium between them. Thus, it is exactly by being suspended from sharing in the experiences of the dead souls that Er is called to be and is capable of becoming their witness. The first suspension is thus not a negative phenomenon, the negation of having or sharing in an experience, but it is rather a setting apart, a separation from the community of souls in order to become a witness. By being drawn out of the common course of affairs, Er becomes a bystander singled out as the one who can and must tell the story of this mysterious place to the living. Hence, also in this story the witness is the one who has to mediate between an experience that goes so deep that it cannot be expressed by the souls themselves: even in their new lives they cannot articulate these experiences, as we shall see, because these experiences are immemorial.

The first experience of the souls and its suspension are accompanied by two other experiences from which the warrior witness is also excluded. It is remarkable to see that Heidegger and, more recently, Agamben, who both offer a reading of this myth, each emphasizes only one of these three experiences, namely the third and the second experience, respectively.[21] Yet it seems to me that the question of the nature of this story requires one to take all three experiences into account and to understand how only the *suspension* of these experiences is the condition of possibility of the warrior's bearing witness, without which there would be no story, no communication between these two dissimilar communities and places. Let me therefore discuss these other two experiences and their suspension in the next two sections.

Limbo of Separated Souls

The second suspension occurs at the moment when the souls are about to receive the lots that determine in which order they are to choose their next life: "When he had said this, the Speaker threw the lots among all of them, and each—with the exception of Er, who wasn't allowed to choose—picked up the one that fell next to him."²² Er is not allowed to choose, and for good reason. Rather than being born again in the newly chosen life in another cycle of existence, Er is supposed to return to his former life, as an adult who can speak and bear witness to what he sees. Yet, because this is one of the experiences in which Er is, par excellence, the bystander, the scenery of this choosing is of special importance to the testimony Er is supposed to deliver—and it is therefore rather surprising to see that it is fully absent from Heidegger's interpretation of this myth. Its importance is affirmed by Agamben, though, who argues that this spectacle allows us to understand the nature and the meaning of this *topos daimonios*. For Agamben, to borrow Heidegger's expression, it is this spectacle above all that marks this realm as *das Un-geheure*, "the uncanny, the extraordinary."²³ Agamben approaches this spectacle by distancing himself from a particular interpretation of how this story could exemplify justice. One could think that this place represents in Plato's thought the realm of pure justice in which not only the souls' lives are properly judged but in which it is also made clear that the souls are fully and solely responsible for their next life: rather than fate or necessity, it is the soul that chooses its life. Yet Agamben immediately makes clear that such an interpretation of Plato's uncanny realm does not do justice to the testimony Er gives of it. In particular, he emphasizes how Er articulates the impression this spectacle makes on him: "Er said that the way in which the souls chose their lives was a sight worth seeing, since it was pitiful, funny, and surprising to watch."²⁴ The words that are used here to express how this scenery affects Er are *eleeinēn*, which means pitiful; *geloian*, which means absurd, ludicrous, or ridiculous (which also appeared in the first experiment); and *thaumasian*, which means wonderful, absurd, and strange.²⁵ These three words, in my appropriation of Agamben's interpretation, show that the land of the dead is not a land of pure justice; these words express above all the particular misery or poverty in this obligation of the soul to choose. For Er, this misery shines forth in the absurdity of the spectacle. On the one hand, the souls are offered the freedom to choose their next lives, indicating that these lives are not determined by fate or necessity. Yet, on the other hand, for the most part the souls do not have the means or the capacity to choose well. The Loeb edition captures this tension by translating as follows: "He said it was a strange, pitiful, and ridiculous spectacle, as the choice was determined for the most part by the habits of their former lives."²⁶ Because it is the habit of the soul's former life—that is, the second nature the soul has attracted by the social environment and experiences in that life—that determines its choice rather than true or pure righteousness, most souls are bound to choose badly.

Indeed, if one reads the examples to which Er bears witness, and if one hears how badly the souls choose, one cannot refrain from the idea that the responsibility granted to the souls by this choice is much higher than they can bear. For instance, of one of those who make a terribly wrong choice, it is said that he "lived his previous life under an orderly constitution, where he had participated in virtue through habit and without philosophy."[27] This is a striking example because it indicates how much habit and its usefulness depend on the particulars and the givenness of an environment. While virtue through habit may offer the possibility to live rather well in this particular environment, it remains to be seen what happens to this soul when the orderly constitution upon which its habits depend disappears. Plato's *topos daimonios* is the literary invention in which this possibility is experimented: by its *apodēmia*, its leaving its community and orderly constitution behind, the soul is thrown back upon its own resources. This "spectacle" indicates that without philosophy, that is, without the soul's striving for righteousness during the lifetime, there are no resources to prevent it from making the most disastrous choice: "In his folly and greed he chose [the greatest tyranny] without adequate examination and didn't notice that, among other evils, he was fated to eat his own children as a part of it."[28]

My appropriation of Agamben's reading of the myth deviates from the conclusion Agamben draws from this spectacle. Based on this absurdity, he writes that "Plato intended to suggest that [the *topos daimonios*] was precisely not an image of justice and harmony."[29] Indeed, Agamben is right that Plato's depiction of the land of the dead does not portray it as a heaven of pure justice. Unlike the Christian God, the divinities, judges, and so forth are not meant to represent pure Justice. Yet one has to understand more precisely the exact connection of this place to justice. It is somewhat surprising that Agamben at this point does not draw from his own resources, in particular from his account of exile from *L'uso dei corpi*. After all, this land of dead souls is a land that is truly separated from the land of the living. Interestingly enough, when Heidegger notes that Socrates first calls this story an *apologos*, rather than a *muthos*, he suggests translating this as *Abrede*, which is a mode of saying (*Sagen*) in which the speakers separate (*abscheiden*) what they say from everything else that is said. Thus, he emphasizes that this story is meant to create a separation, an exile from the common *polis* and the common *logos* because the question of *dikaiosunē* demands to consider the given polis from the position of exile and separation. This *Abrede*, this particular form of saying, preserves (*bewahren*) its proper truth (*Wahrheit*), as Heidegger adds.[30] It seems to me—and this is no longer simply Heidegger—that this truth concerns the role of righteousness. What the literary experiment of the exile from the orderly constitution in which one happens to live shows is that the human tendency to base one's choices solely on habits depending on this constitution renders the human utterly defenseless and vulnerable when this constitution disappears. It is only by taking care of the polity of one's own soul that one might build up a resistance against the habits, some merely fragile and some simply evil, and participate in righteousness. To bring out the importance of this latter polity of the soul, the *apologos* of Er separates the soul from the contingent community in which it lives its life. In this barren, desolate situation, in this misery of the soul, it becomes clear why the pursuit of righteousness is indispensable to the soul and to the lives it lives. As Agamben rightly notes, this care of the soul in the pursuit of righteousness "refers also and above all to the living."[31] After all, the souls in the afterlife are only capable of choosing right if, in their previous life, they prepared for the state of exception in which they find themselves now in *topos daimonios*. Only the philosophical life, according to Socrates, is the life that has truly prepared its soul to choose. This is the reason why Er is sent as a messenger and witness to the living. His testimony of the *topos daimonios* articulates the demand of the dead souls on the living to offer them the means to choose; this demand, in turn, corresponds to the promise of righteousness, to the promise of knowing "the best way to choose, whether in life or in death."[32]

In line with Agamben's attention to the complex term of use in *L'uso dei corpi*, one might perhaps add that humans do not own their souls. They are not theirs. They rather borrow them. They inherit them from the soul's previous lives. They receive their life from the soul that chose it. They hand the soul on to future lives. In this sense, the living live their life indeed for another and an other's time.[33] Yet, in the time of their life, while using their soul, all depends on the traces and marks they inscribe on it. To live, to use the image from the *Phaedrus*, is to write on the soul. All depends on whether the living are indeed "most concerned" (*malista epimelēteon*) to seek what enables their soul to "distinguish the good [*chreston*, literally 'usable'] life from the bad."³⁴ The use of the soul is useful only if it is marked by the concern that responds to the demand of the soul to which Er, the messenger, bears witness.³⁵

The Plain of the Unforgettable

After the souls have chosen their new life, their choice is made irreversible.³⁶ Subsequently, they start a journey that will bring them to their new life. At the end of this journey, we encounter the third experience from which Er is excluded:

> [T]hey travelled to the Plain of Forgetfulness [*to tēs Lēthēs pedion*] in burning, choking, terrible heat, for it was empty [*kenon*] of trees and earthly vegetation [*hosa gē phuei*]. And there, beside the River of Unheeding [*ton Amelēta potamon*], whose water no vessel can hold, they camped, for night was coming on. All of them had to drink a certain measure of this water, but those who weren't saved by reason drank more than that, and as each of them drank, he forgot everything [*epilanthanesthai pantōn*] and went to sleep. But around midnight there was a clap of thunder and an earthquake, and they were suddenly carried away from there, this way and that, up to their births, like shooting stars. Er himself was forbidden to drink from the water. All the same, he didn't know how he had come back to his body, except that waking up suddenly he saw himself lying on the pyre at dawn.³⁷

In the last part of the journey, the souls reach a truly desolate place, as if it was not already miserable enough for them in the *topos daimonios*. Remarkably, this place has no place in Agamben's account of the myth of Er. For Heidegger, on the other hand, the Plain of Forgetfulness is the culmination point of this story—and he only truly reads this fragment of the story.³⁸ Heidegger interprets *lēthē* as the counter-essence of *phusis*. The Plain of Concealment, as he translates it, is a plain in which nothing grows, which allows nothing to "spring forth" (*aufgehenlassen*).³⁹ For him, the myth of Er is important because it preserves the remembrance of this *lēthē*, this counter-essence of truth in his sense of *alētheia*. At the end of this plain, the souls encounter the River of *Amelēs*, the River of Unheeding or Carelessness of which the water makes the souls forget everything. In the myth, the plain and the river are in line, and Socrates even substitutes *amelēs* and *lēthē* when speaking of the River of Forgetfulness (*ton tēs Lēthēs potamon*) as if they concern one and the same "phenomenon," namely that of the forgetting that prepares the souls to be born again.[40] Yet Heidegger insists that these two terms need to be carefully kept apart because they are fundamentally different.

It remains to be seen whether such a strict distinction makes sense. Yet it is helpful because it makes perfectly clear what for Heidegger is preserved in this myth. The following long quote may help us in this regard and explain why for Heidegger the Plain of *Lēthē* is the most characteristic (and for him only relevant) figure of the *topos daimonios*:

> The field of *lēthē* prevents every disclosure of beings, of the ordinary. In the essential place of *lēthē* everything disappears. Yet it is not only the completeness of the withdrawal [. . .] that distinguishes this place. [. . .] The "away" of what is withdrawn and concealed is surely not "nothing," for the letting disappear that withdraws everything occurs in this place—in this place alone—and presents itself here [*das alles entziehende Verschwindenlassen its das, was sich allein an diesem Ort begibt und in ihn sich dargibt*]. The place is void—there is nothing at all that is ordinary in it. But the void is precisely what remains and what comes into presence there [*Aber die Leere ist hier das Bleibende und Anwesende*]. [. . .] The place of *lēthē* is that "where" in which the uncanny [*das Un-geheure*] dwells in a peculiar exclusivity [*in einer eigentümlichen Ausschließlichkeit*]. The field of *lēthē* is, in a pre-eminent sense, "demonic."[41]

What is characteristic for this Plain of *Lēthē* is not that it is simply nothing, but rather that it is the place where "the letting disappear that withdraws everything occurs" and where this "presents itself." In this plain as the culmination point of the myth, *lēthē* comes to presence. Heidegger goes on to claim that this is par excellence the "demonic," uncanny, and extraordinary dimension of the *topos daimonios*. The River of Unheeding, on the other hand, represents for him the sheer forgetting of this Plain of Concealment. Therefore, river and plain are all but in line. Rather, they are opposed to each other. Let me note simply that such an opposition is somewhat odd in light of the story. This is not only so because Socrates mixes them up but also because drinking from the river's water results in *forgetting* everything; the forgetting of *epilanthanomai* is not simply a matter of carelessness but is rather an intensification or completion of the forgetfulness of *lēthē*. This has two implications for our assessment of Heidegger's understanding of this story and its culmination point, namely one appreciating and one criticizing Heidegger's interpretation.

First, the river's water represents a complete forgetting of all that happened to the souls in their afterlife, preparing their new birth. This implies that if we follow Heidegger's intriguing interpretation of the Plain of *Lēthē*, we should understand it in line with what Agamben called the unforgettable, which I think is best summarized in the following quote from Mortier's *Godenslaap*: "There is so much that will never be forgotten, because no one will ever have known that it existed."[42] For Agamben as well as for Mortier, it is exactly in its being unforgotten that this place remains with us—not in the form of a memory, a commemoration, or a commemorative place, but in the form of the emptiness and the void it represents. The word *kenos* that is added in the story to characterize this plain indicates that it is empty, fruitless, and void—empty of all experience, all appearance and growth.[43] Or, rather, this plain offers the souls and the readers of the story the experience of emptiness, the experience of that there is nothing to be experienced. This is much in line with Heidegger's own description of this place, the *topos daimonios*, as the void that remains (*das Bleibende*) as the surplus over all to which we do have access in ordinary life. The story thus indeed exemplifies that which lies beyond our experience; yet as the philosopher, non-poet Heidegger insists that what lies beyond our experience is, strictly speaking, a void. The awareness of this void, and the withdrawing of everything as what always remains with us, is for Heidegger *the very reason that humans need to care for truth* as unconcealment. If truth were of the order of permanence, which we might think when we forget the Plain of *Lēthē*, no care for its disappearance would be necessary. *Alētheia* demands care because the place of its withdrawal is inscribed into its core and is named *lēthē*.

When Er is prohibited to drink from the water, he becomes the one that bears witness to this void and plain's withdrawal of everything. In this way, he articulates the *demand* for care that speaks from this story. Hence, on a structural level, Heidegger also recognizes the fundamental dimension of the demand for care that speaks from this story. On the water from the River of *Amelēs*, Heidegger writes:

This water does not know care (*meletē*) concerning what is opposed to disappearance, to going away, and consequently to withdrawing concealment. This water [. . .] does not know *meletē tēs alētheias*, care over unconcealedness, the care that beings be secured [*geborgen*] in the unconcealed and therein remain constant.[44]

By being not able to drink, Er exemplifies the care over unconcealedness and bears witness to the demand made on the living to care for unconcealedness. In this way, for Heidegger, Er seems to be the example for the philosopher because those who drink too much of this water are the "men who lack philosophy" (*Philosophie-losen*), those who "are at the mercy of the withdrawal and the concealment of beings (*des Seienden*)."[45]

Second, however, to come back to our hesitation concerning the strict and somewhat unconvincing distinction between forgetfulness and to forget, *lēthē* and *epilanthanomai*, important questions remain. Because *all* souls have to drink from the water and will forget everything of this place when they are born and because Er is so explicitly introduced as an absolute singularity, excluded from the experience that all must have, is it truly convincing to interpret the water from the River of *Amelēs* as the source of carelessness in humans, as Heidegger does? Moreover, what happened to the concern for righteousness in this myth and in the *Republic* as a whole in Heidegger's interpretation of it?

If, for a moment, we suspend the distinction Heidegger introduces and rather follow Socrates's account that considers *lēthē* and *amelēs* as part of the same constellation at the end of the journey through the mysterious place, a different picture arises. The souls' journey ends abruptly when they are "suddenly carried away from there," to be born. If one wants to understand what type of forgetfulness or lack of care is at stake in this final stage of the myth, one should perhaps consider the lack of care we find in infants, in the newborns. If we use the term "lack of care" for the infant, it is clear that it does not coincide with the sense Heidegger awards to this term, which is connected to the sense of fallenness and the everyday that we find in *Sein und Zeit*. The infant is characterized by an incapacity to take care of themselves. When they are born, they lack the most basic means to keep themselves alive. As Protagoras describes the human infant in Plato's dialogue that carries his name: "naked, unshod, unbedded, and unarmed."[46] Infants have a voice, though, that does not speak but demands. It demands care from others for its very survival because it is not able of self-care.

This figure of the infant naturally imposes itself on the reader of the myth of Er. After all, at the end of the journey through the *topos daimonios*, the souls who return to the land of the living as humans, return as infants. They have no name; they are not educated; they are not formed; they cannot speak; they cannot defend or protect themselves; they cannot warm themselves; they are marked by the formlessness or potentiality that characterizes the child: even their capacity to speak particular languages is only potential. One might be tempted to say, based on the spectacle that Er paints, that, just as the human infant has the potential to speak any language although it will only speak particular languages, the soul has the potential to choose every life and thus does not carry the form of any life in particular. This is the state of the soul at the end of the *Republic*, and Er, the one who does not return to the state of infancy but retains his capacity to speak, is therefore called to be a witness and to articulate the demand of the soul to be taken care of.

Socrates concludes the story as follows: "And so, Glaucon, his story wasn't lost but preserved, and it would save us, if we were persuaded by it, for we would then make a good crossing of the River of Forgetfulness [*ton tēs Lēthēs potamon*], and our souls wouldn't be defiled."[47] The story is preserved and not lost. What remains is saved and guarded by this testimony. What remains is, indeed, the ritornello of the souls, which is nothing but a demand to save them from their misery in choosing a life. This ritornello also discloses, as Socrates recalls in the last remarks of the *Republic*, that the soul is capable of everything: it is capable [*dunatēn*] to endure all evil and all good. The soul can suffer and endure everything and still survive. In a different context, Agamben writes about a similar capacity as "the mark of the inhuman" that humans "bear within themselves": the human is "atrociously consigned to its own being capable of everything," and he adds: "It is this *capacity*, this almost infinite potentiality to suffer that is inhuman."[48] What remains, what is preserved and saved, thanks to this messenger on the threshold of the living and the dead, is a testimony that articulates the ritornello of the souls, their capacity to endure everything and their demand to take care of them and to take care of righteousness.

Part II

A Distinctive Sense of Testimony

Chapter 8

Elements of Testimony

> [R]eflection on testimony has always historically privileged the example of miracles. The miracle is the essential line of union between testimony and fiction.[1]
>
> —Derrida, *Demeure*, 98/75

Orientations to Testimony

Proceeding from the idea that the six literary experiments of Part I provide a specific orientation to a continental philosophy of testimony, Part II and Part III are devoted to a systematic account of testimony developed in discussion with some basic reflections on testimony in contemporary continental thought. To this end, however, it is necessary to determine the instances or elements of testimony that require further elucidations. This is the task for the second part of this chapter. Let me first say something about the particular approach to testimony that I develop here.

The continental approach to testimony that I want to develop in this study, and that is oriented by the six literary experiments, is different from other important present-day contributions to the reflection on testimony. It is different from the blooming epistemology of testimony in present-day analytic thought as well as from the blooming reflections on the particular ethical-political concerns that critical race theory and feminism have brought to the notion of testimony. From an analytic epistemological point of view, testimony is mainly approached as the source of the beliefs we derive from the reports of others.[2] This epistemological approach researches conditions under which it is justified to call beliefs at which we arrive through testimony well-founded, questions of whether testimony is a basic source of knowledge, and questions of how testimony leads to a more social (rather than subject-oriented) account of knowledge. One could say that this approach privileges the question of the trustworthiness of testimony, rather than that of its object and how it discloses this object. In the wake of these social epistemological developments, different feminist theories of testimony have been developed, both from analytical and continental origin, for instance in the work of Fricker and Oliver, respectively. These approaches inquire into the political, ethical, and social circumstances of which testimony is given more credit.[3] Also here the question of trustworthiness is central, but explored from a different angle: why is it the case that people's identity, whether in terms of race, gender, or religion, causes hearers of testimony to attribute more or less credence to their testimony? How to understand the forms of bias and discrimination we encounter here?

Obviously, these epistemological, political-philosophical, and critical theoretical approaches to testimony are very important.[4] The approach I want to develop here goes in a different direction, and it seems to me that the direction I'm developing here resonates strongly with a basic motivation in some important twentieth- and twenty-first-century continental thinkers to turn to testimony as an indispensable philosophical topic for their thought. To explicate this direction, let me point out briefly which orientation the six literary experiments offer for an account of testimony.

(1) The most striking characteristic shared by all experiments is that the witness or the interpreter bears witness to what cannot speak for itself or what does no longer, does not, or does not yet have a voice that can speak. Bearing witness is thus in the first place giving a voice to what cannot speak so that it can be heard or understood in the first place. Thus, it seems to make sense to speak of an "object of testimony" to refer to how what-is-borne-witness-to is presented to an audience by a witness.[5] Testimony is indispensable if it speaks of occurrences or events unknown to the hearers it addresses. If the hearers themselves were present and experienced those events, testimony would be redundant. Yet, in the former case, this indispensability means that it is only in and by testimony that the object is (re)present(ed) to the hearers. Thus, what-is-borne-witness-to is *first* and *only* given by testimony to its hearers.

One might expect that, in turn, what-is-borne-witness-to is fully given to or fully experienced by the witness, who therefore and subsequently can bear witness. However, the experiments paint a more complex picture. Consider, for instance, the first experiment. Neither the speaking Socrates nor the silent Theodorus has an experience of Protagoras's lost voice *without* the witness's interpretation. The interpreters enact the lost voice by either speaking or remaining silent; without this interpretation, this voice is *simply* absent, without any trace of its absence in the dialogue. Bearing witness, however, allows the interlocutors—interpreter and listener—to relate to this voice *as* absent and lost. Hence, there is not first the witness's experience of the object and subsequently their rendering this object in language. In the sixth experiment, we do see that there is first an experience of the *topos daimonios* and subsequently a story that bears witness to this realm. Yet in this experiment the structure of experience is complicated: Er can only be a witness *because* he does not fully experience the *topos daimonios* as the dead souls do. Here, a gap exists between the experience of the dead soul and the experience of the one who actually registers and narrates. The misery of the former robs them of their capacity to speak their experience in life; the distance from this misery allows Er to speak. Consequently, also here the witness has not direct or full access to what-is-borne-witness-to, and his testimony stands for more than his own experience.

Consequently, in each of these experiments, it is not sufficient to speak of an object of testimony, at least if we take object to mean that which appears for an audience or for the witness. Rather, the expression "what-is-borne-witness-to" also refers to a gap in what testimony presents, to what is kept in reserve by this testimony. This *reserve* of what-is-borne-witness-to is the reserve of what appears as the object of testimony. It is the "real" of what-is-borne-witness-to, and testimony is the trace of this reserve that is only "given" as the dark shadow surrounding the object that testimony brings to presence for its audience. Without testimony, this reserve is *simply* absent. With testimony, we relate to this reserve *as* absent, as the shadow of the object. The expression "what-is-borne-witness-to" thus harbors a basic ambiguity, referring to both object and reserve. What-is-borne-witness-to is thus the reserve/object of testimony.

One might be tempted to say that this reserve implies that what-is-borne-witness to only appears *partially* in testimony. Yet the adverb "partially" implies that the possibility exists, if only in thinking or as regulative idea, of a complete appearance available to a complete and absolute witness capable of completely experiencing (and perhaps even completely articulating) this reserve/object. There is no complete appearance of the reserve/object, and the reserve might therefore also be understood as the ontological excess of what-is-borne-witness-to over every appearance in testimony. In the experiments, we saw this. There is a reserve to the experience in the limbo of the dead souls from which Er is also excluded. In the experiment on Bartleby, the narrator explicitly says that Bartleby, "the austere reserve," is only accessible up to a point—he "enlists our best affections" up to a certain point—but beyond that point there are only distance and inaccessibility. Therefore, the reserve is not what remains to be disclosed, and the object cannot be understood as partial object. Rather, with the term "reserve," we mark the very *misère* of what-is-borne-witness-to, its basic exile from testimony and its basic poverty. Reserve expresses the specific *phenomenological* and *linguistic poverty* of what-is-borne-witness-to. It is poor in language and poor in appearing.[6] This poverty, like that of naked existence or bare life (*nuda vita*), bespeaks an urgent need and distress. The impact of the reserve as poverty on testimony is that of a *demand* as in Agamben's *esigenza* and Lyotard's *demande*. The reserve is the demand of what-is-borne-witness-to to be said and heard. In the next chapter, I explore this further.[7]

(2) Before handing us over to the orientation offered by the experiments, let us hold back for a moment. Confronted with these notions of object, reserve, and misery, the following suspicion might arise. Do the experiments not offer a sense of testimony that is derived from a rather particular, limited set of testimonies? Do they not give priority to what is closed and does not speak? If I, with Lyotard, privilege the root *mu* in the conception of the linguistic poverty of the reserve, then indeed we enter a vocabulary inspired by the Greek verb *muein*, which means "to close," "to be shut" (see LSJ s.v. *muō*), and "to compress the lips" (see LSJ s.v. *muaō*), and can still be discerned in terms such as "mute," "murmur," "myth," "mystic," and "mystery."[8] Is this a limitation?

In addition, following the reading of Kierkegaard's *Fear and Trembling*, the preferred testimony that speaks from the experiments seems to be the one that speaks of exceptions. Testimony seems to lure us into a realm in which exceptions reign. Again, we can ask: is this a limitation? With respect to the exception, testimony may have a specific, disclosive effect: it may open up the audience's horizon of understanding to what exceeds it and even to what is an exception to it. My working hypothesis is that this effect explains why testimony plays such a pivotal role in contemporary continental thought. In fact, this effect combines—and I only provide a list here, postponing arguments for further chapters—Badiou's interest in the declaration of the event, Foucault's account of *parrēsia*, Heidegger's notion of self-attestation, Derrida's sense of testimony, Deleuze's account of literary language, Agamben's interpretation of the witness and the oath, and Lyotard's testimony of the *différend* and of infancy. At the same time, the literary experiments—as well as some but not all of the philosophers just mentioned—are hesitant about this "effect" of testimony. They depict a situation in which the witness's recourse to bearing witness is *not* grounded in the certainty of testimony's linguistic efficacy, but rather in the uncertainty of a *promise* by which language responds to the reserve/object's demand, namely the promise—in the precise sense of the German *Zusage*—that bearing witness is possible.

It seems to me that this particular orientation leads up to a distinctive sense of testimony different from the other approaches that I mentioned above, while resonating rather powerfully with the way testimony has been dealt with in both the history of philosophy and more contemporary continental discussions. Let me provide one example of this, which briefly positions my approach to that of some more analytic approaches. One of the basic questions in the epistemology of testimony is whether or not testimony is a basic source of knowledge, that is, whether it is on the same level as perception, memory, and reason, or whether the justifications of beliefs derived from the reports of others can ultimately be accounted for in terms of these other three sources. The stakes of this question are not too difficult to understand. If testimony is a basic source of knowledge, it would offer an important ingredient of a properly social epistemology that cannot be reduced to an epistemology in which the subject and its perception, memory, and reason are the basic sources. In the analytic tradition, this strictly epistemological question is usually understood in terms of a discussion between Hume and Reid. Whereas Hume argues that testimony is not a basic source of knowledge, Reid argues that it is—and there are good reasons to say that, for instance, Augustine, long before Reid, already developed a similar position as Reid.[9] Yet what is often lacking in the systematic epistemological argumentation is that the fundamental difference between Hume and Augustine is not strictly or merely epistemological but rather ontological because their conflict concentrates on the type of "events" testimony is supposed to bear witness to. For them, the basic question of testimony does not primarily concern all kinds of everyday reports by others. Rather, the pivotal question is what to do with testimonies of miracles such as the transubstantiation or the resurrection of Christ. It seems quite clear that Hume's dismissal and Augustine's affirmation of testimony *coincide* with their dismissal and affirmation of the reality of miracles. As soon as one is aware of this, one cannot but help wonder why, as Derrida suggests in the epigraph of this chapter, "reflection on testimony has always historically privileged the example of miracles."[10] It seems to me that any systematic account of testimony that tries to understand what is actually meant by this term has to deal with the question of testimony's peculiar relation to events that might be beyond the horizon of what we consider to be reasonable. One cannot simply "abstract" the epistemological arguments and their soundness from the context of reflections on things as incredible as miracles, without displacing the sense of testimony.[11]

In what follows, I therefore address the following question: Where does this distinctive—or exceptional—sense of testimony that marks the continental debate come from?[12] Is this emphasis based on an arbitrary decision or a nominal definition? Or is there something in the phenomenon of testimony that elicits this emphasis? The three chapters of which Part II of this study is composed are concerned with offering a more conceptual account of testimony by addressing this question concerning the distinctive, exceptional, or privileged sense of testimony in continental thought. In this chapter, I continue with distinguishing what I consider to be the four basic elements of testimony, of which the reserve/object is the first. In the third section of this chapter, I continue the considerations above that brought the notion of the miracle within our horizon: if indeed the miracle is so important, how does the sense of the reserve/object relate to it? I want to treat this question by a discussion of Hume's account of testimony in order to show how the author, who is often referred to in the analytic epistemology of testimony, might be conceived from a more continental perspective and, more precisely, in which sense his account of testimony seems to affirm the continental emphasis on a distinctive, privileged, or exceptional reserve/object of testimony.[13]

The Reserve/Object, Subject, Act, and Hearer of Testimony

Four basic elements need to be distinguished in testimony: the reserve/object of testimony, the act or event of testimony, the subject of testimony or the witness, and the hearer of testimony. Let me explain what I mean by these elements and describe the scope of problems and questions that need to be addressed in relation to them.

The Reserve/Object of Testimony

As I explained above, what-is-borne-witness-to is, on the one hand, an object that testimony places before the hearer of testimony. It is by bearing witness that what-is-borne-witness-to becomes a phenomenon, enters the horizon of understanding of the hearer, and enters the discourse of the hearer (this all on the presupposition that the hearer *accepts* this testimony). On the other hand, this appearing in a horizon or discourse goes together with a shadow, a reserve held in reserve in the act of testimony as the act that makes the object appear. The object-side of the reserve/object of testimony concerns in the first place that which appears by the disclosure of testimony, and thus that which can be known—it marks the contours of the epistemological and phenomenological realm of testimony. The reserve, in turn, rather refers to the concealment from which something is brought to presence and is, therefore, the ontological reserve with respect to the merely epistemological range of testimony. Reserve is, therefore, also the name for the primacy of the formless reality—or materiality—of what-is-borne-witness-to over the forms that are presented to the hearers and that they can know. The term "reserve/object" thus also marks the split-reference of what-is-borne-witness-to with respect to the form or the object it offers to be known and the formless reality or materiality that is always kept in reserve in the presentation of this object. Concerning this split reference, let me recall the notion of the unforgettable as analyzed in the experiment on *Godenslaap*. On the one hand, the stories told by Helena offer us a particular form of what happened and thus offer what-is-borne-witness-to as an object that can be known, interpreted, and explicated. On the other hand, these stories refer to what is never told because it is not even experienced *as* lost by any of the surviving witnesses and can therefore be neither remembered nor forgotten. They bring to mind the important passage from *Godenslaap*: "There is so much that will never be forgotten, because no one will ever have known that it existed."[14] The dimension of the unforgettable concerns what is "pulverized silently" and marks the true misery at stake in testimony: the formless reality, the reserve, of the stories that do receive a form. Unlike Derrida, I do not think that the miracle is "the essential line of union between testimony and fiction." It may be *a* line of union that complicates the epistemological status of testimony, but the *essential* line of union between testimony and fiction is formed by this notion of the unforgettable, of what is "pulverized silently" but can appear as the reserve of the forms that testimonies present to their hearers.

This sense of the reserve allows me to clarify why I have chosen this term rather than another to capture this dimension of the unforgettable. The term "reserve" gathers together four related senses.

(a) The Latin *reservo* means what is kept in reserve, what is held back or withdrawn from what is actually stated in testimony. In fact, this verb is derived from *servo*, which means "to make safe, save, keep unharmed, preserve, guard, keep, protect, deliver, rescue."[15] Thus, to bear witness is not only to say something and to present an object to the hearers of language, but also to keep back, to protect, and to offer a leafage to a misery that cannot speak for itself. The reserve marks the way in which what-is-borne-witness-to, the unforgettable and its misery, is rescued and preserved.

(b) In the notion of reserve, one should also hear the sense of the reserve from which testimony draws. If testimony is to interrupt and transform the horizon of understanding of the hearers, it needs a reserve from which it can draw the resources to speak in this way. It thus also refers to the *dunamis* that allows it to generate this specific poetic effect to initiate its object in a given discourse or horizon of understanding without reducing this object to an effect of this discourse or a variation within this horizon of understanding.

(c) The notion of the reserve implies that testimony cannot simply and completely present what it speaks of. In this particular sense, the witness is sworn to secrecy. In line with the second experiment, the witness and their testimony is a secretarious, that which keeps a secret. One could suggest that this means that what-is-borne-witness-to may be characterized as "mystical" or unsayable, which would be in line with the root of *muein* at the core of this word. Yet this suggestion runs the risk of privileging the apophatic mode of speech that marks common forms of mysticism. Rather, testimony's mode of speech can be qualified neither as mere *apophansis*, because there is a reserve of the object, nor as mere *apophasis*, because there is an object. More precisely, the reserve is only given as the shadow of the object; consequently, the practice of apophatic speech would not only empty out the form of the object of testimony, but would efface this reserve as well. Instead, beyond the apophatic and apophantic modes of speech, the secrecy of the reserve is at work in testimony in a specific way: testimony is always also an *euchē*, a prayer of the witness and the testimony to the hearer to believe. (In chapter 9, I explain why I use the term *euchē*.[16]) Reserve thus also marks, in the act of testimony, a reserve with respect to the apophantic dimension to state something on its object. I've already noted that the reserve of testimony corresponds to the misery and poverty of what-is-borne-witness-to and to its specific *demand* to appear and be borne witness to. As call on the hearer to belief, testimony is also the speech act that expresses and enacts the reserve's demand. The "mystical" is thus not a dimension in testimony that exists in pure form outside it, and the "unsayable" is nothing less than a *demand for sayability*, which is testimony.

(d) Finally, reserve is, in a derived sense, also the name for the attitude of the witness and the attunement of their mode of speech. Although they have to speak to an audience that has a particular horizon of understanding and that is to be addressed in a particular discourse, they should speak out of a reserve or reservation with respect to this discourse and horizon so that a space for the play of language is available to initiate an object in this discourse that does not follow the rules that mark its genre and in this horizon that does not resemble what falls within the range of what is expectable in it. Moreover, because the witness finds themselves always on the threshold of a given discourse and what-is-(to-be-)borne-witness-to, the witness is also marked by a particular reservation with respect to the reserve of testimony itself because otherwise the witness pretends to have a full access to this reserve, and this would only be possible for the only type of witness I exclude, namely, an absolute witness.

Let me conclude these first remarks on the reserve/object of testimony with the observation that this split reference also grounds the duplications or split-senses of the other dimensions of testimony. We have already seen how the *subject of testimony* is split between what remains silent and what speaks. In the first experiment, we encountered a momentarily unstable equilibrium in the *Theaetetus* when Theodorus refused to speak and with his silent voice represented the reserve of Protagoras's voice, and Socrates, driven by his concern to do justice to Protagoras's offspring, offered a particular form of Protagoras's voice. It is only in the form of this split-witness of testimony that the reserve/object is traced in the subject of testimony. The *act of testimony* is split between its apophantic dimension and the call or promise it always also is, thus mirroring object and reserve, respectively. Moreover, testimony is supposed to speak in a split language, doing justice to both the idiolect or glossolalia of Abraham and Bartleby and the shared language of reason and common sense, as discussed in the fourth and fifth experiments. The poet's or narrator's language thus finds itself on the threshold of the exception and the common or universal, and finds itself placed before the task to initiate and to give to understand new possibilities of understanding for the hearers of testimony. The *hearer of testimony*, who is placed for new, unheard-of possibilities, is thus also placed before a characteristic bifurcation point:

are this testimony and witness that appeal to the hearer trustworthy or not? Do they speak truth or falsity? Do they reveal or hide the events of which they speak? Consequently, there are always two hearers, or, rather, the element of the hearer of testimony has to be understood out of this ambiguity at the heart of the hearing of testimony that only breaks up in a disagreement between hearers when they take a decision. Along these lines, interpreting testimony out of the particular ontological duplication of what-is-(to-be-)borne-witness-to, the reserve/object, offers a distinctive or exemplary sense of the phenomenon of testimony that is paradigmatic for this study.

The Act of Testimony

The *(speech) act* of testimony is the act of bearing witness itself, that is, the *linguistic event*—or simply *event*—of the subject bearing witness to a reserve/object while addressing a hearer. To refer to this element of testimony, I mainly use the term "act" and sometimes that of "event." If we may call the reserve/object the ontological dimension of testimony, the act of testimony concerns the *logic* of testimony and requires, more precisely, an inquiry of the specific mode of the *logos* involved in bearing witness. I do not develop this here, but leave this account mainly for the next chapter, in discussion with both Aristotle and Heidegger. Pivotal for this logic is the latter's account of *logos* in terms of *Rede*, discourse or discursivity, and its specific interpretation in terms of *Bezeugung*, attestation, which in the German has a direct relation to *Zeugnis* and *zeugen*, testimony and to bear witness. In Part III, I discuss the relation of my account of the act of testimony to Foucault's "speech act theory" of *parrēsia* and (to a lesser extent) Badiou's account of declaration, and I discuss in more detail the oath and the promise that are part of the act of testimony.

In line with what I noted above, the distinctive sense of the act of testimony concerns the *possibly irruptive* effect of the discursive practice of bearing witness in a particular situation by *announcing* an object of testimony. Moreover, if one prefers to say that bearing witness is done *in the name of truth*—but I also problematize this expression—one might choose to describe the distinctive, exceptional quality of bearing witness in terms offered by Foucault as the "irruption of the true discourse" that "opens the situation and makes possible effects which are, precisely, not known."[17]

The Subject of Testimony

The *subject* of testimony is the *witness* or testifier. This element of testimony concerns the *ethos* or *ethics* of testimony for (at least) three related reasons.

(a) First, it is witnesses themselves who put themselves forward as witness by offering testimony; hence, the witness is not identified beforehand in the social situation as the one who "automatically" is awarded the subject "function" in this discursive practice. Rather, the witness takes the initiative to adopt this role. This also means that the (truthful) subject begins to bear witness by what one could call a primordial affirmation of the practice of testimony: by adopting the role of the witness, the subject says—implicitly and in silence—"yes" to language: they affirm and adopt for their testimony the promise of language to be able to articulate the demand of what-is-(to-be-)borne-witness-to. This primordial affirmation transcends the sheer act of testimony because it is the inscription or the subjectification of the witness to the practice of testimony.

(b) Second, by positioning themselves as witness, the subject is committed to their testimony and sworn to its truth. If they changed their testimony or when it became clear that they were lying or otherwise turned out to be untrustworthy, they would disqualify themselves as witness. This is reflected in the implicit or explicit *promise* or oath of the subject of testimony to tell the truth. Together with the primordial affirmation discussed under (a), the oath or promise forms the subject's *resolute commitment* to testimony. For later purposes, it might be helpful to add that a resolute commitment to testimony is not a resolute commitment to the reserve/object of testimony: Johannes, the poet, displays a resolute commitment to his testimonial task as narrator, but that does not imply that he displays a resolute commitment to the human possibility of faith he is bearing witness to. Nevertheless, there are important examples—as I discuss in the following chapter as well as in Part III—that tend to conflate these two forms of commitment. In order to maintain this difference, I distinguish a third element of the witness's ethos.

(c) Third, the subject is marked by a particular attunement or attitude of reservation with respect to both the reserve of testimony and the general horizon of understanding or genre of discourse in which they bear witness. It is only by this particular attunement that the engagement or commitment of the subject concerns the testimony and not its object, and by which the subject is capable of staying at the threshold. It is by this ethos of restraint or reserve that the subject is truly committed to testimony alone and attests: "I'd prefer to be at the threshold." The type of concern that motivates me here to add this third aspect of the subject's ethos is explained in more detail in chapter 10, which offers a small typology of the witness.

The Hearer of Testimony

The fourth element of testimony, the *hearer*, *addressee*, or *receiver*, opens up the truly (social) *epistemological* sphere of testimony. Implied with the notion of a hearer is a language, a horizon of understanding, a (life) world, and a prevailing (genre of) discourse. Following the previous analyses that testimony in our distinctive sense is marked by a particular irruptive quality and that the witness addresses the hearer with the demand to believe them, the *basic* epistemological question concerning the *justification* of the beliefs to which testimony gives rise gets a distinctive drift. This may be clarified in terms of the distinction between belief and faith, which in this case is the distinction between the *belief that* testimony's account of its object is true and *faith* or *trust in* the witness and this testimony. Parts of the often referred to debate between Hume and Reid on testimony may be conceived in terms of the question of which of these two has primacy: faith or belief. From one perspective, it seems that faith—and the implied principle of credulity, which states that humans tend to believe what others say—has a certain primacy. Yet one may also argue that, in fact, our faith in others depends on our belief that humans are usually trustworthy—a belief at which we arrived after many encounters with many people and testimonies. From this necessity of faith and this interplay or even possible tension of faith and belief, two lines of inquiry follow.

First, one can consider another example that portrays the tension between faith and belief. For the purposes of our distinctive sense of testimony, this example might be even exemplary. We may trust someone completely—whether it be by the principle of credulity, a belief concerning them based on past experiences or a combination of both—and, hence, be more than willing to accept their testimony. However, if they subsequently tell us something that lies beyond our horizon of understanding, if they speak, for instance, of an experience that we simply cannot even imagine to be true, there might arise such a strong resistance in us against accepting this testimony that it affects and even inverts our faith in this witness. Locke offers a striking example of the king of Siam, who at first believes what the Dutch ambassador tells him, but after the latter's claim that "the water in his country would sometimes, in cold weather, be so hard that men walked upon it, and that it would bear an elephant, if he were there," the king is sure that the ambassador is a liar.[18] For the king of Siam, it is the belief concerning the contents of the testimony that affects and even inverts his faith in the witness. The orientation of our reflections so far indicates that the distinctive sense of testimony that is developed here may very well find itself in such a situation. For that reason, I turn in the third section of this chapter to Hume's account of testimony because it offers, especially in section 11 of his *Enquiry*, titled "On Miracles," an exemplary testimony that is characteristic for such a situation.

Second, although beliefs may offer a support or a ground for one's trust in testimony, this ground is never a *sufficient* ground, but only offers a probable support. Therefore, there is always a remainder or a lack in this support that can only be filled by an act of faith that either accepts or rejects the testimony. Consequently, the hearer never only "hears" a statement on the testimony's object, but always also, implicitly or explicitly, is confronted with a demand for an act of faith. When confronted with this demand, the hearer has not yet chosen—they only hear this demand as demand before a decision. This means that the hearer always finds themselves in the space of the *perhaps* or the *maybe*. When in the *Letter to the Hebrews*, the author famously writes that *pistis*, faith, is a *hupostasis*, the ground and the support, of the things one hopes, he makes it clear that faith is itself the basic guarantee and is not itself supported.[19] Yet what this sense of faith presupposes is such a space of the perhaps or the maybe—or of the undecidable, if one likes. In this way, the epistemological problem opens up an ontological one, which one can hear better in the *maybe* or the French *peut-être* than in the *perhaps*. An act of faith or a decision worthy of its name is necessary where we do not simply confront what is, but rather *what can, perhaps, be*.[20] I stress this ontological sense of the perhaps in order to make clear that the uncertainty is not simply a matter of our finite, limited capacities to know reality. Rather, in the case of testimony, it concerns the particular structure of the reserve/object. The "perhaps" the hearer confronts and which they decide on is grounded in the "perhaps" of testimony's object, which I determined as the reserve that lurks in the shadow of this object.

Relating to Lyotard

In order to clarify what is gained by the introduction of the four elements of testimony—reserve/object, subject, act, and hearer—I want to conclude this reflection by juxtaposing and contrasting the above considerations to some of Lyotard's reflections on testimony. I want to do so because my own enterprise is both inspired by and critical of Lyotard's attempts to think the urgency and the concept of testimony.

Lyotard's theory of phrases, as developed in Le différend, is successful in two senses. First, it develops a sense of the fundamental plurality of language by arguing that there are multiple-phrase regimes that are truly "heterogeneous" and "cannot be translated from one into the other."[21] Moreover, the linkage of different phrases happens according to a genre of discourse that connects phrases in light of a specific end or goal—and, also, these genres of discourse are multiple and heterogeneous. Second, this plurality allows him to introduce the basic category of the differend. Because only particular regimes or genres are followed, some of them cannot actualize themselves. For Lyotard, this non-actualization is a wrong. Moreover, because these regimes and genres cannot speak in the prevalent regime or genre, this wrong deserves to be called a differend.[22] Differend thus refers to the difference—the different linking of phrases—that other genres and regimes would bring into play if they were allowed to speak, but that remains withdrawn from the prevalent discourses. This thus concerns an *injustice* that cannot be said in the prevalent discourse.

This theory, however, is less successful in another respect, namely in offering a theory or a well-defined sense of testimony. Testimony or bearing witness, in Lyotard's distinct sense of the word, is nothing less than bearing witness to the differend. This means that the practice of bearing witness, which is not reducible to but does involve a linking of phrases, cannot be properly accounted for in his theory of phrases. At best, bearing witness is located at the threshold of this theory. Yet, at the same time, bearing witness is exactly what his theory of phrases calls for, as can be seen from the following note: "In the differend, something 'demands' to be put in phrase, and suffers from not being able to be put in phrases right away."[23] This demand, which cannot be granted by the reigning discourse, nevertheless anticipates the promise of bearing witness, if only in the form of bearing witness to the differend—and note that to bear witness to the differend is not to overcome this differend, but rather and more modestly to bear witness that something that wants and needs to speak remains speechless. The theory of phrases posits a prevalent genre of discourse or, in a more phenomenological and hermeneutical vocabulary, a reigning horizon of meaning and understanding. Yet, by this positing, it excludes exactly that which it calls for, which it hopes for, and which Lyotard throughout *Le différend* cannot help but promising, namely the possibility of bearing witness, that is to say, the interruption of the prevalent discourse and the reigning horizon. Even his modest version of it—to bear witness to the impossibility of the victim to bear witness in a given regime of phrases, to attest to the absence of attestation—is beyond the capacity of the given theory of phrases.[24] At this point, a philosophy of testimony becomes necessary.

Let me contrast the four elements of testimony I distinguish with Lyotard's "four instances that constitute a phrase universe: the addressee, the referent, the sense, the addressor."[25] In contrast with the linking of phrases according to a prevalent regime or genre of discourse, bearing witness to the differend is nothing less than a poetic act that changes the whole universe of a phrase and complies with the differend's demand, as Lyotard writes: "To give the differend its due [*faire droit*, which also means in a legal sense 'to allow a claim or demand,' GJvdH] is to institute new addressees, new addressors, new significations and new referents in order for the wrong to find an expression."[26] Interestingly enough, Lyotard is rather optimistic about this possibility because he adds: "No one doubts that language is capable of admitting these new phrase families or new genres of discourse." Yet if there are indeed prevalent discourses and regimes of phrases that constitute our linguistic practices, bearing witness is nothing less than the creation of a wholly new universe and of wholly new rules and thus the very destruction of the description of the linguistic practices he just offered, namely as the rule-governed and goal-governed linking of phrases. Moreover, this gives rise to the following question: if there is a new genre of discourse invented, will this be the one that subsequently takes over and introduces its own differends? Such a question suggests that one might miss the very point of the notion of testimony Lyotard is proposing if one thinks it in terms of the theory of phrases. Rather, testimony is at best a limit-concept, a notion on the threshold of this theory. What testimony is supposed to do in Lyotard's theory, to borrow Agamben's vocabulary, is not so much to destroy given regimes and genres and to create a wholly new universe, but rather to *suspend* and *deactivate* their rules and laws so that it becomes visible that there are exceptions to these rules and laws, other ways of linking that cannot effectuate themselves under the rule of the prevalent genre of discourse.

Nevertheless, it is interesting to see that in other explications of his account of the poetic dimension of testimony, he seconds Derrida and Deleuze's description of the task of poetics to invent idioms: "What is at stake in a literature, in a philosophy, in a politics perhaps, is to bear witness to differends by finding idioms for them."[27] While my project is quite akin to Lyotard's in the sense of the task it awards to literature and philosophy—and "a politics perhaps"—it seems to me that this reference to the idiom and the type of "innovation" it requires goes beyond the scopes of what a theory of the phrase can offer. Why is this so?

First, testimony requires the capacity to create and innovate the regime of phrases or the genres of discourse to which the hearers belong whom the witness addresses. One could say that the first axis of Lyotard's universe of the phrase, which consists of the poles of referent and sense, needs to be replaced by those of the reserve/object and the act of testimony. The act of testimony replaces the pole of sense because for this act to be effective, it should be capable of widening or transforming the horizon of meaning of its addressees, that is to say, announcing new possibilities of hearing. (Or one could also say that this act should be capable of deactivating this horizon so that the hearers who belong to this horizon become sensitive to what cannot manifest itself within this horizon.) The act of testimony should thus rather be the (ambiguous) opening up of another sense in a given horizon of meaning.[28] In this act, however, the reserve/object, which in Lyotard's theory appears in the form of the differend, is not simply present(ed), and the act does not simply create a new discourse or a new horizon. To understand the act as creating new discourses or new horizons would discard the specific place of testimony on the threshold between, in Lyotard's terminology, differend and genre of discourse. This, subsequently, marks the specific place of the hearer or addressee: in a sense the hearer is transformed, but only in the sense that new possibilities of understanding are offered, next to or in contrast with the old one. Testimony creates—to anticipate Heidegger's formulation discussed in the next chapter—new possibilities of hearing and, by that, places the hearer for the question of whether they trust or distrust the testimony they hear. The question of this trust and distrust only arises *because* there is no new genre of discourse that now prevails: what takes place is a mere displacement and deactivation of discourse; testimony does not create a new horizon or discourse, but only renders them out of joint, out of their characteristic articulations.

On the side of the reserve/object of testimony, it is important to see that a particular concern of the present-day turns to realism becomes rather urgent when considering Lyotard's understanding of the referent. Referent is an instance of the phrase and, hence, of discourse. This means also that the reality of this referent can only be understood as an effect of this discourse: "Reality is not what is 'given' to this or that 'subject,' it is a state of the referent (that about which one speaks) which results from the effectuation of establishment procedures defined by unanimously agreed-upon protocol."[29] In this description, there might not be a primacy of a givenness for the subject, but there is a primacy of being-phrased in discourse over being-real. Consequently, the real is an effect of the discursive order (and this is exactly one of the theses that any form of present-day realism challenges). In order for testimony to be possible, however, it is exactly this sense of the reality of the reference that needs to be tackled. Testimony gives an object to the hearer of testimony, but not according to the rules of discourse that determine what counts as real or not. If the object of testimony is what appears in and by the disruption or deactivation of testimony, by the act that initiates new possibilities of hearing, the reality of this object simply cannot be the effect of a discourse—although it remains true, as Lyotard notes, that this reality is not *given* to the hearer. Therefore, the reality of that which is borne witness to is measured by the reserve of testimony, by the extent to which the appearance of the object leaves a long and dark shadow, which discourse's light cannot illuminate. Language and its products, such as the object of testimony, are in this sense the leafage of this shadow, clothing a nakedness, a misery that marks the real of what-is-borne-witness-to.

Second, it is quite remarkable that Lyotard invokes an utter belief or faith in language: "No one doubts that language is capable of admitting these [. . .] new genres of discourse." Yet this is not the situation that marks testimony. If there is no doubt, if there is no reason or ground to doubt language exactly on what it is capable of in bearing witness, *there is no problem of testimony*; we would only need to wait until someone, like a proper savior, actually and finally lives up to the potential of language. However, as soon as one invokes a *faith* in language, the possibility of doubting the power of language this faith affirms haunts this power and immediately shows the very stakes of testimony. A proper analysis of, for instance, the position of the hearer in testimony will unfold how the possibility of doubting language belongs to the core of what happens in and as testimony, as discussed above in the section "The Hearer of Testimony."

Third, when Lyotard adds: "Every wrong ought to be able to be put into phrases. A new competence (or 'prudence') must be found," one cannot be help wondering what this "ought" and this "new competence" exactly mean. If language cannot be doubted or does not need to be doubted, it *can* put every wrong into phrases, and, consequently, language always already possesses the new competence of which Lyotard speaks here. Yet testimony is necessary because language does not simply *have* this competence or potentiality. It may promise it. Yet, as long as the actual testimony has not taken place, articulating a wrong successfully and without doubt, the promise of language is not kept, but its fulfillment is (indefinitely) postponed. Moreover, because no testimony can guarantee its own success and ground its own articulation *without doubt*, to be exposed to testimony is to be exposed to the possibility of falsehood and deception.[30] Rather than saying that the possibility of testimony is grounded in the lack of any doubt concerning the competence and power of language, as Lyotard seems to do, one should say that testimony is the exemplary locus where the phenomenon of the *promise* of language—the promise of a competence and a power to articulate—comes to light.[31]

In light of these remarks, it becomes clear that Lyotard's attention to testimony in *Le différend* can only be the point of departure of a whole range of reflections, starting with an account of testimony that can no longer be described in terms of a theory of phrases. Perhaps if one insisted on locating the sense of bearing witness in the framework of Lyotard's theory of the phrase, it might best be located on the threshold of the "normal" phrase and what he, in a supplement to *Le différend*, calls the phrase-affect, which we encountered in the second experiment. It is interesting to see that on his way to the notion of the phrase-affect, Lyotard shows how testimony becomes a name for an impossibility: testimony cannot bring the phrase-affect into language. What "remains possible," Lyotard notes in *Heidegger et "les juifs,"* is "to bear witness to this impossibility."[32] The only task Lyotard conceives of for testimony is the task of attesting to an absence of attestation, of bearing witness to what remains silent in language or what is "deprive[d] of speech, rendering it *in-fans*."[33] Yet this depiction of testimony, which can also be found at some crucial passages in Derrida and Blanchot, only offers one side. If we follow the account of the development of Lyotard's oeuvre offered by Woodward, one might say that the Lyotard of *Le différend* only discerns the object of testimony and that the Lyotard of *Heidegger et "les juifs"* and later texts only acknowledges the reserve of testimony.[34] Yet testimony is on the threshold of what is singular, exceptional, mute, or inarticulate and the realm of common sense, of a shared language, a prevalent horizon of understanding, and a reigning discourse or episteme. The act or event of testimony is the (ambiguous) announcement of this object by a subject to a hearer. Therefore, this act needs to intervene in the realm of the hearer—displace and deactivate its language, discourse, and horizon of understanding—and to do justice to the reserve/object, it needs to speak *and* be silent of its singularity, exceptionality, muteness, and so on; it needs to disclose an object and attest to what is held back in reserve by this object.

The Guise of a Miracle

According to Derrida, the historically privileged sense of what-is-borne-witness-to is not the extraordinary reserve/object, as I propose, but rather the miracle. For him, the miracle is the privileged phenomenon raising the particular philosophical questions of testimony. Although there are important parallels between these two distinctive senses of what-is-borne-witness-to—for instance, both concern an exception—there are also important differences. Nevertheless, especially with regard to the epistemological dimension of testimony, it can be helpful to consider the problem of the testimony of miracles, for at least two reasons.

(1) The miracle, because of its extraordinary nature, sharpens our sense of the irreducibility of testimony's appeal to faith. The distinction between the report of a scholar and a genuine testimony may clarify this.[35] Although one might call the first report a testimony, this label obfuscates one crucial point. Unlike a witness, a scholar does not implicitly say: "you have to believe me, because I speak the truth." And unlike a witness, a scholar is not supposed to stick to his report to maintain their trustworthiness. Rather, the scholar implicitly says something like this: "If you did the same research that I did—which, by the way, you actually *can* do because my work is reproducible—you would reach the same or similar conclusions. However, if in fact you found other results, I would stand corrected and would be obliged to revise my position." Hence, the scholar appeals to the hearer's capacity to check and, possibly, correct the results. Therefore, in principle, the relation between scholar and audience is symmetrical, despite the fact that in practice it often is not. The relation between subject and hearer of testimony, however, is strictly asymmetrical. This asymmetry is reflected in the indispensability of the act of faith as irreducible ground in testimony.

For Derrida, the miracle exemplifies this. Let me state up front that I do not subscribe to this example and its paradigmatic status. For me, it is somewhat too extravagant, and I explain later why. Yet, it clarifies how Derrida thinks the irreducibility of the act of faith—of the principle of credulity, if you like—in relation to the miracle:

> Any testimony testifies in essence to the miraculous and the extraordinary from the moment it must, by definition, appeal to an act of faith beyond any proof. When one testifies, even on the subject of the most ordinary and most "normal" event, one asks the other to believe one at one's word as if it were a matter of a miracle.[36]

As is often the case with Derrida's striking, extravagant examples, they can be read in at least two ways, depending on what one considers to be "the real issue." One can argue that this quote indicates that there is no essential difference but, at best, only a difference in degree between testimonies of normal events and testimonies of miracles and that, therefore, there is no essential or principle reason to discard or reject testimonies of miracles. Yet one can also argue that this quote is marked by a fundamentally skeptical thrust. Such a reading would run as follows. Because miracles are impossible and because testimonies of normal events invoke the same principle of credulity on which the faith in testimonies of miracles depends, it is only rational that all testimony should be met with initial disbelief rather than with initial faith, and that testimony can only rationally be accepted if we have positive reasons for it. This latter perspective leads us to the second reason to consider the testimony of miracles, because it brings us in the immediate vicinity of Hume's skeptic assessment of testimony.

(2) The analytic debate on testimony is often said to find its origins in a controversy between Hume and Reid. Reid argues that the principles of veracity—that humans tend to be honest in what they tell us—and credulity—that humans tend to believe what others tell them and thus tend to have faith in others and their testimony—are truly *basic principles* of social interaction on which we can rely even in our judgment concerning the epistemological value of beliefs we form based on what others tell us.[37] Therefore, just like perception, memory, and reason, testimony deserves to be called a *basic* source of knowledge: to ground a belief on testimony is justified *unless* there are good reasons not to.

Yet, from a continental perspective, one would immediately object to Reid's analysis by pointing out that social interaction is not a direct, unproblematic interaction between subjects, but rather is mediated by genres of discourse and regimes of phrases. Veracity and credulity are, thus, not genuine principles but are limited to testimonies that fall within the reach of what is commonly known and what resembles what we know. For instance, credulity would be suspended when one is confronted with a testimony of a differend because it challenges what can be said and understood in one's genre of discourse and one's horizon of understanding, respectively. Hence, from the continental perspective, the true philosophical question of testimony arises only where the principle of credulity loses its ground. This does not only mean (i) that this principle is not a first principle, but rather grounded in resemblance, but also (ii) that the question of testimony is not yet truly raised if we simply embrace Reid's version of this principle; only by turning to the problem of the miracle does one get a proper sense of the problem of testimony. One could perhaps say that Reid shies away from invoking credulity or the act of faith where it is needed most—or to be distrusted most—namely in relation to extraordinary testimonies. The continental version of this principle would, thus, rather point to the irreducibility of faith in all testimony and point to the basic similarity. With respect to (i) and (ii), Hume's considerations resonate much more deeply with the concerns raised in continental thought. In fact, his skeptical analysis of both the principle of credulity and the testimony of miracles may help us to understand the problems we are confronting here.[38]

Hume on Credulity

For Hume, the principle of credulity is a fundamental weakness in the machinery of the constitution of human beliefs: "No weakness of human nature is more universal and conspicuous than what we commonly call *credulity*, or a too easy faith in the testimony of others; and this weakness is also very naturally accounted for from the influence of resemblance."[39] Credulity is not a principle, but is itself grounded in the influence of resemblance. Perhaps, credulity might best be described, in Aristotle's terminology, as a *pathos*—a passion, as Hume would say, or a *Stimmung* or attunement, as Heidegger would prefer—that attunes us in a particular way to what we are being told. For Hume, credulity is thus our *pathos* or attunement to *uncritically* accept what accords with what we are accustomed to and thus resembles our beliefs, which are themselves shaped by custom, habit, and probability. Our beliefs are formed on the basis of the experiences we have; and Hume argues: "A wise man [. . .] considers which side is supported by the greater number of experiments: To that side he inclines, with doubt and hesitation; and when at last he fixes his judgment, the evidence exceeds not what we properly call *probability*."[40] Hence, our beliefs, based on custom and habit, only have a particular probability. This explains why resemblance can have an influence—in fact, it is more probable to expect what is in line with our beliefs. Yet this expectation should always be accompanied by "doubt and hesitation." At this point, resemblance becomes a weakness: the *pathos* of credulity suspends the *pathos* of doubt and hesitation, which should always accompany our beliefs. This latter *pathos* speaks out of the conviction that reality can be otherwise than we think or expect it to be. This *pathos* is needed especially in relation to successful liars, who know how to abuse the pathos of credulity to speak for their lies. In this context, Arendt writes strikingly: "reality has the disconcerting habit of confronting us with the unexpected, for which we were not prepared."[41] With respect to the unexpected, the lie can do its work most effectively—after all, even the understanding of what is past, different, or foreign is usually built on resemblance: we understand what resembles our own expectations and experiences, as Ricoeur notes.[42] Yet he adds that this basic form of understanding cannot help us at all when we encounter a testimony of something that does *not* resemble our experiences or expectations.[43] Thus, in relation to testimonies of the unexpected or the singular, our tendency to accept only what resembles what we expect and have experienced is most deceptive. With regard to testimonies of the unexpected, this other *pathos* of doubt and hesitation is indispensable because it not only keeps the possibility open that someone's report, even when it resembles what we expect, may not be true, but it also keeps the possibility open that, when we encounter a testimony of an extraordinary event, it *can perhaps be true* even though it is against all odds, probabilities, and expectations.[44]

This allows us to understand in which sense the miracle can be an important phenomenon in the reflection on testimony. The genuine problem, I would suggest, is not the one posed by Augustine or Arnauld, who mobilize testimony as an instrument to grant credibility to the divine miracle, but rather the one posed by Locke's "king of Siam."[45] The extraordinary always appears in "the guise of a miracle."[46] There is a fundamental difference between the miracle and its guise. The miracle is, because it is originally presented in an epiphany or revelation, always too present, its appearance for the first believer too full and complete. Epiphany and revelation grant the miracle a pure presence and an utter, indubitable truth for the one who is truly overwhelmed by its glory, so that it can only be affirmed.[47] Thus, while the miracle's ground for the hearer might be the act of faith, for the original witness it is a kind of pure immediacy and presence. When something only appears in the guise of a miracle, however, there is no ground of the witness's testimony in their pure experience of the miracle in epiphany or revelation.

Because of this pure presence presupposed in the notion of the miracle, I tend to distance myself from Derrida's invocation of the miracle in his account of testimony. It almost seems that Derrida forgot that the miracle is also marked by an experience, by an epiphany. In its epiphany, the miracle loses all connection to the sense of what-can-perhaps-be because it purely is. In this sense, I also think that Derrida is wrong when stating that the miracle is the line of union between testimony and fiction, where fiction is par excellence the realm of the guise and of what-can-perhaps-be. It is therefore only the *guise* of a miracle that may offer such a line of union.

Hume on Testimonies of Miracles

Let us now return to Hume while keeping the distinction between miracle and guise of a miracle in the back of our minds. Hume proceeds in two steps. First, after having argued that our experience grounds the *general* trustworthiness of humans, he goes on to explain why a testimony nevertheless can become questionable.[48] He does so by referring to testimonies of, for instance, extraordinary events, which are improbable.

It is interesting to see that, apparently, Hume limits his attention to only one of the three elements that, according to Aristotle, contribute to how convincing (*pistos*) someone is. Aristotle distinguishes *ēthos*, *pathos*, and *logos*, and each of them is relevant in the case of testimony.[49] The *ēthos* or character of the witness contributes to or harms the trustworthiness of the testimony. For instance, the ardent believer, who for many years declares his faith in the same way, contributes to their reliability by this behavior. Steadfastness is an ingredient of a witness's trustworthiness. While Hume speaks of the *pathos* of credulity, the general trust in people, he does not, at this point, discuss the singular *pathos* that a singular witness may stir among a singular audience so that this pathos may contribute to the witness's power of persuasion. But he does address it a few pages later, as we shall see. Hume focuses here solely on the improbability of the *logos*, of the testimony's statement or proposition on the extraordinary event. In these cases, as he furthers his probability account, our experience of the usual trustworthiness of testimony in general is opposed to our experience of the rarity of these extraordinary and marvelous events of which this testimony speaks. When we hear a testimony of a rare event, we are more likely to discard it as less probable. In these cases, we have to judge which experience deserves to be followed and which is, in this particular case, more probable.[50]

From here, it is a small step to the miracle itself, at least for Hume: "But in order to encrease the probability against the testimony of witnesses, let us suppose, that the fact, which they affirm, instead of being only marvellous, is really miraculous."[51] Interestingly enough, the particular "violation of the laws of nature" that he mentions is "that a dead man should come to life"; a testimony that claims this is refuted by "an uniform experience," that is, by "a direct and full proof."[52] Because the resurrection of Christ seems to be exactly an event that is refuted by a full proof, he adds "nor can such a proof be destroyed, or the miracle rendered credible, but by an opposite proof, which is superior."[53] (It is important to note that the "opposite proof, which is superior," repeats the suggestion I made above: in cases of miracles such as the resurrection, the ground of its testimony is a proof that is superior to a full proof—what else can this be than a type of experience comparable to the one I described above as the full and overwhelming experience of an epiphany or revelation, which for Hume is "a continued miracle in its own person"?[54] Hence, although Hume might have done so merely to protect himself from the accusation of heresy, he does mention here the possibility an indubitable givenness of a miracle.)

Because the miracle goes against all our experiences, it does not resemble any of our expectations—except, however, for those testimonies of miracles that are accepted by custom and tradition. Yet there is another source of human credulity in addition to resemblance, namely that of pathos. Without mentioning Aristotle, he invokes Aristotle's account of pathos as a basic element to help a speaker persuade an audience.

First, he points to the "passion of *surprize* and *wonder*, arising from miracles," which is an "agreeable emotion" giving "a sensible tendency towards the belief of those events, from which it is derived." This passion of surprise and wonder is indeed to be expected given the very name "miracle." Here, the very topic of the testimony stirs the *pathos* of wonder. Yet it is interesting to see that Hume only portrays this pathos in a negative way. Perhaps if he had adopted the distinction between miracle and guise of a miracle, he might have offered a more positive account of this *pathos* in relation to this guise. After all, the *pathos* of wonder is the very attunement that, according to the tradition, ignites and initiates philosophy, whether it is the Greek *thaumazein*, the Latin *admiration*, or the German *Verwunderung* and Dutch *verwondering*, which both include the reference to the miracle, *Wunder* and *wonder*, respectively. This obviously is not meant to say that philosophy is concerned with the miracle, but rather that the encounter of reality *in the guise of a miracle* is exactly what initiates thinking. The distinction between miracle and guise is thus a crucial distinction to understand what the *pathos* of wonder does and means for thought: it is the very beginning of thought. This *pathos* need not result in thoughtless acceptance of what appears or what is said, but it can initiate an attitude of questioning and wondering concerning what we encounter as well as an attitude of doubting of and hesitating over our accustomed beliefs.

Second, Hume points to the rhetorical quality of testimonies of miracles. Apparently the miracles that are most deceptive are those that are told most eloquently, as he remarks in his own articulate way, "eloquence, when at its highest pitch, leaves little room for reason and reflection, but addressing itself entirely to the fancy or the affections, captivates the willing hearers, and subdues their understanding."[55] Yet there is no testimony without this rhetorical dimension, and it seems to me that in its most primordial sense, this rhetoric dimension is not in the first place concerned with eloquence as such, although eloquence may support it. As I claimed above and as I develop in the chapters that follow, testimony cannot be thought without a fundamental rhetorical dimension, which basically consists of the witness's appeal and demand to the hearer to believe them. This appeal itself is necessary because the hearer is dependent on the testimony to get to know its reserve/object. Because this appeal is indispensable, it inescapably includes the possibility to deceive. Again, at this point, it becomes clear why the distinction between miracle and guise is important: whereas the (true) miracle can always appeal to a more superior full proof, that which only appears in the guise of a miracle cannot. Hence, the basic undecidability of what-can-perhaps-be(-or-not) only belongs to the *guise* of a miracle.

It is therefore now time to leave the miracle behind and concentrate on the entreaty of what actually resides in a guise, demanding to be said and heard. Testimony mediates what lacks the ability to speak for itself and appear out of itself, as each of the literary experiments has taught us. The importance of testimony can only be discovered if we remain at this threshold refraining from epiphanies and revelations.

Chapter 9

An Exceptional Attestation

> To bear witness [*Zeugen*], that just signifies to testify [*Bekunden*], but it also means to be answerable for [*Einstehen für*] what one has testified in one's testimony. Man is he who he is precisely in the attestation of his own existence.[1]
>
> —Heidegger, *Erläuterungen zur Hölderlins Dichtung*, 36/54

For this study, Heidegger's account of attestation (*Bezeugung*) is indispensable. The claim, however, that Heidegger's account of attestation is helpful for understanding testimony is not uncontested. Levinas, for instance, explicitly opposes his own account of "the truth of testimony" to Heidegger's account of *alētheia*, truth as disclosure.[2] Moreover, if one characterizes the continental debate on testimony as one that privileges the testimony of the victims of different forms of societal oppression and thus argues that the social-political question is crucial for the turn to testimony, it is not clear why one should involve Heidegger's account of attestation.[3]

In this chapter, I show how Heidegger's account of attestation contributes to deepening our understanding of the sense of testimony and its problems of testimony that arose in Part I and the previous chapter. It does so in a threefold sense. First, this account of attestation contributes to a further elaboration of one of the basic determinations of testimony that arose in Part I, namely that testimony belongs at the threshold of *phōnē* and *logos*, of the inarticulate and the articulate voice. Heidegger's analysis of voice (*Stimme*) and discourse (*logos* or *Rede*), which leads up to his account of attestation (*Bezeugung*), allows me to further explore this threshold and relate it to the account of testimony offered in the previous chapter. Second, I use Heidegger's account of attestation as a whetstone to sharpen my understanding of the four elements of testimony distinguished in the previous chapter. Third, in the analysis of testimony so far, a particular dialectic or dual relation between demand—Agamben's *esigenza*—and promise imposed itself: the demand of the reserve/object and the inarticulate voice to be said and heard, on the one hand, and the promise of (testimonial) language to comply with this demand and to articulate what is inarticulate, on the other. Testimony involves both this demand and this promise, and Heidegger's analysis of attestation and of promise (*Zusage*), as developed in *Unterwegs zur Sprache*, helps me to develop this. Before starting with these three tasks, I first contextualize some of Heidegger's remarks on *logos* and *Rede* in the important methodological § 7 of *Sein und Zeit*.

Logos Hermeneutikos and an Aristotelian Example

Heidegger's well-known definition of phenomenology in § 7 of *Sein und Zeit* is marked by an interesting twist. Phenomenon, as he explains, means in the first place *"what shows itself in itself,* what is manifest."[4] The crucial verb here is *zeigen*, "to show," and the crucial noun is *das Offenbare*, "what is manifest."[5] *Logos* mirrors this sense of phenomenon, as Heidegger elucidates by interpreting Aristotle's *apophainesthai*: *logos* makes manifest (*offenbar machen*) and lets to be seen (*sehen lassen*).[6] The combination of these two senses leads to the following formal definition of phenomenology: "to let what shows itself be seen from itself, just as it shows itself from itself."[7] At this point, Heidegger adds a crucial twist by asking the following remarkable question: "What is it that is to be called 'phenomenon' in a distinctive sense?"[8] The word *ausgezeichnet*, translated as "distinctive," means "extraordinary" or "exceptional" in the sense of "excellent." The exceptionality of this phenomenon in a distinctive sense consists in the following:

> it is something that does *not* show itself initially and for the most part [. . .] is *concealed* [. . .] But what remains *concealed* [*verborgen*] in an exceptional sense, or what falls back and is *covered up* [*Verdeckung*] again, or shows itself only in a *"distorted"* [*verstellt*] way, is [. . .] the being of beings.[9]

This exceptional phenomenon, the being of beings, is thus marked by a *reserve* with respect to that which shows itself from itself. This phenomenon does not only "initially and mostly" but always retains its reserve. Consequently, the accompanying *logos* cannot simply "mimic," correspond to, or comply with that which the (formal) phenomenon always already offers from itself. Rather, this exceptional phenomenon is *in need of* a *logos* or to make this phenomenon known or manifest *in the first place*.[10] In the terminology I adopted earlier in this study, I would suggest to say that it *demands* such a form of *logos* to make it known, that wrests this phenomenon from its concealment.

To characterize the type of *logos* that is needed here, Heidegger turns to Aristotle's notion of *hermēneia*, interpretation. With respect to the exceptional phenomenon, we are not dealing with a *logos apophantikos* but rather with what one could call a *logos hermeneutikos*, which is characterized by *Kundgabe*, an announcement that makes known and makes manifest.[11] In the context of the discussion on the exact meaning of hermeneutics in *Sein und Zeit*, it is often pointed out that Heidegger introduces two senses: the more well-known sense of explication (*Auslegung*) and the sense of announcement (*Kundgabe*). In *Unterwegs zur Sprache*, Heidegger argues that the former sense of explication (*Auslegung*) is a derivative one, whereas the latter one of announcement (*Kundgabe*) is the primary sense of what the Greek *hermēneuein* expresses. It is sometimes argued that this hierarchy is not present in the same way in *Sein und Zeit*.[12] Nevertheless, it seems to me that a similar difference must already be at work in *Sein und Zeit*, for the following reason. One explicates what is implicated or complicated. In this sense, if one considers the example of a text, one may indeed say that one interprets a text by explicating its implicated or complicated meaning. Yet the text *itself*, before and beyond this explication, *announces* this (complicated or implicated) meaning in the first place, *calling for* explication. This text thus first announces or declares: "I have something meaningful to say," or perhaps the text even implicitly implores: "Please, read me, I have something meaningful to say"—and the reader answers to this call favorably when they begin to read and explicate it in, ultimately, the form of a statement, *Aussage* or *logos apophantikos*.[13] Thus, *Kundgabe* is distinct from *Auslegung* in the exact sense that this announcement calls for or demands explication. Although the notion of the call is not present in § 7 of *Sein und Zeit*, this account shows that there must be an intrinsic connection between announcement and call or demand; it is only in his account of attestation that this intrinsic connection is brought to the fore.

In the description of Aristotle's *logos* as *apophansis* in § 7 of *Sein und Zeit*, Heidegger mentions, albeit only in passing, an important distinction in Aristotle. In addition to the distinction between *phōnē* and *logos*, which distinguishes the human *logos* that gives something to understand from the mere voice and its vocalization (*Verlautbarung*),[14] Aristotle points to a distinction internal to human *logos* itself: the *logos apophantikos*, that is, those sentences "in which there is truth or falsity" are distinguished from those in which there is no truth or falsity. Aristotle's paradigmatic example of the latter is the prayer: "a prayer [*euchē*] is a sentence [*logos*] but is neither true [*alēthēs*] or false [*pseudēs*]."[15] The Greek *euchē* refers to what we would call a performative, in particular to the vow or promise that I make or to the call on something or someone that I do in prayer. Promise and call or demand are thus both contained in this sense of *logos* as *euchē*. Exactly this mode of speech is not only a separate mode of speech, but can also stand at the threshold of the order of the *logos apophantikos*, the speech that can be true or false, and that of the mere voice, *phōnē*. For Aristotle, the mere voice is only the expression of the (human) animal's disposition; hence, it can never be *in itself* a demand or a promise. Yet it can be articulated as a demand for or promise of justice in human *logos*. This articulation of the mere voice as a demand is not of the order of the *logos apophantikos*, but rather is of the order of the call or the prayer. Only when the mere voice is *interpreted*—in the ambiguity of "heard" and "articulated" in human *logos*—as a demand, *euchē*, it *is* a demand. Of course, with this statement, we transcend the boundaries of Aristotle's *On Interpretation*, which limits itself to an analysis of the *logos apophantikos*. Yet we encounter here a possibility, on the threshold of *logos* and *alogos*, what is without *logos*, to announce a demand or a call on *logos* and on the being that has *logos*. This idea of an announcement of a demand or call might not be at stake for Heidegger in § 7, but his analysis of attestation is based on it. In the account of the attestation, Heidegger's analysis of *logos* and truth truly departs from the guidance of the *logos apophantikos* because it introduces a mode of discourse in which a demand and appeal are addressed to a hearer to hear what cannot speak for itself or to pay heed to what cannot show itself in itself, to what cannot phenomenalize itself.

To conclude this analysis of the structure of an announcement of a call or demand, let me add one element. To speak of announcement in relation to a truly exceptional phenomenon—of being, for Heidegger—means to say that the hermeneutic *logos* gives the exceptional phenomenon to understand *in the first place*.[16] This initiative or genuine gift-character of the hermeneutic *logos* has to be taken seriously and, indeed, for Heidegger, concerns the *basic* meaning of interpretation. Consequently, we can no longer simply say that interpretation *as such* always already presupposes a fore-understanding (*Vorverständnis*) or fore-structure (*Vor-Struktur*). What is presupposed in this presupposition is that we are always already in the light of an implicated or complicated sense. Yet, taken in a strong sense, an announcement is the event of a gift that *inaugurates* and *generates* a (pre-)understanding by calling on the hearer, thus making explication possible in the first place.[17] While this generative sense of the *logos hermeneutikos* might not so clearly visible in the first part of *Sein und Zeit*, and especially not in the analyses of understanding and explication in §§ 31–34, it is a crucial ingredient of the analysis of attestation. Perhaps this generative sense need not surprise us given Heidegger's sensitivity to the idiomatic and etymological relations of the German language: *Kundgabe* or announcement in the strong sense of the word is a form of *Zeugen* or *Erzeugen*, the generating, of the understanding by the announcement of its privileged, exceptional reserve/object.

Disclosed to Uncanniness

While in § 7 of *Sein und Zeit*, the demand or appeal is only implicitly present, this call of being actually addresses Dasein in the experience of *Angst* or anxiety. It is important to turn our attention to this phenomenon, because it *both* introduces the Heideggerian version of what we called the reserve/object of testimony, which I only truly develop in the next section, *and* allows me to reinterpret the phenomenon of the voice or voicing *preceding* the famous analysis of the call of conscience in §§ 54–60. It is this voice that offers us a sense of the mere *phōnē* that goes beyond a mere expression (or indication) of pain or pleasure; in addition, to anticipate the analysis, the voice of conscience is a genuine call to voice the demand of this mere voice. My analysis that follows is motivated and inspired by Agamben's interpretation of Heidegger's concepts of *Stimme* and *Stimmung*, but departs from and disagrees with Agamben's suggestions in some fundamental respects.

Like the being of beings, anxiety is one of those phenomena in *Sein und Zeit* that Heidegger deems worthy of characterizing as exceptional: it is an "exceptional [*ausgezeichnet*] disclosedness of Dasein."[18] This means that the primary meaning of truth as *alētheia—Erschlossenheit* or disclosedness—receives a distinctive or exceptional sense in relation to anxiety. To capture this extraordinary sense, Heidegger introduces the notion of uncanniness (*Unheimlichkeit*), which we already encountered in Part I and which in the German literally articulates the experience of not-being-at-home and acquires for Heidegger the meaning of not-(or-no-longer-)being-at-home-in-the-world. The world is the environment in which everything we encounter is meaningful; it is our familiar horizon of meaning and understanding, which is always already there. In this realm, the human *logos* functions normally, allowing understanding of the meaning of the innerworldly beings of which we always already have a fore-understanding. Against the background of this ordinary form of disclosedness, the experience of anxiety is exceptional because it shuts down and revokes the ordinary disclosedness of the world. Yet by this breakdown of the common horizon of understanding, the exceptional phenomenon of Dasein's being, its being-in-the-world, is itself disclosed. This is why Heidegger describes anxiety as a fundamental attunement, *Grundstimmung*: anxiety attunes Dasein to the world in such a way that all we encounter in the world loses its significance—that is, all normal attunements to the world and the innerworldly beings it offers are broken down; yet, thanks to this detachment from the innerworldly being, Dasein's being-in-the-world itself can "obtrude."[19]

The German notion for attunement or mood is *Stimmung*, which translates the Greek *pathos* or disposition, and in the German is derived from *Stimme* or voice. Following the chain *Stimme, stimmen, Stimmung*—voice, to voice, to vocalize or to tune, attunement—one could suggest translating *Stimmung* poetically as "voicing."[20] Perhaps beyond the limits of what Heidegger exactly states, I would like to suggest that, for Heidegger, anxiety is the voicing of Dasein's bare or naked being-in-the-world, that is, its being-in-the-world stripped bare from the significance with which innerworldly beings normally encounter Dasein and exiled from the normal horizon of understanding. Because the voicing of anxiety is in the first place "heard" as the breaking down of the horizon of significance in which Dasein is at home, this voicing belongs among the different inarticulate voices we encountered in Part I.

To mark this exceptionality, Heidegger suggests that the exceptional disclosedness of anxiety can disappear again so that the world is perceived once more in its familiar significance. When this happens, anxiety's voicing can only be interpreted as saying nothing, as being utterly voiceless in the sense of being speechless, a voice without meaning: "When *Angst* has quieted down, in our everyday way of talking we are accustomed to say 'it was really nothing.'"[21] Hence, the same type of exclusion of mere *phōnē* from meaningful *logos* marks Heidegger's account of anxiety. Thus, one might say, it is exactly in the everyday, entangled (*verfallen*) state of Dasein that anxiety's voicing has to be articulated as a call or a demand to be heard, because in this entangled state, it counts as nothing. From there, it becomes comprehensible why Heidegger needs the structure of attestation because attestation will be exactly the announcement by which anxiety is given a voice in *logos* to call on Dasein in its everydayness.

Consequently, Dasein's being-in-the-world itself is the uncanny reserve of the significance of the familiar world that can only be made known when this everyday significance of the world is deactivated, and when the regular voicings or attunements are revoked. If it is the task of the *logos hermeneutikos* to announce Dasein's being, then this notion of *logos* is introduced as the *promise* of language or of speech to *say* and *voice* this demand of being to be heard and to articulate the bare voicing of anxiety as a call on Dasein, so that this voicing is not reduced to "it was really nothing." Hence, we see that a particular form of *logos* is required on the threshold of anxiety's inarticulate voicing and the everyday voicings.

It is in this context that we should understand Agamben's claim that Heidegger's analysis of anxiety and *Stimmung* seems "to reach a limit that he is unable to overcome."[22] Strictly speaking, the analysis of anxiety and its attunement only offers a dichotomy, and before the analysis of attestation or the human, there is nothing created on or as a proper threshold between the two elements. This is the reason why Heidegger subsequently introduces the notion of the voice, *Stimme*, that articulates this call. Let me first indicate in which sense I think that Agamben's analysis points to, but does not fully capture, the Heideggerian way of dealing with the problem of the threshold that imposes itself here.

Agamben notes that *Stimmung* indicates that Dasein finds itself "always already" in a particular horizon of meaning or particular mode of disclosedness of world. After all, this notion goes back to Heidegger's concept of thrownness (*Geworfenheit*) and its character of "always already." This, for Agamben, marks the basic negativity of Dasein's existence. As he puts it in *Language and Death*, Dasein did not enter language—that is, the realm of meaning and understanding—with his own voice by starting to speak. Hence, although *Stimmung* is related to *Stimme*, *Stimmung* rather indicates that Dasein is without (animal) voice and always already in the realm of meaning and understanding, that is, the disclosedness of world. Up to this point, Agamben's analysis resonates with the account I offered above of *Stimmung* in its everydayness. Yet Agamben extends this conception of *Stimmung* to the *Grundstimmung* of anxiety. This extension, however, does not make sense because it does not capture how this basic attunement deactivates this "always already."²³

As soon as we do insist on the dissimilarity between an everyday *Stimmung* and anxiety's *Grundstimmung*, we may see that Agamben's own concerns are actually very close to those of Heidegger. In his essay "Vocazione e voce," Agamben suggests translating Heidegger's *Stimmung* as *vocazione*, vocation or calling.²⁴ The Italian translation sounds just as remarkable as its English version. Yet if we understand *Stimmung* as the pregiven disposition with which we relate to beings and by which we encounter them as meaningful, it becomes comprehensible *why* this translation is not too far-fetched: we are always already called in a particular way by the reality we encounter. Yet if we position the *Grundstimmung* of anxiety in relation to this idea of *Stimmung* as *vocazione*, and capture its exceptional status for Heidegger, it would be, in line with what I suggested above, best to interpret the exceptional vocation of the *Grundstimmung* as a *revocation* and deactivation of everyday vocations and dispositions: it interrupts and revokes all those vocations that are "always already" predisposing us to the world.²⁵ This, then, becomes the task of the exceptional call, namely to enact this interruption, revoking the everyday callings and initiating another disclosedness.²⁶

In Heidegger's own version of this revocation in "Was ist Metaphysik?" he notes that anxiety robs us of words, leaves beings meaningless, and leaves us with an *empty silence*:

> Anxiety robs us from speech. Because beings as a whole slip away, so that precisely the nothing crowds around, all utterance of the "is" falls silent [*schweigen*] in the face of the nothing. That in the uncanniness of anxiety we often try to shatter the vacant stillness [*leere Stille*] with compulsive talk only proves the presence of the nothing. [. . .] In the lucid vision sustained by fresh remembrance we must say that that in the face of which and concerning which we were anxious was "properly" nothing. Indeed, the nothing itself—as such—was there.²⁷

In his reading of this quote, Agamben points to the words silence (*Stille*) and to keep silent (*schweigen*). He interprets these to mean that Heidegger's nothingness is "not simply grounded in a having-been of the voice, but in a *silence* lacking any further trace of a voice."²⁸ In one sense, Agamben is right: indeed, Heidegger's reference to silence intensifies the exclusion of anxiety's voicing from the familiar horizon of meaning. Yet, in another sense, his reading is run aground because the lack of the voice concerns "only" everydayness. Rather than speaking of a lack, one should insist here on the particular demand that appears at the horizon of the strange movement of Heidegger: it moves from stating that it "was 'properly' nothing" to an affirmation that "Indeed, the nothing itself [. . .] was there." How is this movement enacted? The empty silence, interrupted by arbitrary chatter, is the inarticulate voice of Dasein that keeps its breath in pure anxiety. If in the animal—and this includes the human animal—the inarticulate voice of pain is a cry of pain and that of pleasure is a cry of joy, the inarticulate voice of anxiety could be a cry of distress, but it could also be a voice keeping its breath in awe of what it confronts and encounters; this inarticulate voicing is "like a breathlessness, a panting, an effort to be," to borrow Levinas's words.[29] Agamben insists so much on the voice as what produces sounds that he seems to forget how by anxiety one may be struck dumb. Is it not this loss of a voice, this mute voice, that asks for *another* voice? For a witness who speaks for this mute voice, who makes known anxiety's faint lament? In line with these questions, should we not emphasize that anxiety, Dasein finds itself "fully incapacitated"?[30] Indeed, the movement that Heidegger's quote indicates secretly brings into play another such voice: the empty silence is accompanied by a call that allows Dasein to experience: "Indeed, the nothing itself [. . .] was here." Thus, we find that indeed his analysis of *Angst* as *Grundstimmung* reaches a limit and requires "*another voice*" that *attests* to this realm disclosed by anxiety—and it is Dasein in its everydayness that is now actually the *hearer* of this attestation.[31] This brings us to the notion of the voice of conscience, which Heidegger introduces under the heading of attestation in §§ 54–60 of *Sein und Zeit*.

The Voice of Attestation

When reading Heidegger's account of attestation (*Bezeugung*) as an account of bearing witness, it is rather straightforward to identify the four elements of testimony: the *reserve/object* of attestation is Dasein's being-in-the-world as disclosed by anxiety; its *subject* is Dasein's conscience and the voice of conscience; its *act* is the call (*Ruf*); its hearer is Dasein in its everydayness, with its horizon of meaning marked by the they (*das Man*). In this section, I discuss what Heidegger's analysis of attestation offers for a further understanding of these four elements of testimony.

The Witness, the Voice, and Its Giving to Understand

Heidegger opens § 54 with the remark that he is looking for a distinctive, exceptional attestation, namely the attestation by which Dasein attests to its "authentic *potentiality-of-being-one's-self*" (*Selbstseinkönnen*).[32] Because selfhood is determined as a mode of existence,[33] the distinctive phenomenon at stake in these sections is nothing less than Dasein's authentic potentiality to be according to its very own mode of existence.

In the introduction to Part I, I briefly mentioned how Agamben describes thinking and poetry as engaging in experiments that fundamentally affect our mode of living and existing, leading to a "transformation" and an "anthropological change." The stakes of Heidegger's reflection on attestation are nothing less than such an experiment that transforms one's mode of existence; here, the "one" is none else than the hearer of attestation who is given to understand the basic potentiality of their mode of existence. Thus, the object of this attestation is not always already implicitly given to Dasein in a (fore-)understanding according to the fore-structure developed in the first part of *Sein und Zeit*. Rather, the giving of "to give to understand" (*zu verstehen geben*) should be understood as a genuine gift: attestation is the event of the very gift or giving of understanding. Attestation *inaugurates* a particular understanding that, before or beyond this event, does not belong to the horizon of significance in which Dasein is at home. Hence, attestation interrupts the structure of what we *always already* understand and what we are *always already* familiar with.[34] That the "to give to understand" should indeed be understood in this primordial, exceptional sense is marked by the reference to the family of *zeugen*, to bear witness, in the German language. As noted before, *zeugen* does not only mean "to bear witness" or "to testify," but also "to generate," "to create," "to beget," or even "to produce" (*erzeugen*).[35] Thus, attestation is a birth, a second birth, and a sheer gift by which Dasein is disclosed (*erschlossen*) to the exceptional or distinctive phenomenon of its own authentic mode of being. This gift requires the irruption of Dasein's everyday existence, as Heidegger writes:

> But because Dasein is *lost* in the "they," it must first *find* itself. In order to find *itself* at all, it must be "shown" to itself in

its possible authenticity. In terms of its *possibility*, Dasein *is* already a potentiality-for-being-its-self, but it needs to have this potentiality attested.[36]

It is no mistake that "shown" is written here in quotation marks: this distinctive phenomenon is first and foremost concealed or distorted and "shows" itself only as attestation. The phenomenality of this mode of being is rooted in a primordial *logos hermeneutikos* that is the event of the announcement or the very gift of the meaning of being by which Dasein comes into its own in the first place. It announces an element that, up to the act or event of attestation, exceeds the horizon of being-at-home-in-the-world; it is therefore an exception to and a reserve of this horizon.

When Heidegger, in addition to his earlier references to *Stimmung* and *Grundstimmung*, finally actually employs the notion of the voice, *Stimme*, he uses it in this particular sense of "to give to understand," as he explicitly writes: "'voice' is understood as giving to understand."[37] Agamben clearly sees that this notion of the voice is not only different from Aristotle's mere *phōnē*—this is why Heidegger distinguishes it from the voice as "vocalization" (*Verlautbarung*)—but also from the sense of meaningful speech, *logos*, which falls within the range of the hearer's horizon of understanding. This latter difference is more surprising than the first because it indeed means that this voice is not simply Aristotle's human voice, that is, a sound provided with meaning, but rather belongs in the gap that separates the animal sound from the meaningful voice.

While I acknowledge the importance of this insight from *Il linguaggio e la morte*, it seems to me that Agamben does not capture the genuine implication of this voice on the threshold of an immediate exclamation of a disposition and a meaningful utterance. In fact, Agamben suggests that Heidegger's account of the voice as "giving to understand" would be yet another version of the mere intention to signify. By identifying the motive of "giving to understand" as "a pure intention to signify without any concrete advent of signification," Agamben reads Heidegger's voice of conscience as yet another version of what he calls the Voice with a capital V in *Il linguaggio e la morte*, which is always removed in meaningful speech.[38] Recall, as I noted in the final section of the chapter 3, that this realm of the intention to signify is, for Agamben, basically the realm of the semiotic and of the *gramma*, the letter, and articulation. The intention to signify marks for him the double negativity of language: it is the presupposition of meaningful speech that is concealed in meaningful speech, but it is also the presupposition that, as every presupposition, excludes something from language, namely the inarticulate voice. Yet can we truly identify here Heidegger's voice with Derrida's letter?

The problem with Agamben's analysis is that it completely bypasses the specific sense of attestation and testimony that mark this "giving to understand" of the Heideggerian voice. This voice is not presupposed—as the intention to signify is—but it *is* only in its happening, in its enactment, in its addressing. When it addresses, it attests to the realm of uncanniness at the heart of Dasein's existence. It is therefore nothing less than the very gift that offers the possibility of understanding this realm of uncanniness to a hearer who, left to their own devices, lacks the possibilities to understand it; it is this voice that calls on this hearer to understand. Hence, we are not dealing here with a Voice in Agamben's sense, that is, with the removed presupposition of an intention to signify for any meaning or the presupposition of the realm of the semiotic for the realm of the semantic. We are not dealing with such a Voice *because*, unlike the realm of the semiotic, which excludes the mere voice, the Heideggerian voice is a call on Dasein to hear and understand exactly the realm of uncanniness that cries in the silence of the basic "voicing," *Grundstimmung*, of anxiety.[39] The voice does not exclude or remove this basic distress but rather brings it into the open in the form of a call and a demand on the hearer of this voice.

The Act that Generates: Bezeugung as Zeugen

The suggestion that the sense of *zeugen* as "to generate" should be taken into account is amplified by Heidegger's subsequent comments. He notes that the voice of conscience "gives us 'something' to understand, it *discloses*," thus showing how attestation is concerned with the "*most primordial* phenomenon of truth" of disclosedness, *Erschlossenheit*.[40] In fact, in relation to, for example, § 44, Dasein's disclosedness reaches a new depth and attains a new determination in the analysis of attestation. Attestation, as Heidegger insists, is a particular mode of discourse (*Rede*), namely a call (*Ruf*). In its most basic sense, the announcement that marks the disclosure of *logos* is thus call. The new depth attained in Dasein's disclosedness thus concerns the following: the voice of conscience addresses and calls Dasein to be open to its reserve/object. As a call, this mode of disclosedness is a "shock," a "jolt," and a "waking up."[41] Moreover, the attestation announces its reserve/object as that which is withdrawn from the direct experience of the hearer: what the hearer *directly* experiences is the call, the being called to the reserve/object.

Yet there is a basic problem in the address of attestation because everyday Dasein "*fails to hear*" this call; it does not and cannot hear anything related to its authentic mode of existence.[42] Hence, the general discourse (*Rede*) of the they (*das Man*), which Heidegger describes as idle talk (*Gerede*), plays the role of the shared discourse and horizon of understanding out of which Dasein tends to understand itself. By belonging to—or "listening to" (*hören auf*) the they—this general discourse, the phenomenon of an authentic self remains mute and inaudible for Dasein in its everydayness. Yet if the hearer of attestation lacks the capacity to hear, how can the call of attestation reach such a hearer?

For Heidegger, there is only one possible solution. The attestation itself should by its nature be capable of interrupting and breaking Dasein's adherence to the discourse of the they and be capable of generating new possibilities of hearing:

> This listening must be stopped [*gebrochen*, that is, broken, GJvdH], that is, the possibility of another kind of hearing that interrupts that listening must be given by Da-sein itself. The possibility of such a breach [*Bruch*] lies in being summoned [*Angerufenwerden*] immediately. Dasein fails to hear itself, and listens to the they, and this listening gets broken by the call if that call, in accordance with its character as call, arouses [*wecken*] another kind of hearing.[43]

In this quote, Heidegger uses the verb *geben*, to give, to indicate that something has to be granted to Dasein of which it is not possible in its everydayness. Attestation generates and creates "the possibility of another kind of hearing." Thus, attestation affects the discourse of the hearer on a very basic level. This other kind of hearing attunes the hearer differently and brings them in another disposition or *pathos*, namely that of the basic attunement of anxiety.[44] Attestation and the voice of conscience thus indeed play an intermediary role at the threshold of the (authentic) being of Dasein and Dasein in its everydayness.

This particular capacity of attestation to generate new possibilities of hearing is an important feature that all testimony must possess if its credibility is not limited to what hearers always already expect or always already understand (implicitly). It also shows in which sense the act of testimony is different from a standard performative or speech act. In the commonplace examples of a performative, the words that are spoken indeed *do* something, but the effects they generate are expected and foreseen. When a civil servant says the words: "Now I pronounce you husband and wife," the two people concerned are from that moment onward married. These words thus effectuate their married state but do so according to the expectation of all those present. In the case of the act of testimony, however, the discursive possibilities of the hearers' discourse are changed and the situation is thus opened up to *unforeseen* possibilities. This specific characteristic of the act of testimony is itself grounded in the specific nature of its exceptional reserve/object, which is other than and foreign to the discourse or horizon to which the hearer belongs. Heidegger's account of attestation is exemplary in this respect for any analysis of testimony in contemporary continental thought.

In this sense, bearing witness is first and foremost concerned with the possibility of an *encounter* with the other, the exception or the foreign. Rather than simply repeating Heidegger's emphasis on the phenomenon of conscience in the formula "the voice of conscience," one should rather emphasize the *giving* that is at stake in attestation. Whereas Dasein in its everydayness fails to hear Dasein's fundamental uncanniness because it does not hear or neglects the voicing of anxiety, the act of attestation *gives a voice* to Dasein's anxiety, promising an encounter with this uncanniness. Similarly, by giving an articulated voice to its reserve/object, the act of testimony *promises* the hearer an encounter with the other, the exceptional and the foreign. Yet, and this is a crucial addition, *neither* this promise *nor* this encounter is *secured* by the act of testimony itself. Heidegger's explication of the voice of conscience as attesting to the potentiality-of-being-one's-self is in this respect very precise: it is not the actualization of this potentiality or this mode of existing, but only the promise and the possibility or the chance of such an existence. It is the hearer who has to *affirm* this possibility so that the encounter may, perhaps, take place. It is therefore not a sign of a metaphysics of the will that, for Heidegger, to understand the call of conscience means at the same to *want* to have a conscience; it is simply an indispensable mark of the gift of attestation or testimony. To "understand" a call simply means to *affirm* what the voice calls for—or to reject it and miss understanding it. For Heidegger, this affirmation is addressed in the form of a resoluteness (*Entschlossenheit*) to maintain itself in this affirmation and to keep this potentiality or possibility open because once the call has been heard, Dasein is answerable for it.

The Deception and the Faith of the Hearer

Let me go one step further and introduce a term that is conspicuously absent in Heidegger's analysis and suggest that such a call is always also an appeal to *faith*. Why is this latter term absent in *Sein und Zeit*? If we emphasize the "perhaps" of the encounter, as I did at the end of the previous section, we should take care not to forget that a "perhaps" only makes sense for Heidegger in terms of the hearer whose *feebleness* might cause the encounter not to take place; this is why he requires resoluteness of the hearer. On the side of attestation and conscience, however, such a "perhaps" seems simply absent or unthinkable for Heidegger. On the side of conscience, we are dealing with an "unequivocal" (*eindeutig*) call of which we can be certain that "the direction it takes is a sure one" (*die sichere Einschlagsrichtung*; *Einschlag* also means (deep) impact).[45] On this side, no deception is possible:

> "Deceptions" occur in conscience not by an oversight of the call (a mis-calling) but only because the call is *heard* in such a way that, instead of being understood authentically, it is drawn by the they-self into a manipulative conversation with one's self and is distorted in its character of disclosure.[46]

Apparently, for Heidegger, the voice of conscience can only be misheard if, on the side of the hearer, the rupture with the discourse of the they-self is not clear-cut enough; in such a case, the encounter with what calls is distorted and contaminated by everydayness. This means that, apparently, the disclosedness of the call itself is *pure*. Yet this also means that a lack of affirmation on the side of the hearer can only be understood in terms of the hearer mistaking the call and approaching it too much in terms of the discourse of the they. Exactly at this point, Heidegger's analysis loses the focus on the mediating role of attestation. Rather than giving a voice to the mute uncanniness of existence, the task of attestation has now become to draw the hearer out of the discourse of the they, completely and purely. The voice becomes the pure entrance to the realm to which the everydayness has no access whatsoever, and there is no reason whatsoever for the hearer not to believe or accept the call.

At this point, our analysis could go in one of two directions. We could follow the more well-known path and insist that we see here how the dichotomy between authenticity and inauthenticity as well as the rejection of everydayness determines Heidegger's analysis. Following this line of thought, we would accompany the analyses of Arendt, Nancy, and others. This is, for many reasons, an important line of thought and also seems to bear on the question of testimony, especially when it concerns the specific possibilities awarded to the general discourse of the they: Why, for instance, can't this discourse be transformed by the call? And does a testimony not always address an audience? Yet it is not fully clear what the answers to these questions should be in the case of testimony. It is not unthinkable that while addressing an audience and offering a seemingly public speech, the way in which a testimony addresses is by calling on someone in their singularity.

The other direction does not (yet) ask for the social dimension of the hearer but rather concerns an inquiry into the sense of the witness in Heidegger. This is the line of thought I pursue here because the sense of the witness remains underdeveloped in his analysis. We have identified conscience as the witness in this scheme. However, in testimony the witness is not the one who can simply be *identified* with speaking the truth. Rather, the witness is always the one who *claims* to speak the truth and who, as we saw, always implicitly or explicitly adds to this claim: you have to believe me because I am sworn to tell the truth. Up to now I have emphasized, because Heidegger's analysis of attestation brought this to our attention, that attestation means for the hearer that new and other possibilities of understanding are generated. If this were the only relevant aspect for the hearer, the only true task of the hearer would be to listen carefully enough to these new possibilities so that they truly unbind the hearer from their original horizon of understanding. Yet, in testimony, the question of the hearer's affirmation of what they hear is complicated by the fact that the hearer is confronted with *two* questions: not only the question of whether their horizon of understanding can be widened or transformed to such an extent that they can actually and truly hear the call, but also the question of whether the witness is actually trustworthy. For the hearer, the witness is the one whose *credibility* is at stake. The "perhaps" that characterizes the realm of the hearer does not only concern the boundaries and possibilities of their horizon of understanding but also the question of whether the call and the testimony being heard can and deserve to be believed.

This aspect is completely absent from Heidegger's account of conscience: the voice of conscience is simply and without exception the voice of *truth*. With such an idea of a voice that cannot deceive, one is actually referred back to something like the inarticulate *phōnē*. After all, this mere voice presents nothing but its own immediacy and presence, indicating only the affect it cries out; it does not demand; it does not state whether the disposition in which the (human) animal finds itself is just or not. Deception comes into play when we, for instance, mimic and stage such a cry and, for instance, merely pretend that we are in pain. Yet such an imitation of the *phōnē* belongs to *logos*. In this sense, interpretation implies the possibility of deception. Notwithstanding, as I argued above, it is also only by means of an interpretation that the inarticulate voice can actually become an articulate *call* and demand. Consequently, the possibility of (self-)deception is given with every call and demand. Even if one argued that Heidegger's notion of the voice aims to overcome the distinction between inarticulate *phōnē* and *logos*, and thus is both at the same time, one would have to acknowledge that, because of its character of *logos*, the possibility of deception cannot be excluded.

Heidegger's exclusion of the possibility of any form of deception conceals the very *claim* to truth that is characteristic to testimony and attestation and that can never be grounded or supported beyond the witness's exclamation: "You have to believe me!" On the part of the hearer, this implies that they never "simply" accept the truth. Rather, the interplay of the witness's claim to truth and the hearer's acceptance or rejection of this claim can best be characterized as the play of convincing or persuasion, which in the German is expressed by another variant of *zeugen*. To convince is *überzeugen*; and the hearer who resolutely affirms the call expresses his conviction, *Überzeugung*, that the attestation is true.[47]

In light of Heidegger's lack of attention to this realm of faith and conviction in his account of attestation, it is rather intriguing to see that Derrida claims the exact opposite. According to him, Heidegger's notion of attestation would attest to "a sort of faith" preceding all philosophy and "a certain *testimonial sacredness*" or even "a sworn word <*foi jurée*>" that would be reaffirmed in "Heidegger's entire work" and that would reside in "the decisive and largely underestimated motif of attestation (*Bezeugung*) in *Sein und Zeit* as well as in [. . .] *all* the existentials and, specifically, that of conscience (*Gewissen*), originary responsibility or guilt (*Schuldigsein*) and *Entschlossenheit* (resolute determination)."[48] This remark intrigues because of the tension with my own comments. On the one hand, it seems evident that a notion such as attestation *has to be* concerned with a primordial faith on the basis of which the disclosure of the possibility of an authentic existence is possible. After all, an attestation needs to be *believed* before it can be effective. In this sense, Derrida's remark expresses the obvious.

On the other hand, however, by insisting that the call cannot lead to deceptions and is unequivocal and certain in its direction and impact, Heidegger himself hides or, rather, expels any appeal to faith. Instead, he insists that the voice of conscience is directly the voice of the truth of Dasein's authentic mode of existence.

Therefore, rather than reading Derrida as offering a proper account of Heidegger at this point, we had better read him as offering a critique of this aspect of attestation in Heidegger. This critique implies that the value and meaning of truth cannot be sheer disclosedness, *Erschlossenheit*, but incorporates the precarious sense of *truthfulness*—and I call this sense "precarious" because truthfulness is never without the possibility of deception. In turn, this displacement of truth displaces the value of resoluteness, *Entschlossenheit*, that marks the hearer's attitude to the call of conscience. With the Derridean twist that reads in every attestation an appeal to faith, this is *not only* the resoluteness to distance oneself from the discourse of the they and to maintain oneself in the possibilities of understanding opened up by the call, *but also* the resoluteness to *believe* and affirm the call as the call of truth, that is, to maintain oneself in one's *conviction* that the call deserves to be affirmed.

As soon as one says conviction, as Ricoeur has shown in the Heideggerian language of *alētheia*, it can be separated from neither the possibility of deceit nor the critical necessity of suspicion.[49] It is as if Heidegger resolutely excludes deceit and suspicion on forehand, as if he is indeed guided by a sort of faith that does not allow doubt. Probably Heidegger's response to this latter suggestion or allegation would be simple: these doubts and suspicions would only hand over Dasein back into the hands of the they because the realm of the they is the only alternative for authenticity.[50] Yet this response is problematic because the very distinction between authenticity and inauthenticity depends on, is grounded in, and is generated by the attestation that "shows" the realm and the possibility of the authentic to Dasein *in the first place*. The logic is thus already grounded in a faith preceding it. Indeed, following Derrida, we should insist that neither testimony nor attestation has any sense without this sense of faith in their truth. As soon as one insists on this precarious nature of testimony, one shows that the stakes of the affirmation of testimony are twofold: not only to ward off the deceptions due to the horizon of meaning to which the hearer belongs—in Heidegger's example, Dasein's everyday mode of being—but also to expose oneself to the possibility of a deception rooted at the heart of any primordial faith.

This latter comment, I would like to suggest, provides another understanding of the sense of guilt to which Heidegger refers in §§ 54–60. Affirmation is not simply a matter of avoiding deceptions and unbinding oneself from the they, but is more profoundly a form of *being guilty of binding oneself to a faith*, and in the wake of this faith to the particular reserve/object of testimony, which cannot be exempt from the possibility of deception. Therefore, the hearer's affirmation indeed means resolutely maintaining one's position, but it also means the hearer's being answerable for embracing this basic possibility of deception in every faith, of following the deceitful miracle, event, movement, or mode of existence. Thus, the reserve/object is not simply Dasein's potentiality-for-being, *Seinkönnen*, but this potentiality is marked by a "perhaps," which so clearly resounds in the French *peut-être*, which is the third-person singular of *pouvoir-être*, the French translation of *Seinkönnen*. Because Dasein's potentiality-for-being depends on an attestation, it can never be more than a *Vielleicht-Seinkönnen*, a what-can-perhaps-be. That Heidegger suppresses this perhaps is due to the fact that, concerning this particular aspect, his value of truth as the disclosure of an authentic mode of being prevails over what I consider to be his true discovery, namely, that it is by attestation that this mode of being is made known and opened up. This raises a more general question we cannot yet answer at this stage of our investigation: can testimony explicitly bear witness to this *perhaps*, which is integral to the reserve/object of testimony? This question has to wait until the final chapters.

NAKED EXISTENCE

It is in § 57 that Heidegger finally addresses the reserve/object of attestation. He arrives at this point not with an argument but rather with a rhetorical question in which he identifies the reserve/object as the uncanniness of Dasein's being-in-the-world:

> Uncanniness reveals itself authentically in the fundamental attunement of *Angst*, and, as the most elemental disclosedness of thrown Dasein, it confronts being-in-the-world with the nothingness of the world about which it is anxious in the *Angst* about its ownmost potentiality-of-being. *What if Dasein, finding itself in the ground of its uncanniness, were the caller of the call of conscience?*[51]

As opposed to the familiarity of everydayness, the uncanniness is for Heidegger the best candidate to be the basic other of everydayness. Interestingly enough, Heidegger also identifies the *caller* of the call, that is, the witness. The witness is Dasein in the basic attunement of anxiety. Dasein calls and Dasein is called. "The calls comes *from* me, and yet *over* me," as Heidegger writes.[52] Yet this duplication of Dasein follows the strict distinctions of authenticity and inauthenticity, singularity and everydayness, uncanniness and being at home in a meaningful world, "something like an *alien* voice" and a familiar voice.[53] Yet, despite the apparent clarity of these distinctions, one cannot help but wonder, furthering an earlier suggestion, whether Dasein (in its everydayness) is not so much called by its opposite or by a strictly distinct version of itself, but rather by its *double*. We could draw a parallel with the second literary experiment, chapter 3, in which the protagonist, Alice, is confronted with Ariane, her twin sister and double, who represents the very distress and uncanniness of Alice's very existence. If one draws such a parallel in order to clarify what Heidegger is doing here, one is immediately struck by the peculiarity of his approach. Apparently, in the moment of attestation, Dasein can find itself *at once* in two positions. It is *both* Dasein calling in anxiety and distress *and* Dasein called in everydayness. It is as if Dasein were schizophrenic or schizopathic according to the basic meaning of this word: it is split (*schizō*) into two hearts (*phrēn*) or two passions or dispositions (*pathos*) *at the same time*. The importance of the call is exactly that it generates a relation between the two—it belongs at the threshold, capturing the zone of indifference between these two. Yet, exactly because attestation has this intermediate role on the threshold of this doubled Dasein, Heidegger is not precise enough when he identifies the caller with only *one* of the two attunements or modes of being of Dasein. Although the call has only one direction—it calls the hearer to the object and not the other way around—this does not justify the identification of the subject with the reserve/object of attestation. Rather, the caller belongs to the threshold itself, in between the reserve of which it voices the demand and the hearer that it calls.

Let us phrase this in terms of Heidegger's own description from "Was ist Metaphysik?" where he writes that the attunement of anxiety is attuned by the voice (of conscience).[54] This description makes sense if we understand it *from the side of the hearer*: Dasein in its everydayness is attuned by the call and thus attuned to the attunement of anxiety. It does not make sense, however, if we read it the way Agamben suggests, namely that the attunement of anxiety would itself be grounded in this voice. Such a reading does injustice to the particular status and function of the reserve/object of testimony in general and in Heidegger's attestation in particular. It seems more in line with Heidegger's analysis of anxiety to identify the uncanniness of not-being-at-home-in-the-world with the most fundamental and basic distress of Dasein's existence, which itself is and remains mute—as the inarticulate, mere voice that does not call—but is given a voice in attestation.

Heidegger's analysis of the reserve/object of attestation concerns the most elementary ontological level, but it would not be difficult to think of examples on less elementary levels to get a sense of what is at stake here. One could think of the nakedness and helplessness of infants, of the refugees who have lost their dwelling place in the world, or of the Alzheimer patients who have lost their language, their voice, and with that the very texture of their world and existence. These are all examples in which in a more or less distinct way the distress of Dasein's existence can be heard—in the very precise sense that in this distress, innerworldly beings have no or hardly any meaning for Dasein—and in each case an inarticulate voice expresses this distress and demands articulation, demands to be given to understand. Yet if we follow this line of interpretation, the latter sentence is, again, not precise enough; it is not enough, as Heidegger does, to identify the caller with this distress itself. Exactly at this ambiguity, Agamben's somewhat distorting reading finds its justified point of departure. How would it be possible that one who is indeed in a distress described by anxiety, in which the world loses all significance, would be capable, out of oneself, to address or to call? To address or to call is to move beyond oneself to another—or to oneself in another state—but there is no reason or ground for someone to do so or to be able to do so in a state of the type of distress to which anxiety corresponds. Therefore, the capacity to call belongs to the realm *in between* anxiety and everydayness: Dasein in everydayness is called to care, but not by an always already caring Dasein in anxiety. The distress of anxiety is exactly that there is *nothing* to care for in this state of not-being-at-home-in-the-world. In this disposition, the call does something: it *articulates* this distress in a demand for care, which is the care for a potentiality-for-being-in-the-world.[55] Thus, it is necessary to distinguish the sheer distress and its inarticulate voice, which Heidegger in an excellent way termed *Stimmung*, from the particular *demand* of this distress that calls in the call, which coincides with Heidegger's *Stimme*. This demand is the call *to* care: when Heidegger speaks of the call as the call *of* care, this cannot mean that there is already caring in anxiety, but it rather means that it is the call *to* care, to take care of the fundamental anxiety and uncanniness that mark one's very own existence.[56]

In this last paragraph, we are reading Heidegger according to a motif that can be found in his analysis, but that does not account for his tendency to identify the caller with Dasein in anxiety. It seems to me that at this particular point, it makes sense to say with Agamben that, "perhaps, humans are even poorer" than we might think.[57] The naked "that" of their existence does not have the capacity to call itself, but needs a supplement, a witness who is answerable for this deepest human distress and who gives an articulate voice to this inarticulate, silent voice of the deepest human poverty.

Let me rephrase the duality of everydayness and anxiety in terms that bring it even closer to some of the motifs encountered in Part I. The different forms in and by which we lead our everyday lives do not coincide with who we are. With respect to these forms, human existence is marked by a particular formlessness, which other authors such as Lyotard and Agamben have also identified as human infancy or potentiality. In itself, this formlessness does not mean anything and is as helpless and naked as an infant; in itself, it is pure misery, as Lyotard would say. In relation to the forms of our everyday existence, however, this formlessness gives rise to a particular demand to care because, with respect to it, every form is a deformation. This formlessness is therefore a source of critique and a resource or reserve of a call to care for one's own existence beyond the particular forms with which one tends to identify or interpret one's existence. Thus, the call and demand for care are not simply the call "of" this formlessness, as if this formlessness were its author or subject, but rather that this call is *located* at the interplay or threshold of the forms and the formlessness of existence and is specifically calling existence in its particular forms to its concealed and underlying formlessness, to what Heidegger so strikingly names "the naked 'that' in the nothingness of the world."[58]

When Dasein in its everydayness is called to care for this dimension of its own existence, it is proclaimed to be answerable for its "naked 'that,'" as Alice is answerable for Ariane. Heidegger's remarkable account of being-guilty basically means this: attestation proclaims that Dasein is answerable to itself for its naked existence even though this existence is not created or grounded by or in itself. Resoluteness and wanting to have a conscience describe the attitude of Dasein of being prepared for this answerability and to maintain itself in this preparedness: "Wanting to have a conscience becomes a readiness for *Angst*."[59] This latter formulation is rather important because it indicates that anxiety does not become a reality in an affirmative response to the call of conscience. Rather, resoluteness is described as the preparedness or readiness for anxiety. When we are prepared to face our enemies in combat, we are willing to face them, but do not, at the moment of this preparedness, actually face them. This means also that the duality of Dasein in anxiety and Dasein in everydayness is not reduced to a monism (of Dasein in anxiety); rather, another duality arises of Dasein in anxiety and Dasein being prepared to be affected by this anxiety. This duality is the structure of the basic care for one's naked existence in which attestation is still sworn to secrecy—the reserve of the reserve/object is not canceled in Dasein's purely coinciding with its anxiety—but in which the hearer affirms and dwells in the new possibilities of understanding generated by attestation. Resoluteness is thus the preparedness for the *interruption* of testimony and describes the attitude of the hearer who believes, affirms, and accepts.

Does Heidegger's exploration of attestation thus not repeat the Platonic scene of the myth of Er? Is not the Platonic soul like the other, alien, inarticulate voice in ourselves that attunes our existence, but does not have the capacity, because of the water it drank from the River of Carelessness and Forgetfulness, to draw itself from its silence? Is the myth of Er not the *Sage*, the mythic saying that gives a voice to the inarticulate, mute voice in us—the voice that speaks from the deepest distress and anxiety of human existence and that calls the human to take care of its soul? Is the *topos daimonios* and in it in particular the plane of *Lēthē*, this most uncanny element in the uncanny place where nothing grows or appears, not the predecessor of Heidegger's "nothingness of the world"? And does "the naked 'that' in the nothingness of the world" not resume the soul's sojourn in this most uncanny of places?

The Promise of Language

I want to conclude this chapter by referring to one aspect of testimony that we do not find in Heidegger's account of attestation but that, due to the "sloppiness" explained above, Derrida does relate to this account, namely the sense of *Zusage*, which Heidegger in his later works introduces as a crucial name to elucidate the essence of language. Note that, on several occasions, Heidegger suggests naming the essence of language with the word *Sage*, which is usually translated as "saying." While this translation has its own merits, it is important to keep in mind that in the German language, *Sage* means "legend" or "folktale." This explains why, for Heidegger, *Sage* translates the Greek *muthos* and why he refers to the myth of Er as "die letzte Sage," the last myth.[60] Much in line with our own concerns, he argues that this myth is actually a testimony and attestation: the myth "attests to [*bezeugt*] the essential rank" of language in relation to *alētheia* as disclosure.[61] By this testimony of the myth of Er, we hear in Plato's works of the essence of language as that which discloses and brings into the open.

The subsequent specification of *Sage* as *Zusage* or promise complicates this understanding of language in relation to disclosure. *Zusage* is not so much faith or trust itself, although Derrida sometimes suggests it is; nor is it the simple granting of language, as English translations sometimes suggest. To understand *Zusage*, one should always keep in mind the sense of promise; *zusagen* can mean "to promise to grant" but never simply "to grant." It is therefore related to the oath and the vow. Thus, these notions complicate the understanding of the essence of language: they add to the sheer disclosure of language the structure of the promise and of the vow.

In one very striking passage in "Das Wesen der Sprache" from *Unterwegs zur Sprache*, this structure of the promise is introduced to capture the very poetic experience of language. The poet is the one who learns from language what is promised, *zugesagt*, to him, but what nevertheless "hesitates in its withdrawal," *zögert im Entzug*, and "holds itself in reserve."[62] This means that the promise or *Zusage* of language does not simply give or grant what it promises to give; it speaks to the poet, but in what the poet hears, in what he receives, he also hears this withdrawal and this reserve of the actual fulfillment of the promise. This brings the experience of the essence of language very close to that of testimony: not only because the object testimony announces is always marked by a reserve but also because the language of testimony itself can only exist as a promise and as a promise that can never fulfill itself. It exists as a promise of the witness to speak the truth, and as the promise of the act of testimony to offer what is withheld from the hearer's own horizon of understanding. The promise to speak the truth is never fulfilled but always needs to be affirmed and resolutely maintained by the witness. Also, the promise of the act of testimony to offer what is withheld never offers its reserve/object in a full presence. There always remains a silence, even in the object that is given a voice; silence is the double of this object, its reserve. Bearing witness is therefore always marked by this promise:

Socrates promises to do justice to the lost voice of Protagoras, but this promise is always accompanied by the silence of Theodorus that interrupts the Socratic testimony and attests to an absence of attestation. One cannot be thought without the other.

Let me conclude with one etymological consideration, which Heidegger himself does not seem to offer—at least, I did not find it—but which is not foreign to Heidegger's own approach to language. *Entzug* is the word that expresses the withdrawal of the reserve/object of the poetic announcement. It is related to *entziehen*, to withdraw, and *ziehen*, to draw. Derrida has shown how important this chain of words is for Heidegger, and he discusses them together with the notions of *Riss* and *reissen*.[63] Yet in the German, there is another verb that etymologically belongs to *ziehen*, namely *zeugen*: these verbs are derived from the same root. *Zeugen* might then occur for the first time in the sense of "drawing" someone to or before the court, making this person a witness in a court case.[64] *Zeugen* then does not find its origin in the witness who decides to speak up, but rather in the reserve/object that somehow draws the witness to testifying. The witness experiences in this reserve/object a demand and a being drawn to assume the position of the one who bears witness, that is, of the one who draws the demand of the reserve/object from its withdrawal, articulating it in an act that is always also a vow and a promise. Perhaps more than any of Heidegger's poets, it is the witness who, by being drawn to bear witness, is placed before the promise of language to offer what is indeed "the highest and what remains," namely to generate the possibilities of understanding for the hearers and to voice the demand of what is withdrawn in reserve. Is there a greater mourning or sadness—*Trauer*—thinkable than the one experienced by those who, when starting to bear witness, speak out from (their trust in) this promise of language, and then find that language hesitates and wavers, complicating each and every testimony with an additional testimony to an absence of testimony? And still, though mournful, such a doubled bearing witness is how testimony voices a demand par excellence.

Chapter 10

A Typology of the Witness

Truly I do not know how to speak.¹

—*Jeremiah* 1:6

In the previous chapter, I passed over one rather striking element in Heidegger's account of the voice of conscience. In order to avoid any confusion and to make it perfectly clear that the call that comes "*over* me" also truly comes "*from* me," Heidegger dismisses the idea that the voice of conscience is the voice of another power that speaks in me:

> Thus we need not resort to powers unlike Dasein, especially since recourse to these is so far from explaining the uncanniness of the call that it rather annihilates it. [. . .] Why should we look to alien powers [. . .] before we have made sure that [. . .] we have not given too *low* an assessment of the being of Dasein [. . .]?²

Apparently, Heidegger feels compelled to emphasize that we are not dealing here with the voice of another being that calls Dasein. His argument is quite straightforward, although not without problems. The alien powers represent something "objectively ascertainable," as Heidegger writes in the next paragraph, and this means that the being of such a power can only be of the order of "objective presence" (*Vorhandenheit*). As soon as this is granted, the conclusion he aims at is within reach: to identify the source of the voice of conscience as an objectively ascertainable power is simply "a flight from conscience, a way out for Dasein along which it slips away."

My hesitation in accepting this argument is fueled by the above quote: Heidegger speaks of "alien powers" (*fremde Mächte*), and in which sense is the alien nature of these powers different from the alien nature of the voice by which Dasein is called? How can such a power be genuinely "alien" yet at the same time "objectively ascertainable," that is, be a being that ultimately is grounded in the sphere of everydayness? Would it be unthinkable, and if so why, that such a power is truly alien and thus also belongs to the realm of the uncanny? If this is not unthinkable, how could Dasein as the *hearer* of the call be able to distinguish its "own" alien voice from that of a truly alien power?

I raise these questions not so much to create a marginal space in Heidegger's reflections on Dasein in which alien powers could take up their residence, but rather to show their strategic function. Heidegger insists, without proving it, on a strict distinction or separation of attestation from other modes of speech that resemble it, such as the divine speech we encountered in Part I under the name of glossolalia. When the voice calling from Dasein to Dasein may rightly be called an *alien* voice, does this not mean that Dasein in its everydayness is seized and overcome by something in itself that is at the same time alien to it? Would it subsequently be out of line to say that Dasein's existence is thus *enthralled by* or *delivered to* this alien voice? Let's call this latter sense of being enthralled by . . . or being delivered to . . . by its appropriate name "enthusiasm," from the Greek *entheos*, to be full of the god, inspired, or possessed by the god. What these concerns thus show is that Heidegger's reflections on the voice of conscience retain the formal structure of a divine-like inspiration that *speaks in* me—as in glossolalia—but empties out this divinity from all content, handing Dasein over to an enthusiasm without *theos*, to being enthralled by the naked "that" in the nothingness of the world. Is Heidegger's analysis of the voice thus not a secularized, emptied-out version of such a divine speech?

This remnant of enthusiasm in his account of attestation might explain why the element of the subject of testimony remains underdeveloped. To integrate a sense of enthusiasm, or a derivative form of it, into a conception of testimony problematizes especially the figure of the witness. If the witness is to speak in a common language, they cannot be speaking a divine language because the latter is truly alien and without any common measure. The witness is therefore not only the one who experiences something—in Heidegger's case, bare existence—but the witness should also be able to *disengage* in a certain way from this singular experience so that it can be announced to those who did not have this experience.

If there is an ethics to testimony, one that concerns the witness, it derives from a certain imperative force—a being-drawn—to speak that the witness *adopts* when they bear witness. Exactly for this latter reason, it cannot be a divine force that simply overtakes and speaks in the witness as a divine voice. It is this concern that forms the point of departure for this chapter devoted to a typology of the witness.

Glossolalist, Prophet, Poet, and Interpreter

The striking resemblance between Agamben's analysis of Heidegger's voice of conscience in *Il linguaggio e la morte* and his analysis of glossolalia in *Categorie Italiane* offers enough ground to suspect a relation between Heidegger's voice of conscience and glossolalia. Similar but distinct accounts of a foreign voice speaking in someone can be found in explications of the figures of the poet, the prophet, and sometimes even the interpreter. In each of these figures, the voice that speaks is traditionally of a divine nature. I address these figures with the following two basic questions in mind: first, how are these figures related to the witness and in which sense is their speech different from or similar to that of testimony? Second, what does the value of the divine in these figures imply, and which role, if any, does this value play in bearing witness?

THE GLOSSOLALIST

Reconnecting to my previous discussion of glossolalia in chapter 5, let me add one more quote from Paul's 1 *Corinthians* 14 to get a better sense of what is at stake in this mode of speech. For Paul, someone who speaks in tongues has a private, fully singular communication with the divine. Therefore, it is impossible to comprehend what the glossolalist says. For Kierkegaard, this is the reason to compare Abraham's speech with glossolalia: the patriarch gives expression to a completely singular relation with the divine. For Derrida, Abraham's divine language is comparable to that of Bartleby, and he implies that we encounter in Abraham's and Bartleby's ironic, enigmatic sentences the *suggestion* of signification.[3] Agamben identifies glossolalia as a pure intention to signify, marked by the absence of both the *phōnē* of a living being and of any actual meaning.[4]

Yet I am not convinced that for either Paul or Kierkegaard such a pure intention to signify or such a suggestion of signification is at stake in this extraordinary mode of speech. To see this, consider the following remark of Paul on the tongue (*glōssa*) and on speaking in tongues, in which all ingredients I mentioned in chapter 5 are gathered together:

> When you come together, each one has a hymn, a lesson, a revelation, a tongue, or an interpretation. Let all things be done for building up. If anyone speaks in a tongue, let there be only two or at most three, and each in turn; and let one interpret. But if there is no interpreter, let them be silent in church and speak to themselves and to God.[5]

For Paul, glossolalia is a singular speech between a singular spirit and the god. In this sense, there is a strong, formal resemblance with Heidegger's account of the call of conscience. This latter call also calls to a purely singular relation. Paul and Heidegger differ in two respects, though. First, for Heidegger, the "external" power is replaced by Dasein's own alien dimension disclosed in anxiety. Yet glossolalia in Paul refers to an alien power that is *not* of the order of the "objectively ascertainable": the direct communication with this god is utterly inaccessible from a communal point of view and thus definitely from the point of view of objective presence, which is a derivative of everydayness.[6] Second, although Paul appreciates the value of this mode of speech, he is mainly concerned with the question of how this singular voice can be "upbuilding" for the community. This is the type of question Heidegger is not interested in because the call of conscience draws Dasein out of its everydayness into a sheer singularity.

In this particular sense, and perhaps despite the reference to the divine, Paul's account of glossolalia offers something Heidegger does not think, namely how, when such an incomprehensible voice is given, it can be present in a community in such a way that it is not simply an exception to the community that, when present and heard in the community, only confuses. It is at this point that Paul introduces the notions of interpretation (*hermēneia*), interpreting (*diermēneuō*), and interpreter (*diermēneutēs*). For Paul, the question of meaning and the recognition of the glossolalist's voice as giving something to understand only *takes place* when interpreters are present. Hence, it is unlikely that glossolalia *itself* can be accounted for in terms of a pure intention to signify; glossolalia first appears as a linguistic "phenomenon" that is purely closed in on itself and that truly has nothing to say and intends to say nothing to the community. If it affects the community, it does so as a *force* that confuses. Paul considers this duality to be counterproductive for the community and therefore commands the silencing of any speaking in tongues when no interpreters are present. Yet this banishment is conditional: Paul allows for the possibility of interpreters mediating between these two languages. The interpreter thus *intervenes* in this duality that separates the language of the community from the divine language and places itself on their threshold. Because Paul argues that the interpretation aims at the upbuilding of the community, as opposed to its confusion, it would seem to go against the basic tenet of his remark to argue that the interpreter is brought in only to *reduce* the divine language to the language of the community or to comprehensible meaning. Rather, a *building up* of the community is at stake. Therefore, it seems more likely that the interpreter is indeed concerned with *giving to understand* what is said and, by interpreting, creates new ways of hearing and understanding that transform the community: the community and its language are changed; they are built up.

Our previous reading of Kierkegaard has shown more pertinently what this upbuilding can mean.[7] The interpreter or narrator is not the one who reduces Abraham's divine language or singularity to something that can be shared, but they intermediate between singularity and community and bear witness to a singularity as something that, in Abraham's case, concerns—for Kierkegaard's poet—one of the most basic possibilities of human existence, which is excluded from reasonable, universal discourse.

This has a particular consequence, namely that the witness in this particular context cannot be identified with a single individual alone. The witness should rather be understood as a certain indifference between two figures: on the one hand, the glossolalist—or *Fear and Trembling*'s Abraham—who actually experiences this mode of speech and who actually expresses the inarticulate, incomprehensible, and confusing sounds, and, on the other hand, the interpreter or narrator—*Fear and Trembling*'s poet who adopts the role of the *diermēneutēs* demanded by glossolalia—who is close to the experience of glossolalia but is disengaged from it. In the language of Kierkegaard's poet, this proximity requires both admiration and repellence with which the poet is drawn to and repulsed from the "glossolalist"; and it requires the capacity to poeticize, to disclose the singular existence to a community, and thus to create new, unheard-of possibilities of understanding and hearing.

Thus, with respect to the glossolalist, the witness is marked by a fundamental duality, is a composition of two figures. Without the experience there is no object; without the (partial) disengagement there is no possibility to speak for a community. This strange duality of engagement and disengagement in the split figure of the witness will return again and again. There seems to be a rather remarkable resemblance between the consuming nature of the experience of the unification with the divine, as in glossolalia, and the experience of utter nothingness, as in Heidegger's anxiety: both are so fully demanding that they leave no room for a proper address.

Our discussion needs to be complemented with one crucial aspect of Agamben's account of glossolalia. In *Quel che resta di Auschwitz*, he argues that in the speaking of tongues a "desubjectification" takes place. This means that the one whose voice is heard is no longer simply the *subject* of the speech that is uttered.[8] The speaker does not master or know what they say. They speak in a barbaric language, as Agamben adds, which is not of the order of the *logos*, of the shared universal language of reason. He then adds something that not only deviates from his earlier insistence to read glossolalia as a pure intention to signify but also comes quite close to my concerns as expressed above: "Glossolalia thus presents the aporia of an absolute desubjectification and 'barbarization' of the event of language, in which the speaking subject gives way to another subject, a child, angel, or barbarian who speaks 'unfruitfully' and 'into the air.'"[9] The normal functioning of language presupposes a subject that speaks, which is the product of a process of subjectification in which the individual becomes "fit" to speak in a particular discourse. Glossolalia, however, is the event of language that does the opposite. It deactivates the process of subjectification and *de*subjectivizes the one who speaks. Consequently, it is no longer the subject of a dominant discourse who speaks but, in this divine speech, the individual who speaks "gives way to another subject." Clearly, this other subject cannot be the subject of another common *logos*; it cannot be another determined subjective form of another, particular discourse. It rather refers to a form of "subjectivity" that transgresses all forms of subjectivity, that desubjectivizes all forms of subjectification.

Although Agamben suggests in *Quel che resta di Auschwitz* that Paul speaks rather condescendingly of this mode of language, my own reading has shown that Paul is not condescending. Rather, because this mode of speech does not respect the order of common discourse, Paul considers it to be a highly dangerous form of discourse that threatens to dissolve the given order of discourse and to confuse the community that depends on this discourse. Moreover, when, in turn, the community and its discourse try to immunize themselves against this threat and confusion, glossolalia runs the risk of being discarded and excluded, as the foreigner and the child are often excluded and banished from the discourse that perceives itself as being at home, mature, and reasonable. For Paul—and Kierkegaard—this would amount to disregarding its upbuilding reserve for the community. Therefore, interpreters are necessary so that the alien "subjects" that appear in this speech are not trampled upon but brought to the attention of the community in such a way that the community may be built up by this encounter. The task of the interpreter-witness is thus to mediate between the discourses that subjectivize and normalize, on the one hand, and the discourses such as glossolalia that desubjectivize and singularize, on the other. In this way, the interpreter-witness bears witness to these alien subjects before a tribunal that still lacks and requires the capacity to comprehend or receive them—a capacity the interpreter has to offer and generate for them. The discourse of bearing witness thus belongs at the limit of discourse theory, on the threshold of subjectivizing and desubjectivizing modes of speech.[10]

Consequently, rather than following Agamben's remark that Paul is condescending regarding the one who speaks in tongues, it might be better to compare the apostle's relation to the divine language with Plato's relation to this other divine language, poetry. Concerning this latter relation, Agamben's assessment is actually more convincing and closer to how I would interpret Paul's remarks on glossolalia. He notes that Plato considers poetry not to be a lower mode of language but rather to be truly dangerous and a possible cause for ruin.[11] I would add to this assessment: "if not guided by interpreters." In Plato's dialogues, poetry is never simply dismissed, not even from the philosophically ideal *polis*. In the *Republic*, Socrates calls on the *philopoiētēs*, the friend of poets, to speak on the poet's behalf in the discourse of philosophy.[12] This intermediary figure of the *philopoiētēs* is required because the poet cannot speak in the prose of *logos* or argument. Socrates demands a philosophical trial in which the poets are on trial and are defended by their friends in the language of "prose" without meter (*aneu metrou logon*). This is why the *philopoiētēs*, the one who speaks for the poets in the language of this philosophical court, is called the *prostatēs*, the guardian of this alien voice, the one who stands for the poets, who speaks the language of the court but aims to give a voice to what cannot speak this language. This example demonstrates a structural kinship with the one from the *Theaetetus* discussed in the first literary experiment. There, Socrates asks Theodorus to speak for Protagoras because he is Protagoras's friend. Also in the *Republic*, it is the task of the friend of the poets to offer a defense and to protect what they love. It is the friend's benevolent, intimate, and engaged glance that might see something that others don't. What is at stake here is therefore not simply a multiplication of arguments, but rather the question of how to share in a voice that *cannot* speak the language of the addressees. This is one of philosophy's basic concerns. In fact, because Socrates concludes his discussion in the *Republic* with an *apologos*, the myth of Er, which is upbuilding to the self and contributes to the care of the soul, would it be unlikely to suggest that, ultimately, it is Socrates himself who is the true *prostatēs* standing up for and guarding *muthos* in relation to *logos* and showing in which sense *muthos* is both dangerous and upbuilding for the philosopher and their care for the soul? Would it be too farfetched to suggest that Socrates positions him not once but at least three times as the guardian of an alien voice or discourse? In the *Ion*, Socrates is the interpreter and guardian of rhapsodic enterprise, who interprets for and on behalf of Ion because the latter does not understand his own discourse. In the *Theaetetus*, Socrates interprets Protagoras's voice because the latter can no longer speak and offers himself as the guardian of Protagoras's intellectual offspring. In the *Republic*, Socrates summons the *philopoiētēs*, the lover or friend of poets, to speak on the poet's behalf and adopts this task himself as a true *prostatēs* or guardian of myth.

The Prophet and the Poet

The second figure, the prophet, also appeals to one's imagination.[13] Let me, to introduce this figure, briefly refer to one of the characteristic passages in which we find an actual calling of a prophet and read this against the background of my inquiry into the witness. This passage, found in the first chapter of *Jeremiah*, is interesting in comparison to the usual portrayal of enthusiasts in Plato's dialogues. Whether it concerns the ones who "practice" divination in the *Timaeus* or the poets and rhapsodes in the *Ion*, in each case it seems that these enthusiasts are "simply" out of their mind because the gods have overtaken them.[14] That there might also be a story to be told that marks the very beginning of this "enthusiasm"—that is, a story of the transition from someone in possession of their powers of understanding and judging to someone who is no longer in possession of what they say and what their voice discloses, sings, or commands—does not seem to be a theme for Plato. Yet it is a theme that interests us here because it concerns a moment of desubjectification that is intrinsic to the exceptional mode of speech of prophets and poets.

At this point, a difference between the figures of the poet and the prophet, on the one hand, and the figure of the glossolalist, on the other, imposes itself. The latter confronts us with a mode of speech that does not aim to communicate with a larger audience, but is rather engaged in a singular communication with the god. In the case of the former two, however, a different picture arises. Their speech does not require another interpreter for communication to take place. Prophets address an audience and convey divine messages and commands to these addressees. The poet addresses others as well. If we take Socrates's account in the *Ion* as our basic reference for the understanding of the poet in this sense, the poet is not the one who communicates a particular meaning or understanding—how could they, because they are out of their mind—but rather a divine power, as Socrates informs the rhapsode Ion: "It's a divine power that moves you."[15] The poets themselves are possessed by a power that makes them speak or sing; and their song communicates this power to their audience, which subsequently is captivated by the same power and enthusiasm.

In the context of these figures, the first chapter of *Jeremiah* deserves to be read because it offers us an interpretation of the constitutive dynamics between divinity and prophet. When called on by Yahweh to speak for him, Jeremiah's response is "I cannot speak."[16] He blames his incapacity to speak on his youth. In response to the call, Jeremiah thus attests to his own incapacity to speak but also to a specific nullity or insignificance as the ground for this incapacity. More precisely, it would be better to say that by attesting to his incapacity, the prophet attests to his nullity, his *Nichtigkeit*, as Heidegger would call it.[17] After all, the figure by which Jeremiah expresses his insignificance—he is only a child, a boy or a youth—is the figure of this incapacity itself: is the child not par excellence the one who is not in a position to speak? If we asked what exceeds Jeremiah's capacity to speak, the first answer would be that he considers himself a child with respect to the community of adults *to which* he is supposed to speak as well as to the divine matters *of which* he is supposed to speak. Yet Jeremiah's incapacity and nullity culminate before the god *for which* he is called to speak. This marks the specific rhetorical setup of *Jeremiah* 1: we encounter a messenger *who cannot speak* and who discovers this incapacity and his nullity exactly when he is called to speak. What does this mean?

If we consider the rhetorical strategy of the narrative that unfolds, one immediately suspects that the prophet's attestation has a strictly economic role. After all, the story of Jeremiah's calling aims to establish that it is *not* Jeremiah who speaks when we hear meaningful sounds formed by his breath, tongue, and mouth. As the story tells us, directly after his "I cannot speak,"

Yahweh touches Jeremiah's mouth and puts divine words in it so that the human incapacity to speak and the human's utter insignificance before this Yahweh turn out to be the best of fortunes.[18] Because Jeremiah has nothing to say of and for himself, his own voice does not add anything to the words that Yahweh puts in his mouth. This is the best of fortunes because such an addition would only contaminate and distort the divine message. The possibility of such a contamination is now excluded, and Yahweh may convey his pure message through the prophet's mouth. Hence, by the prophet's attestation of his incapacity to speak, his mouth, breath, and tongue become the *pure* and *purely external* vehicle and mouthpiece for divine messages and commands. The result of this rhetorical strategy shows in which sense the figure of Jeremiah stands out among the group of divine messengers as an *exemplary* messenger: he is a paradigm that shows us something essential common to all members of the group of enthusiasts.

Following its ancient definition, there is one thing we can say about the human, namely that they *can* speak. The human is defined by the capacity to understand and inhabit the world with reason and language. It is in this setting that the attestation of the prophet's insignificance and incapacity to speak with his own voice for Yahweh is indeed a *necessary* condition for the proper functioning of the machinery of divine communication. Without this attestation, the divine communication would forever be contaminated by human reason and understanding, by the human voice that even when speaking for Yahweh cannot help but speak also (for) itself. Thus, the secret of the divine messenger unveiled in *Jeremiah* concerns the strange structure of a double voice inhabiting the prophet when he prophesies: on the one hand, the divine voice that actually speaks in the prophet and fills the prophet's mouth and, on the other hand, his human, finite voice whose *only, but indispensable,* task it is to say that it cannot speak and cannot but remain silent confronted with the call to speak for the divine.

When noting that Tynnichus of Chalcis, the poor poet who apparently only wrote one worthwhile poem, shows that it is not poets themselves who speak but rather the gods, Socrates confirms the same idea in his reflections on the poets in the *Ion*.[19] The double voice—human and divine—is marked by a hierarchy: the human voice is incapacitated so that the divine voice can speak in an uncontaminated way through and in the human voice. Yet what is absent in the *Ion* is that in order to function, this hierarchy requires an attestation of the human incapacity to speak. *Jeremiah* thus presents a more complicated picture than the *Ion*: not only is

Jeremiah never diagnosed as being out of his mind or as being possessed, but his attestation also precedes the moment in which the divinity takes over his voice. Jeremiah wittingly places his voice at the divine's disposal. This act of desubjectification is Jeremiah's response to the call by Yahweh. This desubjectification gives way to another subject to make itself be heard with the voice of the prophet so that the latter's voice is indeed filled with the divine voice. Hence, for the divine machinery to work, it is crucial that Jeremiah withdraws his own voice and holds on to this withdrawal so that Yahweh can speak through him. This initial withdrawal happens in and as the prophet's attestation of "I cannot speak." Only in and by this attestation—this performative contradiction that speaks of its own incapacity to speak—his voice can become the nullity that the divine voice needs to be able to make itself heard.

At this point, I would like to add another element to the argumentation so far and locate this figure of the enthusiast within the context of present-day thought. This figure is not absent from present-day philosophical reflections, but it is approached in a specific way, namely under erasure of the divine sovereignty that regulates the divine machinery of prophetic and poetic communication. The divine sovereignty that rules its interpreter is emptied out. One could say that present-day thought approaches the figure of the enthusiast therefore with a particular melancholic attunement. If mourning is always over the loss of an object that one once possessed, melancholy refers to the way in which an object that was never possessed can be related to, but only *as lost*.[20] In the case of the enthusiast, this loss of the object has a specific meaning, which can immediately be connected to our previous analyses on the distinctive task assigned to the witness. The loss is here in the first place the loss of the power of a particular voice: the divine power to overtake the voice of the poet and the prophet is nullified or deactivated; the divine voice that *wants* to speak—in the sense of *demands* to speak—has lost its capacity to overtake the poetic and prophetic voice; it can no longer steer or control this voice and is unable to articulate and master its own voice in the human voice.

Perhaps Derrida as no other has grasped this melancholic sense in *Donner la mort*. Putting himself in the position of the hearer of testimony, he argues that nobody hears the divine word directly, but always mediated: "I hear tell what he says, through the voice of another, another other, [. . .] an intermediary who speaks between God and myself."[21] Because of this inescapable mediation, we never know for certain whether we indeed hear the pure, uncontaminated word of God, "the Other," or whether we hear a version of his words affected by the mediator, "another other." This is not merely an epistemological concern, but rather aims to show that the picture painted in *Jeremiah* is insufficient. Derrida's comments dispute the basic presupposition that the divine power itself is the very ground and guarantee of why the mediating prophetic voice cannot contaminate or distort the message the gods convey. According to the logic of divine sovereignty, the distinction between the true and the false prophet is guaranteed by the divine calling: the false prophet is the one who has not been called and who did not lay down their own voice. The death of God in Nietzsche's sense or the critique of the onto-theological constitution of metaphysics in Heidegger's sense is exactly concerned with disputing this principle of divine speech. Once the basic sense of the divine calling is disputed—the sense of incapacitating the human's voice so that the divine voice can use it as its pure vehicle—the divine voice no longer speaks directly or immediately.[22]

If this is the constellation within which the figure of the enthusiast is received in present-day thought, it makes sense to repeat the question with which we started: what does the prophet's attestation of his nullity and incapacity to speak actually mean? If the divine machinery is deactivated and the sovereign power is incapacitated, this attestation can no longer be understood as the negative consequence or reverse of the positive phenomenon of the divine voice articulating itself accurately in the prophet's voice. Rather, *this attestation is the only positive phenomenon that is left*. Derrida's analysis offers us the possibility to get a sense of the positive signification of the prophet's attestation that he cannot speak. What Derrida's comments aim at is showing the double bind at the heart of the prophet's giving a voice to someone else. If the prophet's voice actually lets the other voice be heard by making it speak, the prophet's voice must indeed be characterized by a particular "incapacity" to speak: the prophet must be capable of incapacitating his own voice in such a way that it gives way to the other's voice to speak in them.

I would like to suggest that in this way, Jeremiah's attestation is displaced. It is no longer simply "I cannot speak," expressing an impossibility, but rather "I can also not speak," expressing a possibility not to. . . . This means that the prophet is the one who can withdraw their own voice while speaking and allow another voice to be heard in their voice. Thus, the prophet's attestation bears witness to the capacity of a desubjectification in speech so that the subject is no longer the only one who speaks. This moment of desubjectification does not rob something or someone of their speech, as is suggested in some of the available literature on testimony.[23] Rather, it concerns the doubling of the voice of the one who speaks. The prophet's attestation only offers the *chance* of the other's voice to speak in the prophet's voice. Yet, as Derrida often reminds us, this chance cannot be separated from the *risk* that in the prophet's voice, only the prophet speaks in the guise of letting another speak. The prophet *letting* the other speak—the "true" prophet or witness—cannot be separated from the possibility that it is the prophet *making* the other speak—the "false" prophet or witness.[24] Thus, for the other voice to be heard, it is not simply the prophet's or poet's voice as such that is needed, but their voice in their nullity, in their capacity of withdrawing themselves, so that in this contraction a space opens up for another voice to resound. This contraction is, according to Derrida's logic, never complete. A complete contraction of the prophet's voice would lead to a collapse of the structure of the double voice: the voice of the other needs an attestation to be able to speak. Thus, this contraction affects and enables the breath and the spirit of the other voice we, perhaps, hear.

The loss of the divine voice and sovereignty thus has significantly displaced the sense of the prophet's attestation. In a certain way, this change demonstrates the birth of the witness out of the prophet. It is only by the effacement of the divine sovereignty that the structure of the prophet changes into that of the witness in which the attestation "I can also not speak" no longer describes the absence of engagement, but rather attests to a particular task assigned to the witness. This task is not to find one's own voice, but rather to find and articulate the voice of the other in one's own voice.

The structure of the witness that arises in this way thus begins with a desubjectification of one's own voice because this dispossession is never simply given (*gegeben*) but only assigned as a task (*aufgegeben*). What remains is the attestation of the capacity not to be the subject who speaks. The account of the prophet mediated through Derrida's analysis has led us to a positive phenomenon in the human voice that addresses us in the attestation of the human capacity not to speak that, perhaps, turns into a capacity not to speak (for) oneself alone. This "perhaps" or "maybe" is crucial here. It shows that this attestation is not nothing but a promise marked by a basic hesitation of the perhaps. If the only chance and hope of hearing the inarticulate voice speak is to be found in this capacity of the messenger not to speak (for) itself, this chance is followed by a risk as its shadow, namely the risk of ventriloquism, the risk that the messenger only mimics the capacity not to speak and does not *let* the divine voice speak but rather *makes* it speak, as yet another masterful creation of the messenger's voice. In this letting and making the other voice speak, we hear how the witness is sworn to and born from the secrecy of its reserve/object, and we hear the promise, perhaps, to let the voiceless and their misery speak.

Martus, Testis, Superstes, and Auctor

The analyses of glossolalist, prophet, and poet thus offer another account of the *double* voice of the witness. Whereas in earlier chapters, we encountered this double voice in the form of the silent and the articulate voice, the previous analyses in this chapter show how to let another voice speak requires a particular desubjectification, a potential, and a task not to speak oneself. Yet to speak of a double voice *of the witness* might nevertheless sound troubling. After all, should a witness not speak with *one* voice, and be consistent in what they say? For the purposes of this study, it is not so difficult to see what the role of the structure of the double voice is and why, therefore, this detour along glossolalist, poet, and prophet is worthwhile: this structure corresponds to the particular mediate position of the witness on the threshold, which it shares with the interpreter, the poet, and the prophet. To clarify how this detour help us to elucidate the problem of the witness, I now explore some of the terms in Greek and Latin that (also) mean "witness" and that have marked the continental discussion on the witness, such as the Greek *martus* and the Latin *testis*, *superstes*, and *auctor*. Yet I want to begin with a brief comment related to Benveniste's explication of the Greek *istōr*.[25]

Istōr and the Absolute Witness

Benveniste introduces the term *istōr* in the context of his analysis of the oath (*horkos*), and in this context *istōr* means (also) witness. As he shows in reference to Homer, this term is used to describe the gods as the ones who know because they see or have seen. *Istōr* thus expresses in the first place the eyewitness. In fact, as Benveniste notes, this particular word for witness corresponds to the root Indo-European root **wid-*, which is the basis of the English word "witness," and which means to have seen and therefore to know: when it comes to choosing between witnesses, it is best to believe the witnesses who actually saw what happened. The ones who saw truly know, and therefore the witnesses who saw, are the ones who are deemed irrefutable, as Benveniste notes.

The reason why this sense of the witness is interesting for me does not so much concern the value of seeing that it introduces, and I would definitely not endorse the idea of an "irrefutable" witness based on the fact alone that they saw. What interests me, though, is the context in which *istōr* is used. Benveniste notes that the Greeks appealed to the sight of the gods as their true witnesses, whereas the Romans appeal to the gods to listen (*audi*) to them. Yet what these two types of witnesses share, the Greek gods that see and the Roman gods that hear, is that an oath is always sworn before them. I've already noted a couple of times that the witness is sworn to the truth. Yet what do we actually do when we swear to speak the truth? What is it in swearing an oath that somehow binds the witness to their words? In the analysis of *istōr*, we get a proper sense of the binding force of this practice. To swear an oath is to pledge to speak the truth not to other human beings but rather before the ultimate witness, namely the gods that see and hear everything and don't forget anything.[26]

In our society, perjury is punishable by law. In earlier times, however, there was no punishment inscribed in the ancient Indo-European codes because perjury is only punishable by the gods, as Benveniste claims, because the gods "are the guarantees of the oath."[27] This means that in this ancient sense, the witness themselves is not the ultimate guarantee of testimony and its truth, but their oath is, and because the gods are the witness of the oath, the gods are the ultimate guarantees.[28] Although the witness swears to speak the truth, the ground of this promise is found in another witness who primordially and irrefutably founds the connection—or, in the case of perjury, the disconnection—between the word the witness speaks and the object of which this word speaks. The reason why such an ultimate divine witness might be considered necessary is not difficult to comprehend. After all, only an infallible witness suspends the intrinsic undecidability of the truth or falsity of a testimony. It is therefore not strange that the divine witness is also considered to be the judge. As Benveniste notes, the Greek *istōr* and the Latin *arbiter* mean both witness and judge because it is the divine witness who judges on the issue of perjury and thus on whether the human witness indeed preserves the connection of word and thing in their testimony.

In the opening pages of his study on the oath, *Il sacramento del linguaggio*, Agamben suggests that the oath is concerned not only with offering an alternative to "the unreliability of men, incapable of staying true to their word" and forcing them to stay true to their word, but also with supplementing "a weakness pertaining to language itself, the capacity of words themselves to refer to things."[29] If the oath is the enunciation that establishes the connection of word and thing, its reference to the divine order only becomes more reasonable and pertinent because this weakness of language is exactly due to language's capacity to distort reality and things, that is, to be false in the sense of Plato's *pseudos*. Only the language of the gods, as Socrates argues in the *Cratylus*, does not suffer from this condition. An oath done before the gods as its witnesses offers the assurance that the weakness of language is not the inevitable, final word about language.[30]

Yet when this divine, permanent realm is no longer in place, as we also discussed in the previous section, the reference to an absolute or ultimate witness no longer makes any sense. Consequently, the oath has nothing to offer but the justice and the truthfulness of the speaker and of the witness. Surely, this insight is not of recent date because it is already announced by Cicero when he states there is no such thing as a punishment by the gods: removing this punishment takes the sting out of the absolute witness.[31] When there is no absolute witness to whom the oath can refer as the ultimate ground of its truth, the human practice of bearing witness comes into its own mode of finitude, by which even an oath cannot take away not only the possible unreliability of the witness, but also the possible weakness of language itself, producing effects by which the reserve/object of testimony is distorted.

This latter becoming finite of bearing witness is of crucial importance to the present-day debate on testimony. Not only does Agamben's account of the oath take this finitude as its point of departure, (not entirely justifiably) projecting it back on its history, but it also is the very condition of the sense of testimony deployed by Lyotard, as Derrida notes: "[Lyotard] problematizes the idea of God as absolute witness."[32] To be precise, Lyotard problematizes the idea of an absolute witness, which in the history of thought as well as in the history of the oath is often identified with God or the gods. Indeed, as Lyotard notes: "the idea of an 'absolute witness for a reality' is inconsistent."[33] His argument is straightforward and goes back to the finitude of the witness, who has nothing to offer beyond their own word as guarantee for their testimony: "He or she has not seen everything.

If he or she claims to have seen everything, he or she is not credible. If he or she is credible, it is insofar as he or she has not seen everything, but has only seen a certain aspect. He or she is thus not absolutely credible."[34] The argument is strikingly similar to what Benveniste claims about *istōr*. Also for Lyotard, the reference to seeing forms a core of the argument. The witness who has seen everything can be the only real, absolutely credible guarantee of testimony. Yet one can easily adjust this argument, which privileges the finitude and perspectivity of human vision, and apply it to the other senses. Moreover, one could adapt the argument and apply it to the very weakness of language itself: every testimony always tells, formulates, articulates in a certain way, keeping silent and concealing other ways of narrating what happened. The oath is no longer done before a divine, absolute witness. The oath has rather become part of the witness's attestation itself; it is a ritual and a performative between the witness and the tribunal, circling around an empty place that once was occupied by the idea of a witness who truly and absolutely sees everything. It is, therefore, by this oath that the witness is sworn to secrecy, to the secrecy of this empty place in which we only find the witness's own word and promise. The implication of the sense and the absence of the absolute witness is explored further in the next chapter.

Martyr, *Superstes*, and *Testis*

That the two Latin terms *testis* and *superstes* often appear together in, for instance, Derrida's and Agamben's discussion of the witness is due to Benveniste's attention to the verb *superstes*, of which the basic meaning is "surviving" but which also came to mean "witness."[35] The verb *superstito* means to stay alive (to survive) or to remain. As Benveniste explains, *superstare* means to remain or survive beyond "an event that has annihilated the rest"; or, in terms of another example that he immediately adds: "A death occurred in a family; the *superstites* subsisted [or lived on] *beyond* the event."[36] Thus, *superstes* in the sense of witness refers to someone who has experienced or lived through an event in which others died—perhaps we could simply say the event of the death of others—but the witness survived and lives to tell the tale. To grasp the specific sense of witness as *superstes*, Benveniste contrasts it with the sense of witness as *testis*.[37] *Testis* is the third party present as a witness at an affair in which two parties are interested. For instance, when two people marry, the witness is the third party who is not involved in the contract, but only present to witness the conclusion of the agreement between the two interested parties. *Superstes*, on the other hand, is the witness who was himself present and engaged in—in the sense of suffering, experiencing, or living through—the event.

To this twofold meaning of witness, one could add the sense of martyr derived from the Greek *martus*. The Greek notion relates neither to a sense of the third (*testis*), nor of the survivor (*superstes*), nor of the one who has seen and knows (*istōr* and "witness"), nor of the one who is drawn and generates (*Zeuge* and *zeugen*), but rather to that of proof, as the word *marturion* suggests.[38] Historically, *martus* as martyr has taken on a specific sense of the one who offers their life for their conviction and who *proves* their own conviction by the sacrifice of their life. The martyr is thus the witness who attests to a conviction by proving an absolute, resolute adherence to it. To sacrifice one's life means first to die for one's faith, but also, and second, to act absolutely faithfully in the service of one's conviction or faith. The martyr thus offers their own life as the very guarantee of the truth and truthfulness of their cause.[39]

Finally, it might be good to distinguish one last category on the threshold of the witness, namely the mere *sufferer* who undergoes and experiences an event but neither survives it nor bears witness to their suffering by offering their life as sacrifice—they simply die or are killed. This sufferer represents an experience that is not borne witness to. It is important to distinguish this sheer suffering without testifying voice not because this figure is a witness in the complete sense of the word, but rather because the figure of sheer suffering without testifying voice is the complement or the *double* of the *superstes*. The survivor survives an event that is not survived by all. In this particular sense, the *superstes* is the remainder and the one who perhaps does not fully share in the experience of the sufferer, but has a share in it, up to a point, that is, up to the point of death.

These three senses of the witness—the *testis* as the third, disinterested party, a bystander who is engaged in what happens by being a witness; the *superstes* as the survivor of a disaster, who is already engaged in this event but is not consumed by it and therefore lives to tell the tale to those who were not present at the event, and who has the sufferer as its necessary complement; and the martyr who attests by sacrificing one's life and who engages absolutely in their conviction—offer a brief but crucial typology of the witness allowing us to differentiate between the ways in which the subject of testimony is at stake in some of the present-day philosophical debates to which I return in the chapters that follow.

Recall that this typology aims in the first place at differentiating between the forms of the engagement of the witness in the object of testimony. Therefore, I would like to address two more issues in this chapter. First, I would like to explicate how this typology concerns the way in which the witness is engaged or involved in the reserve/object and the act of testimony; and, second, under the heading of the *auctor*, I would like to develop the relation between the witness as *superstes* and the sufferer as this witness's complement.

Derrida privileges the sense of *superstes* or surviving in this typology and tends to bring *testis* and *superstes* together under this heading:

> Allow me to call to mind an essential kind of generality: is the witness not always a survivor? [. . .] One testifies only when one has lived longer than what has come to pass. One can take examples as tragic or full of pathos as the survivors of the death camps. But what ties testimony to *survivance* remains a universal structure and covers the whole elementary field of experience. The witness is a survivor, the third party, the *terstis* as *testis* and *superstes*, the one who survives.[40]

In an abstract sense, this comparison between *testis* and *superstes* makes sense. The *testis* is called on to testify that the conclusion of the contract has taken place after the actual conclusion. Yet to conclude from this that the *testis* is a survivor stretches the sense of survival to the mere and too unspecific sense of "living on after. . . ." It does not capture Benveniste's specific sense of the survivor of a deadly event. To simply say that the survivor is the one who lives on after an event is to discard that in the notion of *superstes*, survival means not only to outlive an event but also to outlive those who are left behind and died in the event, and it means to be capable of telling their story. In the third literary experiment on Mortier's *Godenslaap*, we briefly encountered Etienne Leboeuf. Although he lives after an event in which many were killed, his quivering body, which harbors the horrific experience of the trenches, is incapable of articulating them. He is the sufferer who remained in the event because the event has robbed him of the capacity to tell about it and to find the words to articulate his experiences. When identifying every witness as a survivor, Derrida discards the specific differences in the way in which the subject of testimony is involved in testimony.

I mention this disagreement with Derrida to show that the typology offered here concerns in the first place the different ways of the subject's involvement in testimony. The *sufferer* (that is, the double of the *superstes*) represents an absolute involvement, which leaves no space for testimony and language. This figure cannot be the subject of testimony because it represents a full desubjectification, an existence stripped bare by an experience that does not necessarily transgress what one can suffer, but that does draw humans to the very threshold of their humanity. This experience shows that, as Agamben notes, "the human being is capable of not having language, [. . .] capable of its own in-fancy."[41] If we identify humanity with its having language, this experience confronts the human with the inhuman in itself, as Agamben continues: "This means that humans bear within themselves the mark of the inhuman, that their spirit contains at its very center the wound of non-spirit, non-human chaos atrociously consigned to its own being capable of everything."[42] Although "everything" seems somewhat exaggerated, the tenet of Agamben's comment is clear. The sufferer (as the complement of the *superstes*) is the one who suffers more than their humanity can handle. Yet it is exactly this experience of the sufferer that may confront us, the bystanders, with the naked "that" of their human existence—at least, if it is borne witness to by the *superstes*.

The *superstes* is the one who is also involved in the reserve/object of their testimony, but is at the same time somehow detached from it, or is at any rate not so much *in* the event that they cannot bear witness to it. As Benveniste indicates, the *superstes* is beyond the event. Whatever the exact sense of this "beyond" is, it means that the *superstes* does not remain in or is left behind in the event as the sufferer is. There is a striking passage by Kafka, quoted by Arendt in *Men in Dark Times*, which exemplifies the witness as *superstes* and allows us to portray the relation to its double, the sheer sufferer:

> Anyone who cannot cope with life while they are alive needs one hand to ward off a little their despair over their fate—in a very imperfect way—but with their other hand they can jot down what they see among the ruins, for they see different and more things than the others; after all, they are dead in their own lifetime and the real survivor. Presupposing that they do not need both hands and more than they have for their battle with despair.[43]

There is perhaps no better image imaginable to capture the position of the *superstes* than that of these two hands. To survive an event is indeed to live beyond the death this event causes; and this is not only the complete death of others, but also the death and despair in the one who survived as Kafka suggests: "they are dead in their own lifetime."[44] To state, as I did above, that the *superstes* is in a sense detached from the event can therefore only mean this: that the survivor has one hand at their disposal to "ward off a little" the utter despair that dwells in them. The last sentence, which Arendt for some reason did not quote, portrays the sliding scale that distinguishes the *superstes* from the sufferer. The *superstes* is only a *superstes* as long as "they do not need both hands and more than they have for their battle with despair." As long as one hand is enough to create some distance to the utmost despair—a despair that would render the *superstes* speechless, as it does the sufferer—the *superstes* has the other hand available to "jot down," to note and register what they have seen. Because "they see different and more things than the others," the *superstes* is a genuine witness who has something to say that lies beyond the horizon of understanding of the hearer of testimony.

Testis and martyr bring into play yet other senses of engagement. The third party is the disinterested party who, by being called on to be a witness, is in a certain way involved as a supplement to the contract or the relation established by two interested parties, but the *testis* is not affected by this event, and the attunement of the *testis* is not a struggle with despair, as for the *superstes*, but rather a basic *indifference*. As soon as the *testis* would no longer be indifferent, as a witness, to the contract that has been made by the two parties, the *testis* could no longer be involved as third party. The martyr is the inverse of the *testis*. The martyr is sheer involvement with the object of testimony and is *resolute and absolute affirmation* of this involvement up to the point of dying for or sacrificing their full life for this testimony. The attunement of this witness, to combine Heidegger's and Badiou's vocabulary, is an absolute, resolute faith in and fidelity to the object of testimony. The testimony of the *superstes* refers to the sufferer, thus offering always a doubled sense of the witness, of the one who can speak and the one who cannot speak but merely experiences. In the case of testis and martyr, a similar codependency might occur. In the case of *Fear and Trembling*, Abraham is a martyr, that is, one who is willing to engage absolutely in his cause. Yet, by being such a witness to truth, he is deprived of the capacity to speak: the absoluteness of the engagement makes the martyr incomprehensible to those who do not share their conviction. Therefore, in *Fear and Trembling*, it seems to me that the poet is actually the *testis*, the third party who witnesses the singular bond between God and Abraham and who bears witness to what has taken place there, but without himself being engaged in or in any way sharing this bond. Similarly, the *testis*, the independent third party, always refers back to interested parties who are engaged in the bond and therefore cannot attest to it.

Auctor

The last term used for witness that I want to discuss is *auctor*. This notion refers in the first place, as Benveniste and Lewis and Short explain, to the one who promotes, produces, takes an initiative, or generates.[45] In a derived sense, via the sense of the authority (*auctoritas*) with which one advises or persuades, *auctor* comes to mean "One that becomes security for something, a voucher, bail, surety, witness."[46] *Auctor* is the guarantee for someone else and bears witness for this other party, and so it becomes the one who assists or supplements someone who cannot vouch or bear witness for themselves. From this latter sense, Agamben's analysis of the *auctor* departs by adding the idea that the *auctor* is also the one who completes "an imperfect act."[47] This particular meaning of *auctor* still resounds in our modern use of the verb "to authorize." In certain circumstances, I need the authorization of someone else to actually be able or allowed to do something; the *auctor* is the one who makes the actualization of the intended act possible. Similarly, when it comes to the sense of assistance or persuasion, the *auctor* is the one who offers the additional act or ground that is needed for the other to complete their act (or to simply act). This also applies to the sense of *auctor* as witness, as Agamben suggests: "*auctor* signifies the witness insofar as his testimony always presupposes something [. . .] whose reality and force must be validated or certified. [. . .] Testimony [. . .] always implies an essential duality in which an insufficiency or incapacity is completed or made valid."[48] In many of the previous analyses, we have already encountered this duality as being constitutive of testimony: the reserve/object of testimony is what is incapable of showing itself from itself; it depends on testimony. In turn, testimony does not create its object, but is added to it so that it is made manifest. In this sense, the reference to the *auctor* does not offer anything new to our analysis.

However, in relation to the *superstes*, the sense of *auctor* as witness does offer new insights. Agamben makes the following, somewhat enigmatic suggestion concerning the relation between the *superstes* and the sufferer: "the survivor's testimony has truth and a reason for being only if it is completed by the one who cannot bear witness."[49] This statement is not enigmatic because now, all of a sudden, it is the incapable one who is said to complete the act of bearing witness: this completion simply indicates that, for Agamben, *auctor* and what it completes, survivor and sufferer, are complementary and always presuppose the other. The suggestion is enigmatic, however, because it is not clear in which sense the survivor's testimony completes or validates the absent testimony of the one who cannot bear witness: How and in which sense can the survivor's testimony *stand for* the absent testimonies of others? And in which sense is the survivor's testimony untrue if it does not refer to the absent testimonies and witnesses?

To find a way of answering these questions or, at least, to find a way into this enigma, it might be helpful to read Agamben's comment as a direct response to Lyotard's idea that there is no absolute witness. The survivor attests to an event in which many died. This means that their attestation is indeed completed by the experiences of those who cannot bear witness. In other terms, if one wants to attest to the naked "that" of existence, to the ultimate experience of the deadly event, which only the ones who remained in it experienced completely, we see that the sufferers are the presupposition of the testimony of the *superstes* and that the testimony of the *superstes* allows the hearer to perceive something of what also the sufferer experienced, albeit only partial. The *superstes* is in this sense *auctor*.[50] Based on this sense of *auctor*, Agamben writes: "to bear witness is to place oneself in one's own language in the position of those who have lost it."[51] This means that the incapacity to speak—the naked "that" of existence, human in-fancy, or bare life—is the reserve/object of the *superstes*'s bearing witness. In chapter 3, we already encountered the figure of Hurbinek. The latter's incomprehensible words, his "non-language," "*mass-klo, matisklo*" reappear exactly at this point in Agamben's study where he draws the utmost conclusion from his account of the witness as *auctor*.[52] What the *auctor* presupposes is the inarticulate voice of the one who cannot speak, and the completion of the *auctor* consists in articulating this inarticulate voice. It brings to language a particular incapacity of language, that is, a domain of human existence to which language has no access, the infancy or the experience of the naked "that" of existence. This is the melancholy of language and testimony: the naked "that" of existence can only be said or borne witness to as lost; language can only find or possess this object as lost and as dispossessed. This, perhaps, marks the poverty of language: it promises to meet the demand of the inarticulate voice, but can only articulate this voice as lost. Perhaps these are the stakes of testimony: "Perhaps man [. . .] must experience his poverty even more radically."[53]

Yet this is also the way in which the survivor's testimony *stands for* the absent testimonies of others. The *auctor* is the one who stands for, protects, and guards. To borrow a term from Ricoeur, testimony is a *représentance* or *lieutenance*, a *Stellvertreter*, as the Germans would say, of the sufferers' experiences but in a particular sense.[54] *Lieutenance*, literally "placeholder," does not represent its object when representing means taking it up and making it part of the discourse of phrases, but the placeholder is the representative of its object that keeps its place free and empty in language. Bearing witness is the performative occupying of a place in a discourse—this place is kept free for what exceeds this discourse and for what cannot speak for itself in this discourse, for what "holds itself in reserve."[55]

Part III

On the Threshold of Being and Language

Chapter 11

An Ontology of Testimony

> And what else is left to resist with but the debt which each soul has contracted with the miserable and admirable indetermination from which it was born [. . .] It is the task of writing, thinking, literature, arts, to venture to bear witness to it.[1]
>
> —Lyotard, *L'inhumain*, 15/7

The field of ontology is nowadays marked by a call for realism, such as Ferraris's and Gabriel's "new realism," Meillassoux's and Harman's "speculative realism," and Benoist's phenomenological realism. These realisms share one thesis, namely that ontology is not identical to or depending on epistemology.[2] My own account of testimony affirms the shared thesis of these realisms. I showed that testimony cannot be accounted for in epistemological terms alone, but derives from a "reality" that testimony articulates in the reserve/object it makes known. Testimony is a particular mode of *logos* that allows us to encounter this reserve/object, marking the difference between ontology and epistemology as well as that between being and appearing in its very testimony. In the context of testimony, these differences imply that the relation between language and being needs to be rethought.[3] If testimony is a mode of *logos* that makes being known to us, it is located at the threshold of being and language; testimony is an instantiation of the hyphen in onto-logy, the locus where being comes to language. Heidegger's account of *Bezeugung* is exemplary in this respect, although limited to Dasein's mode of being. The examination of this onto-logical role of testimony orients the third and final part of this study.

To clarify in which sense there is a "realistic" twist to my analysis of testimony, let me explicate, this time in ontological terms, why an account of testimony must be parting ways with Lyotard's account in terms of a theory of phrases. In Lyotard's theory, testimony appears as a discursive miracle. Although he seems to be driven by a sense of bearing witness he attributes to philosophy and literature, this sense is actually a vanishing point in his theory of phrases, as if bearing witness is the very *other* of a regime of phrases. His attention to the phrase-affect in his later works invests even more in this otherness up to the point of making testimony *impossible*. This is unsatisfactory and calls for a different theory that explicates how bearing witness is located at the threshold of being and language. The detour in chapter 9 along the exceptional sense of testimony in Heidegger was in this respect a necessary (first) step in responding to this task. Lyotard's analysis limits itself to the *discursive* level and does not take into account the ontological stakes of testimony.

Yet one should also note that a realist critique is somehow already present in these "postmodern" reflections, albeit in the form of a flower's bud not yet opened up. Consider, for instance, Lyotard's following comment: "In the absence of a phrase regimen or of a genre of discourse that enjoys a universal authority to decide, does not the linkage [. . .] necessarily wrong the regimens or genres whose possible phrases remain unactualized?"[4] This quote compels us to raise the question of ontology for at least three reasons.

(1) First, it speaks of a remarkable primacy of the *being* of discourse itself. There is not only discourse, active and actual in which all that is, is given or presented, but there is also discourse that maintains itself in mere potentiality, because other forms of discourse obstruct its actualization. Thus, the Aristotelian pair of potentiality and actuality is introduced to describe different *modes of being* of discourse. Without this pair, Lyotard's theory cannot think a wrong. Moreover, it only makes sense to speak of a wrong if there is a particular ontological *demand* of all that is possible or potential *to be actualized*. In discourse, the linkage of phrases happens according to specific rules. Yet, apparently, beyond these rules and regimens that prevail, there is a demand of phrases that cannot be actualized.

(2) Second, the wrong and the differend corresponding to this wrong do not belong to any phrase regimen. It remains absent from any regime as an inarticulate voice, as incapacity to be phrased. The absence of a universal genre of discourse implies that the most fundamental concern of this theory of phrases or discourses is that which lies in between, on the threshold of these discourses and which, therefore and by definition, cannot be put into phrases belonging to either discourse. If discourses, or at least certain genres of discourses, offer us a conceptual framework, the very language with which we can understand the world, and if we call this "postmodern" account a desubjectified version of Kant's episte-

mology in which the schemes of understanding are offered by language,[5] it makes sense to claim that (a) the ontological problem transcends the epistemological one and that, in fact, (b) the realm that announces itself here as being beyond the epistemological one gives to understand itself first and foremost as a demand for transformation of the linguistic schemes and frameworks with which we speak about the world: it is the finitude of these schemes and frameworks that gives rise to a wrong in Lyotard's sense of the word.

(3) Third, there is one more implicit ontological concern at stake in this passage. The differend and the wrong are not only about linguistic, discursive operations, but also concern victims who suffered something very real and who are unable to phrase their suffering in the linguistic schemes that are offered to them by the tribunal to whom they turn for justice. In more general terms, the following ontological thesis imposes itself: the differend as Lyotard defines it *is* nothing but *language's incapacity to do justice to the victim's reality*. Yet, as if wanting to be saved by a miracle, Lyotard turns to bearing witness as a mode of language, beyond the given regimens of phrases, capable of attesting to this incapacity and, thus, to demonstrating that in bearing witness language does have the capacity to do justice to its own incapacity.

Hence, although the ontological questions remain underdeveloped in Lyotard's analysis, one may allow this bud to open up and see that the true differend at stake in testimony is the difference and the wrong that happens between being and language. There is a *necessity* of testimony, not in a logical sense but in the sense of an urgent demand and need from which we cannot back away, *ne-cedere*. Therefore, testimony is "critical" in name of a reality it announces and which it aims to make known as an object despite the available discourse's incapacity to make this object manifest. Or, if we want to push it a bit further and do justice to the senses of wrong and differend, we could also argue, in the words of Mortier's protagonist, Helena, that testimony is called for in a situation in which our basic attunement to the available, actualized discourses is marked by "suspicion and bewilderment" because they are incapable of addressing or even articulating the reality of the wrongs done to victims. The imperative to speak or to communicate is not found in the simple fact that we are, always already, speaking beings, but rather in this reality that somehow demands to be said. As Agamben writes: "only if language bears witness to something to which it is impossible to bear witness, can a speaking being experience something like a necessity to speak."[6]

In this third and final part of this study, the testimonial encounter of discourse and reality is examined in different steps. My point of departure is the threefold ontological surplus that announces itself in Lyotard's work: (1) First, I discuss the role of the pair of potentiality and actuality and its implication for testimony and its object, with a particular concern for the demand in light of which the potential phrases occur. (2) Second, I turn to the specific sense of alterity and formlessness that does not only play a role in Lyotard's conception of the differend, but that we, for instance, also encountered in Deleuze's conception of literature in the fifth literary experiment. There is a whole range of concepts in present-day thought that represents the category of formlessness, but I privilege one: the notion of infancy, which resonates strongly with motives found in Lyotard, Agamben, Derrida, and Heidegger. To privilege this concept allows me to naturally gather together the senses of formlessness, nakedness, non-speaking-ness, potentiality, newness, misery, and otherness. (3) Third, I discuss the question of language's capacity (and incapacity) to do justice to an encounter with reality. This third point leads us in the direction of the issues of truth(fulness) and falsity of discourse, the trust in and the distrust of discourse, the nature of testimony as veridiction, and so on. (1) and (2) concern first and foremost the question of the reality of the reserve/object of testimony, and it is discussed in this chapter. (3) is addressed in chapter 12. (1), (2), and (3) together form the stepping stone toward the question of the engagement of the witness and the hearer in testimony, and this question concerning the ethos or ethics of testimony is discussed in chapter 13. Finally, chapter 14, in lieu of a conclusion, offers a reading of another literary testimony, a truly poetic one in which many of the discussed themes come together.

Demand as Onto-Logical Category

Lyotard's remark on the "possible phrases" that "remain unactualized" is echoed in a more profoundly ontological sense in Agamben's reading of the concluding scene of *Bartleby, the Scrivener*. My reading of this story in Part I was centered on the narrator-witness. Yet there is one important element that I passed over: according to the narrator, rumor has it that Bartleby used to work in a "Dead Letter Office," which is an office in which letters that did not arrive at their intended addressees were collected and burned.[7] These letter, as Agamben suggests, are the indices of possibilities that were never actualized.⁸ Melville beautifully describes the misery these letters represent—one containing a ring for marriage does not find "the finger it was meant for"; another containing the "bank-note" that promises relief from hunger does not arrive, and "he whom it would relieve, nor eats nor hungers any more." The narrator's conclusion is heartbreaking: "On errands of life, these letters speed to death." Bartleby thus draws our attention to a realm of possibilities that were not actualized but that, as possibility, are nevertheless marked by a specific demand: they could have been. This story, by offering only one example of what could have been, is an index of a vast "ontological squandering."⁹ In the story, the demand of what is squandered is attested to by the various forms of relief, salvation, and care these letters promised to offer, but never actually offered.

Agamben insists—and not without reason—that the final scene of Melville's story thus repeats the Pauline opposition between letter and spirit as between that which leads to death and life, respectively.¹⁰ Yet the letters in the Dead Letter Office do simply lead to death. The letter is a mere vehicle for a possibility to arrive or *not* arrive at an intended addressee, and for a letter to arrive at this office is the failure of this possibility to be ever actualized. Yet for Bartleby, these letters have become something more. They have turned into testimonies of these failed possibilities and the specific demand that speaks from them. As such a testimony, the letter is an index and a remembrance of a failed possibility: while this possibility is eliminated from the mere presence of all that actually is, the letters bear witness to it. They hold the place—*lieutenance*—of those possibilities and their demand amid all that actually exists. Thus, above all, Bartleby experiences the *demand* of these possibilities. This experience does not claim or believe that these possibilities can be actualized in some sort of messianic miracle—or "by virtue of the absurd," as Kierkegaard put it. This experience only asks for attesting to these possibilities and their demand. This, perhaps, cannot be done any better than with the letter, with literary means. Like Helena in *Godenslaap*, the concluding scene of *Bartleby, the Scrivener* does not offer simply a description of what was, but also a sign and index of things that "come and go unseen, and are pulverized silently."¹¹

Leibniz's Account of the Demand of the Possible

With which ontological problem does this part of the literary experiment of *Bartleby, the Scrivener* engage?¹² Agamben connects the scene from

Bartleby's Dead Letter Office to the striking scene from Leibniz's theodicy in which the demiurge returns, now and again, to the "pyramid of possible worlds" to enjoy his choice for the best world that he allowed to come into existence.[13] This scene shows that Leibniz does not consider the realm of possible worlds *as that which is eliminated* in and by the creation of the actual world; otherwise the demiurge would not be able to return to it. Consequently, for Leibniz, there is a primacy of potentiality over actuality, not only because the realm of the possible is the realm from which the demiurge chooses but also because he can return to this realm to confirm this choice and take pleasure in it. This has an important implication for any account of testimony. Leibniz's demiurge is an absolute witness of the realm of pure potentiality, of all possible configurations of the world. For this absolute witness, this realm is marked by permanence and presence because he can return to it again and again. For Agamben, the god's response to this scenery is perverse: once again confronted with all that is possible, he sticks with his previous choice and discards "the incessant lamentation" of what "had to be sacrificed for the present world to be as it is."[14]

Although Agamben's reading is appealing for many reasons, it is important to carefully consider what he does, because the category of exigency or *demand*, here turned against Leibniz, is in fact Leibnizian.[15] The demand forms the core of Leibniz's principle "*omne possibile exigit existere*"; "*everything possible demands existence*."[16] This is an indispensable addition to Aristotle's conception of potentiality. For Leibniz, given the primacy of potentiality, the relation between potentiality and actuality has to be understood in terms of such a demand of the possible to come into existence. For Leibniz, demand is an ontological category, and as soon as one considers how this category functions, it becomes clear that Agamben's argument in *Potentialities* that the demand is not heard in Leibniz's theodicy is not adequate. If the possible is marked by a demand to exist, the demiurge as absolute witness cannot but "hear" this demand. It is inadequate to claim, as Agamben does, that the demiurge closes his ears to this demand. In fact, Leibniz is rather the philosopher par excellence who recognizes that this "inferno of potentiality" is marked by lamentation and demand, that this inferno or limbo of the possible is the very misery of being that continues to cry out to be actualized. Yet Leibniz integrates this demand in an ontology ruled by the principle of reason. Therefore, the demiurge is not only the absolute witness but also the absolute judge of this demand: God judges which demands to existence can be complied with and which not.[17] For Leibniz, the chaotic multiplicity of demands made by the possible requires a rule that orders the corresponding possible worlds according to their degree of perfection. The principle of reason and God thus offer the "regimen [. . .] that enjoys a universal authority to decide." It is according to this rule that the demands of the possible are complied with or not.[18] To acknowledge the right of the demand beyond or before this rule thus requires the suspension of the principle of sufficient reason and its related conception of God. Such a suspension also suspends the idea of the universal judge and his universal authority to decide, *and* the absolute witness who registers all demands and lamentations. The true problem is not a perverse deity closing his ears to "incessant lamentations." Rather, in Leibniz's scenery the lamentations and demands are fully heard and experienced. In fact, their being heard is *secured* by the demiurge as the absolute witness. Yet they are affirmed or denied according to the principle of reason. Hence, contrary to Agamben's claim, the erasure of the idea of this deity *takes away* (rather than makes space for) the certainty of the lamentations being heard and the demands being acknowledged. Yet, in line with Agamben's claim, the suspension of the principle of reason is necessary to open up the possibility of these demands being witnessed *beyond* and *before* the rule of this principle. Thus, we see the double bind of this suspension or deactivation of the principle of reason and its related conception of God: on the one hand, it opens up the possibility of a conception of the demand of the possible beyond the rule of reason or *logos*; on the other hand, it robs us of the certainty of an absolute witness that perceives all demands.

The Demand of Being to Be Said

In *L'uso dei corpi*, Agamben positions Leibniz's notion of the demand not only between the possible and the existing but also on the threshold of being and language: demand is the "hyphen" connecting world and language, thus making onto-logy possible: "If language and world stand opposite one another without any articulation, what happens between them is a pure demand—namely a pure *sayability*. [. . .] The thing demands its own sayability."[19] In Part I, we encountered the inarticulate voice of which we said that it demanded articulation. In *L'uso dei corpi*, Agamben zooms in on this demand: without articulation, there is a demand from the world and from the thing to be said in language. What is at stake is thus a specific potentiality of reality, namely its sayability, its potential to be said. Ontology is therefore a response to the demand of the thing to be said.

Yet Agamben's account of the relation between demand and sayability seems ambiguous. First, he equates demand and sayability. Second, he writes that the thing demands its own sayability, as if it does not yet have this potential. If there is no absolute witness, which for Leibniz is the very instantiation of reason or *logos*, it is no longer certain that reality can be said or that its demand to be said is heard. Because things do not simply speak or call, their demand for sayability is in fact a mute one. Unlike Leibniz's pyramid of possible worlds, which can be revisited by the absolute witness, there is nothing to secure that reality is witnessed or that the demand of the thing to be said is heard. Therefore, to speak of the "sayability" of the thing, as Agamben also does, is simply to skip the intermediate figure and mode of speech that, however, is indispensable because of the suspension of the absolute witness.

So how is sayability linked to the demand of the possible? In Leibniz, reason or *logos* determines which demands are complied with and which possibles are allowed to come into existence. Consequently, for Leibniz, all that exists is of the order of *logos* and thus sayable in Agamben's terminology—after all, the problem of sayability concerns the very possibility of onto-logy. The suspension of this rule of *logos* means that the demand of the possible is no longer ruled according to *logos*; rather, this demand takes place where *logos* is out of joint or inarticulate. This has two consequences. First, this suspension creates a margin for a demand beyond or before *logos*, thus demanding another form of justice and compliance than the one offered by reason. Yet, if it is beyond or before reason and the shared language of *logos*, the question is, who is capable of hearing this barbaric and inarticulate demand? It is exactly at this joint, this threshold connecting the demand of the *alogos* to *logos*, that testimony can take place. Here, I would say, we see the basic meaning of the historical privilege of the miracle in connection to testimony, which we can still trace in Lyotard's account of testimony when he calls it an "event" in the strong sense of the word: what matters in this category of the miracle for a reflection on testimony is not that it is a divine intervention, but rather that it no longer obeys the rule of reason and *logos*. In its most miserable form, stripped of all divine attributes, what remains of the miracle is only a demand of the *aloga*. Second, if what comes into existence out of the realm of pure potentiality is not understood according to the principle of reason, that which is, *to on*, is never guaranteed its sayability. If sayability is the demand of the potential to be said, and the demand is that of the *alogos*, how will it enter, arrive in, or be said in language, for the tribunal of reason? At this joint, testimony finds its crucial ontological meaning because either testimony is the hyphen that connects onto-logy offering an "articulation between being and language," establishing sayability, or there is no ontology.[20]

A Mere Potentiality in Aristotle

In Aristotle, *dunamis* has different meanings. To understand better how the sense of the demand, borrowed from Leibniz, is connected to the sense of the possible or potential that demands existence, but is not granted existence—as in the possible that could have been, but never was—it might help to clarify which sense of *dunamis* is actually at stake. I would like to suggest that this sense is in a certain way anticipated by following sense *dunamis* and *adunamia* Aristotle distinguishes in the *Metaphysics*, Book Delta: "The capacity of performing this well [*epitelein*; accomplish or bring to perfection] or according to choice; for sometimes we say of those who merely [*monos*] can walk or speak but not well or not as they choose, that they *cannot* [*ou dunasthai*] speak or walk."[21] This is determination of *dunamis*, and its accompanying "*ou dunasthai*" or *adunamia* is interesting because in this context *adunamia* does not simply mean impossibility or incapacity, and *dunamis* not simply possibility or capacity. Rather, in this specific usage of the word, *dunamis* and the verb *dunamai* mean being capable of something in such a way that one can actually bring it to its *telos* or perfection (*epitelein*). This sense of *dunamis* resonates in Leibniz's argument that offers a reason for why some possibilities are actualized and others not: it is due to their *perfection*, or their lack thereof; "each possible thing having the right to claim existence in proportion to the perfection which it involves," as Leibniz writes.[22] Two possibles are both capable of existence, but the first one is truly good at existence and brings the world to a higher degree of perfection and, therefore, it comes to existence, whereas the other is *merely* capable of existence, that is to say, *barely* capable of existence—merely and barely here translate the Greek *monos*, because in this example this other possible is *only* possible and nothing more. Perfect potentiality is not actuality itself, but is capable of *epitelein* and is *kalōs*, it is capable of actuali*zing* itself in a beautiful manner. A possible thing that is not perfect according to this specific entry in Aristotle's vocabulary of *dunamis* is called *adunaton*, marked by *adunamia*. Thus, we encounter here something that can both be called *dunamis*, because it is possible, and *adunamia*, because it is not capable of perfectly actualizing its *dunamis*.[23] In this specific context, *adunamia* is not sheer impotentiality or incapacity, but it is rather mere or bare potentiality, without the capacity to actualize well. It is potentiality *alone*, without the (urgently needed) power or potency to bring itself to perfection and fulfillment. It is deprived of a source, an *archē*, in itself for the change into completion to take place. While having a capacity, it lacks the capacity to perform this capacity well or to complete it.[24] Thus, the term *adunamia* refers here to a poverty or misery in the *dunamis* itself. By this poverty, the merely or barely possible cannot find the form to complete itself, but rather retains itself in a particular deprivation of form.

Aristotle tends to offer examples for the different meanings of *dunamis* and *energeia* in the realm of human capacities. Following this custom, we may suggest that this bare potentiality is exemplified in human life at those stages where human existence remains on the *threshold* of its humanity, that is, outside or on the threshold of the public realm or *polis* or outside or on the threshold of language and discourse. Aristotle himself actually offers this latter example, to speak or *legein*. To be incapable of speech means in the quoted passage: not to be capable of actualizing (well) one's capacity to speak and not to be able to say what one wants or chooses to say. The obsession with the philosophical determination of speech as wanting-to-say (*vouloir-dire*) or intention-to-signify therefore always misses the specific inability with which humans can have their capacity to speak, namely as not being able to say what one wants or chooses to say. The true stakes of the category of testimony and attestation are found in the demand for attestation that is experienced in confrontation with these forms of *adunamia*, of not being able to say. The original figure of the witness is, in this sense, the *auctor*, the one who confronted with these forms of mere or bare capacities, is assigned the task to complete them, to give a form to what is deprived of a form so that this form brings to language the formlessness held in reserve.

Before turning to this formlessness, let us join for a second Bartleby in the Dead Letter Office. All that is, to fathom the immeasurable depth of what Agamben calls the "ontological squandering," is for Leibniz only the peak of a pyramid that "goes on descending to infinity."[25] Yet when the principle of reason is suspended, it means that existence can only be thought of as a random, albeit compossible, choice from this pyramid rather than merely from its peak, confronting us with possibilities that can exist—they are not impossible—but lack the capacity to exist well—they are examples of *adunamia*. The misery that Leibniz reserved for all that is below the pyramid's peak and cannot be found in a reality that follows the rule of *logos* thus turns out to be part and parcel of what is. These mere potentialities can exist, but they cannot exist well. The mound of letters piling up in the Dead Letter Office attests to this: the possibilities of relief and alleviation they contain did not come into existence. Hence, the letters, by contrast, attest to the misery of what is and of what happened—and not simply of what did not happen or of what could have been. Thus, perhaps, the letters found in the Dead Letter Office are Pauline after all, but not according to the logic of dead letter and living spirit in which Agamben inscribes them, but rather because they articulate the lamentations and mourning of all that is.[26] Testimony is the form the *logos* of onto-logy has to adopt to be able, perhaps, to articulate the *aloga* in what can be, what could have been, and what is. The witness of this *adunamia*, this poor and miserable capacity in existence, shares in the split between being and *logos*, and is itself divided in Bartleby's experience that remains silent, in Jeremiah's lament that cries out to be heard, and in Paul's articulation of a transcendental, communal mourning permeating all that is.

Bare Existence

What is this form of existence that does not have the capacity to exist well or, in terms of human existence, does not have the ability to speak (well) and therefore is deprived of what classically is understood as the human form or essence, namely the capacity to speak? What is this form of existence that depends on testimony to be given a voice and to be articulated in language? In the previous parts of this study, I have suggested speaking here of the reserve/object of testimony, and I have characterized the specific *dunamis*, which is also an *adunamia*, in terms of the French *misère*, meaning misery, poverty, want, distress, or (de)privation. In addition to the more theoretical discussion of the concepts of demand and mere potentiality, this section discusses three related figures of this deprivation in the human being that allow us to get a better sense of the distinctive reserve/object of testimony in the context of present-day continental thought and a better sense of where it is found.

The Naked "That" of Bare Existence

The first figure, derived from a mere adjective that ties these reflections in with those from chapter 9, is taken from Heidegger's *Sein und Zeit* and his description of the reserve/object of attestation: "the naked 'that' in the nothingness of the world."[27] The adjective "naked" or *nackte* is used five times in *Sein und Zeit*, and in four of these occurrences, it characterizes the uncanniness of existence disclosed in anxiety: "Angst is anxious about naked Dasein thrown into uncanniness. It brings one back to the pure That of one's ownmost, individuated thrownness."[28] In German, the first sentence reads: "Die Angst ängstet sich um das nackte Dasein als in die Unheimlichkeit geworfenes." Because expressions such as *das nackte Dasein* or *die nackte Existenz* mean "bare existence," one could also translate this as "Anxiety is anxious about bare existence as it is thrown in uncanniness." The truly uncanny dimension of existence is to be found in bare existence, *nacktes Dasein*, that is, existence deprived of any horizon of significance from within which it can understand anything—the formless, meaningless "that" of existence, which is definitely not nothing but mere and bare potentiality that the human always bears within themselves.

Among the five quotes, this quote connects this "that" of bare existence to the notion of *Geworfenheit* or thrownness. Often, when the relation of Arendt and Heidegger is discussed, it is argued that Heidegger is the one who concentrates on death, whereas Arendt prioritizes birth. Yet one should not forget that there is a remarkable idiomatic dimension to *werfen* and *geworfen*. In German, as well as in Dutch, the verb "to throw," *werfen*, *werpen*, can also be used to express the giving birth of animals such as dogs: "dogs throw their young," as the literal translation of the idiomatic expression reads. In the notion of *Geworfenheit* therefore resonates the very sense of an animal form of being born. It would therefore not be too far-fetched to read in Heidegger's notion of *Geworfenheit* also that of birth and more precisely that of the human being born as a human animal, as an infant, "naked, unshod, unbedded, and unarmed."[29] It is important to note that the type of potentiality that is thus brought forward differs from that of those existentialists who see in the undetermined state of this "that" of existence the possibility to choose any form for one's life: this potentiality does not come equipped with a will. Moreover, to be born naked, unshod, unbedded, and unarmed also means that this beginning is not the same as the one Arendt has in mind as the entrance of a world and that for her is duplicated in the human capacities to speak and to act. Heidegger rather refers to a mere or bare potentiality, *eine nackte Möglichkeit*, that is at the same time an *adunamia* in Aristotle's sense: there is existence and a potentiality-of-being, but this is not a potentiality that one can be well.[30] The human infant's vulnerability exemplifies this par excellence: when a child is born, it is not at home in a world; it still needs be formed in such a way that it can deal with the worldly structures of meaning in which it is born. Thus, this bare potentiality of human existence is the very uncanniness of existence. It is the sheer contingency of being-born to which every dimension of human existence is indebted. At the same time, human existence is deprived of this potentiality as an active one. One could also say that the poverty of human existence is exactly to never *have* or *be able* of this potentiality to be. To be able of this potentiality would, after all, require *to be able* to not-be, in the precise sense of being able of this *before*, in actuality, being this bare "that." Birth is the gift of our potentiality-of-being—without this contingent beginning of existence, there would be no potentiality-of-being at all—yet birth does not give this potentiality as one we are capable of.

The Birth of Humankind

The very brief (footnote) reference to Plato's *Protagoras* in the previous example is due to the work of Stiegler. He argues that technics and technology are the capacities that complement or, rather, supplement their *adunamia* so that humans are awarded some ways of becoming capable of existence. For this argument, he refers back to the intriguing myth on the origin of the human kind as told by Protagoras in Plato's dialogue of the same name.[31] This scene might be considered as a third example or, if one wishes, as an elaboration of the second example. I do not offer a proper reading of this intriguing story here. I only want to note that in this myth, the human is conceived as the one who is *deprived* of the capacities and powers, *dunameis*, that are handed out to the animals, *ta aloga*.[32] This means that while the *aloga* enter the world as a place they can inhabit, the birth of human kind is the entrance of humans into a world they *cannot* inhabit. In fact, this birth brings into existence a species that is not defined by its capacity to speak or its political nature, but rather by a potential for existence that it cannot fulfill or complete. The human cannot exist well because human kind, as the story tells, lacks any "means of survival" (*sōtēria*, deliverance or preservation). All beings are marked by *conatus*, a striving or a demand to persist in their existence, except for the human. Human kind consists of beings who lack the basic powers to fulfill this demand at the dawn of their birth.

Confronted with this *aporia* in the existence of human kind, so the story goes, Prometheus steals the wisdom of arts and fire from Hephaestus and Athena. These are the non-natural powers granted to the human kind after their birth so that they may survive. These powers are thus the supplements for the essential human deprivation and poverty. As the story continues, it is thanks to the arts that the humans are given "speech and words," *phōnē* and *onomata*.[33] The human's meaningful voice or speech is not an essential or natural part or possession of the human. It is a gift, a complementary capacity enabling human survival, *enabling the human to take on and become capable of the potentiality of existence*. Thus, the incentive to speak and the demand to speak are not found in the presupposition of language itself, but rather in the absence of a natural human *phōnē sēmantikē* and in the absence of a natural human capacity for survival. Using Leibniz's vocabulary, we could say that the human lacks the right to claim existence because they lack any perfection in their potentiality-of-being.

Infancy

The fourth example continues the second and third. Language is a supplement, an addition. Hence, the human *phōnē* as the *phōnē sēmantikē* is an *auctor* in the sense discussed in chapter 10: it presupposes the vulnerable, miserable mode of existence that is born and that is non-speaking, namely *infancy*. Testimony comes into play when language is not only the mode of preservation of the human kind, that is, the mode of being in which the human has simply left behind this infancy, but when this (in)capacity is always somehow presupposed and demands to be attested to. We could call this (in)capacity the inarticulate voice or demand of a miserable, vulnerable existence. Especially in the work of Lyotard—and to some extent also in the early work of Agamben—infancy is in fact the name for the reserve/object of the type of bearing witness to which literature and philosophy are called.[34] For him, the originary being-guilty to which Heidegger draws our attention in his analysis of the voice of conscience should be understood as a debt of all human existence to this dimension of infancy from which it stems: humans are born from a "miserable and admirable indetermination" by which they have contracted a particular "debt to infancy," and this debt "is one which we never pay off. [. . .] It is the task of writing, thinking, literature, arts, to venture to bear witness to it."[35] The infant is an important figure because it brings together a particular sense of potentiality, formlessness, and poverty or misery.[36] In the first place, the human infant is marked by a lack of speech, but this deprivation of speech is to be understood as a potentiality: the human infant has the capacity to speak. In fact, the potentiality of human speech is present in the child in a way that transgresses any actualization of this capacity in any human adult: the human child is truly capable of speaking *all* languages. In this sense, the truth of Protagoras's myth could consist in the fact that none of the languages the child learns comes naturally; they are only appropriated historically.[37] Yet, at the same time, this potentiality is not yet a capacity one has: the infant depends on its environment to actually develop particular linguistic skills so that, one day, it may actually speak; it cannot choose a language of its liking, but is marked by a certain poverty in this capacity.[38] The infant is handed over to others and does not find its own voice or language, but only the language of (some particular) others. In this sense, the child's potential to speak does not prefer any language; it is truly formless with respect to the particular form of language it can actualize. This potentiality is a passive one and not an active one as in the adult. Yet without this infant potentiality, no adult would speak, and in this sense the adult is indebted to infancy. At the same time, the adult has lost this basic potentiality in the particular language or languages they can speak. As Heller-Roazen suggests, it is in the child's gibberish, this *lalein*, that we find the inarticulate voice of this potentiality that does not yet speak any language, but that is also not identical to the animal voice in the sense that it is marked by and voices this potentiality to speak any of the human languages.[39]

Lyotard appropriates this particular sense of infancy in terms of a difference between the human's infancy before their formation (*Bildung*) and the human after their formation and their being integrated in and adjusted to the human institutions such as that of particular languages (but any form of arts, science, technics, and politics are implicated as well in this formation). If we call the latter properly human, as he suggests, the former is inhuman and vice versa: there is no (dialectical) identification possible between these two domains, and this is why the realm of infancy and our debt to it needs to be borne witness to in the other realm. One could indeed say that, as Kierkegaard suggests in *Fear and Trembling*, language offers the leafage to cover the nakedness of the human, which is given in an exemplary way in human infancy, but the question then is how this infancy can be attested to.

In sum, humans are not born fully human; they need to be educated to become properly human. The human infant does not automatically become human. Rather, infants need to be formed and adapted to the social structures in which adult life takes place—and these structures include language but also "communal life, adult consciousness and reason."[40] The human infant thus requires a supplement, a particular set of *technai*, to become human and to share in adult life. Thus, human life has a double provenance: on the one hand infancy, with its lack of speech, its lack of reason, and its particular "misery and poverty," as Lyotard writes; and on the other hand education and the social and political institutions to which the infant needs to be adapted and by which the infant needs to be (in)formed. Given this *double* provenance of *the* human, it remains to be seen what exactly we mean when we say "human," as Lyotard makes clear by asking the following question: "What shall we call human in humans, the initial misery of infancy, or their capacity to acquire a 'second' nature [. . .]?"[41] Infancy and the capacity to be educated belong together and are both basically human; there is no human without either of them: without the former, the human would not come into existence, and without the latter, according to Protagoras's story, there would be no preservation of and no future for the human.

Moreover, this educational process leaves a "remainder": adult life does not integrate infancy without remainder. Hence, the more precise question of Lyotard's inquiry into the human and the inhuman is: who exactly is the adult human? In the course of his work, Lyotard's answer is clear. Infancy is not only the raw, formless potentiality of the human that is formed into an adult form by the processes of education. Rather, in the product of this shaping and forming the human being according to a certain model, infancy remains in the human as this potentiality that has not adopted the adult form but rather *resists* it. It is not only the provenance of the human who, once having become properly human in its own anthropogenesis, has left this infancy behind, but it is also, as what remains, a principle of deformation or critique of the adult form of life and all that comes with it. This sense of "indetermination" of infancy is captured in the following quote: "shorn of speech, incapable of standing upright, hesitating over the objects of its interest, not able to calculate its advantages, not sensitive to common reason, the infant is eminently the human because its distress heralds and promises things possible." The infant is not only the figure of human distress, of the human that cannot preserve itself when left to its own devices, but also the figure of things possible—and this means of course in the first place of possibilities that have not been actualized but that are, in infancy, given as possibilities; it is thus a figure of what could have been but also of what-can-perhaps-be, at least when this potentiality is still given as potentiality in what is and has become of this human. Infancy is, in the human, the reserve toward all attained human forms attained, and it is that which is held in reserve with respect to all human forms. The human is thus a double, and in its adult configuration it can only complement itself when it testifies to its own infancy. This reserve of what cannot speak demands to be attested to because it marks what it is to be human. Infancy is, in the human, the possible that demands existence and that demands to be said because it is the reserve of the horizons of meaning and the discourses within which we find ourselves.

Each of these four figures offers a particular sense of the reserve/object of testimony that shows on which threshold testimony is located, always between the realm of *logos* and its rule, on the one hand, and the realm of *alogos*, of what lacks the capacity to speak (well) and exist (well or by itself), on the other. If the beings that testimony bears witness to are on the other side of *logos* and its rule, the stakes of testimony are nothing less than their communicability, their sayability, and the encounter of these beings and *logos*, that is, these stakes are nothing less than onto-logy.

Chapter 12

The Truth and Untruth of Testimony

for it is here, in the tragic life, that one finds the vast majority of myths and falsehoods.[1]

—Plato, *Cratylus* 408c

For Aristotle, as discussed before, only the *logos apophantikos* is a mode of discourse that is either true or false. Other modes of speech, such as *euchē*, a call, a promise, or an oath, are not. Yet that does not mean that the notion of truth and untruth is absent from these other modes of speech, albeit that we no longer use the notion of truth to signify a true proposition. Heidegger's account of truth as *alētheia* as well as Aristotle's own notion of *dēloō*, which is a form of making manifest, suggest a different concern with truth in language. In relation to testimony, this different concern implies a specific focus on the announcement of testimony. Yet, as indicated in chapter 9, this notion of announcement is complicated by other issues, namely those of truthfulness and credibility, which arise in relation to bearing witness.

First, truthfulness concerns the witness, who is sworn to the truth. Their bearing witness always includes on oath that grounds their appeal for belief: "Please, believe me! I swear and promise to tell you the truth!" In this sense, truthfulness guides us almost naturally toward the question of the oath and its meaning for testimony. With the suspension of the absolute witness, discussed in chapters 10 and 12, the oath only has itself or its utterer to offer as ground: there is no divine, absolute witness who can attest to the truth of a testimony or the witness's truthfulness. This lack of a more solid ground, as I argue in this chapter, mirrors the twofold nature of what is attested to: the object and the reserve of testimony.

Secondly, the question of truthfulness concerns language itself. The epigraph to this chapter immediately explains why this is so. As opposed to the truthful language of the gods, the tragic life of humans is mirrored in the fundamental ambiguity of their language. When Socrates argues in the *Cratylus* that human language can be false, it is not just a matter of the falsity of a proposition; it rather concerns the very trustworthiness of language. With the suspension of an absolute witness, this experience of language is intensified, and humans seem to be fully handed over to myths and falsehoods. This particular experience of language needs to be integrated in the sense of announcement that marks testimony.

As becomes clear in this chapter, these two concerns of truthfulness—in relation to the witness and to the experience of the tragic falsity of language—belong together. To show how they belong together, let me begin with the observation that two lines of inquiry developed in chapter 10 and 11, respectively, concern one and the same issue. For Heidegger, the *logos hermeneutikos* is basically concerned with announcement. In *Unterwegs zur Sprache*, this leads to a concept of hermeneutics that privileges announcement over explication. Furthering Heidegger's line of thought, Nancy argues that this account of hermeneutics points to a sense of the Greek *hermēneia* that is lost in the more classical sense of hermeneutics as developed by Gadamer and Ricoeur. Nancy's claim is obviously right when we consider, for instance, how Ricoeur limits his use of the term "hermeneutics" to the practice of the *explication* of symbolic expressions. Yet the fact that Ricoeur limits the term "hermeneutics" to the practice and the theory of explication, that is, to the epistemic questions to which symbolic expressions give rise, does not mean that he does not see, like Heidegger and Nancy, that any explication presupposes a more primordial announcement of meaning. In fact, Ricoeur's account of this primordial announcement offers the means to show how the problem of the trustworthiness of language goes to the heart of this announcement.

The Ambiguous Kerygma of the Symbol

For Ricoeur, hermeneutics is not an epistemological enterprise closed in on itself.[2] Rather, he recognizes the primordial nature of a reality that elicits the need for explication. Yet this reality only becomes a concern for us once it is articulated in the symbol, which grants reality its ontological appeal for us. The symbol, as he argues, is a linguistic phenomenon characterized by its *kerygmatic* function. The symbol proclaims hidden elements of human existence that the addressees cannot know or experience by themselves or by means of their own faculties, but for which they truly depend on the symbol. In this sense, the symbol has a testimonial structure: it bears witness to a primordial dimension of human existence for which the human depends on it. The symbol is thus an announcement in the strong sense of the word: it generates a new horizon of meaning for those who are capable of hearing the symbolic call. Thus, as the early Ricoeur notes, the symbol announces what is *other* than the horizon of meaning to which the addressees belong. In his account of the religious symbol, he refers to this ontological dimension as the "wholly other," adopting Karl Barth's famous terminology.[3]

The kerygmatic function of the symbol stresses its *mediating* function: the symbol is neither the other itself nor what is other itself, but it proclaims and announces the other. The symbol is the herald, *kērux*, of the other, engaged in a *kērugma*, public announcement, and provided with a capacity of *kērussō*, to proclaim or to herald. If we follow Plato's *Statesman*, where the Stranger connects the activity of the herald with that of the interpreter—neither of these two figures announces their own orders or messages, but they pass on what they received, and they announce it to those who could not hear it from the original source—we see in which sense Ricoeur's idea of the *kērugma* is also involved in an account of the primordial announcement of hermeneutics.[4] As announcing the other, the symbolic mediation does not bring into play what resembles or varies on the addressee's horizon of meaning, but truly transforms it.

At this point, therefore, I disagree with Nancy's assessment of Ricoeur's hermeneutics in *Le partage des voix*. In fact, Nancy claims that Ricoeur's hermeneutics departs from an "adhesion of sense" and a "participation in meaning," as if this sense and meaning is always already presupposed in every interpretation and never truly accounted for.[5] In fact, as he argues, this participation in meaning is the very belief that constitutes hermeneutics in a classical sense: "Hermeneutic *belief* [croyance] in general is not anything other than that presupposition."[6] By this unquestioned belief, Ricoeur's hermeneutics would forget the primordial hermeneutic sense of announcement.[7] That—and why—I disagree with this account is clear from the previous paragraph, but I want to stipulate two further reasons. First, Nancy does not recognize in which sense there is, prior to any explication of meaning, a symbolic announcement of meaning, which for Ricoeur is a kerygma of what is wholly other. Second, he misinterprets the sense of "belief" here. *Every* attempt to interpret presupposes that there is something meaningful to be found in what is interpreted. There is no need to call this a belief in the strong sense of a conviction (*croyance*); it is rather the basic working hypothesis of any interpretation, but as every hypothesis it may turn out to be invalid.

This does not mean, however, that there is no conviction or belief at work in Ricoeur's hermeneutics, but it should be located at the right level: not on that of explication but on that of the symbolic kerygma. Ricoeur emphasizes that at this latter level, there is a basic belief, namely the belief in the symbol, the trust *that* the symbol has something to say. Although it announces something that is unclear and even does not fit within the already given horizons of understanding, the interpreter approaches the symbol with the trust that its testimony on human existence is truthful and informs us about a dimension of human existence of which we would otherwise be deprived. This more nuanced account of Ricoeur's position is, I think, important because it allows us to find in Ricoeur's understanding of the symbol the outlines of a sense of (symbolic) announcement in a Heideggerian sense of the word in which the question of trust and belief is naturally integrated. This would thus be a significant step forward with respect to Heidegger's analysis of attestation and the lack of any reference to trust and belief, as discussed in chapter 9. Let me therefore examine this analysis of the symbolic kerygma of the wholly other in some more detail and start with its "reserve/object," the wholly other.

One has to move carefully here: is the "wholly other" of Barth not another version of the Christian God? And should we therefore not wonder with Nancy whether the form of alterity this wholly other brings into play is genuinely other? As Nancy writes: "[I]t would be necessary to analyze up to what point the alterity *of* meaning is put into play, and not only an originating meaning of an identified other (and because of that, endowed with an unchanged other [*non-altérité*])."[8] The hesitation that speaks from this quote needs to be taken seriously. If the wholly other is yet another instantiation of the absolute witness or another version of the metaphysical God, then this notion does not bring into play a genuine alterity or exception to the Christian horizon of meaning from which Barth and Ricoeur often speak.[9] Yet we should also not forget that, conceptually, the wholly other offers a notion that is capable of being a genuine exception.

What interests me at this point is exactly the role awarded to the symbolic kerygma. As Ricoeur notes, the function of the symbolic kerygma is to allow the wholly other to *address* and does not simply remain totally other, but transforms the addressees' horizon of understanding.[10] Rather than remaining other, unperceivable, and unhearable, the kerygma is and acts as announcement in the strong sense we encountered also in

Heidegger's account of the call: the kerygma generates new possibilities of understanding and truly gives to understand or, as Ricoeur prefers to say, "gives to think."[11] This means indeed that by being borne witness to, the wholly other loses its *mere* otherness, which consists exactly in its non-addressing and its sheer absence, but only because it transforms the horizon of the hearers that it addresses. In turn, however, this does not mean that thanks to the kerygma the otherness is reduced and eliminated. As Ricoeur suggests, the kerygma offers "new symbolic expressions situated at the point of rupture and suture between the Wholly Other and discourse."[12] The symbol is located on the threshold of what is wholly other and discourse, at the very point where these two are torn apart *and* stitched together, as Ricoeur writes. This description shows how similar this symbolic kerygma is to the structure of testimony that I explore in this study. In terms of object and reserve, Ricoeur's description can also be rendered as follows: by presenting the wholly other as object, the symbol "annihilates" its radical otherness—it stitches together—but in the same movement, this otherness is not exhausted in what the symbol presents, and in this sense, the symbol holds back in reserve—it tears apart. Being on the threshold, the symbol draws from both sides and, therefore, also announces a meaning divided in itself, sharing in the other and in the addressee's discourse.

It seems to me that, like no one else, Ricoeur has taken this division at the heart of the symbolic kerygma seriously. In fact, this is the reason why, for Ricoeur, the question of interpretation is always a question of multiple, *conflicting* interpretations. This conflict is grounded in the divided sense of the symbol, which is itself elicited by the reality of its object. By its very nature, being on the threshold of two different domains, the symbol allows for and necessitates different, conflicting interpretations. Here, announcement is not a unitary disclosure but rather a mutual contamination of discourse and reserve/object in the symbol.

The basic conflict that goes hand in hand with this form of symbolic announcement can be traced in two basic, different attitudes or attunements with which the hearer may listen to the symbol: the attitude of belief or trust and that of suspicion or distrust. In the first attunement, the hearer listens to the symbol in order to hear in it something meaningfully disclosed about the wholly other and human existence. The second attunement, which Ricoeur famously connects to the works of the masters of suspicion, Marx, Nietzsche, and Freud, is not marked by trust in what the symbol has to say but rather looks for what it hides and what it does not or cannot say. Whereas the attunement of trust insists that the symbol announces something of the other and thus privileges the appearance of this otherness in symbolic language, the attitude of distrust insists that the symbol is actually an effect of a reigning discourse and is not in any way the announcement of something new, but only the illusion of something new and thus also the distortion and concealment of what is truly other. This duality reflects the symbol's position on the threshold of wholly other and discourse. In what Ricoeur calls the annihilation of the radical otherness, we find the resources of this suspiciously attuned interpretation: the object presented by testimony refers beyond itself and thus allows also for a mode of interpretation that insists that the object, taken in itself, distorts and conceals the reserve.

Hence, Ricoeur's account of the symbol is important in the context of this study because it does not identify the sense of hermeneutic announcement with sheer, unequivocal disclosure—unequivocality (*Eindeutigkeit*) marks Heidegger's call of conscience—but rather shows that the symbol's announcement is fundamentally ambiguous or *zweideutig*. It is ambiguous because it operates on the threshold of two incompatible domains. Much later, in *Soi-même comme un autre*, Ricoeur indeed connects the symbol's ambiguity to that of attestation in his account of the latter's truth and untruth. The truth of attestation, as he explains, cannot be simply be understood as truth in *opposition* to untruth.[13] Rather, the announcement of attestation always *involves* untruth and cannot be separated from it. It is exactly in this sense that the modes of discourse of neither symbolic language nor testimony or attestation can be understood as a *logos apophantikos* in Aristotle's sense: these former modes of discourse are not *either* true *or* false, but truth and falsity are intertwined.

Ricoeur's account of hermeneutics as a practice divided up by the epistemic attitudes of conviction and suspicion thus reflects this double sense of announcement. To say that a testimony is either true or false is to say a view from nowhere exists, an absolute witness, capable of regulating and judging the interplay between two incompatible domains. Yet this is not the case. Even when a witness revokes their testimony and says "I lied," the element of trust cannot be removed. It is for this reason, as both Ricoeur and Derrida emphasize, that every testimony is and remains haunted by the possibility of false testimony; the same applies to attestation, as Ricoeur notes: "[Suspicion] haunts attestation, as a false testimony haunts a true testimony."[14] Given the absence of an absolute witness, we cannot overcome this possibility. As Ricoeur writes: "But there is no recourse against false testimony than another that is more credible; and there is no recourse against suspicion but a more *reliable* attestation."[15] This is not just a matter of our finite epistemic capacities: it concerns the being-true and being-false of attestation *itself*. This means that the poetic power of the act of bearing witness to generate new possibilities of understanding in the discourse of its addressees is never guaranteed, but is always under scrutiny and critique because it always *may be* concealing or distorting the reserve/object of testimony. It is for this ontological reason—concerning the *being*-true and *being*-false of testimony—that the witness has to pledge their adherence to the truth and that the hearer is confronted with a basic undecidability of two opposed attunements they can adopt: trust and distrust.[16] The truth and the untruth of the announcement that takes place in the act of bearing witness are thus inseparable and indistinguishable. The chance of a genuine encounter with the reserve/object of testimony cannot exist without the risk of being caught up in a mere illusion.

I'm aware that Ricoeur ultimately privileges trust and belief over distrust and disbelief. However, this tendency in his thought is due to a "personal wager," as he notes in an interview with Richard Kearney.[17] This privileging is problematic. Yet to privilege distrust and disbelief is problematic as well. After all, the initial belief in testimony is never a blind belief, but is rather comparable with the basic trust that we all seem to have in language. By using language, as Derrida notes, we attest to a basic affirmation of our trust in language; by using language, we say "yes" to it and turn out to be an "implicit believer" in language.[18] Yet, in turn, this does not mean that this trust can be taken for granted and that distrust would be a gratuitous attitude. Our reading of Mortier's *Godenslaap* has indicated this. Language can also *not* deliver what it promises and belie the speaker's implicit affirmation of language. This ignites distrust. Yet this distrust does not seem to be complete because it is this very distrust *that forces some to speak up*, as if answering to a demand in language itself; sometimes they do so in the most captivating way, as we see not only from Helena's attempts to give her past a voice but also from the works of authors such as Kierkegaard, Nietzsche, and other masters of suspicion. Thus, a fundamental undecidability is and remains inscribed in the type of announcement that operates on the threshold of two mutually excluding domains and that is supposed to generate in the addressee's discourse the possibility of the other to be heard.

Testimony, thus, cannot secure its own certainty. It cannot ward off the possibility of perjury, deception, lie, fiction, hallucination, or forgetfulness. Note that this list shows that the uncertainty of testimony is not only concerned with the fact that the hearer can never be sure that the witness speaks the truth, but also concerns the witness because, for instance, they do not speak from the immediate perception or experience of what they bear witness to, but rather from their memory that can play tricks on them; and it concerns the object/reserve of testimony that in certain situations cannot but depend on a certain fictional or literary element, for instance, when the speaking witness is "only" the *auctor* of what the experiencing witness experienced and of which the latter cannot speak. To capture this basic fragility and vulnerability of testimony, Derrida speaks of the "perhaps" of testimony. Although no testimony that is introduced or concluded with a "perhaps" would be acceptable in a court of law, there is no testimony without this "perhaps" of perjury, lies, fiction, or hallucination—as Derrida suggests—but also the "perhaps" of "the incapacity to tell a story, the refusal to recount, the insistence of the unreliable," as Ricoeur adds.[19] The "perhaps" is the silent voice that accompanies whatever the speaking voice testifies. To expel this "perhaps" before a court of law, because testimony has nothing else to offer but itself and its speaker, the witness is sworn to the truth. A similar vow—in Greek also *euchē*, stressing its intrinsic relation to the call and the appeal—is at stake in any testimony: because the witness has nothing else to offer but themselves to ground their testimony and to expel the danger of the "perhaps," they implicitly or explicitly promise or swear to speak the truth as soon as they testify.

The Blessing and Curse of the Vow

A distorting testimony is a complicated and diverse phenomenon. The witness may suffer from "error or hallucination in good faith" or may actively deceive.[20] Language itself is marked by an intrinsic weakness: it cannot ward off distorting rhetoric or propaganda and it sometimes suffers from a basic incapacity to express what demands articulation. And one can easily think of mixtures of these possibilities, such as, for instance, the witness who in good faith is the victim of propaganda by which their testimony in good faith nevertheless results in a distorting testimony.

To ward off the risk of testimonial distortion, the witness is sworn to truth. Obviously, on the level of such a vow, promise, or oath, the problem of distortion and falsity simply repeats itself, because every oath is haunted by the possibility of perjury.[21] Yet the phenomenon of swearing in testimony shows how the possibility of false or distorting testimony is not added to the practice of testimony, but rather belongs to this practice from the outset. There is no testimony without an oath or without an explicit or implicit promise to tell the truth because oath and promise are supposed to guarantee a testimony's reliability.[22] Yet, as indicated above, the unreliability of testimony (without an oath) is not only that of human speakers, but also concerns language. As Agamben notes: "The 'scourge' that [the oath] had to stem was not only the unreliability of men, incapable of staying true to their word, but a weakness pertaining to language itself, the capacity of words themselves to refer to things and the ability of men to make profession of their condition as speaking beings."[23] Although *Il sacramento del linguaggio*, Agamben's study of the oath from which this quote stems, is in some respects problematic and not always convincing,[24] the specific orientation of his study is quite important for my own purposes in the following respect. For him, the oath is an act of language that is supposed to guarantee the relation (or the encounter) of language and being and that of language and action. Although Agamben treats these two elements in one grand, sweeping gesture, I limit my attention in this chapter to the connection of language and being and turn my attention to the relation of language and action in the next chapter. The relation of language and being concerns the question of whether the reserve/object of testimony can be borne witness to and articulated in the discourse of the hearer. The relation of language and action, by contrast, concerns the question of whether the witness is indeed committed to their testimony, affirming the relation of being and language this testimony puts forward and putting themselves at stake in testimony as the guarantee for this act of language. These two relations together concern the very possibility of testimony and mark the specific relevance of the oath and the promise in an account of testimony. Only if the oath actually safeguards both relations can a testimony take place.

Agamben's remarkable archeology of the oath in its Greek sense of *horkos* shows that the vow belongs to the structure of language: for humans, language is of crucial importance because language vows to say being. In this vow, language can either be trustworthy, *pistos*, deserving faith, *pistis*, or its swearing to touch on and announce being becomes a curse, *ara*, for the humans who let themselves be guided by language. Much stronger than "perjury" or "lie," the notion of the curse captures the impact of language that cannot live up to the human's basic faith in and affirmation of it. When language distorts or conceals reality, language becomes a genuine curse to the human. If indeed the oath is that which guarantees language's relation to being, it becomes clear *why* in ancient times an oath is done before the gods as witnesses. The gods witness "the 'joining together' [. . .] that [. . .] unites words and things, that is, the *logos* as such," and the articulation as such.[25] As witnesses, Agamben suggests, the names of the gods—one swears in the name of a god and before a god—"expresses the positive force of language," but this very name can become a curse, and as curse, it "expresses a weakness of language, namely the breaking of this relation."[26] The oath is thus marked by a "co-originarity of blessing and curse," and the curse is the very possibility of language to deprive the one who trusts in it of being and reality. Consequently, Agamben discovers in the oath the same ambiguity that Ricoeur discovers in symbolic testimony and attestation: preceding any sense of propositional truth, the truth and untruth of language basically concerns blessing and the curse of language, which found our trust in and suspicion of language, respectively.

In the ancient understanding, hence, the value of the god and its name consists in being the very guarantee of language's testimony of reality. In line with my previous analyses, the oath of language can only come into its own when the sense of an absolute witness is suspended and, also, the divine ground of the oath is deactivated. That it is, in fact, not a trivial task to arrive at such a suspension in a conception of the oath may be exemplified by Agamben's peculiar account of what Aristotle writes on the oath in his *Metaphysics*: "for what is oldest is most honourable, and the most honourable thing is that by which one swears."[27] Agamben claims that the latter part of this sentence is translated incorrectly and should rather say that the oath *itself* is the most honorable thing.[28] Such a reading effaces the reference to any absolute witness and indeed positions the oath as the most honorable—or, perhaps, uncanny—thing itself. However, this reading is not very convincing. In fact, if we follow Agamben's own logic of the *pistos/pistis* and the *ara* of language, it seems more in line with Aristotle's account that not the oath itself is most honorable but that the oath is rather *sworn in the name of* what is most honorable. This name is not the oath itself, but this name grounds the trustworthiness of the oath. *Pace* Agamben, Aristotle seems to be saying that by swearing by what is most trustworthy, the oath itself is granted trustworthiness. Subsequently, in a derived sense, the *pistos* or trustworthiness of the witness is "thus essentially the correspondence between language and actions."[29] This means that by the reference to the name of the god and by understanding both the blessing and the curse of language in terms of the oath's reference to this name, the sense of an absolute witness is not suspended or deactivated but still very much operative in Aristotle's remark. Consequently, it is not clear how Agamben arrives at this suspension and how, in his analysis, the vow at the heart of language's testimony comes into its own, profane nature. In fact, in Agamben's archeology of the linguistic act of swearing the name of god seems to be insisting itself, granting the act of swearing an almost magical force or power. It seems to me however, that a true deactivation of the absolute witness is necessary. Only then has the subject who adopts the role of witness nothing else to offer than this oath by which they attest to the capacity of language to articulate the object as well as to their own capacity to maintain faithful to their uttered words.

Derrida's account of the vow leads me to a similar hesitation. He discerns in the vow and the *foi jurée*, the sworn word, a reference of god as absolute witness, as the one who is evoked and invoked by the act of swearing.[30] Naas suggests that this may be understood as Derrida's very own appropriation of the term "god," in his own "idiom."[31] Indeed, Derrida moves very carefully, as always, when invoking this term. Yet his account insists on a presence-absence of the absolute witness, that is, on a remainder of this absolute witness in the concept of the vow and the oath. Derrida does not seem to be aware that his own invocations of the notion of God are themselves remainders of this absolute witness who testifies for every witness who swears an oath before it or in its name.[32] In texts such as *Foi et savoir* and *Sauf le nom*, there is an undeniable presence of the *apophasis* that insists on the absence of God in language, which goes hand in hand with God as the very empty place in language. This affects Derrida's account of testimony in such a way that the oath and the vow are placed on the threshold of this apophatic language as an adherence and affirmation of a present-absent God as the present-absent witness.

In this context, it seems to me that a fundamentally different sense of testimony and its vow can be found in Celan's important phrase "Niemand // zeugt für den Zeugen," "no one // bears witness for the witness"—a sentence to which Derrida is very attentive in other contexts. There is no god or linguistic remainder of god in a magical act of language present in Celan's phrase. He is much more insistent than Agamben and Derrida on this point: *no one* bears witness for the witness. The context and the situation of testimony today is that there is no other guarantee than the witness and their oath, than the witness and their trust in language, than the witness and their promise to keep and perform their vow. That Celan writes *Niemand* where Agamben in his archeology of the oath and Derrida in his deconstruction of the oath write the name of God—the former under the aegis of a problematic Messianism and the latter under erasure and in a strict, but still problematic, apophatic mode of presence-absence—marks a significant and crucial difference to which I return in chapter 14. For Celan, the witness has nothing other than themselves and their testimony to offer in the oath they swear. It is in this sense that the witness and the human capacity of language themselves are at stake and that the blessing and curse of language are truly language's. By contrast, every remainder of the absolute witness in a conception of the vow and oath of testimony secretly, insistently, and perversely claims to offer something more than the "perhaps" of human testimony.

Veridiction and Testimony

Despite my hesitations concerning the question of whether Agamben's archeology of the ancient conception of the oath allows testimony to come into its own, later stages of *Il sacramento del linguaggio* move the analysis of the oath in a direction that seems better capable of profaning human speech without losing sight of the specific function of discursive practices such as the oath and testimony. Toward the end of his study, Agamben returns to the Aristotelian distinction between the *logos apophantikos* and other modes of *logos* such as *euchē*. Agamben takes recourse to the practice of *parrēsia* or veridiction, which Foucault carefully analyzed in his last lecture courses at the *Collège de France*, and posits this practice as the paradigm for non-assertional modes of speech. This particular turn in Agamben's study is not completely transparent. Neither is it immediately clear why this mode of speech would be a paradigm for all forms of non-assertional modes of speech, nor is it clear why an analysis of the oath should lead up to an analysis of veridiction. Yet what is clear is that the difference between *logos apophantikos* and *parrēsia* allows Agamben to distinguish *between* modes of speech in which truth "is measured with logical and objective parameters" so that in assertional modes of speech this truth does not depend on the subject that speaks *and* modes of speech in which "the subject constitutes itself and puts itself in play as such by linking itself performatively to the truth of its own affirmation."[33] Hence, the contrast of statement, *logos apophantikos*, and veridiction, *parrēsia*, does not follow the rule of Aristotle's distinction—is there truth in this mode of *logos*?—but rather concerns the difference between two ways in which truth can be at stake in language, either objectively and logically or subjectively because the subject is the guarantee for the truth. This latter specification also makes clear what the importance of veridiction is: it is a mode of speech in which the speakers put themselves at stake. Thus, for Agamben, veridiction is exemplary for what a profanation of the oath aims at: a mode of speech in which the speaker themselves become the guarantee of the relation between word and thing and between word and action; they become the guarantee and measure of the truth and trustworthiness of this speech. Veridiction or truth-telling is a form of bearing witness to the truth with one's life: in *parrēsia*, the witness is sworn *with their life* to the truth they bear witness to. For this reason, linguistic practices such as swearing an oath, bearing witness, and truth-telling in the sense of *parrēsia* are practices by which humans take their place in language. For Agamben, the enactment of these practices is nothing less than the event of becoming-human, of anthropogenesis, in which the human is sworn to language and to what they say in it.[34]

This parallel with the practice of testimony is important for the purposes of this study. Apparently the human still needs to become human and becomes human at the very moment in which it adopts the position of a parresiast or, as Arendt would say, courageously takes the initiative to speak. It will probably come as no surprise that at exactly this point there are important similarities with Badiou's account of the subject and their particular form of bearing witness to the truth. This is our concern in the next chapter. For now, however, in order to prepare this analysis, I want to explore in more detail which form of subjectification is at stake in *parrēsia* and how it relates to the subjectification and desubjectification that mark testimony, as discussed in chapter 10. Especially in light of the ambiguity of the truth and untruth of testimony, of its reliability and unreliability, one can easily suspect that there might be a distinction between a practice that defines itself as *truth*-telling, in which the possibility of untruth is not reflected upon, and a practice that is *sworn* to the truth and that, in Agamben's terms, consequently is "co-originarily exposed to the possibility of both truth and lie."[35] Although Agamben tries to connect this analysis of the event of language in which both blessing and curse, both truth and falsity are at work to the practice of *parrēsia*, this cannot be traced in Foucault in the same way, and it seems to me that there are good reasons for Foucault not to do so. This leads to the question of what the similarities and differences between veridiction and testimony as linguistic practices are.

Both testimony and veridiction are in an imprecise or metaphorical sense "performative" because they are linguistic acts that do something in the world. Yet, as Foucault carefully points out with respect to *parrēsia*, these practices are different from what is normally and more precisely termed "performative." As Foucault explains, this is due to the fact that in speech act theory, the performative always refers to an institutionalized and codified mode of speech. Let us consider the basic example of the civil servant who, by a performative, marries a couple. Let us adapt Foucault's analysis of *parrēsia* to clarify in which sense (also) testimony is not a performative in the standard sense of the word, although it is an act of language that performs something.[36]

First, a civil servant must have a particular *status* in the situation that gives them the institutional authority to perform this marriage. This particular person should be the one who holds this particular office in this given situation. In this sense, the subject-role or subject-function of this speech act is already defined in the discursive situation in which the speech act takes place. The witness, however, may have all kinds of institutional functions or roles before bearing witness, but none of them is being a witness. The witness is in this sense not an institutionalized mode of subjectivity. In fact, witnesses constitute themselves as witness *by the very act of bearing witness*, as Ricoeur notes: "it is the witness who first declares himself to be a witness."[37] The subjectification of the witness thus happens in and as testimony—in a certain sense, one could say that to become a witness is to deactivate institutional roles and functions one has and to become in the first place the subject of testimony. Differently put, whereas the civil servant can easily be replaced by another civil servant, the witness is always *singular* and can, therefore, not be institutionalized.

Second, the institutional authority of the civil servant does not depend on the civil servant's own convictions. The pronunciation by which the couple becomes husband and wife does not depend in any way on the personal engagement or involvement of the civil servant in this procedure. All aspects of this procedure are well-defined, and the human who holds the rank of civil servant in the apparatus of the state may be fully indifferent, uninvolved, and disengaged to the marriage. The sincerity of the civil servant does not matter.[38] In the case of testimony, however, the witness offers themselves as the guarantee of their testimony; they and their trustworthiness are the "proof" and "evidence" of their testimony.

It is in this context that the phrase to which I already referred a couple of times, and to which both Ricoeur and Derrida refer in their own way, finds its proper place. The witness implicitly or explicitly says: "you have to believe me, because I engage myself to tell you the truth."[39] The personal involvement of the witness is required, and it remains a requirement because the witness is supposed to adhere to their testimony. If they fail to do so, they become less trustworthy or lose their trustworthiness altogether.

These first two points concern the specific type of subjectification that takes place in bearing witness and veridiction alike. Yet, with respect to the third point, testimony and veridiction part ways. With respect to a regular performative utterance, Foucault notes that the effect of the performative act on the situation "is known and ordered in advance, it is codified."[40] In the case of veridiction, however, the truth that is announced is not inscribed in the reigning discourses. Therefore, this announcement is nothing less than "the irruption of true discourse," and this "determines an open situation, or rather opens the situation and makes possible effects which are, precisely, not known. *Parrēsia* [. . .] opens up an unspecified risk."[41] We have already encountered these two notions, "irruption" and "unspecified risk," in our discussion of testimony. Yet the role they play in our analysis of testimony and in Foucault's analysis of veridiction is not exactly the same as we see when we ask for a further clarification of these terms: what and how does the irruption irrupt? With which risk, to what or to whom, are we dealing here?

For Foucault, "a man who stands up to a tyrant and tells him the truth" "is an exemplary scene of *parrēsia*."[42] If indeed this is the paradigm of veridiction, the risk involved is in the first place the risk for the one who speaks. After all, it is not guaranteed that tyrants will look favorably upon those who tell them the truth, when there are so many flatterers around willing to tell them otherwise. Yet this is not the *primary* risk at stake in bearing witness. The primary risk is the risk that the reserve/object is distorted or remains hidden. This difference thus concerns the discursive value of "true discourse." For Foucault, *parrēsia* presupposes this constellation: there is a true discourse—at least according to the speaker—and this needs to be communicated to, in the exemplary case, a tyrant. Consequently, as Foucault explicitly states, he is not interested in the problem of truth itself in his analysis of veridiction.[43] This also means that the basic problem that lies at the basis of Lyotard's work on the differend, namely whether or not there might be a difficulty in *understanding* the parresiast's interruption of the tyrant's discourse or, for the parresiast, a difficulty in articulating the truth that needs to be told, is not part of Foucault's analysis of veridiction. His sole concern is how the one who speaks may be afflicted by this engagement in *parrēsia*. This means in particular that the risk does not involve distorting the truth or not being able to transmit the truth but rather solely concerns the political and social risk for the speaker. Hence, for Foucault, the question of risk is raised to introduce the importance of *courage* to adopt the position of the parresiast in a situation in which the tyrant is surrounded by flatterers.

This, however, is not exactly the issue in the case of testimony. There, it is not even clear whether a true irruption *can* take place. After all, the act of bearing witness in its distinctive sense should not only constitute the subject of testimony, but should also generate genuinely new possibilities of hearing. In this sense, there is no "truth" available, which only awaits to be told. It is in the act of testimony that an irruptive discourse can take place, and if it takes place, it opens up the reserve/object to an unspecified risk, and it opens up the hearer's discourse to an unspecified risk because it confronts the hearer with the demand to believe. In the case of testimony, the risk is thus a double one. First, the witness who risks to speak does not (necessarily) run a risk in terms of a danger for their lives—this *may* also be involved, as is discussed in the next chapter, but is not essential to testimony—but rather a risk that their attempt to speak fails to give a voice to its reserve/object. Second, the discourse (and not just the conviction) of the hearer is to be transformed so that the call of this object is actually heard. This transformation of discourse is at the same time the formation of a discourse in which the object of testimony can speak or can be articulated. The difference between Foucault's analysis of *parrēsia* and our account of testimony is thus in the first place a difference between, on the one hand, an analysis that is concerned with the subject-function of veridiction and the different aspects of the subjectification involved and, on the other hand, an analysis for which in the first place the relation of being and language is at stake and in which, therefore, the problem of *the curse of language* has to be taken into account as well.

These considerations amount to the following. Whereas the categories of risk and courage of which Foucault speaks are well equipped to address one specific element of the relation of language and action that plays a fundamental role for the subject of both veridiction and testimony—as I discuss in the next chapter—they are not suitable for addressing the problem of the relation and the encounter of being and language that is posed by testimony. To some extent, this is a somewhat unexpected result. First, it shows that Agamben's attempt to rethink Foucault's veridiction in light of the oath cannot do justice to the oath's being exposed co-orginarily to the blessing and the curse of language. Second, in terms of Foucault's own analysis, one might have expected a closer proximity of *parrēsia* to that of testimony because Foucault adopts the terminology of testimony at crucial stages—especially in his analysis of the Cynics. The basic context in which Foucault raises the question of *parrēsia* in ancient thought and culture is that of the relation between truth and subject: the subject is not "ready" to receive the truth, but needs to be made ready to be able to receive the truth. In this vague sense, the question of *parrēsia* seems almost the same as that of testimony: how to prepare the hearer for the truth for which they are not yet ready? Yet in Foucault's work, this "making ready" is integrated in a whole set of techniques and technologies by which the self works on itself (or is worked on by masters who have reached a higher level of self-transformation). In this way, the realm of preparation is fully thought in terms of a process of subjectification, that is, in terms of a whole machinery of (self-)governance. What Foucault seems to miss in this insistence on these works, techniques, and governance is that these in ancient thought are only *preparatory*. Ultimately, the chance of an encounter with truth depends on a moment of desubjectification, on a moment of the ungovernable. In fact, this desubjectification is the very *completion* of the preceding, preparatory process of subjectification; this desubjectification *authorizes* the process of subjectification because in it, the truth that is other than what can be governed is encountered. Although I briefly criticized Derrida earlier in this study for remaining too close to a certain mystic paradigm of negative theology, there is one aspect of this paradigm that is crucial, namely that the *work* of language, in the insistent mystic *apophasis*, is a work for something that is not governed by the work or the techniques of language, something that is not effectuated by this activity but that simply needs to *happen* as a chance encounter, in an ultimate *suspension* of these techniques. In this event, the mystic subject who utters its apophatic formulas comes to a silence and is taken up in what, in these terms, can only be called desubjectification, taken up in something that is ungovernable.[44] The witness now does the exact opposite of the mystic, because the witness *speaks*. Yet what the witness retains from the mystic is the importance of contraction: in what the witness says of the object of testimony, the voice and demand of the reserve should also be perceived. In this sense, testimony requires that this formless reserve, which is ungovernable because it cannot be approached by any formation process, comes to language. In chapter 10, this was called "desubjectification" to indicate that this process is not so much about the subject coming into its own form by techniques and technologies that subjectify it, but rather about a subject of speech that can, *perhaps*, allow to speak the (silent) voice of misery. This other voice and this "perhaps" are not governable. The ambiguity of testimonial announcement, which guided the course of this chapter, thus complicates the unproblematized sense of truth in the parresiast practice of speaking for the truth. Finally, in this comparison between testimony and veridiction, another theme entered our reflections that goes beyond the theme of this chapter because it brings the engagement of the witness in testimony into play. The next chapter is devoted to this topic.

Chapter 13

Subject and Commitment

Martyr of the truth understood as "witness to truth."[1]

—Foucault, *Le courage de la vérité*, 160/173

the survivor lets the other speak inside himself.[2]

—Derrida, *Béliers*, 20/139

By the particular focus on how the announcement of testimony relates being and language, the previous chapter had to sidetrack the other basic relation that is part and parcel of the vow of testimonial language, namely the relation between language and action. This second relation concerns the fidelity of the witness to their word(s) and the engagement of the witness in their own testimony. To address the witness's fidelity and engagement, we need to return to the typology of the witness in which I distinguished the witness as the third or *testis*, the witness as the survivor (*superstes*), and the witness as the one who testifies with their lives to their conviction, to which I refer as the martyr because this is one of the senses of *martus* or *marturos* in the ancient world. Especially a reflection on the last two—survivor and the martyr—guides us to substantially different models to think the commitment of the witness. Therefore, I first examine these two models and, finally, question how the commitment of the witness as the third relates to these two models. Because the questions that guide this chapter were first raised in the discussion of Foucault and Agamben's account of oath and veridiction, it is only natural to start with the model of fidelity and engagement that their work offers.

Conversion and the Witness to the Truth

To indicate the impact of ancient Cynicism on certain forms of ancient Christianity, Foucault refers to the term *marturōn tes alētheias*, witness to the truth, in the vocabulary of Gregory of Nazianzus, the bishop of Constantinople.[3] Despite my own attempts to show not only the similarities but also the difference between *parrēsia* and testimony, Foucault's analysis of *parrēsia* culminates in a particular sense of testimony, inspired by the Cynic form of *parrēsia*. Because Foucault is mainly interested in the mode of subjectification at stake in it, he interrogates this version of testimony mainly in terms of the type of witness it presupposes, namely the witness to the truth. The *marturōn tes alētheias* is not so much concerned with speaking the truth, the whole truth and nothing but the truth, but rather extends bearing witness to their existence as a whole. The *marturōn tes alētheias* does not simply speak the truth but rather *lives* the truth. Thus, for Foucault, the figure of this witness is concerned with a particular *form of life*, which is the full and real testimony to the truth. The life of such a witness should be a complete serving this truth. The notion of truth in the expression *marturōn tes alētheias* thus stands for a conviction to which one can devote one's entire existence. (This conviction overflows the epistemic realm into the ethical because it is not merely a *doxa*, but a form of life that demands to be lived.) Consequently, in the martyr, language and action are united in a complete unity. The witness's commitment to their testimony and conviction—*Zeugnis* and *Überzeugung*—is seen in their mode of life; the martyr aims to establish "a relationship between forms of existence and manifestation of the truth."[4]

Foucault's analyses of Cynic *parrēsia*, and the particular sense of the witness as martyr they arrive at, are interesting for two reasons. First, they resonate with a motive that not only appears in ancient thought, but also can be traced, for instance, in Kierkegaard's insistence on the figure of the witness to the truth in his last struggle with the Danish church and, more recently, in Badiou's attention to a form of subjectivity that shares all the characteristics of this martyr.[5] For Badiou, it is in fact Paul, the apostle, who is one of the founders of this sense of subjectivity. Hence, both Badiou and Foucault refer back to the importance of a particular development in Hellenistic thought.[6] Second, and more generally, when discussing Cynicism, Foucault makes it perfectly clear that his basic interest in the question of *parrēsia* is ultimately to be found in ancient philosophy's self-understanding as a project that is not solely concerned with knowledge but first and foremost with attaining a certain mode of life in which the truth is expressed that guides *philosophy's* quest. Philosophy itself is in this sense a practice in which the philosopher attests to the truth with their life. Philosophy *is* bearing witness and *is* attestation. Exactly this basic characteristic of ancient philosophy has "worn out" today.[7] Thus, testimony in the sense of the cynic *parrēsia* is not a sub-question for philosophy or a sub-discipline of social epistemology, but rather *is* the basic question of philosophy: "The philosophical life is a manifestation of the truth. It is a testimony. Through the type of life one leads, the set of choices one makes, the things one renounces and those one accepts, how one dresses, and how one speaks, et cetera, the philosophical life should be from start to finish the manifestation of this truth."[8] For Foucault, as I noted in the previous chapter, the paradigm of the parresiast is found in the one who puts one's life at risk by standing up to a tyrant to tell them the truth. Yet this risk is not the *telos* of *parrēsia*. In this particular example, the goal of veridiction is to form the tyrant or prince it addresses. Hence, veridiction is a mode of speech that aims to subjectify the addressee. This capacity of *parrēsia* marks veridiction as a "technique" to govern and form subjects so that they adopt a mode of life by which they express the truth.[9] In more emphatic terms, this governance aims at a conversion or transformation of the self: it is only by a conversion that the soul, initially incapable of the truth, becomes capable of it and becomes capable of living it.[10] Thus, Foucault's analysis shows not only that (efficacious) testimony leads to a transformation of discourse, but also that this transformation implies a particular subjectification on the side of the hearer. This connection between what testimony gives to understand and the existential effect on the hearer is already at stake in Heidegger's account of attestation, but Foucault shows how this connection is not limited to a secretive self-communication of Dasein, but can also be accounted for in terms of the mode of speech of veridiction as testimony.

Yet we should add that in Foucault the question of the truth itself is not thematized, as if one can analyze the speaking of the truth while not analyzing truth.[11] Heidegger's analysis, by contrast, departs from the bare "that" of existence that shows the necessity or the demand—as in Agamben's *esigenza*—to attest and to testify. Although Foucault argues that already in (Plato's) Socrates the question of self-knowledge is part and parcel of the more primordial concern for self-care, he does not seem to see that this concern itself is driven by an existential distress, as I analyzed before, not to become a ludicrous spectacle and to understand where the human belongs in the ambiguity of *Typhon*, the animal with its many inarticulate voices, and *logos*, the meaningful voice. This distress motivates any subsequent attention for governance and care but cannot be reduced to or grounded on it. To speak of "truth" in Foucault's formal, presuppositional sense suspends this basic distress that motivates and demands testimony.

Nevertheless, Foucault does show us the importance of the identity of language and action. As Aristotle already noted in his reflection on rhetoric, the persuasiveness of any speech depends, among other things, on the *pistos*, the trustworthiness of the speaker. This *pistos* increases when the *ēthos* of the parresiast itself is in accordance with the *ēthos* they proclaim. The *identity of speech and action* must be visible in the parresiast for their speech to be effective as a technique to form and govern the other's mode of existence. Thus, also on the side of the subject of testimony, there is a specific process of subjectification. As Foucault notes, the parresiast is bound to what they state as the truth: "*Parrēsia* [. . .] [includes] the statement of the truth, and then, on top of this statement, an implicit element that could be called the parrhesiastic pact of the subject with himself, by which he binds himself both to the content of the statement and to the act of making it."[12] All witnesses bind themselves by the act of speech to the truth of what they say. However, because in the context of *parrēsia* this truth concerns in the first place a conviction and a form of life, the parresiast is bound in a particular way to what they say. Their own mode of existence should be in accordance with the bare truth of existence. Because this bare truth of existence itself goes beyond Foucault's specific interest, his account of this form of testimony or veridiction indeed gets a profound ethopoietical twist: not the relation between language and being—which is the question of ontology and truth—but the question of the relation of language and life is his sole concern. It seems to me that this is not only a methodological choice of limiting oneself to one specific field of research—for instance, governance and processes of subjectification—but it also has an impact on the analysis of this mode of speech. Unlike that which the examples of Heidegger, Lyotard, and (a certain) Agamben suggest, the demand of veridiction for a particular *ethos* does not correspond to a certain incapacity or im-potentiality. Although Cynicism is dealing with the bare truth of existence, this truth somehow *grants* the power to transform the subject in the first place. In this sense, this truth is not so bare or formless but in fact rather powerful and capable of prescribing and imposing a form. This ultimately means that Foucault's account of ancient thought ends up following a rather familiar model, namely that of *technē* and *poiēsis*: the presupposed truth or conviction is the very idea or form that prescribes the form that the human life should adopt—by techniques and technologies such as *parrēsia*—if it wants to live philosophically.[13] Consequently, the witness is in the first place the one who embodies the truth, in the sense that their body exemplifies and empowers the truth. Because of this, the question of testimony still involves a mode of speech but no longer finds its goal therein. This almost bodily identification of truth and the witness's mode of existence is not innocent. In fact, if we conceived of it from the perspective of Heidegger's and Lyotard's account of human misery and the bare "that" of existence, we would find an altogether different bareness of existence: their account of this bareness *prohibits* any embodiment because the embodiment of this bareness would rob the human of their capacity to speak and to bear witness. This is one of the main bifurcation points in the present-day debate on the witness and their commitment to their testimony: does this commitment culminate in embodiment or does it rather prohibit this?

In order to further develop and illustrate this insight, let me point out three elements that characterize the type of witness who appears in Foucault's analysis of the *marturōn tes alētheias*.

To Live an Other Life

First, the Cynics insist that the true life is "other than the life led by men in general"; thus, they radicalize the idea that marks the ancient philosophical attention to a *philosophical* life as "an *other* life (*vie autre*)."[14] The theme of this other life, as Foucault suggests, should be distinguished from the idea of an other, higher world.[15] This is an important distinction because it shows how the critique of Plato's dualism and its reverberations in the present-day analysis of the onto-theological constitution of philosophy and metaphysics tend to overlook the importance of another "otherness" than that of the other world, namely that of the other way of living. The attention to this theme also explains why, after Nietzsche's devastating critique of Paul's Christianity, philosophers such as Agamben and Badiou reread Paul's letters as texts of which the basic concern is that of an other life. Even the idea of the resurrection and a life after death is interpreted by these readers in light of Paul's claim that the believers have resurrected with Christ, that is, the resurrection does not concern an imaginary other world, but rather a fundamentally other mode of living.[16]

Militantism

Second, this other mode of life resembles that of "revolutionary militantism," as Foucault suggests. This mode of living insists in each of its actions on the necessity "to break with the conventions, habits, and values of society."[17] In this register, one could easily inscribe Badiou's conception of the subject, which is also emphasized in his reading of Paul's letters.[18] For Badiou, the truth to which the subject bears witness results from the event. This truth is by definition what breaks with the common order in a given situation. From within the order of such a situation, the event cannot but appear as a miracle, and humans become subjects only if they proclaim that this miracle indeed has taken place and if they subsequently live their lives in pure fidelity to this event. For Badiou, fidelity means to embody the truth of this event in one's actions. If one wants to object to Badiou's concept of the event that it leads to yet another version of Plato's dualism, one should keep in mind Foucault's distinction and the basic Pauline dimension of Badiou's thought: the event is not a concept to describe another world, but simply the most minimal ontological machinery that is needed to think the possibility of what Foucault terms *une vie autre*, that is, a mode of life that expresses and embodies a truth.

If we combine the analyses of the other life and militantism, we find what defines a proper *conversion*. The convert changes their basic mode of existence and bases the rest of their existence on this transformation. In this model of the martyr, to bear witness is in the first place to live every aspect of one's life in light of this conversion. This conversion is never simply complete(d) and continues to require the work and the techniques that render one ready to express the truth. Badiou captures the same idea when he suggests that the subject is a Two. The first, old mode of existing according to the rules and norms of the situation to which one belongs is basically the matter that needs to be transformed so that the new mode of existence appears as the rupture with the old one.[19] The life of the convert is thus not simply transformed, but is lived as continuous transformation: although everything begins with a conversion—or, as Badiou would argue, the event—this beginning requires the continuous ethopoiesis of subject and world, and this is the process of living the truth. Hence, for both Badiou and Foucault, the reserve/object of testimony cannot properly exist in the linguistic form of testimony, but requires an expression in one's mode of life, that is, requires the embodiment of the truth.

By this specific emphasis, the phenomenon of testimony changes in nature. The importance of embodiment and fidelity to the truth become the central features of the martyr. The martyr's speech is of secondary importance. Whereas I have always insisted that, in a privileged sense, testimony concerns the articulation of what cannot be articulated in a particular discourse or horizon of understanding, the model of the martyr can even render speech redundant. Although this might not be immediately visible in Diogenes of Sinope, who spoke, or in the Badiouan subject, who declared and named, we encountered one genuine witness to the truth who remained silent, namely Kierkegaard's Abraham, whose way of living his faith has all the characteristics of the martyr. To bear witness by remaining silent is the heightened sense of the form of testimony to which Foucault and Badiou point. Although the Badiouan subject seems to speak—they name and declare—this speech is not a form of communication because it is only comprehensible to those who live the same other life and who are faithful to the same event; because the tongue of the Badiouan subject is overtaken by the event, for those who do not affirm the event, the Badiouan subject speaks in tongues. In this sense, Badiou's subject is a clearly secularized version of Kierkegaard's Abraham, but what Badiou lacks is a poet such as Johannes de Silentio, who does speak and aims to communicate on the threshold of the witness who cannot speak but only believes and an audience that can speak but cannot believe.

In the previous chapter, I introduced the notions of *pistis* and *pistos* to capture the basic sense of the witness's oath. In the case of the Cynic or Pauline *parrēsia*, however, the meaning of these terms has changed: in this case, to be sworn to the truth means to live it. This, however, has a strange consequence because it seems to place certain constraints on the truth: truth should be something that can be lived and embodied and that can only be done justice by being lived and embodied. The witness bears witness by a particular form of life, with its own habits, clothes, speech, attitudes, and so on. Yet if we compare this, once more, to the privileged object to which Heidegger's account of attestation guided us, to a certain nakedness and misery in human life, we may safely say that there is no form of life thinkable that can express this: there are no habits, practices, and so on that express this misery. Forms, rather, keep this misery at bay. Perhaps this refers to a basic difference between Abraham and Bartleby: whereas Abraham offers a form of life that inspires many, Bartleby only offers the slowly but surely occurring de-formation of all forms of life.

The Scandal of the Truth

In *Le courage de la vérité*, Foucault notes that the form of life developed by the Cynics and their (Christian) heirs such as the Franciscans offers the spectacle of a *skandalon*, a stumbling block and an offense for their environment because it shows existence in its bare truth.[20] Or, as Foucault also explains this scandal, Cynicism has discovered a tension between what people accept as true "at the level of principles," that is, at the level of their theoretical insights and understanding of the world, and how they actually live their lives, in which they do not express the very principles according to which they understand the world.[21] In this sense, the Cynics confront the others with the truth that they live under a false pretense. The tension between thought and life is thus the very condition of possibility of the Cynic scandal. What is interesting about this analogy between testimony in general and one's mode of living is that it shows a particular supposition of human existence. Apparently, humans are somehow bound or expected to be bound by an existential oath that pledges that their understanding or *logos* of the world is in accordance with their actual *ēthos* and *praxis*. The Cynic mode of life proves this presupposition to be reasonable. Others are offended by them because they are reminded of their incapacity to keep this existential oath. Conversion, both in the Pauline and Cynic case, is thus the transformation of one's existence so that it becomes possible to keep the existential oath to act and live in accordance with one's thought.[22]

Consequently, this notion of conversion basically concerns human fidelity and trustworthiness. Are humans capable of being trustworthy, that is, of living in accordance to their *logos* and, thus, of overcoming what seems to be a fundamental human weakness and incapacity? Those who side with the Cynics or with Paul must respond affirmatively to this question; otherwise the reference to a conversion to another mode of living, to living the truth in one's life, loses its sense. They thus presuppose that there is a natural state, as Diogenes of Sinope claims, or a redeemed state, as Paul suggests, in which the human is marked by a particular natural power and sovereignty to act in accordance with one's thinking.[23] It seems to me that this sense of a conversion that allows the human life to adopt a form that is powerful and sovereign to act in accordance to the *logos* is, in Agamben's terminology, a fundamentally messianic notion.[24] Although terms such as weakness, destitution, poverty, bareness of existence, and misery are used to describe this mode of existence that deserves the name of the true life in ancient culture, these terms *only* capture this mode of existence from the perspective of the common mode of life. The famous passage from 1 *Corinthians* 1:18–31, which plays a crucial role in Badiou's *Saint Paul*, strikingly demonstrates this when Paul describes his teaching and his existence in terms of foolishness, stumbling block (*skandalon*), weakness, being low born and despised, things which are not: each of these terms describes the perspective from the common order and the worldly mode of existence.[25] Yet, by a messianic operation, God transforms all of these terms into what is truly wise and powerful. In its own terms, Cynicism follows the same type of conversion, according to Foucault: weakness, destitution, and misery turn out to be the actual and even natural sovereignty and power of human existence.

For these reasons, it seems to me that the figure of witness as martyr that appears in Foucault, Badiou, and (a certain) Agamben is overtaken by a particular messianic, redemptive dimension, suggesting that human existence can be transformed into true existence. Ultimately, because of these redemptive overtones, these authors are not capable of truly thinking the more tragically attuned account of the misery of human existence discerned in other chapters of this study. This misery tends to disappear from sight in these authors because they take it up in a messianic and ethopoietical process of salvation that offers the way to a true and proper human existence—immortal and infinite, as Badiou boldly suggests.

Thus, in the model of the martyr, the ultimate task of testimony to invent new idioms in the discourse of the hearer so that the unspeakable can be said, is displaced in favor of the ethopoietical invention of a form of life that embodies the truth. Yet if the genuine problem of the correspondence between *logos* and life is placed on the side of life, the problem of *logos* is assumed to be solved—and, thus, the testimony of the martyr is no longer concerned with the problem of the *sayability* of its object, but rather with obtaining a true *ethos* and *form of life*. There, perhaps, lies the genuine difference between the Socratic irony and the Cynic scandal. In the Socratic irony, *logos* cannot redeem itself from its weakness and is therefore always humbled and called to testimony. In the Cynic scandal, by contrast, the Cynic mode of life has embraced the *hubris* and the phantasm that human existence is capable of expressing the truth.[26] This short-circuits not only the problem of articulation at the heart of testimony, but also the tragic misery of human existence as such.

The Desubjectification of the Survivor

When shifting our attention from the Greek *martus* to the Latin *superstes*, we change our attention from the witness who offers their own existence as proof to the witness for whom existence has turned into survival—or, in Derrida's vocabulary, *survivance*, survival and remainder.[27] To get a primary sense of the difference between these two models of the witness's commitment, let me contrast the *superstes* to Badiou's conception of the subject. The *superstes* is the one who survives an event that deprived (many) others of their existence. Badiou's subject is also preceded by an event. Yet there is a striking difference. The survivor is the one who confronts loss; the loss of their previous life before the event that shook their existence to the core and deprived them of so many; the survivor feels the burden to bear witness to this loss and to bear witness for those who cannot speak themselves. The Badiouan subject, however, is the subject who arises after an event and is constituted in and by a conversion. For the convert, the previous life is not a lost life, but rather one that has been overcome and that is resurrected to a new life, as Badiou repeats Paul. By contrast, the life of the survivor is not marked by an affirmation of the event that turned it into that of a survivor. In this sense, there is a certain primacy of negation and loss, which is subsequently taken up in testimony: it is a lost object that is borne witness to. To be a remainder is exactly this: to be, but only by the grace and in relation to what is not (or what is no longer).

Derrida's *Demeure* offers a remarkable account of the structure of survival in his reading of Blanchot's short story *L'instant de ma mort*. The narrator in this story tries to capture what it means for a young man to be put in front of firing squad and to be saved at the last second before being killed. What does it mean to experience such a traumatic event, and how can we speak about it? The young man, as the story suggests, experienced the moment of his own death, which he nevertheless survived. When the story unfolds, it becomes clear that, although the narrator and the young man first seem to be different people, they are in fact one and the same person. Yet the narrator is separated from his younger self by this traumatic event in which, according to the story, the young man died and the narrator survived. Hence, this traumatic event is a rupture in the self-identity of this man. The narrator is a witness of this traumatic event, but at the same time does not have access to the experiences he had when he was this young man experiencing his own death. In this precise sense, the traumatic event doubles the man in, on the hand, the survivor who tells the story and tries to make sense of what the young man must have experienced and, on the other hand, the young man as the true witness who experienced something that he, however, cannot narrate anymore because he died or was fundamentally transformed in this event.[28]

To capture this complicated structure, Blanchot also doubles the *I* in the story.[29] This doubling and its impact on the testimony is exemplified by the interplay of knowledge and doubt and of life and death. The narrator begins his testimony by saying: "I remember a young man."[30] The trustworthiness of this memory is affirmed every time the narrator says "I know" when describing the experiences of the young man and the impact the event had on him. However, this "I know," which occurs at least twice in the story, is immediately doubled and thereby withdrawn. The first time, it is echoed in the question "Do I know it?" The second time, it is doubled by "I imagine."[31] By this doubling, memory and knowledge become indistinguishable from imagination and doubt.

The key word with which Blanchot relates to this epistemic doubling is *peut-être*, perhaps, which he uses five times in a short story of fewer than five pages. It is crucial to note that the *perhaps* and the uncertainty it expresses are not simply due to an epistemic uncertainty or finitude. In the previous chapter, I briefly discussed the ambiguity of the testimony's announcement in terms of this perhaps. Here, I want to explore the meaning of the "perhaps" for the witness and their commitment. In this story, this epistemic doubling is rooted in an ontological doubling of voices.[32] There are two voices. The first one says: "I am alive." The second immediately responds with: "No, you are dead." Hence, like the convert, the survivor relates to both life and death, but in the case of the survivor, their mode of existence is characterized as both life and death, as both being and non-being. Therefore, their mode of being is that of a third excluded from the opposition between being and non-being, which is nothing other than "what can, perhaps, be," the *peut-être*.[33] The martyr-convert cannot live the "perhaps"; they live the truth of their conviction and emphasize how certain they are of it by dedicating their complete life to the truths or the gods they serve. The survivor, however, lives the mode of uncertainty, of the perhaps, which is introduced by the traumatic event, which bifurcates life into death and life, into a survival in which life and death are both, at the same time, valid.

The narrator-witness in Blanchot's story bears witness but does not simply speak the truth, the whole truth, and nothing but the truth, as a witness is supposed to in a court of law and as, in a completely different setting, the witness as a martyr does by their form of life. The *perhaps* that Blanchot uses to qualify the narrator's testimony is nothing less than an *epochē* of this truth, as Derrida rightly notes: "and in both cases a principle of uncertainty, a *perhaps* that modalizes, 'epochalizes,' and suspends all assertions of the narrator-witness. He never affirms anything, never commits himself to any assertion."[34] The reason for this suspension is clear. Every time the narrator-witness bears witness to what the young man experienced in this traumatic event, he feels compelled to add the doubt of whether he actually knows it and whether it is not merely a figment of his imagination. Moreover, because the experiences of the young man are at stake in this testimony, of whom the narrator-witness is that which remains, the term "perhaps" marks the mode of being of the reserve/object of testimony: the young man is *and* is not the narrator-witness.

Blanchot's story is thus a self-attestation in which the young man's experience of the event is the reserve/object, and it is narrated by the one who is truly the only one who can say something about it, namely the man himself, at an older age. It is therefore the reserve/object itself which does not have its very own truth, but only its *peut-être*, its "what can, perhaps, be." This mode of being is not simply kept secret due to a contamination of testimony and fiction. Rather, this mode of being is the only one that *preserves* what Agamben calls the unforgotten, that which is not even remembered by the survivor himself. If we take the story's suggestion seriously that this event deserves to be called a death of the young man before actually dying, it indeed concerns something to which the survivor never had any (full) access: if something truly died in the young man, there is no experience of this; the only experience one has is thus that of something to which one has no access and of which one cannot testify. The true stakes therefore are indeed the attempt of the survivor to attest to an absence of attestation, to something that one does not remember because one did not experience it oneself.[35]

To characterize this doubling of young man and narrator, Derrida describes the narrator as a witness *for* the witness: "he testifies *for* a witness, in a different sense this time, *in the place* of the witness he cannot be *for* this other witness that the young man was, and who is yet himself."[36] The narrator is a supplementary witness. The narrator-witness testifies in the place of the true witness he himself cannot be and whom only the young man could have been had he not died (partially). This means that the structure of testimony and the figure of the witness at stake in the *superstes* or survivor are intrinsically connected to that of the *auctor* as discussed in chapter 10. The survivor completes the experience of the real witness, the young man, who cannot speak. When we use the verb "to complete" in this context, it should be clear by now that the completed testimony does not say everything (or the whole truth). To complete is rather to bear witness for the one who cannot bear witness. Although the latter is the one who fully experienced what happened, this experience is of such a nature that it rendered them speechless. To complete such a "witness" thus also means to attest to the absence of attestation marked by the incapacity of the young man to speak for himself.

In the analysis of the witness to the truth, it became clear that this type of witness is fully marked by subjectification: this witness arises in the process of governance guiding them to the *other*, true mode of life. In the case of the *superstes* and the narrator-witness from *L'instant de ma mort*, a different picture arises. Much in line with the analyses from chapter 10, the subjectification of the survivor is co-originary with a desubjectification because the survivor can only be a witness when they are also a witness for the "real witness"—for example, for the young man in Blanchot's story. Only if the survivor can lend their voice to "this other witness," the one who fully experienced the traumatic event, does bearing witness take place.[37] What is at stake in the testimony of the survivor is not only the articulation of their own experiences, but also the giving of a voice to the mute experiences of those who are no longer there. The young man represents the silent, inarticulate voice, whereas the narrator-witness represents the one who speaks on behalf of the young man and who attests by narrating but who also, for instance by interjecting his "perhaps," attests to an absence of attestation. The narrator-witness speaks for the young man as Socrates speaks for Protagoras in the *Theaetetus*, but the narrator-witness also interjects a *perhaps* that represents a silent voice as Theodorus does in the *Theaetetus*.

There is a striking passage in Agamben's *Quel che resta di Auschwitz* that unfolds a similar structure. For him, the *superstes* is an *auctor*, and the *auctor* is not the one who simply tells everything, tells each and every experience. To tell everything, to tell the whole truth, as we already indicated in a discussion of Lyotard, would require an absolute witness. The completion to which the notion of *auctor* refers must therefore be interpreted in a different way. Let us consider the passage from Primo Levi's *The Drowned and the Saved*, which Agamben quotes *in extenso*. In this passage, Levi refers to a similar doubling at the heart of testimony. On the one hand, he distinguishes the "true witnesses," the ones who experienced everything fully and, on the other hand, people like himself who survived and who were the exception. "[These survivors] tried [. . .] to recount not only our fate but also that of the others, indeed of the drowned; but this was a discourse 'on behalf of third parties,' the story of things seen at close hand, not experienced personally."[38] Interestingly enough, Levi uses almost the same image to describe the *Muselmänner* as the one Blanchot uses to describe the young man who died before his actual death. The "drowned would not have testified because their death had begun before that of their body." The witness as survivor does not only speak on their own account, but also for those who were lost in the event of which they testify. By this doubling of testimony, in a "true witness" and a narrator-witness—or "pseudo-witness," as Agamben proposes to call them—the narrator-witness becomes the intermediate who speaks on behalf of a third party to the hearer of testimony. This means that testimony is in itself divided because it appeals to an experience to which the speaker has no access but which the speaker completes, in the precise sense that they bear witness to it. Agamben comments: "The survivors speak in their stead, by proxy, as pseudo-witnesses; they bear witness to a missing testimony. And yet to speak here of a proxy makes no sense; the drowned have nothing to say, nor do they have instructions or memories to be transmitted."[39] The formulation "to bear witness to a missing testimony" mirrors Blanchot's idea of attesting to the absence of attestation. In fact, as the sentences that follow explain, one should take this absence seriously. It is not a linguistic incapacity, as if the true witness does have something to say or some memory to transmit, but only lacks the capacity to do so. Rather, it is a genuine absence. The real witnesses have nothing to communicate; they have no "instructions or memories" that they want the survivors to disclose in their testimonies. We are dealing here with the category of the unforgettable, with the "ontological squandering" of an experience that is so devastating that it does not leave any space for memories. This does not mean that the narrator-witness does not have anything to tell—in this sense, Agamben's account is one-sided. Rather, the survivor attests to what happened and to the absence of attestation. Both voices—the one that speaks and the one that keeps silent—speak in the survivor's testimony. To complete is thus, in one particular sense, to render incomplete, to bear witness to what cannot be said in this testimony: to complete is *both* to speak and to lend a voice to what cannot speak *and* to keep silent and attest to an absence of attestation.[40]

Derrida rightly notes that to capture the problem of testimony, it is not necessary to turn to the testimonies of Auschwitz, as Lyotard and Agamben do.[41] However, Agamben's reading in *Quel che resta di Auschwitz* does make one thing clear. Derrida's insistence on the possibility of perjury to account for how testimony can never tell the whole story tends to obscure the fundamental role played by the absence of attestation. What is at stake in testimony is not simply the absence of the attestation that it might be false as a linguistic act: the *perhaps* that is kept silent before the law is not simply the *perhaps* of the act of testimony—that is, the fact that it has to be believed but for that very reason can also be doubted—but rather pertains to the reserve/object, to that which the testimony bears witness to and to which it is committed. By the incompleteness of testimony, it preserves the absent attestation in its absence, in addition to what it tells. It thus shows that the witness of testimony is not simply the one who speaks, but is also concerned with the desubjectification of the one who speaks so that the speaker's voice can become a voice *for, in place of* another voice so that the latter may be heard in its silence and absence. This is uncanny, but it is not something mysterious. The silent voice *is* the absent attestation; it marks the void left behind by those who could speak but can no longer, who had something to say but say no more, who had an articulate voice but were rendered mute. In this sense, as Derrida writes, "the survivor lets the other speak inside himself."[42]

The vow or promise at the heart of the survivor's testimony is thus different from that of convert and martyr. Yet this vow is still a vow concerning the relation of language and action. It is no longer concerned with attaining a particular form of life, to mold one's existence in the shape or the form that one's understanding of this existence offers. If the survivor's task is to bear witness to what is lost, one cannot embody or live this. Commitment is thus fundamentally different and concerns first of all maintaining oneself on the threshold of *logos* and *alogos*. It means in the first place to adopt a form of speech that allows the formless to be attested to, albeit in its absence. While the martyr or convert is closed in on themselves and their truth, the survivor has no such option. While the martyr or convert is the new life that starts with attaining a new form of life, the survivor and their testimony is what remains of what is lost. The survivor's fidelity is thus to those third parties whose existence they cannot adopt or resurrect, but to which they can only bear witness. While the martyr or convert is concerned with embodying the truth they aim to live, such an embodiment is impossible for the survivor because for them embodiment would mean to die, to become mute, to turn into the ghostly existence of the *Muselmänner*.

Differently put, there is no testimony when the survivor would identify themselves with this bare existence as their form of life. Rather, the survivor's testimony thus presupposes, despite the proximity, a certain distance from and a non-identification with the bare life or naked existence in the reserve/object of their testimony. This ambiguity of proximity and distance from the "real" witness marks the survivor's commitment. In Kafka's striking image, if the "real" witness is the one who needs "both hands and more than they have for their battle with despair," the survivor is the one who "needs one hand to ward off a little their despair" so that the other one is free "to jot down what they see among the ruins." The commitment of the survivor-witness, the agreement between their language and their actions, may best be exemplified in this way: to keep one hand free, for as long as they can.

The Distance of the Third

The figure of the witness as the third—*testis* or *terstis*—imposes itself in two different ways. First, we encountered it in Levi's quote in which he describes his own testimony as "a discourse 'on behalf of third parties.'" The third parties here are the *Muselmänner* who are, for Levi, the true witnesses who, however, are not capable of bearing witness to their experiences. They are the third party with respect to the dialogical situation of the narrator-witness and the hearer. The third party here is nothing less than the reserve/object of testimony itself. To this reserve, the narrator-witness, in addition to all that they tell of the object, can only bear witness by directing the hearer's attention to the absence of an attestation. What marks the *Muselmann* as a third party—and in this sense, there is a fundamental difference between the poet, the prophet, and the glossolalist, who are inhabited by a divine force that speaks in them—is that they have nothing to convey. They did not communicate to the narrator-witness any instructions, forces, or memories that need to be told. In this sense, although the third party marks for the narrator-witness the full weight of the testimony, this third party is not engaged in the testimony. It does not even call; it is the narrator-witness who calls on their behalf and who calls the hearer toward the void of their absent voices.

Second, the theme of the third appears in Derrida's *Demeure*. There, Derrida seems to mirror Levi's reference to the third party and describes the narrator-witness as the third instead: "What is the third party to a secret? What is the place of the witness? Is the witness the one who takes part in a secret dual, or is the witness not already a third in the secret?"[43] Although Derrida does not mention Kierkegaard's *Fear and Trembling* in this context, this story might be helpful to capture in which sense the witness might indeed be seen as a third with respect to what Derrida calls a secret. In Kierkegaard's story, the secret is, in the first place, an intimate and singular encounter or relation between Abraham and God. *Mutatis mutandis*, we might say that in Blanchot's story, the secret concerns the singular relation of the young man with the event of his quasi-death. With respect to these two secrets, the narrator-witness is the one who somehow has "seen at close hand, not experienced personally." This means that the narrator-witness is indeed a third party to the event. The narrator-witness is engaged and marked by a close proximity in the sense of "seen at close hand" but has "not experienced personally," that is, does not *completely* share in the secret and the singular encounter that is at stake in their testimony. It is this distance from this secret, the fact that they are not fully engaged in it, that allows them to speak publicly.

Although Derrida and Levi use the term "the third" in different ways, they nevertheless use it to indicate a similar structure, namely how the survivor belongs to and is distant from the event they survived. In relation to the survivor, the place of the witness as the third is captured by the following question's undecidability: "Is the witness the one who takes part in a secret dual, or is the witness not already a third in the secret?" The witness as survivor is and should be thought as a double.

It is this sense of distance introduced by the figure of the third that is absent from the witness to the truth. There is no distance between the martyr and the secret in which they are engaged because it is the truth that is to be expressed by and in the martyr's own existence. This embodiment of the truth is the true testimony in the case of the witness to the truth. Therefore, the martyr is indeed engaged in a dual secret, as between Abraham and his God or between the Badiouan subject and the event to which they are faithful: in both cases, their lives express the truth to which they are committed, but it also means that in both cases there is no mediation possible with those who are not committed in the same way in the same secret. As I noted earlier in this chapter, there is a fundamental lack of communication between the Badiouan subject and those who reject their event, just as there is no communication between Kierkegaard's Abraham and those who insist on the ethics that universally condemns murder. In these cases, there is no general making manifest anymore—a communication only takes place between those who share in the same secret. Yet, in the case of Kierkegaard's Abraham, there is still a third, a poet admiring Abraham and repelled by Abraham, who takes it upon himself to stay at the threshold so that communication becomes, perhaps, possible. This is no longer a form of communication that is derived from a kind of general form of belonging to humankind and its *logos*; it is a form of communication that is demanded by the lack of communication. If the martyr and their existence is supposed to speak beyond the community of those who share in the secret, testimony and bearing witness only become possible when a third enters the scene, willing to address those who do not share in the secret.

This latter account of the role of the third with respect to the martyr allows us to reassess the relation of language and action. It seems a rather straightforward idea that the correspondence between word and act should ultimately consist in adopting a mode of life that is in agreement with what one considers to be true. Yet language is never owned; the word is never my own, my property. It is always shared. This means that adherence to a conviction, as an act, should also and in turn be brought into relation to a *logos* that surpasses the community of the initiated, of those who share in the secret. It is in need of a witness who offers an *apologia*, a defense, or simply an *apologos*, a story of the *ēthos* that is being shaped in the embodiment of this conviction. It seems to me that only with the introduction of the witness as the third that the witness may fulfill the specific testimonial oath, which is not to coincide with the reality to which the witness testifies but to be on his or her threshold, which is to announce a reserve/object rather than to live or unconditionally affirm it.

Chapter 14

In Lieu of a Conclusion

Celan's Poetics of Testimony

For what is there to do in this life but write for nothing?[1]
—Soucy, *La petite fille qui aimait trop les allumettes*, 174/133

It seems only natural for a study that took its point of departure in poetic orientations, to return, after the conceptual work is done, to poetics in order to affirm how, perhaps, the language of poets—of some poets—more than any other language can bear witness to human misery. In this last chapter, I turn to the work of Paul Celan because in certain instances of his poetry and his prose on poetry, one finds exemplified the sense of testimony I've aimed to put forward in this study. To show this, I discuss some elements of his rich work that resonate with my attempt to think bearing witness, with special attention to the figure of *Atemwende*, turn-of-breath, which is not only the title for one of his collections of poems but also a basic motive in his speech *Der Meridian* with which he accepted the Georg Büchner Price.

Perhaps, a Turn of Breath

Let me start with a hesitation. More than the literary examples I discussed in the first part of this study, Celan's poetry seems to speak in such a way of the reality to which it bears witness that, rather than articulating this reality, it renders language itself inarticulate. This is noted by several interpreters. As Gadamer for instance suggests: "In his later volumes of poetry, Paul Celan increasingly moved toward the breathless stillness of muted silence in words which have become cryptic."[2] His poetry apparently mimics muteness and stillness; it is as if it holds its breath. This reference to breath, which in his poetry goes hand in hand with a reference to wind and storm, shows how Celan inscribes the Hebrew *ruach* and the Greek *pneuma* in his poetry and how he refers with these words to the basic constituent of the (inarticulate) voice: how can we speak without breath?[3] Moreover, breath is concerned with a change, albeit in the most "quiet," "barely perceptible," and "subdued" way possible, namely the turning of one's breath, *Atemwende*.[4] One turns one's breath, perhaps, to begin to speak or to begin to use one's voice.

This subdued, muted speech can easily be interpreted as a form of obscurity. Celan himself notes in *Der Meridian* that one often reproaches poetry for being obscure. Primo Levi's and Agamben's comments on Celan are examples of this reproach, and I return to their comments below. Celan himself, however, adds that this obscurity concerns the very stakes of poetry. Poetry is allotted this obscurity for the sake of an encounter with what comes from afar and what is strange or alien. To speak of that with which we are not familiar thus may necessitate a certain obscurity in the language one uses. Moreover, Celan complicates this obscurity. The encounter to which poetry strives depends not only on the alien nature of what the poetic words hope to give way to, but also on a particular *doubling* of what is strange. As he writes in *Der Meridian*: "there are perhaps two kinds of strangeness."[5] This twofold nature of the strange is not a certainty.[6] Therefore, Celan uses the word *vielleicht*, "perhaps," which he repeats twenty-five times in his speech and which he increasingly uses when he approaches the figure of *Atemwende*. The encounter with the strange is, in the first place, an experience that leaves one without any breath. It confronts us with what robs us of "breath and speech," *den Atem und das Wort*. In this sense, Celan's account of poetry fits with the particular sense of a reality that lies beyond or before the human capacity to speak and is more related to the sense of mere *phōnē* than that of *logos*. Yet for Celan, even the voice is silenced in the encounter of which poetry wants to speak. It is an experience by which one's breath stops short, by which one is robbed not only of language but also of breath. The encounter thus appears in the first place as what incapacitates us; it is an experience that is accompanied by silence and muteness not because it confronts us with a secret or a mystery, but simply because it takes away the possibility to speak and to breathe. We are here, both historically and poetically, in the situation that Agamben has in mind when he speaks about the human as being capable of everything, as the one who can suffer beyond the limits that define their essence, their *logon echon*, rendering them *alogon*.

It is in the context of such an encounter and experience that the figure of the turn-of-breath is introduced: "Dichtung, das kann eine Atemwende bedeuten"; "[poetry]: that can signify a turn-of-breath." Although this sentence does not include the word *vielleicht*, it would be justified to include it. In fact, as if to compensate for forgetting to include in this particular sentence the careful "perhaps" that determines the rhythm of his speech, Celan doubles the uncertainty in the next sentence: "who knows, perhaps," poetry "travels its path [. . .] for the sake of such a breath turning?" Thus, poetry is what can, perhaps, be a turn of breath. The turn of breath is not the regular turning of our breath when we breathe normally. It is rather the interruption of the interruption of our breath. It is the breathing in of a new breath so that we, perhaps, can speak or at least make our voices be heard. It is in this exact sense that poetry is engaged in distinguishing the strange from the strange, that is, distinguishing the strange that merely robs the human of breath and speech *from* the strange that allows for a turn of breath and another poetic speech. It is in this sense, face to face with the misery in human existence, that a demand arises for another turn of breath and a poetic testimony. Let me quote in full how Celan describes this:

> Perhaps [poetry] succeeds since strangeness [*das Fremde*], that is, the abyss *and* the Medusa's head, the abyss [*Abgrund*] *and* the robots [*Automaten*], seem to lie in the same direction—perhaps it succeeds here in distinguishing between strangeness and strangeness [*Fremd und Fremd*], perhaps at precisely this point the Medusa's head shrivels, perhaps the robots cease to function—for this unique, fleeting moment? Is perhaps at this point, along with the I—with the estranged I, set free *at this point* and *in a similar manner*—is perhaps at this point an Other [*ein Anderes*] set free?

The direction of which Celan speaks in this quote, which is the direction where the strange and foreign come from, is the direction of what I have called the inhuman and the uncanny. In fact, Celan refers to this realm in similar terms when he writes: "Here we have stepped beyond human nature, gone outward, and entered a mysterious realm [*unheimlichen Bereich*], yet one turned toward that which is human."[7] In the imagery borrowed from Büchner, he adds that it is the task of poetry to distinguish between what petrifies us, that is, the Medusa's head and the robot, and another type of strangeness.

The Gorgon-Head

Let us first consider this remarkable figure of the Medusa's head and its ramifications in the context of my study. There is an important similarity and dissimilarity between Celan's reference to the Medusa's head and the very brief mentioning of Celan's work in *Quel che resta di Auschwitz*. Following Levi, Agamben suggests that Celan's poetry is obscure because it is comparable with the "inarticulate babble or the gasps of a dying man."[8] For Levi, and Agamben does not contradict him on this point, Celan's poetry offers "a dark and maimed language, precisely that of someone who is about to die and is alone." Therefore, Agamben refers to Celan in the same context in which he refers to Hurbinek and his non-language "*mass-klo, matisklo.*"[9] Agamben suggests that there is a parallel between the "secret word" of Hurbinek, which seems to have all the characteristics of a private language, that is, of a "non-language that one speaks when one is alone." Testimony, in turn, is assigned the task of giving way to this non-language. Hence, Agamben does give a role to Celan's poetry in the problematic of testimony, but he positions it on the side of what is to be borne witness to rather than as what bears witness; he interprets it as what is in need of an auctor, an additional narrator-witness articulating the gasping and gargling of the dying man.

It seems to me that Agamben does not do justice to the poetry of Celan and does not position it rightly in relation to the problem of testimony. The most direct way to see why Agamben's characterization is problematic is by considering what Celan says immediately after his introduction of the turn-of-breath and his hesitation and reservation to embrace this turn-of-breath as the reality or the certainty of poetry. Despite his hesitation, suddenly he exclaims: "But the poem does speak!"[10] This is not a stifled, bare voice or the inarticulate gargling of a dying man, but the insistence on a particular mode of speech. Poetry happens when human language in a confrontation with something that far exceeds its capacities to speak regains its breath and finds the means to say and to speak, perhaps. With Celan's poetry, we are in a similar situation here as the one portrayed by Mortier when he writes that faced with language's incapacity to confront the reality of war, either in the form of propaganda that simply lies or in the form of the incapacity of language to offer to human suffering the means to speak it. Thus, if there is a gasp in Celan's poetry—and I think there is—it is not simply that of a dying man, but rather that of someone, perhaps, who knows, and with a subdued hope, regains their breath and turns their breath to speech.

The figure of the Medusa's head allows us to explicate more clearly in which sense Agamben (or Levi) seems to miss a basic hope in Celan's poetry, in whatever subdued or hesitant way it may be formulated. Poetry "succeeds" when it is capable of distinguishing a form of strangeness that is not that of the Medusa's head. Poetry is for the sake of an encounter with what is strange. Yet the first figure that is to be encountered in this uncanny realm is Medusa, that is, a head that petrifies humans, that robs them of their speech and their breath. It is the same figure, but now in the form of its generic name of the Gorgon-head, that appears in Agamben's account of Levi—and it appears there for the same reason. To explain why the *Muselmänner* cannot speak, Levi describes them as those who have seen the Gorgon. They are the ones who have experienced fully the encounter with the strangeness, that is, the inhuman horror that marks the reality of the camps. For Agamben's Levi, the true or complete witnesses of this encounter with a reality that is as *gorgos*, horrific, as the Gorgon, are therefore those who are robbed of the capacity to speak of it.

Agamben first mentions this figure in the prelude of his account of both Hurbinek and Celan and the impossibility of testimony of which they are both in their own way an example.[11] Yet what Agamben misses at this point is that Celan's poetry does not simply speak of an encounter with the Gorgon. Poetry only begins where a turn of breath takes place and another strangeness is brought into play. I come back to the meaning of this other strangeness below, but it is important to see first that Celan's poetry does not conceive of itself as mimicking or enacting the encounter with the Gorgon. Quite the opposite.

Moreover, Agamben also seems to miss the basic meaning of the Gorgon in relation to the voice and to human speech. In his actual interpretation of the figure of the Gorgon, he focuses fully on the face (or the anti-face) of the Gorgon, and he offers a somewhat mystifying account of this face that cannot be seen and that, consequently, the *Muselmänner* saw something that cannot be seen.[12] Yet it seems to me that his interpretation does not take into account the specific features of the Gorgon-head. Its oldest depictions emphasize not so much the face as such but rather its wide-open mouth and its tongue hanging out. This portrayal suggests that this monster is not in the first place a sight to be feared. Its most striking features of mouth and tongue refer to the Gorgon's roar. In fact, it is suggested that etymologically Gorgon goes back to a root meaning "to gargle." The emphasis on the roar of the Gorgon seems to be confirmed by Pindar, who speaks of "the dismal death-dirge of the Gorgons bold," as Thalia Howe mentions.[13] The Gorgon's roar is a deep lamentation. In fact, Howe's description of the Gorgon-head makes it clear why especially the Gorgon is an important reference in the context of voice, language, and testimony: "It is clear that some terrible noise was the originating force behind the Gorgon: a guttural, animal-like howl that issued with a great wind from the throat and required a hugely distended mouth, while the tongue, powerless to give coherence, hung down to the jaw."[14] What inspires fear and makes humans who encounter the Gorgon choke and hold their breath and voice is not the sight of an unseeable face, but rather its terrible voice. Howe's striking portrayal of the tongue—hanging down "powerless to give coherence"—marks the inhuman and inarticulate nature of this voice. The tongue cannot turn or bend the flow of air and wind into speech, that is, into something comprehensible.

It might make sense to connect the Gorgon to the figure of the Typhon, the creature to which Socrates refers in the *Phaedrus*, as I discussed at the beginning of this study.[15] These figures may very well confront us with a terrible sight, but what is crucial is not their sight but their voice. Their inhumanity is in their terrible roar and their horrific voices, which are completely strange to the human. In this context, it becomes clear why Celan suggests that the task and the only possibility of poetry is a turn-of-breath that is capable of distinguishing the sheer sight of the Medusa's head and the roaring sound of the Gorgon, which renders humans utterly speechless and hands them over to an utter incapacity of speech, *from* another strangeness.

Poetic Testimony

From the previous discussion, it is clear that for Celan, poetic testimony finds itself called for in a situation that is marked by an encounter with a misery that renders the human speechless. This situation has a threefold poetic consequence for Celan: first, it has its effects on language; second, it calls for a distinction between strangeness and strangeness; and third, it aims at another encounter with this other strangeness. Let me discuss each of these elements to clarify in which sense poetic testimony is a struggle with language for the sake of reality.

Death-Bringing Discourse and Dreadful Silence

The catastrophe that the encounter with the Medusa's head portrays implies the death of language. With this latter death, I do not mean what this expression usually means, namely that this language is no longer spoken because of a historical process of decay. Rather, as Celan indicates in his short *Bremer Rede*, amid all that was lost, language "remained unlost," *blieb unverloren*.[16] This adjective "unlost" sounds like "undead," which perhaps is the best description of a survivor of such a catastrophe. Rather than being or feeling alive, the survivor remains as un-dead, as what or who did not die in this death-bringing event. Moreover, because language cannot be owned, this language that remains as unlost is also the language of the perpetrators who have left their traces on the language in which the poet speaks. Therefore, Celan describes this language as a "death-bringing discourse," *todbringende Rede*. The language and propaganda of the perpetrators was the call to destroy. At the same time, reminiscent of what we found in Mortier, this language is marked by a "dreadful falling silent," *furchtbares Verstummen*, because it is incapable of giving a voice to what is lost.[17] This means that the speechlessness and breathlessness to which the encounter with the Gorgon leads is not only that of the *Muselmänner* or of the victims, but renders language itself incapacitated to attest to this catastrophe and to bear witness for the victims. We encounter here the curse of language in its most uncanny form.

In his essay "Poétique et politique du témoignage," Derrida offers a reading of Celan's poetry centered on the phrase from the poem *Aschenglorie*: "Niemand // zeugt // für den Zeugen"; "no one // bears witness // for the witness."[18] This is a basic sentence in Celan's oeuvre because of its fundamental ambivalence. First, it captures exactly the situation in which language, as what remains unlost, finds itself. Where the victims, the true witnesses, cannot testify themselves, language is called on to offer possibilities for testimony. Yet no one bears witness for the true witness. Second, it captures this bankruptcy of language and testimony in terms of a reference to the absolute witness. Where it reads "no one," it used to read God or the gods, who were the guarantees of all our oaths and testimonies because they witnessed everything.[19] To call on the absolute witness when taking an oath is to call on an authority that can testify for us and for our testimony; yet this absolute authority or *auctor* is absent. Third, in absence of the gods, this phrase itself is a testimony. At this point I fully agree with Derrida, who writes: "For this poem says something about bearing witness. It bears witness to it."[20] Yet this is not a form of "meta-witnessing" as the condition of possibility and impossibility of an absolute witnessing, as Derrida goes on to suggest. Rather, it is itself a testimony to an *absence* of testimony, to an absence of the absolute witness. In my discussion of the oath in chapter 11, I already noted that at this point, Derrida once more, albeit fully on his own terms, invokes a reference to a God. Celan, on the other hand, does not do so. He mentions *Niemand*, no one. Because this, however, is itself an attestation to the absence of an absolute witness and even to the absence of an *auctor* who could complete the testimony of the true witness, as Agamben suggests, it is the most minimal and mute form a poetic testimony can adopt.[21] If anything, it shows both the death of language and how, despite this death, the catastrophe and those who died in it demand a testimony. We have already encountered, in our discussion of Blanchot, Derrida, and Agamben, the expression of attesting to the absence of attestation. This attestation is, in fact, the *inaugural* testimony because it does not simply keep the misery of existence silent but voices its demand to be borne witness to. Fourth, and this puts the previous comments upside down, the reference to the *Niemand* is at the same time an address. The erasure of the absolute witness makes place for, in Agamben's terminology, the true witness. In *Quel che resta di Auschwitz*, as discussed before, the *auctor* is the one who completes the testimony of the true witness. Yet this also implies that the narrator-witness of any actual testimony refers to the true witness who, however, cannot bear witness for the truth of what the narrator-witness testifies. In this sense, this phrase attests to the loss of the true witnesses, who have lost their identities and existence and who therefore have become no one and nothing, part of a vast "ontological squandering." It is in this sense that this phrase is also addressed *to* this *Niemand*. In the poem *Stehen, im Schatten*—standing, in the shadow—Celan writes: "Standing-for-nobody-and-nothing. // Unrecognized, // for you // alone"; "Für-niemand-und-nichts-Stehn. // Unerkannt, // für dich // allein."[22] This describes what the poem can, perhaps, be. It stands for no one and nothing, but this no one and nothing refers to the space that is kept free in the poem for the you. The poem stands in the place of the you, not to keep the you away, but to hold their place free, to address the you and reserve a space where the you can speak. In this sense, the poem is a placeholder that holds the place free for the you, the true witness. As Gadamer interprets *Stehen, im Schatten*: "Standing and standing firm means bearing witness to something," that is, to the you.[23]

With this last reference to both the shadow and the poem that gives a voice to the you and holds its place and space free in itself, I am running ahead to the two other elements that need to be discussed. Yet before doing so, let me return briefly to the beginning of this section. If indeed testimony is born from the incapacity of a language that remains unlost, the poet cannot simply start to speak. The first task is to tear down this dead language, which is dead in a very precise sense: it is incapable of engaging in an encounter with reality because it lies in its propaganda, and it is incapable to speak for what is lost. In his poem *In die Rillen*—into the grooves—from *Atemwende*, Celan attests to this dismantling so that a space opens up for the possibility of an encounter: "when with trembling fists // I dismantled the roof over us, // slate by slate, // syllable by syllable"; "als ich mit bebenden Fäusten // das Dach über uns // abtrug, Schiefer um Schiefer, // Silbe um Silbe."[24] In light of Heidegger's famous adage that language is the house of being, we see what the catastrophe has done to language. Language should give us and reality shelter and offer us and reality a meaningful and inhabitable place. This is the very meaning of onto-logy. The catastrophe, however, has made this house an inhabitable place from which any approachable reality has been banished. Differently put, the ones who still inhabit this language that remains unlost are exiled from any approachable and addressable reality. It has become a house that suffers from the abandonment of being, *Seinsverlassenheit*, to such an extent that one can no longer presuppose a voice of being because being and reality have become the sheer strangeness that robs humans from their speech and even their breath, that is, their principle of life. Language can no longer be trusted to attest to reality. It has turned into a prison that deprives one of language as what enables an encounter with reality and as what promises to respond to the demand of reality to be said and attested to. It is from this crisis, however, that this demand becomes a "necessity [*esigenza*] to speak."[25] From this demand, the poet's engagement with language is born, and it is for this very reason that the poetic engagement with language is not simply *poiēsis*, a making or creating in language, but a *poiēsis* motivated by an urgency and a demand of testimony, which language in its dreadful falling silent and its death-bringing discourse cannot fulfill or even perceive. Therefore, this *poiēsis* begins as a dismantling, as destruction or deconstruction of the prison of language that remains unlost.

The "Reserve of the 'Perhaps'"[26]

The poetic dismantling or deconstruction of language happens necessarily with linguistic means. Because of this, it is not a straightforward tearing down. Rather, this dismantling is taken up in the hope that there is a reserve of language on which the poet can draw and which up to now is withdrawn. Indeed, as Derrida notes, this uncertain and subdued hope is at stake in Celan's *perhaps*'s in *Der Meridian*. Yet this reserve does not simply mean that Celan does not dare to affirm the poetic experiment. Rather, the modalization of the perhaps goes into two directions. It concerns what language, despite everything, still preserves. Thus, the suspension of the sheer rejection of language opens up the possibility of a poetic drawing on its reserve. When Gadamer suggests that Celan's poetry is marked by such an "indescribable discretion" that it comes close to falling silent, one should be aware that this is not an empty stillness.[27] Its subdued speech, verging on muted silence—and the phrase "Niemand // zeugt // für den Zeugen" is one basic example of this—is a discrete speech that by holding itself back holds something in reserve, in the manner of someone holding his or her breath while waiting for the turning of breath to happen.

One could say that the crisis of language is due to a separation, or a boundary that cannot be passed, between the unspeakable catastrophe and the language that remains unlost. If we put it in this way, it becomes clear where we have to locate the reserve of the perhaps, namely on the threshold between the unlost language and the reality of which it cannot speak. If we follow Celan's suggestion in *Der Meridian* that the turn of breath of language is concerned with distinguishing between strangeness and strangeness, we might simply say that the perhaps is a modality that aims to separate out from this strangeness that incapacitates language a *Singbarer Rest*, a singable remainder, a poetic reserve.[28] The question is, confronted with the sheer nothingness and destruction of the catastrophe out of which Celan writes his poetry, whether there is still someone or some reality that can be addressed and can be attested to. For Celan, this is truly a question. Therefore the perhaps's multiply when he encounters this issue. Yet it is exactly this "maybe" of language that may hold such an encounter in reserve. By this hope of the perhaps, Celan sets out on his poetic path. In *Der Meridian*, Celan describes these poetic paths in these terms: "There are, however, among possible paths, paths on which language acquires a voice; these are encounters, a voice's paths to a perceiving thou, creaturely paths, sketches of existence perhaps."[29] Celan chooses the image of the meridian for this path that captures the sense of an address and an encounter with a you, with a creature, with existence.

The meridian is not only the path by which language finds a voice to address a hearer, but also acquires a voice, namely the voice of this you, this creature and this existence that could not speak. If this is the case, the meridian is not only a figure that goes from one pole to another, exemplifying the address, but is also the figure that separates out from sheer destruction and nothingness a singable remainder. In this context, the figure of the cut of Apelles to which Agamben refers in *Il tempo che resta* imposes itself.[30] If we represent a distinction by a line that separates the space on its left from the space on its right, the question of Celan's poetry is not the question of adding another distinction to the distinction between the unsayable horror of reality and the incapacity of the unlost language, but rather of positioning itself on this threshold and destabilizing it so that it sets free a singable remainder, a reserve of a possible address and encounter. This is what the cut of Apelles represents. Apelles was renowned for his capacity to paint such delicate, thin lines that he could even cut a painted line in half—not transversally but longitudinally. To add a longitudinal line in the line that represents a distinction is to unsettle the separation this line represents. This, perhaps, is the poetic line to be drawn: not adding another distinction, but unsettling the given distinction by inscribing a line of longitude, that is, *a meridian*, in the line that separates, so that a remainder is separated out and set free.

Celan's own imagery also suggests another interpretation of this remainder, namely in terms of the figure of the *Schatten*, the shadow or the shade. We encountered this image before in the title of the poem *Stehen, im Schatten*. What or who stands in the shade? Is it not that which is not directly visible or that which is to be protected from the sun and the light? Is it not what is held in reserve in this sense of the words *servo* and *reservo* in Latin—what is protected so that it can rest? In *Sprich auch du*, the image of the shadow and the shade returns: "Speak— // But keep yes and no unsplit, // And give your say this meaning: // give it the shade"; "Sprich— // Doch scheide das Nein nicht vom Ja. // Gib deinem Spruch auch den Sinn: // gib ihm den Schatten."[31] When yes and no are not separated, we are in a situation where unreserved affirmation and unreserved negation are both equally suspended. This is the realm of the perhaps itself. The reserve with which this realm of the perhaps goes hand in hand is depicted with the image of the *Schatten*. The poem should speak in such a way that the strict separation between yes and no is unsettled and destabilized, and this gives the say, *dem Spruch*, its shadow or shade. The sense of the poem depends on this shadow. It is unclear whether this shadow refers to the space, protected from the light, in which this saying can rest or whether it is a shadow or depth that is cast by the saying itself. I don't think we have to choose between these two interpretations because they both play with the sense of the reserve that is separated out in this realm of the perhaps. In this poem, Celan thus uses an imagery which is strikingly similar to the one used by Sextus Empiricus. The latter portrays suspension, *epochē*, as a body, *soma*, followed by a shadow, *skia*.[32] For the philosophers, it is considered to be a failure when one does not arrive at a judgment, when one does not clearly distinguish one's yes from one's no. Yet in the Skeptic case, the *aporia*, the incapacity to judge, which leads them to the *epochē*, the suspension of judgment, turns out to be an *euporia*, a good passage or pathway leading to what is longed for—the shadow the body grants is what all ancient philosophers longed for, namely *ataraxia*. The Skeptic has discovered that this *ataraxia* is not found in the right judgment, but is simply given as the pure grace of the suspension of judgment. That it is indeed a form of grace is affirmed by Sextus when he adds that this discovery was not expected or foreseen. It happens "as if by chance"; it is a perchance to which the Skeptic owes their fortune and their rest. In fact, Sextus invokes a story about the same painter, Apelles, to capture this chance. Apelles, frustrated by the fact that he is incapable of capturing the foam on the mouth of the snorting horse he tries to portray, stops painting, grasps his cloth, and throws it at the horse; all of a sudden, the foam appears exactly as it should be. The shade and the shadow thus represent the unexpected reserve of language that is withdrawn from us but on which the poet nevertheless draws. To draw on this reserve is to encounter it as what is sayable and addressable. In this sense, the reserved, subdued, and discrete mode of poetic speech is required to grant language its obscurity, its shadow, and its reserve because this shadow can, perhaps, be the place where an encounter is preserved.

To Bear Witness to Reality

It is not so strange that Celan subsequently describes this encounter as a *Geheimnis*, as *das Geheimnis der Begegnung*. To translate this as "secret" is not wrong, but one should note the intrinsic relation, as discussed in chapter 3, between the German *Heim*, *Unheimlichkeit*, and *Geheimnis*. Uncanniness is what is unfamiliar and what offers no place to dwell in. The crisis of language intensifies this problem. Exactly by trying to keep the uncanny out, language does not offer an inhabitable place. If, as Celan does, the strangeness is compared in the first place to the uncanny, *das Unheimliche*, and if, as he also does, the meridian or the path of the poem is compared with "homecoming," *Heimkehr*, it also becomes clear that the meaning of the expression "the secret of the encounter" carries the significance of *Heim* in *das Geheimnis*.³³ Therefore, the chain of *Heim*, *Unheimlichkeit*, and *Geheimnis* receives a specific significance in the course of Celan's *Der Meridian*. The distinguishing between strange and strange is, in this terminology, a distinguishing between *das Unheimliche*, the uncanny, and *das Geheimnis*, the secret, in which the latter is part of a *Heimkehr*, that is, a turn (*Kehre* and *Wende*) that is not a conversion of a subject, but a turn of breath by which language can, perhaps, become once more an inhabitable place (which for Celan is no longer a place on earth, but that is poetically named "heaven").

This secret of the encounter consists, first of all, in the capacity of the poem to speak. As Celan suggests, the poem "speaks only in its own, its own, individual cause [*in seiner eigenen, allereigensten Sache*]."³⁴ Note that Celan writes here "speaks in," which indicates that the poem does not speak *about* its own cause but rather speaks *in defense of* its own cause, that is, testifies to its own cause. Moreover, "cause" translates the German "Sache," which one could also translate as "subject matter" and which in the philosophical vocabulary translates the Latin *res*. The poem testifies to the reality of its very own object. Yet Celan adds a doubling of the voice or the breath of the poem: "it has always belonged to the hopes of the poem, in precisely this manner, [. . .] to speak *in the cause of something or someone other*—who knows, perhaps in the cause of something or someone *wholly other*."³⁵ The change in terminology from *das Fremde* to *das/der Andere* indicates in the first place the dialogical hope of the poem. Whereas *das Fremde* refers to what is foreign to us without a possible linguistic or poetic relation, *das Andere* refers to what is different but nevertheless relatable to us and addressable in and by the poem. Note that the translation personifies the other. This is not wrong because for Celan, whatever is addressed *becomes* a you. That is to say, what Celan calls the dialogical nature of the poem consists not only in addressing other human beings who then become the hearers or readers of the poem, but it also and more importantly concerns addressing *all types of reality in the poem*—you, creature, and existence. It is not only about other humans, but it concerns all reality, as Celan explicitly says when he describes the poetic dialogue in these terms: "when we speak *with things* in this manner."³⁶ By addressing reality in this way, the poem "allows the most idiosyncratic quality [*Eigenste*] of the other, its time, to participate in the dialogue [*mitsprechen*]."³⁷ Let me emphasize that one should be careful not to inscribe too quickly Celan's references to the other, or even the wholly other, into Levinas's vocabulary. There is no transition from being to other taking place.³⁸ Rather, a transition from strange to other takes place, in which both represent a particular modality of being, in which the first concerns being in its inapproachable state and the second concerns being in its approachability. What is at stake for Celan is not only the face of the other in which even the wholly other may be present, but also the linguistic possibility of the poem to address reality. By this address, reality—"things"—becomes a you, that is, it becomes that which speaks to us in the poem. What is at stake for Celan is thus, in the first place, "an approachable reality." Poetry is both "racked by reality," "Wirklichkeitswund," and "in search of reality," "Wirklichkeit suchend," as he writes in his *Bremer Rede*.³⁹ When poetry renders reality approachable and makes an encounter, *Begegnung*, with reality possible, the latter can become an object, *Gegenstand*, of testimony, that is, that which approaches, *entgegenkommt*, the hearer of testimony.

In these reflections, poetry is testimony. To address or approach reality does not simply mean to address as we address a hearer, and it also does not mean to anthropomorphize reality. Rather, it means that "language acquires a voice," namely the voice of this reality so that it speaks in the poem itself as another voice, as the you who is always invited in Celan's poetry to speak. Gadamer's essay on Celan is called "Who Am I and Who Are You," referring to the figures of the I and the you that appear so often in Celan's poetry. Yet it is not a matter of identifying these figures but rather of acknowledging that the poem aims to speak with *two* voices, that it aims to establish not only a voice of its own but also to desubjectivize itself and give the floor to reality as a you, as a voice that speaks and that is thus approachable in language. In this way, poetry attests to reality, or it fails.

If we return once more to Celan's "Niemand // zeugt // für den Zeugen," it becomes clear why so many of Celan's poems indeed stage and address a you. They want to give a voice to the you so that the speechless no one becomes a you that speaks and that indeed bears witness for the testimony that the poem offers. To be testimony, the poem needs the voice of reality. In this sense, the stakes and the hopes of Celan's poetry are in fact those of testimony: what can, perhaps, be an encounter of language and reality? When this, perhaps, happens, would it not be, on the side of the human, a becoming human in its most basic sense? Here, then, to conclude or simply stop short, we perhaps find the *archē tou logou*, the genuine beginning of human speech, which then, just as in the *Symposium*, finds its origin not in the one who speaks but rather in what demands to be said because it cannot speak itself—*ou gar emos ho muthos*, "not mine the tale."⁴⁰

Notes

Introduction

1. Lyotard, *L'inhumain*, 15/7. Throughout this study, I refer to originals and translations as #a/#b, where #a denotes the page number of the original text and #b the page number of the used translation, which is specified in the bibliography.

2. Plato, *Laws* IX, 854d; LCL 192:202–3; or perhaps in reference to *Laws* IX, 873b. LCL refers to the Loeb Classical Library; I refer as LCL #v:#p, where #v denotes the number of the volume and #p the page number. The only other used abbreviations are LSJ to refer to *The Online Liddell-Scott-Jones Greek-English Lexicon*, see http://stephanus.tlg.uci.edu/lsj/#eid=1&context=lsj; and LS to Lewis and Short, *A Latin Dictionary*, see http://www.perseus.tufts.edu/hopper/text?doc=Perseus:text:1999.04.0059.

3. Plato, *Sophist* 237d; LCL 123:340–41.

4. Plato, *Gorgias* 523e; Plato, *Cratylus* 403b, where it reads: *psuchē gumnē tou sōmatos*.

5. Kierkegaard, *Fear and Trembling*, 61. Plato, *Gorgias* 523a–24a; LCL 166:518–21.

6. See Van der Heiden, "Technology and Childhood."

7. Plato, *Protagoras* 321c; LCL 165:130–31.

8. Plato, *Protagoras* 322c; LCL 165:134–35.

9. Plato also refers to a form of naked existence that represents a more paradisiacal situation; see *Statesman* 272a.

10. As Derrida suggests, the "reflection on testimony has always historically privileged the example of miracles" (Derrida, *Demeure*, 98/75).

11. Heidegger, *Sein und Zeit*, 454/315 (translation gives "naked Dasein"), 179/127, and 367/255.

12. Leibniz, *Philosophische Schriften*, 1:448–49; Leibniz, *Discourse on Metaphysics & The Monadology*, 51 (= *La Monadologie*, #24).

Chapter 1

1. Derrida, *La dissémination*, 77/69.
2. Ibid.
3. Badiou, *L'être et l'événement*, 144/126.
4. Derrida, *La dissémination*, 77/69.
5. Plato, *Phaedrus* 276d; Cooper, *Plato*, 553. See also Schmidt, "The Garden of Letters."
6. Lyotard, *L'inhumain*, 15/7.
7. Agamben, "Bartleby o della contingenza," 72–73/260.
8. Ibid., 73/260.
9. See also Ricoeur, *Du texte à l'action*, 115–17.
10. For the verb *ēthopoiein*, see Plutarch, *Pericles* 2.3; LCL 65:6–7, and Foucault, *Herméneutique du sujet*, 227/237.
11. Ricoeur, *Du texte à l'action*, 112–15.
12. Derrida, *La dissémination*, 77/69.
13. Plato, *Phaedrus* 229e.
14. Ibid. 229c; Cooper, *Plato*, 509.
15. Aristotle, *Metaphysics* 981b14–24; Barnes, *Complete Works of Aristotle*, 2:1553.
16. Aristotle, *Metaphysics* 982b17–83a12; Barnes, *Complete Works of Aristotle*, 2:1554–55; LCL 271:12–15. See also Van der Heiden, "Vrienden van het verhaal," 18–20.
17. As Derrida writes: "to free [the myths] from the heavy serious naïveté of the scientific 'rationalists,' and on the other, not bothering *with* them" (Derrida, *La dissémination*, 76/67). Yet it is not about freeing the myths and also not about being bothered with them.
18. Plato, *Phaedrus* 229e; Cooper, *Plato*, 510.
19. Plato, *Phaedrus* 230a; Cooper, *Plato*, 510.
20. Diogenes Laertius, *Lives of Eminent Philosophers* I.14; LCL 184:14–15.
21. Plato, *Phaedrus* 229e–30a; Cooper, *Plato*, 510. One could add to these examples the reference to the *Delphois grammatōn* in Plato, *Philebus* 48c. Here the question also is whether people truly adopt the task of self-knowledge or merely strive for *doxosophia* (Plato, *Philebus* 49a; the "conceit of wisdom" [LCL 164:335]), which is truly vain and empty knowledge or knowledge in matters that are utterly inconsequential. Socrates also describes these people as ridiculous or absurd (*geloious* and *geloiōn*; Plato, *Philebus* 49b–c; LCL 164:336–37).
22. Derrida, *La dissémination*, 172.
23. Plato, *Republic* 619e–20a, 618c. Cooper, *Plato*, 1222, 1221.
24. There are other examples such as the *Delphois grammatōn* in Plato, *Philebus* 48c. Also in this dialogue, Socrates describes the pitiful state of those who do not follow this imperative but merely strive for *doxosophia*, the "conceit

of wisdom," in terms of their being ridiculous (*geloious*). See ibid., 49a–c; LCL 164:334–37.

25. Derrida, *La dissémination*, 77/69. Agamben, *L'uso dei corpi*, 322/255.
26. Derrida, *La dissémination*, 77/69.
27. Ibid.; my italics.
28. Plato, *Phaedrus*, 230d–e.
29. Ibid. 230a; Cooper, *Plato*, 510.
30. "The sun appeared, and many-armed Typhoeus roared for the fray with all the tongues of all his throats, challenging mighty Zeus" (Nonnus, *Dionysiaca*, II.244–46; LCL 344:62–63).
31. Plato, *Phaedrus* 276a; see also Derrida's distinction between "the fertile trace" and "the sterile trace" (Derrida, *La dissémination*, 172/149).
32. This is the term Phaedrus uses and which Socrates affirms, see Plato, *Phaedrus* 276a–b.
33. Plato, *Protagoras* 314a–b; Cooper, *Plato*, 751.

Chapter 2

1. Plato, *Eighth Letter* 355a; Cooper, *Plato*, 1669.
2. Heidegger, *Parmenides*, 131–32/88.
3. Nancy, *Le partage des voix*, 46/227.
4. Heidegger, *Unterwegs zur Sprache*, 115.
5. I've discussed this in *Ontology after Ontotheology*, 83–89.
6. For the image of the iron rings, see Plato, *Ion* 533d–e; for the divine power, see 533d.
7. Ibid. 534e.
8. Plato, *Theaetetus* 167d–68b; Cooper, *Plato*, 186–87.
9. Plato, *Theaetetus* 165a–b.
10. Foucault, *L'herméneutique du sujet*, 16–20/15–19.
11. Plato, *Theaetetus* 142a–b; Cooper, *Plato*, 158.
12. Plato, *Theaetetus* 143b–c; Cooper, *Plato*, 159.
13. It might be interesting to confront this "use" of the slave with Agamben's analysis in the first chapter of *L'uso dei corpi*: in the use of the slave's voice, there is no master-position.
14. Heidegger also stresses this immediacy in his comment, although he understands it as the immediacy of the human's relation to *alētheia*; see Heidegger, *Parmenides*, 132.
15. Plato, *Theaetetus* 152a; Cooper, *Plato*, 169.
16. Plato, *Theaetetus* 161c.
17. Ibid. 162a; Cooper, *Plato*, 180.
18. Plato, *Theaetetus* 162d; Cooper, *Plato*, 180.

19. Agamben, *Quel che resta di Auschwitz*, 58/64.

20. This is exactly how Agamben criticizes the positions of Apel and Aristotle: "Insofar as they are founded on a tacit presupposition (in this case, that someone must speak), all refutations necessarily leave a residue in the form of an exclusion" (ibid., 58/65).

21. Plato, *Theaetetus* 164d; Cooper, *Plato*, 183.

22. Plato, *Theaetetus* 164e; Cooper, *Plato*, 183.

23. A similar issue can be found in the opening scene of Plato's *Republic* in which Cephalus withdraws from the conversation and hands over the *logos* to his son Polemarchus, who is subsequently identified as "heir to the *logos*" of Cephalus (see 331d–e). When the argument continues, it is Polemarchus who has to interpret Cephalus's side of the argument: "But I shall ask you, and I am indeed asking you to interpret (*hermēneusai*) our side of the debate as well, whatever it is" (Plato, *Republic* 453c; LCL 237:461).

24. Plato, *Theaetetus* 165e; Cooper, *Plato*, 184.

25. Plato, *Theaetetus* 166a–68c. See also: "Whatever I report you must imagine you are hearing from them in person" (Plato, *Menexenus* 246c; Cooper, *Plato*, 961).

26. E.g., Socrates interprets Protagoras's discontent with the discussion when his points of view are represented by the young, inexperienced Theaetetus; see Plato, *Theaetetus* 166a–b.

27. Derrida, *La dissémination*, 167–68n64.

28. See also Van der Heiden, "The Voice of the Past in the Present," 432–33.

29. Plato, *Theaetetus* 168c; Cooper, *Plato*, 187.

30. Plato, *Theaetetus* 169a; Cooper, *Plato*, 187.

31. Plato, *Theaetetus* 171c–d; Cooper, *Plato*, 190; LCL 123:113.

Chapter 3

1. Lyotard, "La phrase-affect," 51/238. See also Lyotard, "Les voix d'une voix," 202/130.

2. Aristotle, *Politics* 1253a8–18 (= 1.1.10); Barnes, *Complete Works of Aristotle*, 2:1988.

3. Aristotle, *Politics* 1253a15–16; LCL 264:10–11.

4. Lyotard, "La phrase-affect," 50; Agamben, *Il linguaggio e la morte*, 53/39; Agamben, *Categorie Italiane*, 66–67/68.

5. Lyotard, "La phrase-affect," 52/238.

6. Ibid., 48/236. Lyotard states this in reference to Freud.

7. Lyotard, *L'Inhumain*, 11/3.

8. Lyotard, "La phrase-affect," 47/235.

9. Lyotard himself writes: "Dans le différend quelque chose 'demande' à être mis en phrases" (Lyotard, *Le différend*, 30/13). In the French, "demander" is

not only "to ask," as the English translation suggests, but also "to demand." This latter sense is more pertinent here.

10. Ibid., 51/238.
11. See also Van der Heiden, "De onbestemde taal."
12. See LSJ s.v. *mueō*.
13. Soucy, *La petite fille*, 13/3.
14. Ibid., 119/89.
15. For Alice's comparison of the father with God, see also ibid., 164–65/126.
16. Heidegger, *Parmenides*, 176/118.
17. Plato, *Republic* 621a; Cooper, *Plato*, 1223.
18. For these terms and Heidegger's usage of it, see, e.g., Heidegger, *Hölderlins Hymne "Der Ister,"* 91.
19. Heidegger, *Wegmarken*, 313.
20. Kierkegaard, *Fear and Trembling*, 61.
21. Soucy, *La petite fille*, 97.
22. Ibid., 140.
23. Ibid., 98/73.
24. Ibid., 99/73.
25. Ibid., 157–58/120–21.
26. Ibid., 75–76/53.
27. Ibid., 79/56.
28. Ibid., 142/108.
29. Ibid., 174/133.
30. Plato, *Theaetetus* 142a-b; Cooper, *Plato*, 158.
31. Agamben, *Quel che resta di Auschwitz*, 31–32/33–34.
32. Soucy, *La petite fille*, 150/115.
33. Ibid., 150–51/115.
34. In this sense, there are basic resonances between my approach to Agamben and that of Watkin, *Agamben and Indifference*, who interprets him as a philosopher of indifference. Yet, in order to maintain the difference with other contemporary philosophers of indifference, such as Badiou, it is crucial to emphasize the figure of the threshold: a threshold does not simply render indifferent the two spaces it separates, but it is rather the intermediate place, the point of transition, where the difference becomes indifferent and, therefore, the place where a communicability or a passage, an *euporia*, between these two spaces might be possible; see for two important references ibid., 32, 85.
35. Soucy, *La petite fille*, 152/116.
36. The idea that Ariane is the source of the gift of speech and words is expressed a number of times in the book, see, e.g., ibid., 96, 126, 170.
37. Agamben, *Quel che resta di Auschwitz*, 36/39.
38. Agamben, *Il linguaggio e la morte*, 53/39.

39. Agamben, *Infanzia e storia*, XIII/8. *Ta en tē phōnē* appears in Aristotle, *On Interpretation* 16a5.

40. Agamben, *Categorie Italiane*, 67/68.

41. "The *gramma* is thus the form of presupposition itself and nothing else" (Agamben, *La potenza del pensiero*, 21/37).

42. As quoted in Agamben, *Categorie Italiane*, 67/69.

43. Ibid., 71/74.

44. Levi, *Survival in Auschwitz*, 191; quoted at Agamben, *Quel che resta di Auschwitz*, 34/37.

45. In relation to the figure of Hurbinek, Cavarero notes: "The other deportees therefore attribute to the articulated sounds of the child the intention to signify" (Cavarero, *For More Than One Voice*, 211). She argues that Hurbinek's voice is already on its way to speech and is therefore "not an inarticulate cry" (ibid., 212). There might be degrees in inarticulateness. Yet, by reading the sense of Hurbinek's voice in terms of coming to speech or finding its fulfilment in speech, Cavarero repeats the metaphysical gesture that Agamben problematizes and misses the crucial meaning of bearing witness in his argument as the attempt to reserve in speech a place for the living voice of, in this case, Hurbinek.

46. Agamben, *Quel che resta di Auschwitz*, 36/39.

47. Soucy, *La petite fille*, 157/120.

Chapter 4

1. Agamben, *Il tempo che resta*, 43/40. Translation adapted. In accordance with Kotsko's translation of *L'uso dei corpi*, I translate *esigenza* as "demand" and *esigere* as "to demand" throughout this study.

2. Ibid.; Cooper, *Plato*, 126.

3. Plato, *Cratylus* 407e–8a; Cooper, *Plato*, 126.

4. Plato, *Cratylus* 408c; Cooper, *Plato*, 126.

5. Agamben, *Il tempo che resta*, 43/40.

6. Mortier, *Godenslaap*, 8/10.

7. Ibid., 8–9/10.

8. Ibid., 403/361.

9. Ibid., 20/20.

10. Ibid., 15/16. For the difference between the mother's and the daughter's language, see ibid., 18/18.

11. Ibid., 18/19.

12. Ibid., 327–28/291.

13. Agamben, "Bartleby o della contingenza," 83/267.

14. See also Mortier, *Godenslaap*, 360–61/322.

15. Ibid., 291/327.

16. Ibid., 20/21.
17. Ibid., 36/34.
18. Ibid., 92–93/84.
19. Ibid., 35/33.
20. As the title of an interview with Derrida reads: "La langue n'appartient pas."
21. "Die Welt ist fort, ich muss dich tragen" (Celan, *Gesammelte Werke*, 2:97).
22. Mortier, *Godenslaap*, 306/272.
23. Ibid., 210/189.
24. Ibid., 180–81/162–63.
25. This relation to one's own body is described by Jolly as victims' "*inability to inhabit their 'estranged' bodies within the realm of social discourse*" (Jolly, "Witnessing Embodiment," 308).
26. Ricoeur, *Soi-même comme un autre*, 370/320.
27. Mortier, *Godenslaap*, 48/44–45.
28. I'm using here "stand for" in the sense of Ricoeur's "représentance"; see Ricoeur, *La mémoire, l'histoire, l'oubli*, 320/248.
29. Mortier, *Godenslaap*, 19/20.
30. Ibid., 176/159.
31. Ibid., 386/346.
32. For the connection of breath and voice, see also Cavarero, *For More Than One Voice*, 20–24.
33. Mortier, *Godenslaap*, 20/20.

Chapter 5

1. Agamben, *Quel che resta di Auschwitz*, 59/65. Slightly adapted translation: I've translated *esigenza* as "demand" instead of "necessity."
2. For this sense of *methodos*: "Der Weg heißt griechisch ὁδός; μετά heißt 'nach'; μέθοδος ist der Weg, auf dem wir einer Sache nachgehen: die Methode" (Heidegger, *Der Satz vom Grund*, 92).
3. Kierkegaard, *Repetition*, 125.
4. Howard V. Hong and Edna H. Hong, "Historical Introduction," in Kierkegaard, *Fear and Trembling*, ix–xxxix.
5. Quoted in Hong and Hong, "Historical Introduction," xix.
6. Kierkegaard, *Fear and Trembling*, 61.
7. Ibid.
8. Agamben, *Quel che resta di Auschwitz*, 71–72/77.
9. As Helena, the poetess, writes: this basic misery "we try in vain to tuck in with words" (Mortier, *Godenslaap*, 386/346).
10. Derrida, *Donner la mort*, 131/95.

11. Some call *Fear and Trembling* a novel; see Hong and Hong, "Historical Introduction," xxvi.

12. Kermode, *The Genesis of Secrecy*, ix–x.

13. This quote is attributed, without reference, to Paul de Man in Schumacher, *Die Ironie der Unverständlichkeit*, 98.

14. Kierkegaard, *Fear and Trembling*, 14.

15. More ironically, Johannes writes: "It is supposed to be difficult to understand Hegel, but to understand Abraham is a small matter" (ibid., 32).

16. Ibid., 33.

17. Ibid.

18. "I cannot make the movement of faith, I cannot shut my eyes and plunge confidently into the absurd; it is for me an impossibility, but I do not praise myself for that" (ibid., 34).

19. Derrida, *Marges de la philosophie*, I/x–xi.

20. Kierkegaard, *Fear and Trembling*, 112.

21. Kierkegaard, *Repetition*, 226.

22. This is mainly discussed in *Problema I*, and these characterizations can be found at Kierkegaard, *Fear and Trembling*, 54–55.

23. Ibid., 55. The quote continues: "—yet, please note, in such a way that the movement repeats itself, so that after having been in the universal he as the single individual isolates himself as higher than the universal." This addition is fully in line with the comments in *Repetition* in which Kierkegaard writes that the unjustified exception is the one that wants "to bypass the universal" (Kierkegaard, *Repetition*, 226).

24. See also Derrida, *Donner la mort*, 118/85: "The sacrifice of Isaac is an abomination in the eyes of all, and it should continue to be seen for what it is."

25. For an overview of the different translations of the Greek *thaumazein*, see Llewelyn, *Seeing through God*, 55–69.

26. Kierkegaard, *Fear and Trembling*, 60. As Derrida interprets: "But as soon as one speaks, as soon as one enters the medium of language, one loses that very singularity" (Derrida, *Donner la mort*, 60).

27. What follows here is a reflection on the culmination point of Johannes's narrative on Abraham's incapacity to speak, in which he repeats and gathers some of the issues mentioned before; see Kierkegaard, *Fear and Trembling*, 113–19.

28. Ibid., 113.

29. Ibid., 115.

30. *Gen.* 22:8; quoted in Kierkegaard, *Fear and Trembling*, 115–16.

31. Ibid., 119.

32. *Gen.* 22:7.

33. Kierkegaard, *Fear and Trembling*, 118.

34. Derrida connects this answer of Abraham to the answer Bartleby famously gives to the lawyer who employs him and asks him to copy and read copied texts, namely "I would prefer not to"; see Derrida, *Donner la mort*, 106/74–75.

35. Kierkegaard, *Fear and Trembling*, 114, 119.

36. 1 *Cor.* 14:20.

37. 1 *Cor.* 14:4.

38. Agamben, *Categorie Italiane*, 65/66.

39. Much earlier in his narrative, Kierkegaard's poet already prepares this when he lets the knight of resignation say: "[F]or in the world of time God and I cannot talk to each other, we have no language in common" (Kierkegaard, *Fear and Trembling*, 35).

40. 1 *Cor.* 14:5.

41. See Agamben, *Categorie Italiane*, 64/66, where he connects glossolalia to Augustine's *temetum*, which in turn is understood as "pure intention to signify."

42. Kierkegaard, *Fear and Trembling*, 46.

43. Derrida, *Donner la mort*, 104/73.

44. Kierkegaard, *Fear and Trembling*, 80.

45. Derrida, *Donner la mort*, 104/73.

46. Kierkegaard, *Fear and Trembling*, 80.

47. Lyotard, *Le différend*, 160/108.

48. Kierkegaard, *Fear and Trembling*, 55. As he writes against Hegel's version of dialectics: "The Hegelian philosophy assumes no justified hiddenness, no justified incommensurability" (ibid., 83). Thus, Hegel does not allow for secret, exception, or reserve.

49. Ibid., 7.

50. Ibid., 15.

51. Plato, *Symposium* 177a; Cooper, *Plato*, 462.

52. Derrida, "La langue n'appartient pas," 87/103.

Chapter 6

1. Melville, "Bartleby," 19.

2. For the philosophers' interpretation of Bartleby, see, e.g., Berkman, *L'effet Bartleby*.

3. Derrida, *Donner la mort*, 106/74–75. Deleuze compares the attorney from Melville's story with Abraham; see *Critique et clinique*, 104/80–81.

4. Ibid., 99/77. The enigmatic squid refers to *Moby Dick*: "Whatever superstitions the sperm whalemen in general have connected with the sight of this object [i.e., the squid, GJvdH], certain it is, that a glimpse of it being so very unusual, that circumstance has gone far to invest it with portentousness. So

rarely is it beheld, that though one and all of them declare it to be the largest animated thing in the ocean, yet very few of them have any but the most vague ideas concerning its true nature and form" (Melville, *Moby Dick*, 264). The squid is a figure for what is portentous, what inspires awe, threatens and is inauspicious, and of which one has "but the most vague ideas concerning its true nature and form."

    5. Melville, "Bartleby," 5.

    6. According to Deleuze, this terminology is Melville's; see Deleuze, *Critique et clinique*, 102/79. For the sense of a divine language, see ibid., 93/71–72.

    7. Ibid., 106/83.

    8. Melville, "Bartleby," 32–33.

    9. Deleuze, *Critique et clinique*, 11/1; my italics; translation adapted. The second sentence reads "La littérature est plutôt du côté de l'informe." The translation reads somewhat oddly as: "Literature rather moves in the direction of the ill-formed"; "être du côté de" simply means here "to side with" or "to be on the side of"; and in a context referring to Aristotle's matter-form distinction, "informe" simply means "without form" or "formless" rather than "ill-formed."

    10. Ibid., 15–16/5. See also ibid., 94/72 and 138/109–10.

    11. Ibid., 15/4.

    12. Ibid., 114/89.

    13. Melville, "Bartleby," 4.

    14. Ibid.

    15. The attorney "who never pleads in courts, offers a plea in telling his story" (Meindl, *American Fiction*, 68).

    16. Ricoeur, *La mémoire, l'histoire, l'oubli*, 334/257.

    17. Ibid., 223/175.

    18. See, e.g., Dilthey, "Das Verstehen anderer Personen," 215–16/234–36: "the imagination can increase or diminish the intensity of the attitudes, powers, feelings, strivings, and thought-tendencies that characterize our own life-nexus in order to re-create the psychic life of any other person."

    19. Ricoeur, *La mémoire, l'histoire, l'oubli*, 223/175.

    20. Meindl, *American Fiction*, 64.

    21. Melville, "Bartleby," 18.

    22. Ibid., 9.

    23. Ibid., 30.

    24. Lyotard, "La phrase-affect," 51–52.

    25. Ibid., 51.

    26. Lyotard, *L'inhumain*, 15/7. In this quote, the last "it" refers to *enfance* or infancy, but as Lyotard makes clear in "La phrase-affect": "This time before the *logos* is called *infantia*" (Lyotard, "La phrase-affect," 53/239). See also Lyotard, *Misère de la philosophie*, 41.

    27. Melville, "Bartleby," 18.

28. Plato, *Symposium* 174d–75b. Cooper, *Plato*, 460–61. See also Plato, *Symposium* 220c–d.
29. See also Vila-Matas, *Bartleby & Co*, 12–13, which speaks of Socrates's hallucinations.
30. Arendt, *The Life of the Mind*, 197–202.
31. Melville, "Bartleby," 10.
32. Ibid., 11.
33. Ibid.
34. Ibid.
35. This breakdown of any commonality is also emphasized in a second dispute; see ibid., 12.
36. Ibid., 11; my italics.
37. "Il me suffit en somme qu'on ne confonde pas être affecté, *affectedness*, et être adressé, *addressedness*" (Lyotard, *Misère de la philosophie*, 91).
38. Although Bartleby's voice does not communicate meaning, we can say that what takes place is "a sort of communicability or transitivity of affects without expectation of a return" (Lyotard, "La phrase-affect," 54/240).
39. Melville, "Bartleby," 12.
40. Ibid., 23.
41. Ibid., 20.
42. Ibid., 21.
43. Deleuze, *Critique et clinique*, 106/83.
44. Melville, "Bartleby," 16–17.
45. Ibid., 18.
46. Ibid., 19.
47. Levinas, *Existence and Existents*, 98.
48. Plato, *Timaeus* 72b; LCL 234:186–89.
49. Ibid., 34.

Chapter 7

1. Deleuze and Guattari, *Qu'est-ce que la philosophie?*, 67/69.
2. Ibid., 67/68–69; my italics; translation slightly adapted.
3. Deleuze, *Critique et clinique*, 111–12/87.
4. Ibid., 93/72.
5. *Theaetetus* 176a–b; Cooper, *Plato*, 195.
6. Agamben, *L'uso dei corpi*, 300/235. See also LSJ s.v. φυγή, "banishment, exile" [LSJ = Liddell-Scott-Jones, *Greek-English Lexicon*].
7. Agamben, *L'uso dei corpi*, 299/235. Note that Socrates indeed uses this word to describe his own journey in *Phaedo* 67c; Agamben interprets this journey as the separation of body and soul mentioned in *Phaedo* 67a.
8. See LSJ s.v. ἀποδημία.

9. How much "death frames the *Republic*," see Schmidt, *On Germans and Other Greeks*, 21–26.

10. Plato, *Republic* 614b–21d. See for related, but different discussions of this myth, Van der Heiden, *De stem van de doden*, 267–88; Van der Heiden, *Ontology after Ontotheology*, 280–88; Van der Heiden, "Vrienden van het verhaal."

11. "Das Leitthema der 'Politeia' ist die *dikaiosunē*" (Heidegger, *Parmenides*, 137).

12. For Glaucon's quote, see Plato, *Republic* 361e. For Adimantus's plea, see ibid. 362d–67e.

13. Derrida develops such an argument; see *Donner la mort*, 133–36/97–99.

14. Plato, *Republic* 612d–13e.

15. Agamben, *L'uso dei corpi*, 322/255.

16. Derrida, *Force de loi*, 35/15. Deconstruction is, in this sense, understood by Derrida as the testimony of justice in the realm of appearance—a testimony that depends on the concealment of justice to be possible.

17. This is the expression used by Socrates in Book X; see Plato, *Republic* 608b (also 591e); Cooper, *Plato*, 1212.

18. Schmidt, *On Germans and Other Greeks*, 23.

19. Plato, *Republic* 614b–c; Cooper, *Plato*, 1218.

20. Plato, *Republic* 614d; Cooper, *Plato*, 1218.

21. Heidegger, *Parmenides*, 130–93; Agamben, *L'uso dei corpi*, 315–31/249–62.

22. Plato, *Republic* 617e; Cooper, *Plato*, 1220.

23. Heidegger, *Parmenides*, 147/99.

24. Plato, *Republic* 619e–20a; Cooper, *Plato*, 1222. Discussed in Agamben, *L'uso dei corpi*, 318/251, 325/257.

25. Agamben translates: "pitiful, ridiculous, and marvelous" (ibid., 320/253). For an analysis of this passage, see also Schmidt, *On Germans and Other Greeks*, 41–42.

26. Plato, *Republic* 619e–20a; LCL 276:513.

27. Plato, *Republic* 619c; Cooper, *Plato*, 1221–22.

28. Plato, *Republic* 619b–c; Cooper, *Plato*, 1221.

29. Agamben, *L'uso dei corpi*, 323/256.

30. Heidegger, *Parmenides*, 146.

31. Agamben, *L'uso dei corpi*, 327/258.

32. Plato, *Republic* 618e; Cooper, *Plato*, 1221.

33. Levinas, *Humanisme de l'autre homme*, 45/27–28.

34. Plato, *Republic* 618c; as quoted in Agamben, *L'uso dei corpi*, 326/258; the remark between square brackets is Agamben's.

35. For this latter paragraph, see also Van der Heiden, *Ontology after Ontotheology*, 287–88.

36. For what follows, see Plato, *Republic* 620d.

37. Ibid. 621a–d. Cooper, *Plato*, 1223.
38. Heidegger, *Parmenides*, 185.
39. Ibid., 176/118.
40. Plato, *Republic* 621c.
41. Heidegger, *Parmenides*, 176/118–19.
42. Mortier, *Godenslaap*, 48/44–45.
43. LSJ s.v. κενός, A.I.2. "empty, fruitless, void."
44. Heidegger, *Parmenides*, 177/119.
45. Ibid., 179/120.
46. Plato, *Protagoras* 321c; Cooper, *Plato*, 757.
47. Plato, *Republic* 621b–c; Cooper, *Plato*, 1223.
48. Agamben, *Quel che resta di Auschwitz*, 72/77.

Chapter 8

1. Derrida, *Demeure*, 98/75.
2. Lackey and Sosa, *The Epistemology of Testimony*, 1.
3. From the analytic tradition, see, e.g., Fricker, *Epistemic Injustice*, and from the continental tradition, see, e.g., Oliver, *Witnessing*.
4. See Krämer, Schmidt, and Schülein, *Philosophie der Zeugenschaft*, 13–17, who distinguish between an epistemological and ethical interest in testimony.
5. My usage of hyphens in the expression "what-is-borne-witness-to" is mainly for the sake of readability.
6. One could compare this relation between reserve and object with Sallis's suggestion to interpret the Platonic *idea* as the foreground of *alētheia*; see Sallis, *The Verge of Philosophy*, 23–24. Such a foreground then also has a background, namely concealment or *lēthē*, to which both *alētheia* and *idea* are related. In this comparison, the object would be the foreground of testimony's announcement by which something can appear and can be known in the first place; the reserve would be the background, that which is held back because it lacks the *dunamis* to appear.
7. Misery understood as phenomenological and linguistic poverty is, at this point, a formal characterization and applies equally to the dreadful existence of Alice and Ariane in Soucy's novel; to the existential possibility of faith in Kierkegaard's Abraham; to the category of the event, as developed by Badiou; and to Eckhart's experience of the godhead. These are all phenomenologically and linguistically poor.
8. Lyotard, "La phrase-affect," 51/238. The Greek *muein* also means "to initiate into mysteries"; see LSJ s.v. *mueō*.
9. Cf. King and Ballantyne, "Augustine on Testimony."

10. Derrida, *Demeure*, 98/75.

11. Note that I'm not propagating the miracle here as the preferred "object" of testimony. Yet abstraction from these particular objects in a "purely" epistemological account can lead to curious consequences. King and Ballantyne, e.g., conclude one of their analyses of testimony in Augustine as follows: "Augustine's proposal appears to be that a testifier's mental knowledge that *p* can be transformed into testimony-based knowledge that *p*" (King and Ballantyne, "Augustine on Testimony," 202). Here, for Augustine, *p* is actually the resurrection of Christ. By representing this as *p*, the value of the miraculous is simply effaced as if it were of no consequence. Yet, historically, the philosophical question of testimony is *predominantly* discussed when dealing with miracles. What happens when we write *p* here and erase the very specificity with which the question of testimony is raised in Augustine—as well as in Hume?

12. Krämer distinguishes between the weak and the strong sense of testimony, and she connects this strong sense in the first place to the testimony of victims, and so on; see Krämer, "Les ambivalences du témoignage," 53–54. Yet it seems to me that, first, one should explain what the sense of testimony is of which there is a weak and strong sense and why, second, the determination of the strong sense does not truly take into account the historically privileged sense of the miracle in relation to testimony, which marks Augustine's and Hume's approach to testimony alike and which also has its present-day forms.

13. Interestingly, in *David Hume*, a book that aims to establish Hume as "continental ancestor," Freydberg does not discuss section 11, on miracles, from *An Enquiry Concerning Human Understanding*.

14. Mortier, *Godenslaap*, 48/44–45.

15. LS, s.v. *servo*. This root is also traceable in the Latin *observo* "to watch over, to heed, attend to, guard" and it derives from the PIE root **ser-*, "to protect."

16. See Aristotle, *On Interpretation* 16b26–17a26; Heidegger, *Grundbegriffe der Metaphysik*, 459.

17. Foucault, *Le gouvernement de soi et des autres*, 60/62; for the comment on the difference with performative utterances, see 59–60/61–62.

18. Locke, *An Essay Concerning Human Understanding*, 512 (= 4.15.5).

19. *Hebrews* 11:1; NRSV.

20. I use the expression "what can, perhaps, be"—and for readability I render it sometimes with hyphens as *what-can-perhaps-be*—in order to stress the relation to the important Heideggerian category of *Seinkönnen*. Derrida expresses his disliking of this term in favor of the English "perhaps" and "perchance"; see Derrida, *Politiques de l'amitié*, 47–48/30, 59/39; see also Jacques Derrida and Alexander Garcia Düttmann, "Perhaps or Maybe," *Pli* 6 (1997): 1–18; at 2.

21. Lyotard, *Le différend*, 10/xii.

22. See, e.g., ibid., 10, 50–52.

23. Ibid., 30/13.

24. The formulation "to attest to the absence of attestation" appears in different forms in Blanchot, *Le pas au-delà* 107/76: "*témoignant pour l'absence d'attestation*" or "*testifying to the absence of testimony*"; Derrida, *Demeure* 33/31; and Agamben, *Quel che resta di Auschwitz*, 9/13 formulates it in terms of what one cannot bear witness to (he does not use the word *impossibile* as the translation might suggest): "testimony contained at its core an essential lacuna; in other words, the survivors bore witness to something it is impossible to bear witness to [*non poteva essere testimoniato*]."

25. Lyotard, *Le différend*, 30/13. As he writes elsewhere: "A phrase universe is in principle (that is to say transcendentally) polarised according to two axes: the poles of sender [*destinateur*; or addressor, GJvdH] and recipient [*destinataire*; or addressee, GJvdH] upon the axis of address, the poles of sense and referent upon the semantico-referential axis (which Aristotle names apophantic)" (Lyotard, "La phrase-affect," 46/234). The translation of *destinateur* as addressor and of *destinataire* as addressee stems from the English translation of *Le différend*. Lyotard refers continuously to these four elements throughout *Le différend*; see, e.g., Lyotard, *Le différend*, 23/8, 30/13, 108/70, 201/139.

26. Ibid., 29/13.

27. Ibid., 30/13.

28. This ambiguity is discussed in more detail in chapter 12.

29. Ibid., 17/4.

30. Agamben, *Il sacramento del linguaggio*, 10/6.

31. In this sense, I do not agree with Agamben's attempts to remove the problem of the witness and of testimony in his analysis of the oath, which for him is the very locus of this promise of language; see ibid., 44–47/32–34; it did not come as a surprise to me that at the end of this book, Agamben cannot but reintroduce the terminology of testimony and attestation in the culmination points of his analyses of the oath and its role for human existence; cf. ibid., 91–99/66–72.

32. Lyotard, *Heidegger et "les juifs*," 82/47.

33. Ibid., 41/20.

34. Woodward, "Testimony and the Affect-Phrase," 170, 179, 182.

35. See Derrida, "Poétique et politique du témoignage," 528/77.

36. Derrida, *Demeure*, 98/75.

37. Reid, *An Inquiry into the Human Mind*, 232–33.

38. I refer to section 11, titled "Of Miracles," in Hume, *An Enquiry Concerning Human Understanding*, 79–95 as well as to some important, brief references in Book 1.3, titled "Of Knowledge and Probability," in Hume, *A Treatise of Human Understanding*, 50–120.

39. Ibid., 78 (= 1.3.9.12).

40. See Hume, *An Enquiry Concerning Human Understanding*, 80.

41. Arendt, *Crisis of the Republic*, 6–7. I would like to thank Sanem Yazıcıoğlu for pointing out this reference to me.

42. "[C]omprehension is built on the basis of a sense of human resemblance at the level of situations, feelings, thoughts, and actions" (Ricoeur, *La mémoire, l'histoire, l'oubli*, 223/175).

43. Ibid.

44. For a similar concern on probability and chance as determining factors in cognitive discourse, see Lyotard, *Le différend*, 23–24/8–9.

45. Locke's example of the king of Siam was referred to earlier in this chapter. Augustine is for Arnauld also the basic reference; see Arnauld, *Logique de Port-Royal*, 369–83 (= 4.12–14).

46. This expression is Arendt's, who uses it in the following context: "The new always happens against the overwhelming odds of statistical laws and their probability, which for all practical, everyday purposes amounts to certainty; the new therefore always appears in the guise of a miracle" (Arendt, *The Human Condition*, 178).

47. This sense of the miracle, its glory and epiphany, shows a particular kinship with Levinas's conception of testimony, which invokes specifically these notions, "glory" and "epiphany," to capture that dimension that leaves no reserve. See Levinas, *Autrement qu'être*, 220–38, and Levinas, "Vérité du devoilement et vérité du témoignage," 105–8/265–68, and especially; "The glory of the Infinite is the egress of the subject from the dark corners of its *reserve*, which might offer an escape route from the summons of the other" (ibid., 106/266). This explains why Levinas, despite clear resonances with elements of this study, plays such a limited role: for me, the reserve/object of testimony is not of the order of glory, that is, of a hyper-presence that transcends all phenomenological presence, but rather of a fundamental misery and poverty.

48. See Hume, *An Enquiry Concerning Human Understanding*, 81); see also Hume, *A Treatise of Human Nature*, 58–59 (= 1.3.4) where he reminds us of the ultimate "authority either of the memory or the senses."

49. Aristotle, *Rhetoric* 1356a2–21; LCL 193:16–17; Barnes, *The Complete Works of Aristotle*, 2:2155. See also Heidegger, *Grundbegriffe der aristotelischen Philosophie*, 119–23.

50. See Hume, *An Enquiry Concerning Human Understanding*, 82.

51. Ibid.

52. Ibid., 83.

53. Ibid.

54. Ibid., 95.

55. Ibid., 84–85. He cannot refrain from adding a third argument, namely that "supernatural and miraculous relations [. . .] are observed chiefly to abound among ignorant and barbarous nations" (ibid., 86). As always, the *barbaros*, those who have no access to the Greek *logos*—although this *logos* was supposed to be a shared, universal language of reason—is offered as an argument against the miracle.

Chapter 9

1. Heidegger, *Erläuterungen zur Hölderlins Dichtung*, 36/54. Translation slightly altered.

2. See Levinas, "Vérité du devoilement et vérité du témoignage," and Levinas, *Autrement qu'être*, 220–38; see also Franck, "The Sincerity of the Saying."

3. See the introduction of the anthology: Krämer, Schmidt, and Schülein, *Philosophie der Zeugenschaft*, 13–17. Here the continental approach is characterized by its attention for the testimony of victims.

4. Heidegger, *Sein und Zeit*, 38/25. In the original: "*das Sich-an-ihm-selbst-zeigende*, das Offenbare." He repeats this formulation at ibid., 41/27: "das Sich-an-ihm-selbst-zeigen" or "the self-showing in itself."

5. Ibid., 40/30.

6. See, e.g., ibid., 43/28. Aristotle also refers this sense of *logos* with the verb *dēloō*, "to make known."

7. Ibid., 46/30. In German: "Das was sich zeigt, so wie es sich von ihm selbst her zeigt, von ihm selbst her sehen lassen."

8. Ibid., 47/31.

9. Ibid. I've added the quotation marks to the translation because they are also in the German original. This has been addressed in a detailed way by Parapuf, *Hermeneutics and Relational Ontology*, 86–113.

10. "Und gerade deshalb [. . .] bedarf es der Phänomenologie" (Heidegger, *Sein und Zeit*, 48/31).

11. He uses the same translation in § 72 of *Grundbegriffe der Metaphysik*; see especially 441, 446.

12. See Heidegger, *Unterwegs zur Sprache*, 115/29. Nancy emphasizes the same distinction in *Le partage des voix*.

13. See Heidegger, *Sein und Zeit*, §§ 32–33.

14. Aristotle, *On Interpretation* 16a29; LCL 325:116–17; Heidegger, *Die Grundbegriffe der Metaphysik*, 444. See, e.g., Heidegger, *Die Grundbegriffe der Metaphysik*, 441–83 (= § 72) in which Heidegger basically reads Aristotle, *On Interpretation* 16a1–17a24; LCL 325:114–23; Barnes, *Complete Works of Aristotle*, 2:25–27. Here Heidegger emphasizes the threefold division I discuss next; see also Sheehan, "*Hermeneia* and *Apophansis*." For my purposes, this text of Heidegger does not play any other role because, e.g., his usage of the terms *Kundgabe* and *Zuverstehengeben* in this text is not marked by its specific role in relation to an exceptional phenomenon, but is simply translating the Greek verbs *dēloō* and *sēmainō*; see, e.g., Heidegger, *Die Grundbegriffe der Metaphysik*, 441–46.

15. Aristotle, *On Interpretation* 17a1–7; Barnes, *Complete Works of Aristotle*, 1:26. Heidegger, *Die Grundbegriffe der Metaphysik*, 448. This distinction has variants in Lyotard's distinction between the denotative and prescriptive phrase;

see Lyotard, *Le différend*, 173/117; and in Agamben's distinction between assertion and veridiction, see Agamben, *Il sacramento del linguaggio*, 84/61.

16. This is the specific sense Heidegger lends to the *Kundgabe* of the exceptional phenomenon of being in *Sein und Zeit*. This specific sense returns, it seems to me, in his account of hermeneutics in *Unterwegs zur Sprache*. It seems absent, though, from his reading of Aristotle's *On Interpretation* in *Die Grundbegriffe der Metaphysik*. There, *Kundgabe* and terms related to it simply refer to all types of making manifest; see, e.g., ibid., 441, 446. The same difference applies when we compare Heidegger's account of *Zuverstehengeben* in ibid., 442, where it is introduced as a translation of Aristotle's *sēmainein*, and its usage in his account of attestation in Heidegger, *Sein und Zeit*, § 54, where it concerns the opening up of new possibilities of hearing, as we discuss below.

17. This is the point of view Nancy defends against the interpretation of hermeneutics he discerns in Gadamer and Ricoeur; see Nancy, *Le partage des voix*.

18. Heidegger, *Sein und Zeit*, 244/172.

19. Ibid., 247–48/174–75; see also 250/176.

20. "The term *Stimmung*, which we usually translate as 'mood,' should be stripped here of all psychological significance and restored to its etymological connection with the *Stimme*" (Agamben, *Il linguaggio e la morte*, 70/55). A similar analysis can be found in Agamben, "Vocazione e voce."

21. Heidegger, *Sein und Zeit*, 248/175. In "Was ist Metaphysik?," Heidegger offers the same description: "Daß die Angst das Nichts enthüllt, bestätigt der Mensch selbst unmittelbar dann, wenn die Angst gewichen ist. In der Helle des Blickes, den die frische Erinnerung trägt, müssen wir sagen: wovor und worum wir uns ängsteten, war 'eigentlich'—nichts. In der Tat: das Nichts selbst—als solches—war da" (Heidegger, *Wegmarken*, 112).

22. Agamben, *Il linguaggio e la morte*, 73/58.

23. Heidegger strictly *distinguishes* between the ordinary attunements of everydayness and that of anxiety: "But just when moods [*Stimmungen*] of this sort bring us face to face with beings as a whole they conceal from us the nothing [*das Nichts*] we are seeking" (Heidegger, *Wegmarken*, 111/87).

24. "The etymological connection between *Stimmung* and *Stimme*, vocation [*vocazione*] and voice [*voce*], acquires here its own meaning" (Agamben, "Vocazione e voce," 86/498).

25. For revocation, see also Agamben, *Il tempo che resta*, 29/23.

26. For Heidegger, this enactment marks Aristotle's *euchē* in distinction from the *logos apophantikos* in *On Interpretation*: "Diese Rede ist auch nicht das bloße Wünschen, sonder der konkrete Vollzug des 'einen anderen Bittens'" (Heidegger, *Die Grundbegriffe der Metaphysik*, 448).

27. Heidegger, *Wegmarken*, 112/89.

28. Agamben, *Il linguaggio e la morte*, 72–73/57.

29. Levinas, *Existence and Existents*, 78.

30. "Wie soll es das auch, wo sich doch die Angst gerade in der völligen Ohnmacht gegenüber dem Seienden im Ganzen befindet" (Heidegger, *Wegmarken*, 113).

31. Agamben, *Il linguaggio e la morte*, 74/59; I changed the capitalization of Voice in this quote. The theme of testimony requires me to offer a partly alternative reading of this passage, cf. Van der Heiden, *Ontology after Ontotheology*, 247–53. In the afterword to "Was ist Metaphysik?," Heidegger simply uses the notion of the voice for this voicing or *Stimmung* of anxiety when he speaks of "die lautlose Stimme" and "die Stimme der Stille," which is the voice of being; see Heidegger, *Wegmarken*, 306. Anxiety there appears as "die von jener Stimme gestimmte Stimmung" (ibid., 307). Thus, there is a voice of being (*die Stimme des Seins*; ibid., 307), which, as Agamben argues, is an analogue of the voice of consciousness in *Sein und Zeit*; see Agamben, *Il linguaggio e la morte*, 76/60.

32. Heidegger, *Sein und Zeit*, 355/247.

33. "eine *Weise zu existieren*" (ibid.).

34. This furthers my analysis in Van der Heiden, "The Letter and the Witness."

35. In what follows, I translate this meaning of *zeugen* consistently as "to generate" because in English, it also has the senses of "to beget," "to create," and "to produce."

36. Heidegger, *Sein und Zeit*, 356/248. I've added the original's emphasis on "lost."

37. Ibid., 361/251.

38. Agamben, *Il linguaggio e la morte*, 74/59. See, e.g., Heidegger, *Sein und Zeit*, 363, 368.

39. Agamben's critical account of the Voice in Heidegger misses the value of attestation; in *Quel che resta di Auschwitz* he does address testimony but without reference to Heidegger's attestation.

40. Heidegger, *Sein und Zeit*, 357/249. See the discussion in ibid., § 44; at 292/203.

41. "In der Erschließungs-tendenz des Rufes liegt das Moment des Stoßes, des abgesetzten Aufrüttelns" (ibid., 361/251).

42. Ibid., 360/250.

43. Ibid., 360/250–51.

44. See, in this respect, also what Heidegger writes on Aristotle's *Rhetoric*: it is the task of the speaker (or the call) to transpose the hearer in another *diathesis*, disposition or "frame of mind," by inspiring—or "roused to emotion," *pathos*—the hearer for its cause, *Sache*; see Heidegger, *Grundbegriffe der aristotelischen Philosophie*, 121; and Aristotle's *Rhetoric* 1356a2–21; LCL 193:16–17.

45. Heidegger, *Sein und Zeit*, 364/253.

46. Ibid.

47. In this sense, I would not follow Ricoeur's analysis of conscience along the lines of Hegel, Nietzsche, and Heidegger, as if Heidegger would be the outcome

of the emptying out of a sense of conscience; cf. Ricoeur, *Soi-même comme un autre*, 396–405.

48. Derrida, *Foi et savoir*, 89–92/95–96; see also Naas, *Miracle and Machine*, 327. Derrida ranges attestation here under the heading of faith and oath, whereas elsewhere he argues that testimony is about presentation, thus reinstating the value of the present in Heidegger; see Derrida, "Poétique et politique du témoignage," 530/80. We have already seen why the connection of Heidegger's sense of phenomenology with presence is problematic in terms of his account of the distinctive or exceptional phenomenon, let alone of his account of testimony or attestation.

49. Ricoeur, *Soi-même comme un autre*, 350.

50. Consider, e.g., the following quote: "Das verstehende Hören des Rufes versagt sich die Gegenrede nicht deshalb, weil es von einer 'dunklen Macht' überfallen ist, die es niederzwingt, sondern weil es sich den Rufgehalt unverdeckt zueignet" (Heidegger, *Sein und Zeit*, 392/273).

51. Ibid., 367/255.

52. Ibid., 366/254.

53. Ibid., 367/255.

54. Heidegger, *Wegmarken*, 307.

55. "Das Sichängsten ist als Befindlichkeit eine Weise des In-der-Welt-seins; das Wovor der Angst ist das geworfene In-der-Welt-sein; das Worum der Angst ist das In-der-Welt-sein-können" (Heidegger, *Sein und Zeit*, 254/178). If one asks *how* this call is possible, one can probably only find an answer in the difficult formulations that Heidegger uses in "Was ist Metaphysik?" concerning this nothing: "The nothing nihilates incessantly" (Heidegger, *Wegmarken*, 116/92).

56. Here, I move beyond what Heidegger would probably affirm; consider, e.g., the following: "Das Gewissen ist der Ruf der Sorge aus der Unheimlichkeit des In-der-Welt-seins, der das Dasein zum eigensten Schuldig-seinkönnen aufruft" (Heidegger, *Sein und Zeit*, 383/266). It all depends on how one reads this "aus": it is true that care as a problem depends on this realm of uncanniness, but there is only a call to care to Dasein.

57. Agamben, *Il linguaggio e la morte*, 121/96; "*Testimony takes place in the non-place of articulation*. In the non-place of the Voice stands not writing, but the witness" (Agamben, *Quel che resta di Auschwitz*, 121/130).

58. Heidegger, *Sein und Zeit*, 367/255.

59. Ibid., 392/272.

60. Heidegger, *Parmenides*, 175/118; note that the English translation offers "the last word."

61. Ibid., 132/89.

62. Heidegger, *Unterwegs zur Sprache*, 159/66: "Die eigentliche Trauer ist in den Bezug zum Freudigsten gestimmt, aber zu diesem, insofern es sich entzieht, im Entzug zögert und sich spart. Indem der Dichter den genannten Verzicht

lernt, macht er die Erfahrung mit dem hohen Walten des Wortes. Er vernimmt die Ur-Kunde dessen, was dem dichterischen Sagen aufgegeben, als das Höchste und Bleibende zugesagt und doch vorenthalten ist. Die Erfahrung, die der Dichter mit dem Wort macht, könnte er nie durchmachen, wenn sie nicht auf die Trauer gestimmt wäre, auf die Stimmung der Gelassenheit zur Nähe des Entzogenen, aber zugleich für eine anfängliche Ankunft Gesparten."

63. See Derrida, "Le retrait de la metaphor."

64. See the entries *Zeuge* and *ziehen* in Kluge, *Etymologisches Wörterbuch der deutschen Sprache*, 811–12.

Chapter 10

1. *Jer.* 1:6.
2. Heidegger, *Sein und Zeit*, 369/256–257.
3. As Derrida writes: "the silhouette of a content haunts this response" (Derrida, *Donner la mort*, 106/74).
4. Agamben, *Categorie Italiane*, 64–65/66.
5. 1 *Cor.* 14:26–28.
6. There are good reasons to assume that Heidegger knew this, given his own account of Paul's letters; see especially Heidegger, *Phänomenologie des religiösen Lebens*, 97.
7. The most extensive explication of the meaning of the term "upbuilding," which appears in many titles of Kierkegaard's more religious works, stems from *Works of Love*, in which it becomes clear that the term "upbuilding" is a translation of the verb *oikodomeō* as used in 1 *Cor.* 8:1 and 10, see Kierkegaard, *Works of Love*, 209–24, and Pyper, *The Joy of Kierkegaard*, 130–44. This does not only mean that "upbuilding" is indeed a Pauline term in Kierkegaard's works, but also that it is a word that appears in the same Pauline letter as the reflection on glossolalia. Moreover, and more importantly, Paul refers to the same verb in 1 *Cor.* 14:26, where he uses the term *oikodomē*, the act of building up; in fact, this chapter includes by far the highest count of uses of this verb.
8. Agamben, *Quel che resta di Auschwitz*, 106–7/114–15.
9. Ibid., 106/114.
10. See the opening section of Lyotard, *L'inhumain*: as opposed to the sense of *Bildung* (or disciplining) presupposed in the constitution of subjects, infancy refers to what precedes these modes of subjectification. Therefore, infancy requires a speech that desubjectivizes. The task, for Lyotard, of philosophy and literature is to bear witness to infancy, that is, to let the normal discourses be affected by the speech that desubjectivizes.
11. Agamben, *L'uomo senza contenuto*, 13–14/4–5.
12. Plato, *Republic* 607d; Cooper, *Plato*, 1212.

13. Part of this section also motivates Van der Heiden, "A Hermeneutics of Attestation." Note that there is some ambiguity on the role of the prophet—and in a certain sense, I'm using this ambiguity that one can, e.g., find in Plato, *Timaeus* 71e-72b, where the *prophētēs* is the interpreter who explicates "the pronouncements produced by this state of divination or possession [*enthousiastikēs phuseōs*]" (Cooper, *Plato*, 1272-73). In this passage, Plato also introduces the difference between *entheos* and *ennous* to mark the difference between the enthusiast who is possessed and out of his mind, but can still disclose the most profound insights, and the one who is still in possession of his power of understanding and judgment and distinguishes between the useful and the useless divination. Elsewhere, Plato connects *hermēneutikē* to the work of the enthusiasts who do not properly know or understand; see Plato, *Epinomis* 975c; Cooper, *Plato*, 1619. See also Grondin, *Introduction to Philosophical Hermeneutics*, 21-23, who argues that the sense of *hermēneutikē* or *hermēneia* is marked by a fundamental ambiguity: hermeneutics, apparently, belongs to both domains, to the inspired speech that does not understand and the realm of understanding.

14. See, e.g., Plato, *Ion* 534c-d; Cooper, *Plato*, 942.

15. Plato, *Ion* 533d; Cooper, *Plato*, 941.

16. Jer. 1:6.

17. See, e.g., Heidegger, *Sein und Zeit*, 376/261.

18. Jer. 1:9.

19. Plato, *Ion* 534e-35a; Cooper, *Plato*, 942.

20. Freud, "Trauer und Melancholie"; Agamben, *Stanze*, 24-27/19-21.

21. Derrida, *Donner la mort*, 126/91.

22. This is one of Nancy's basic arguments: the divine voice is not given outside of the chain of possessions, but is only given in the poetic sharing of voices; see Nancy, *Le partage des voix*, 61-81.

23. See, e.g., Trezise, *Witnessing Witnessing*, 2-3; and Haidu, "The Dialectics of Unspeakability."

24. See also Derrida, *Spectres de Marx*, 32/11: "What seems almost impossible is to speak always *of the* specter, to speak *to the* specter, to speak with it, therefore especially *to make or to let* a spirit *speak* [*faire ou de laisser parler* un esprit]." Ricoeur expresses a similar concern in his reflection on how the historian can let (*laisser*) rather than make (*faire*) the past speak; yet Ricoeur does not have the same strict hesitation of Derrida concerning the question of the distinction of these two modes of speaking for the other. See Ricoeur, *La mémoire, l'histoire, l'oubli*, 230, and Van der Heiden, "The Voice of the Past," 443-44.

25. For what follows, see Benveniste, *Le vocabulaire*, 2:173-75.

26. For witness as *istōr*, see also Agamben, *Il sacramento del linguaggio*, 45/32.

27. Benveniste, *Le vocabulaire*, 2:175. See also the critical remarks concerning this "commonplace" in Agamben, *Il sacramento del linguaggio*, 38-40/27-28.

28. As Agamben writes in a comment on this account of the oath: "The oath does not concern the statement as such but the guarantee of its efficacy: what is in question is not the semiotic or cognitive function of language as such but the assurance of its truthfulness and its actualization" (ibid., 7/4).

29. Ibid., 12/8. That the oath was not only concerned with the problem of people lying and committing perjury is illustrated by his reference to Plato's *Laws*: "Thus Plato advises against requiring oaths of the parties to a trial because otherwise it would be revealed that half of the citizens are perjurers (*Laws* 12.948c)" (ibid., 11/7).

30. For a different approach, through Philo of Alexandria, see ibid., 28–31/20–22.

31. "For the question no longer concerns the wrath of the gods (for there is no such a thing) but the obligations of justice and good faith" (Cicero, *On Duties*, 3.29; LCL 30:382–83).

32. Derrida, "Poétique et politique du témoignage," 526/ 74. See also Derrida, *Foi et savoir*, 44–47/64–65, in which he argues that the oath generates God as the presupposition and the ground of itself; in this argument, the name of God is not so much erased as deconstructed and, as Naas suggests, determined as a "*present-absent* witness of every oath" (Naas, *Miracle and Machine*, 96).

33. Lyotard, *Le différend*, 103/66.

34. Ibid., 75/45.

35. Benveniste encounters the notion of *superstes* in his account of the provenance of the word *superstitio*; see Benveniste, *Le vocabulaire*, 2:273–79. For their appearance in pairs in Agamben and Derrida, see Agamben, *Quel che resta di Auschwitz*, 15/17; Derrida, *Demeure*, 54/45; Derrida, "Poétique et politique du témoignage," 526/73–74.

36. Benveniste, *Le vocabulaire*, 2:276.

37. Ibid., 2:277.

38. Derrida also explores these different semantic fields of the different words for (bearing) witness in "Poétique et politique du témoignage," 525–28/72–75; "*Marturion* means [. . .] 'bearing witness,' but also 'proof'" (ibid., 527/75).

39. As Derrida adds, this implies a particular sense of the present; see *Demeure*, 44/38.

40. Ibid., 54/45.

41. Agamben, *Quel che resta di Auschwitz*, 135–36/146.

42. Ibid., 71–72/77.

43. "Derjenige der mit dem Leben nicht lebendig fertig wird, braucht die eine Hand, um die Verzweiflung über sein Schicksal ein wenig abzuwehren—es geschieht sehr unvollkommen—mit der andern Hand aber kann er eintragen, was er unter den Trümmern sieht, denn er sieht anderes und mehr als die andern, er ist doch tot zu Lebzeiten und der eigentlich Überlebende. Wobei vorausgesetzt ist,

daß er nicht beide Hände und mehr als er hat, zum Kampf mit der Verzweiflung braucht" (Kafka, *Tagebücher*, 867); my italics. Except for the last sentence, the translation is taken from Arendt, *Men in Dark Times*, 171–72.

44. A similar idea can be found in Agamben's reference to *superstes*; see *Quel che resta di Auschwitz*, 124/132. To survive one's own death is the basic idea of Derrida's reading of Blanchot's story *L'instant de ma mort* in *Demeure*. Kafka's description, however, seems more sound from a phenomenological perspective and takes this idea away from the rather fictional dimension in which Blanchot keeps it enclosed.

45. Benveniste, *Le vocabulaire*, 2:150. LS, s.v. *auctor* [LS = Lewis and Short, *Latin-English Lexicon*].

46. LS, s.v. *auctor* II.γ.E.; see also Benveniste, *Le vocabulaire*, 2:150.

47. Agamben, *Quel che resta di Auschwitz*, 138/148.

48. Ibid., 139–40/149–50.

49. Ibid., 140/150.

50. Agamben, however, distinguishes the *superstes* from the *auctor*; see ibid., 139/149.

51. Ibid., 150/161.

52. Ibid., 151/162.

53. Agamben, *Il linguaggio e la morte*, 121/96.

54. See Ricoeur, *La mémoire, l'histoire, l'oubli*, 319–20/248; Ricoeur, *Temps et récit 3*, 183/100, 253–54/143; see also Vandevelde, "The Challenge of the 'Such as It Was,'" 145.

55. Heidegger, *Unterwegs zur Sprache*, 159/66.

Chapter 11

1. Lyotard, *L'inhumain*, 15/7.

2. See, e.g., Benoist, "De waarneming als intentionaliteit en als werkelijkheid," 258–64.

3. In this sense, this study on testimony furthers some of the basic insights I tried to develop in Van der Heiden, *Ontology after Ontotheology*.

4. Lyotard, *Le différend*, 10/xii.

5. Ricoeur, *Le conflit des interprétations*, 55/49.

6. Agamben, *Quel che resta di Auschwitz*, 59/65.

7. Melville, "Bartleby, the Scrivener," 34.

8. Agamben, "Bartleby o della contingenza," 86/269.

9. Agamben, *Il tempo che resta*, 43/40.

10. Agamben refers to Paul's comment that the law was ordained to life but led to death.

11. Mortier, *Godenslaap*, 48/44–45.

12. Here I reconsider the account of one element of Agamben's reading of *Bartleby, the Scrivener* that I offered in Van der Heiden, *Ontology after Ontotheology*, 253–61.

13. See, for all Agamben's references, Leibniz, *Philosophische Schriften*, 2.2:260–69 (#414, #415, and #416). Especially at 260.

14. Agamben, "Bartleby o della contingenza," 82/266.

15. As Agamben himself discusses in *Il tempo che resta* and, more extensively, in *L'uso dei corpi*.

16. Leibniz, *The Shorter Leibniz Texts*, 29 (*De veritatibus primis*); quoted in Agamben, *Il tempo che resta*, 42–43/39, and Agamben, *L'uso dei corpi*, 218–19/168.

17. Leibniz, *Discourse on Metaphysics & The Monadology*, 56 (= *La monadologie*, #53–#55). Also here, Leibniz refers to an absolute witness, see, e.g., *Philosophische Schriften*, 1:466–67 (= *La monadologie*, #61).

18. Lyotard, *Le différend*, 29/13.

19. Agamben, *L'uso dei corpi*, 220–21/170.

20. For the hyphen, see Agamben, *L'uso dei corpi*, 220/169. For the quote, ibid., 153/113.

21. Aristotle, *Metaphysics* 1019a23–26; LCL 271:250–51; Barnes, *The Complete Works of Aristotle*, 2:1609.

22. Leibniz, *Discourse on Metaphysics & The Monadology*, 56.

23. Aristotle, *Metaphysics* 1019b17–18; LCL 271:252–53. *Adunamia* means the deprivation (*sterēsis*) of *dunamis*; the *sterēsis* is here not the deprivation of its actualization as such, but rather a deprivation in *dunamis* itself; it is a potential or capacity that is not potential enough to actualize itself well.

24. In the *Metaphysics*, Aristotle notes that among its different senses, *dunamis* in a primary sense is "a source (*archē*) of change (*metabolē*) in another thing or in the same thing *qua* other" (Aristotle, *Metaphysics* 1020a5–6; Barnes, *The Complete Works of Aristotle*, 2:1610).

25. Leibniz, *Philosophische Schriften*, 2.2:266–67. Translation from Leibniz, *Theodicy*, 372.

26. See *Romans* 8:22. There, Paul uses the verb *sustenazō*, to groan, to lament, or to mourn (together), describing the current predicament of creation.

27. Heidegger, *Sein und Zeit*, 367/255.

28. Ibid., 454/315. In addition to the one just quoted, these four are: "Just in the most indifferent and harmless everydayness the being of Dasein can burst forth as the naked 'that it is and has to be.' The pure 'that it is' shows itself, the whence and whither remain obscure" (ibid., 179/127); and "In it, Dasein is taken back fully to its naked uncanniness and benumbed by it. But this numbness not only *takes* Da-sein back from its '*worldly*' possibilities, but at the same time *gives* it the possibility of an *authentic* potentiality-of-being" (ibid., 455/316); see also Visker, *The Inhuman Condition*, 54. The one time in which this adjective is not used in relation to uncanniness is in the following quote: "Interpretation does not, so to

speak, throw a "significance" over what is nakedly objectively present and does not stick a value on it, but what is encountered in the world is always already in a relevance which is disclosed in the understanding of world, a relevance which is made explicit by interpretation" (Heidegger, *Sein und Zeit*, 199/140). Hence, there is no such thing as naked existence in relation to objectively present being or handiness: these modes of being presuppose a horizon of meaning. Thus, by contrast, the adjective "naked" refers to what is without this presupposed horizon of meaning, to what is formless and without essence.

29. Plato, *Protagoras* 321c; Cooper, *Plato*, 757.
30. He accounts for anxiety in terms of "völlige Ohnmacht" (Heidegger, *Wegmarken*, 113).
31. See Stiegler, *La technique et le temps, 1*, 189ff/183ff; this story, told by Protagoras, can be found in Plato, *Protagoras* 320d–22d.
32. Ibid. 321c; LCL 165:130–31.
33. Plato, *Protagoras* 322a; LCL 165:130–31; Cooper, *Plato*, 757.
34. See Lyotard, *L'inhumain*, 9–15/1–7.
35. Ibid., 15/7.
36. Lyotard, *Lectures d'enfance*, 67/149.
37. See also Agamben, *Che cos'è la filosofia?* 26–28/12–13.
38. Ibid., 13–14/1–2.
39. Heller-Roazen, *Echolalias*, 9–12.
40. All the quotes that follow come from Lyotard, *L'inhumain*, 9–15/1–7.
41. In all the quotes from the translation, I have replaced "childhood" with "infancy."

Chapter 12

1. Plato, *Cratylus* 408c; Cooper, *Plato*, 126.
2. In what follows, I take Ricoeur's account of the symbol as a guideline to understand what he has to say on the notion of testimony and attestation, rather than, for instance, his "Emmanuel Levinas: Thinker of Testimony." The latter essay is too much focused on "absolute testimonies to the absolute," and of its task "to speak in the name of the absolute" (Ricoeur, "Emmanuel Levinas," 116). This latter approach bring testimony too close to Levinas's sense of the "glory of the infinite" (ibid., 123–24; Levinas, *Autrement qu'être*, 223–27).
3. For this complex of the wholly other, the call, and the proper positioning of religious symbolism, see Ricoeur, *De l'interprétation*, 504–10/524–31.
4. Plato, *Statesman* 260d–e.
5. Nancy, *Le partage des voix*, 17–21/213–15. See Van der Heiden, *Ontology after Ontotheology*, 74–78.

6. Nancy, *Le partage des voix*, 21/215.

7. "The opening of *hermeneuein* is, in this sense, the opening of meaning and to meaning as *other*: not an 'other' meaning, superior, transcendent, or more original, but a meaning itself as other, an alterity defining meaning. [. . .] *hermeneuein* determines or rather announces that the meaning, this meaning *in question*, is always *other*, in every sense of the expression" (ibid., 39–40/224).

8. Ibid., 40/253.

9. Ricoeur refers here to the Christian Gospel; see *De l'interprétation*, 505/525.

10. Ibid.

11. Ricoeur, *Philosophie de la volonté*, 323.

12. Ricoeur, *De l'interprétation*, 505/526.

13. Ricoeur, *Soi-même comme un autre*, 350–51/302.

14. Ibid.

15. Ibid., 34/22. I added the italics to the translation because it is also in the French original.

16. Belief here is not the equivalent of *doxa*, but means "belief in"; see ibid., 33/21).

17. Kearney, *Dialogues with Contemporary Continental Thinkers*, 27–28.

18. See, for instance, Derrida's account of the "oui, oui" in Joyce's *Ulysses*, Derrida, "Ulysse gramophone," 70/48, 75/49.

19. Ricoeur, *Soi-même comme un autre*, 370/320. Derrida suggests that a testimony without this additional silent voice is a "pure testimony" and that such a pure testimony is in fact an "impossible testimony" (Derrida, *Demeure*, 135/100). Yet there is no reason to speak here of "pure testimony" because there is only human testimony in the *absence* of any absolute witness. This absence affects every testimony and every witness, as Derrida rightly notes; see Derrida, "Poétique et politique du témoignage," 527–28/76.

20. Ibid., 528/78.

21. For Derrida, the oath by which the witness engages himself in testimony is the basic characteristic of testimony by which it deviates from the mere communication of information, see ibid., 531/82.

22. In Dutch and German one could use the verb *bezweren* and *beschwören*, respectively, for "to avert" a danger: these words show their immediate relation to "to swear," *zweren* and *schwören*, respectively.

23. Agamben, *Il sacramento del linguaggio*, 12/8.

24. It is somewhat unclear how Agamben sees the relation between testimony and oath. In the first half of the text, it seems quite clear that Agamben aims to offer a sense of the oath that distinguishes it from testimony, even though he refers to ancient texts that define the oath as affirmation plus a testimony of the gods; see ibid., 45/33. In the same context, however, he reintroduces the sense of

testimony by arguing that the oath is "the testimony [. . .] given by language itself" (ibid., 46/33). Toward the end of the text, the oath as the constitutive, generative moment of human language is understood as a testimony itself—and it is in this context that Agamben emphasizes the ethical sense of language; see 94–95/69.

25. Ibid., 46/34. This reference to the gods is also affirmed by Benveniste, *Problèmes de linguistique générale*, 2:255–56.
26. Agamben, *Il sacramento del linguaggio*, 50/36.
27. Aristotle, *Metaphysics* 983b34–35; Barnes, *The Complete Works of Aristotle*, 2:1556.
28. Agamben, *Il sacramento del linguaggio*, 26–27/18–19.
29. Ibid., 32/23.
30. Consider the following comments in Derrida, *Foi et savoir*, 44–45/65.
31. Naas, *Miracle and Machine*, 96.
32. Derrida, "Poétique et politique du témoignage" is written based on this very phrase of Celan; the reference to Heidegger can be found at 530/80.
33. Agamben, *Il sacramento del linguaggio*, 78/57.
34. Ibid., 16/11.
35. Ibid., 94/69.
36. For these differences, see Foucault, *Le gouvernement de soi et des autres*, 59–63/61–66.
37. Ricoeur, *La mémoire, l'histoire, l'oubli*, 204/164.
38. See also Agamben's discussion of the minister in *L'uso dei corpi*, 106–8/73–75.
39. Derrida, "Poétique et politique du témoignage," 527/76.
40. Foucault, *Le gouvernement de soi et des autres*, 60/62.
41. Ibid.
42. Ibid., 49/50.
43. Foucault, *Fearless Speech*, 169.
44. Thaning, Gudmand-Høyer, and Raffnsøe, "Ungovernable."

Chapter 13

1. Foucault, *Le courage de la vérité*, 160/173.
2. Derrida, *Béliers*, 20/139.
3. Foucault, *Le courage de la vérité*, 160/173, 200/217–18.
4. Ibid., 166/180.
5. See Kierkegaard, *The Moment*.
6. See Badiou, *Saint Paul*; and Foucault, *Le courage de la vérité*, 301/330–31.
7. Ibid., 216–17/234–35. This is also Hadot's analysis in *Qu'est-ce que la Philosophie Antique?*
8. Foucault, *Le gouvernement de soi et des autres*, 315–16/343–44.
9. See also Foucault, *Le courage de la vérité*, 60–61/63–64.

10. This is the conversion (*metanoia*) that is also as the beginning of philosophy, that is, the receptivity of/to truth; see Foucault, *Herméneutique du sujet*, 204–9/214–17, 366/382. Thus, *parrēsia* combines *technē* and *ēthos* (356/372) and veridiction is a *technē tou biou*, a technique of life or a *Lebenskunst* that shapes and transforms a human's mode of living (121/125). Foucault also uses the notion of *ēthopoiein* (227/237).

11. Foucault, *Fearless Speech*, 169.

12. Foucault, *Le gouvernement de soi et des autres*, 62/65.

13. Other techniques are described elsewhere extensively, see, e.g., Foucault, "Self Writing," in *Ethics, Subjectivity and Truth*, 207–22.

14. Foucault, *Le courage de la vérité*, 170/184.

15. Ibid., 226/245.

16. Ibid., 235/255.

17. Ibid., 170/184.

18. In Badiou's book on Paul, this is hardly a hidden theme; see Badiou, *Saint Paul*, 2/2.

19. In this context, Badiou speaks of the division of the subject; see ibid., 59–68/55–64.

20. Foucault, *Le courage de la vérité*, 168–69/183, 174/188.

21. Ibid., 215–16/234.

22. Badiou traces the theme of the *skandalon* in Paul; see Badiou, *Saint Paul*, 48–50/46–47.

23. For Diogenes of Sinope, see Foucault, *Le courage de la vérité*, 254–55/276–78.

24. In Agamben's reading of Paul, the messianic moment concerns exactly the similar sovereign capacity to act good beyond the law, that is, beyond the sin that disconnects *logos* and life; see *Il tempo che resta*, 113/121.

25. See Badiou, *Saint Paul*, 48–50/46–47.

26. Foucault describes the Cynic as "the angel of truth" (Foucault, *Le courage de la vérité*, 283/309). For the relation of Socratic irony and Cynic scandal, see, e.g., ibid., 215–16/234.

27. Zeillinger, "Zeugnishaftes Subjekt" notes that the figure of the witness offers an important motive of comparison between Derrida and Badiou, yet it is necessary to emphasize that Derrida and Badiou offer fundamentally different accounts of the witness.

28. "Death happened to him-them, it arrived *to* divide the subject of this story in some sense: it arrived at this division, but it did not arrive except insofar as it arrived (managed) thus to divide the subject" (Derrida, *Demeure*, 66/54).

29. These two I's that appear in the story are accompanied by a third I, as Derrida suggests, namely by Blanchot the author; see ibid., 126/94.

30. Blanchot, "L'instant de ma mort," 2.

31. Ibid., 4–9.

32. Derrida, *Demeure*, 88/68, 126–27/93–94.

33. In what follows, it becomes clear in which sense the idea that Derrida's work displays an "unconditional affirmation of survival" (Hägglund, *Radical Atheism*, 164) is highly problematic: what is there to affirm unconditionally in a loss?

34. Derrida, *Demeure*, 81/63–64.

35. Ibid., 33/31.

36. Ibid., 84/66.

37. Ibid.

38. Levi, *The Drowned and the Saved*, 83–84; quoted in Agamben, *Quel che resta di Auschwitz*, 31–32/33–34.

39. Ibid., 31–32/34.

40. See also Van der Heiden, "The Letter and the Witness."

41. Derrida, *Demeure*, 54/45. As Trezise notes, Agamben's account of Auschwitz is not about the singularity of this event but rather discloses more universal structures in human speech and the political constellation of this time; see Trezise, *Witnessing Witnessing*, 131–36. I'm less convinced that Agamben belongs to that set of authors who think that Auschwitz is concerned with the unspeakable (123–24): the category of testimony exactly challenges this.

42. Derrida, *Béliers*, 20/139.

43. Derrida, *Demeure*, 35/32.

Chapter 14

1. Soucy, *La petite fille*, 174/133.

2. Gadamer, "Wer bin Ich und wer bist Du?," 383/67.

3. The relation between these notions—in Hebrew *ruach* and *qol* and in Greek *pneuma* and *phōnē*—has been examined for instance by Cavarero, *For More than One Voice*, 20.

4. Gadamer, "Wer bin Ich und wer bist Du?," 388/73.

5. All quotes in the rest of this section are from Celan, "Der Meridian," 195–96/179–80, unless indicated otherwise.

6. To emphasize the uncertainty of this doubling, he even withdraws it at a certain point: "the mysterious, indistinguishable, and in the end perhaps the only strangeness" (ibid., 200/183).

7. Ibid., 192/177. For the relation of this notion to Heidegger's sense of *Unheimlichkeit*, see also Derrida, *Sovereignties in Question*, 125–30.

8. Agamben, *Quel che resta di Auschwitz*, 33–34/36–37.

9. Ibid., 35/38.

10. Celan, "Der Meridian," 196/180.

11. Agamben, *Quel che resta di Auschwitz*, 31/33.

12. Ibid., 47–49/53–54.

13. Howe, "The Origin and Function of the Gorgon-Head," 210–11.

14. Ibid., 212.

15. In Hyginus's theogony, Typhon is the father of Gorgon; see *Fabulae* 151, http://www.theoi.com/Text/HyginusFabulae4.html.

16. Celan, *Gesammelte Werke*, 3:185.

17. Ibid., 3:186.

18. This is the last poem of the third part of Celan's collection *Atemwende*; see ibid., 2:72. See especially Derrida, "Poétique et politique du témoignage," 533–36/87–91.

19. Derrida almost alludes to this in *Schibboleth*, 60/32, but he does so in terms of the inexhaustible interpretability and not in terms of the oath. In Derrida, "Poétique et politique du témoignage," he mentions the absolute witness/testimony twice (at 524/70 and 526/74).

20. Ibid., 524/70.

21. See Derrida, *Demeure*, 78/61 and 84/66. Even in his explicit reflection on this phrase ("Poétique et politique du témoignage," 533–36/87–91), Derrida does not consider the possibility that to bear witness for the witness might, in fact, concern the absent testimony of the *Du* that is needed to substantiate the words of the I.

22. Celan, *Gesammelte Werke*, 2:23.

23. Gadamer, "Wer bin Ich und wer bist Du?," 411/105.

24. Celan, *Gesammelte Werke*, 2:13. Translation taken from Gadamer, "Wer bin Ich und wer bist Du?," 392/78.

25. Agamben, *Quel che resta di Auschwitz*, 59/65.

26. Derrida, *Séminaire La bête et le souverain*, 361; Derrida, *Sovereignties in Question*, 130.

27. Celan's poetry is a "the breathless stillness of muted silence [*Verstummen*]" (Gadamer, *Ästhetik und Poetik II*, 363). See also Gadamer, "Wer bin Ich und wer bist Du?," 398–400.

28. *Singbarer Rest* is the title of one of Celan's poems, see *Gesammelte Werke*, 2:36. Derrida refers to this in *Béliers*, 48/149 to point out the inexhaustible reserve *of interpretation*.

29. Celan, "Der Meridian," 201/184.

30. Agamben, *Il tempo che resta*, 52/49–50.

31. Celan, *Gesammelte Werke*, 1:135. Translation taken from Celan, *Selected Poems*, 43.

32. Sextus Empiricus, *Outlines of Pyrrhonism*, I.29; LCL 273:20–21.

33. Celan, "Der Meridian," 201/184.

34. Ibid., 196/180.

35. Ibid. I've changed "expectation" by "hope" as a translation of *Hoffnung*.

36. Ibid., 199/182. My italics.

37. Ibid., 198–99/182.

38. See Levinas, "De l'être à l'autre," in *Noms propres*, 59–66.

39. Celan, *Gesammelte Werke*, 3:186.

40. Plato, *Symposium* 177a; LCL 166:97; Cooper, *Plato*, 462.

Bibliography

Agamben, Giorgio. *L'uomo senza contenuto*. Rome: Quodlibet, 2013. Translated by Georgia Albert as *The Man Without Content* (Stanford, CA: Stanford University Press, 1999).

Agamben, Giorgio. *Stanze: La parole e il fantasme nella cultura occidentale*. Turin: Giulio Einaudi, 2011. Translated by Ronald L. Martinez as *Stanzas: Word and Phantasm in Western Culture* (Minneapolis: University of Minnesota Press, 1993).

Agamben, Giorgio. "Bartleby o della contingenza." In *Bartleby. La formula della creazione*, by Giorgio Agamben and Gilles Deleuze, 45–89. Macerata: Quodlibet, 2011. Translated by Daniel Heller-Roazen as "Bartleby, or On Contingency," in *Potentialities: Collected Essays in Philosophy* (Stanford, CA: Stanford University Press, 1999), 243–71.

Agamben, Giorgio. *Infanzia e storia: Distruzione dell'esperienza e origine della storia*. Turin: Giulio Einaudi, 2001. Translated by Liz Heron as *Infancy and History: On the Destruction of Experience* (London: Verso, 2007).

Agamben, Giorgio. *Il linguaggio e la morte: Un seminario sul luogo della negatività*. Turin: Giulio Einaudi, 2008. Translated by Karen E. Pinkus and Michael Hardt as *Language and Death: The Place of Negativity* (Minneapolis: University of Minnesota Press, 1991).

Agamben, Giorgio. *La comunità che viene*. Turin: Giulio Einaudi, 1990. Translated by Michael Hardt as *The Coming Community* (Minneapolis: University of Minnesota Press, 1993).

Agamben, Giorgio. *Homo Sacer: il potere sovrano e la nuda vita*. Turin: Giulio Einaudi, 2005. Translated by Daniel Heller-Roazen as *Homo Sacer: Sovereign Power and Bare Life* (Stanford, CA: Stanford University Press, 1998).

Agamben, Giorgio. *Quel che resta di Auschwitz: L'archivo e il testimone*. Turin: Bollati Boringhieri, 1998. Translated by Daniel Heller-Roazen as *Remnants of Auschwitz: The Witness and the Archive* (New York: Zone Books, 2002).

Agamben, Giorgio. *La Potenza del pensiero: Saggi e conferenze*. Vicenza: Neri Pozza, 2012. Partly translated by Daniel Heller-Roazen as *Potentialities: Collected Essays in Philosophy* (Stanford, CA: Stanford University Press, 1999).

Agamben, Giorgio. *Il tempo che resta: Un comment alla Lettera ai Romani*. Turin: Bollato Boringhieri, 2000. Translated by Patricia Dailey as *The Time that Remains: A Commentary on the Letter to the Romans* (Stanford, CA: Stanford University Press, 2005).

Agamben, Giorgio. *Il sacramento del linguaggio: Archeologia del giuramento*. Rome: Laterza and Figli, 2008. Translated by Adam Kotsko as *The Sacrament of Language: An Archeology of the Oath* (Stanford, CA: Stanford University Press, 2011).

Agamben, Giorgio. *Altissima povertà: Regole monastiche e forma di vita*. Vicenza: Neri Pozza, 2011. Translated by Adam Kotsko as *The Highest Poverty: Monastic Rules and Form-of-Life* (Stanford, CA: Stanford University Press, 2013).

Agamben, Giorgio. *Categorie Italiane: Studi di poetica*. Rome: Laterza, 2011. (Originally published in 1996.) Translated by Daniel Heller-Roazen as *The End of the Poem: Studies in Poetics* (Stanford, CA: Stanford University Press, 1999).

Agamben, Giorgio. "Vocazione e voce." In *La potenza del pensiero*, 78–91. Translated as "Vocation and Voice," *Critical Inquiry* 40, no. 2 (2014): 492–501.

Agamben, Giorgio. *L'uso dei corpi*. Vicenza: Neri Pozza, 2014. Translated by Adam Kotsko as *The Use of Bodies* (Stanford, CA: Stanford University Press, 2015).

Agamben, Giorgio. *Che cos'è la filosofia?* Macerata: Quodlibet, 2016. Translated by Lorenzo Chiesa as *What is Philosophy?* (Stanford, CA: Stanford University Press, 2018).

Alloa, Emmanuel, and Stefan Kristensen. *Témoignage et survivance*. Geneva: MetisPresses, 2014.

Arendt, Hannah. *Men in Dark Times*. New York: Harcourt Brace & Company, 1970.

Arendt, Hannah. *Crises of the Republic*. New York: Harcourt, 1972.

Arendt, Hannah. *The Life of the Mind*. London: Harcourt, 1978.

Arendt, Hannah. *The Human Condition*. Chicago, IL: University of Chicago Press, 1998.

Aristotle. *Metaphysics: Books 1–9*. Translated by Hugh Tredennick. Loeb Classical Library, vol. 271. Cambridge, MA: Harvard University Press, 1933.

Aristotle. *Politics*. Translated by H. Rackham. Loeb Classical Library, vol. 264. Cambridge, MA: Harvard University Press, 1933.

Aristotle. *Categories, On Interpretation, Prior Analytics*. Translated by H. P. Cooke and Hugh Tredennick. Loeb Classical Library, vol. 325. Cambridge, MA: Harvard University Press, 1938.

Aristotle. *Art of Rhetoric*. Translated by J. H. Freese. Loeb Classical Library, vol. 193. Cambridge, MA: Harvard University Press, 1926.

Arnauld, Antoine. *Logique de Port-Royal*. New edition. Introduction by Charles Jourdain. Paris: Hachette, 1877.

Badiou, Alain. *L'être et l'événement*. Paris: Seuil, 1988. Translated by Oliver Feltham as *Being and Event* (Continuum: London, 2005).

Badiou, Alain. *Saint Paul: La fondation de l'universalisme*. Paris: PUF, 1997. Translated by Ray Brassier as *Saint Paul: The Foundation of Universalism* (Stanford, CA: Stanford University Press, 2003).

Bambach, Charles. *Thinking the Poetic Measure of Justice: Hölderlin—Heidegger—Celan*. Albany, NY: State University of New York Press, 2013.

Barnes, Jonathan, ed. *The Complete Works of Aristotle*. The Revised Oxford Translation. 2 vols. Princeton: Princeton University Press, 1995.

Benjamin, Andrew, ed. *Judging Lyotard*. London/New York: Routledge, 1992.

Bennington, Geoffrey. *Lyotard: Writing the Event*. New York: Columbia University Press, 1988.

Benoist, Jocelyn. "De waarneming als intentionaliteit en als werkelijkheid: Bijdrage tot de grammatica van de waarnemening." *Tijdschrift voor Filosofie* 78, no. 2 (2016): 251–75.

Benveniste, Émile. *Problèmes des linguistique général*. 2 vols. Paris: Gallimard, 1966. Translated by Mary Elizabeth Meek as *Problems in General Linguistics*, 2 vols. (Coral Gables, FL: University of Miami Press, 1971).

Benveniste, Émile. *Le vocabulaire des institutions Indo-Européens*. 2 vols. Paris: Minuit, 1969. Translated by Elizabeth Palmer as *Indo-European Language and Society* (London: Faber and Faber, 1973).

Berkman, Gisèle. *L'effet Bartleby: Philosophes lecteurs*. Paris: Hermann, 2011.

Bernet, Rudolf. "The Traumatized Subject." *Research in Phenomenology* 30 (2000): 160–79.

Blanchot, Maurice. *Le pas au-delà*. Paris: Gallimard, 1973. Translated by Lycette Nelson as *The Step Not Beyond* (Albany, NY: State University of New York Press, 1992).

Blanchot, Maurice. "L'instant de ma mort." In *The Instant of my Death/Demeure: Fiction and Testimony*, by Maurice Blanchot and Jacques Derrida, translated by Elizabeth Rottenberg, 2–11. Stanford, CA: Stanford University Press, 2000.

Castelli, Enrico. *Le témoignage: Actes du colloque organisé par le Centre International d'Études Humanistes et par l'Institut d'Études Philosophiques de Rome*. Paris: Aubier, 1972.

Cavarero, Adriana. *For More Than One Voice: Towards a Philosophy of Vocal Expression*. Translated by Paul A. Kottman. Stanford, CA: Stanford University Press, 2005.

Celan, Paul. *Selected Poems*. Translated by Michael Hamburger and Christopher Middleton. Middlesex: Penguin Books, 1972.

Celan, Paul. *Gesammelte Werke*. 7 vols. Frankfurt: Suhrkamp, 2000.

Celan, Paul. "Der Meridian." In *Gesammelte Werke*, 3:187–202. Translated by Jerry Glenn as "Appendix: The Meridian," in *Sovereignties in Question: The Poetics*

of *Paul Celan*, ed. Thomas Dutoit and Outi Pasanen (New York: Fordham University Press, 2005), 173–85.
Celan, Paul. *Collected Prose*. Translated by Rosemarie Waldrop. New York: Routledge, 2003.
Celan, Paul. *Breathturn into Timestead: The Collected Later Poetry*. Translated by Pierre Joris. New York: Farrar Straus Giroux, 2014.
Cicero. *On Duties*. Translated by Walter Miller. Loeb Classical Library, vol. 30. Cambridge, MA: Harvard University Press, 1913.
Cooper, John M., ed. *Plato: Complete Works*. Indianapolis, IN: Hackett Publishing Company, 1997.
Deleuze, Gilles. *Critique et clinique*. Paris: Minuit, 1993. Translated by Daniel W. Smith, and Michael A. Greco as *Essays Critical and Clinical* (London/New York: Verso, 1998).
Deleuze, Gilles, and Félix Guattari. *Qu'est-ce que la philosophie?* Paris: Minuit, 1991. Translated by Hugh Tomlinson, and Graham Burchell as *What is Philosophy?* (New York: Columbia University Press, 1994).
Derrida, Jacques. *L'écriture et la différence*. Paris: Seuil, 1967. Translated by Alan Bass as *Writing and Difference* (London: Routledge, 2001).
Derrida, Jacques. *La dissémination*. Paris: Seuil, 1972. Translated by Barbara Johnson as *Dissemination* (London: The Athlone Press, 1981).
Derrida, Jacques. *Marges de la philosophie*. Paris: Minuit, 1972. Translated by Alan Bass as *Margins of Philosophy* (Chicago, IL: The University of Chicago Press, 1982).
Derrida, Jacques. *Schibboleth: Pour Paul Celan*. Paris: Galilée, 1986.
Derrida, Jacques. "Ulysse gramophone: Ouï-dire de Joyce." In *Ulysse gramophone: Deux mots pour Joyce*, 57–143. Paris: Galilée, 1987. Translated by François Raffoul as "Ulysses Gramophone: Hear Say Yes in Joyce," in *Derrida and Joyce: Texts and Contexts*, edited by Andrew J. Mitchell and Sam Slote (Albany, NY: State University of New York Press, 2013), 41–86.
Derrida, Jacques. "Le retrait de la métaphore." In *Psyché. Inventions de l'autre*, 63–93. Paris: Galilée, 1987.
Derrida, Jacques. *Spectres de Marx: L'état de la dette, le travail du deuil et la nouvelle Internationale*. Paris: Galilée, 1993. Translated by Peggy Kamuf as *Specters of Marx: The State of the Debt, the Work of Mourning and the New International* (New York/London: Routledge, 2006).
Derrida, Jacques. *Force de loi*. Paris: Galilée, 1994.
Derrida, Jacques. *Politiques de l'amitié*. Paris: Galilée, 1994. Translated by George Collins as *The Politics of Friendship* (London/New York: Verso, 1997).
Derrida, Jacques. *Apories: Mourir—s'attendre aux "limites de la vérité."* Paris: Galilée, 1996. Translated by Thomas Dutoit as *Aporias: Dying—awaiting (one another at) the "limits of truth"* (Stanford, CA: Stanford University Press, 1993).

Derrida, Jacques. *Demeure: Maurice Blanchot*. Paris: Galilée, 1998. Translated by Elizabeth Rottenberg as *Demeure: Fiction and Testimony* (Stanford, CA: Stanford University Press, 2000).
Derrida, Jacques. *Donner la mort*. Paris: Galilée, 1999. Translated by David Wills as *The Gift of Death* (Chicago, IL: The University of Chicago Press, 1995).
Derrida, Jacques. *Foi et savoir. Suivi de Le siècle et le pardon*. Paris: Seuil, 2001. Translated as "Faith and Knowledge: The Two Sources of 'Religion' at the Limits of Reason Alone," in *Acts of Religion*, edited by Gil Anidjar (London/New York: Routledge, 2002), 40–101.
Derrida, Jacques. *Béliers. Le dialogue ininterrompu: entre deux infinis, le poème*. Paris: Galilée, 2003. Translated as "Rams: Uninterrupted Dialogue—Between Two Infinities the Poem," in *Sovereignties in Question*, 135–63.
Derrida, Jacques. "Poétique et politique du témoignage," *Herne* 83 (2004): 521–39. Translated by Thomas Dutoit and Outi Pasanen as "Poetics and Politics of Testimony," in *Sovereignties in Question*, 65–96.
Derrida, Jacques. *Histoire du mensonges. Prolégomènes*. Paris: L'Herne, 2005.
Derrida, Jacques. *Sovereignties in Question: The Poetics of Paul Celan*. Translated and edited by Thomas Dutoit and Outi Pasanen. New York: Fordham University Press, 2005.
Derrida, Jacques. *Sauf le nom*. Paris: Galilée, 2006.
Derrida, Jacques. *Séminaire La bête et le souverain*, vol. I (2001–2002). Paris: Galilée, 2008.
Derrida, Jacques, and Alexander Garcia Düttmann. "Perhaps or Maybe." *Pli* 6 (1997): 1–18.
Derrida, Jacques, and Évelyne Grossman. "La langue n'appartient pas. Entretien avec Jacques Derrida." *Europe: Revue littéraire mensuelle* 79, no. 861–62 (2001): 81–91. Translated by Thomas Dutoit and Outi Pasanen as "Language is Never Owned: An Interview," in *Sovereignties in Question*, 97–107.
Dilthey, Wilhelm. "Das Verstehen anderer Personen und ihrer Lebensäusserungen." In *Der Aufbau der geschichtlichen Welt in den Geisteswissenschaften*, 205–20. Vandenhoeck & Ruprecht: Göttingen, 1958. Translated as "The Understanding of Other Persons and Their Manifestations of Life," in *The Formation of the Historical World in the Human Sciences*, edited by Rudolf A. Makkreel and Frithjof Rodi (Princeton, NJ: Princeton University Press, 2002), 226–41.
Diogenes Laertius. *Lives of Eminent Philosophers: Books 1–5*. Translated by R. D. Hicks. Loeb Classical Library, vol. 184. Cambridge, MA: Harvard University Press, 1925.
Diogenes Laertius. *Lives of Eminent Philosophers: Books 6–10*. Translated by R. D. Hicks. Loeb Classical Library, vol. 185. Cambridge, MA: Harvard University Press, 1925.

Fóti, Véronique M. "'Speak, You Also': On Derrida's Readings of Paul Celan." *Mosaic* 39, no. 3 (2006): 77–90.
Foucault, Michel. *Ethics, Subjectivity and Truth*. Edited by Paul Rabinow. Translated by Robert Hurley et al. Vol. 1 of *The Essential Works of Michel Foucault, 1954–1984*, edited by Paul Rabinow. New York: The New Press, 1997.
Foucault, Michel. *Fearless Speech*. Edited by Joseph Pearson. Los Angeles, CA: Semiotext(e), 2001.
Foucault, Michel. *Herméneutique du sujet: Cours au Collège de France, 1981–1982*. Edited by Frédéric Gros. Paris: Seuil, 2001. Translated by Graham Burchell as *Hermeneutics of the Subject: Lectures at the Collège de France 1981–1982* (New York: Palgrave Macmillan, 2005).
Foucault, Michel. *Le gouvernement de soi et des autres: Cours au Collège de France, 1982–1983*. Edited by Frédéric Gros. Paris: Seuil, 2008. Translated by Graham Burchell as *The Government of Self and Others: Lectures at the Collège de France 1982–1983* (New York: Palgrave Macmillan, 2010).
Foucault, Michel. *Le courage de la vérité (le Gouvernement de soi et des autres II): Cours au Collège de France, 1983–1984*. Edited by Frédéric Gros. Paris: Seuil, 2009. Translated by Graham Burchell as *The Courage of Truth (The Government of Self and Others II): Lectures at the Collège de France 1983–1984* (New York: Palgrave Macmillan, 2011).
Franck, Didier. "The Sincerity of the Saying." In *Between Levinas and Heidegger*, edited by John E. Drabinski and Eric S. Nelson, 75–84. New York: State University of New York Press, 2014.
Freud, Sigmund. "Trauer und Melancholie." In *Gesammelte Werke X*, 427–46. London: Imago Publishing, 1946.
Freydberg, Bernard. *David Hume: Platonic Philosopher, Continental Ancestor*. New York: State University of New York Press, 2012.
Fricker, Miranda. *Epistemic Injustice: Power and the Ethics of Knowing*. Oxford: Oxford University Press, 2007.
Gadamer, Hans-Georg. *Wahrheit und Methode*. Tübingen: Mohr Siebeck, 1990.
Gadamer, Hans-Georg. *Neuere Philosophie I: Hegel, Husserl, Heidegger*. Tübingen: Mohr Siebeck, 1990.
Gadamer, Hans-Georg. *Ästhetik und Poetik II*. Tübingen: Mohr Siebeck, 1990.
Gadamer, Hans-Georg. "Wer bin Ich und wer bist Du?" In *Ästhetik und Poetik II*, 383–451. Tübingen: Mohr Siebeck, 1990. Translated by Richard Heinemann and Bruce Krajewski as "Who Am I and Who Are You?" in *Gadamer on Celan* (Albany, NY: State University of New York Press, 1997), 67–165.
Gadamer, Hans-Georg. *Gadamer on Celan*. Edited and translated by Richard Heinemann and Bruce Krajewski. Albany, NY: State University of New York Press, 1997.
Greisch, Jean, ed. *Paul Ricoeur: L'herméneutique à l'école de la phénoménologie*. Paris: Beauchesne, 1995.

Greisch, Jean. "Témoignage et attestation." In *Paul Ricoeur*, edited by Jean Greisch, 305–26. Paris: Beauchesne, 1995.
Grondin, Jean. *Hans-Georg Gadamer: A Biography*. Translated by Joel Weinsheimer. New Haven, CT: Yale University Press, 2003.
Hadot, Pierre. *Qu'est-ce que la Philosophie Antique?* Paris: Gallimard, 1995.
Hägglund, Martin. *Radical Atheism: Derrida and the Time of Life*. Stanford, CA: Stanford University Press, 2008.
Haidu, Peter. "The Dialectics of Unspeakability: Language, Silence and the Narratives of Desubjectification." In *Probing the Limits of Representation: Nazism and the "Final Solution,"* edited by Saul Friedlander, 277–99. Cambridge, MA: Harvard University Press, 1992.
Heidegger, Martin. *Wegmarken*. Frankfurt: Klostermann, 1976. Translated as *Pathmarks*, edited by Will McNeill (Cambridge: Cambridge University Press, 1998).
Heidegger, Martin. *Sein und Zeit*. Frankfurt: Klostermann, 1977. Translated by Joan Stambaugh as *Being and Time* (Albany, NY: State University of New York Press, 1996).
Heidegger, Martin. *Erläuterungen zur Hölderlins Dichtung*. Frankfurt: Klostermann, 1981. Translated by Keith Hoeller as *Elucidations of Hölderlin's Poetry* (New York: Humanity Books, 2000).
Heidegger, Martin. *Parmenides*. Frankfurt: Klostermann, 1982. Translated by Richard Rojcewicz and André Schuwer as *Parmenides* (Bloomington, IN: Indiana University Press, 1992).
Heidegger, Martin. *Einführung in die Metaphysik*. Frankfurt: Klostermann, 1983. Translated by Gregory Fried and Richard Polt as *Introduction to Metaphysics* (New Haven, CT: Yale University Press, 2000).
Heidegger, Martin. *Grundbegriffe der Metaphysik. Welt—Endlichkeit—Einsamkeit*. Frankfurt: Klostermann, 1983. Translated by William McNeill and Nicholas Walker as *The Fundamental Concepts of Metaphysics: World, Finitude, Solitude* (Bloomington, IN: Indiana University Press, 1995).
Heidegger, Martin. *Hölderlins Hymne "Der Ister."* Frankfurt: Klostermann, 1984. Translated by William McNeill and Julia Davis as *Hölderlin's Hymn "The Ister"* (Bloomington, IN: Indiana University Press, 1996).
Heidegger, Martin. *Unterwegs zur Sprache*. Frankfurt: Klostermann, 1985. Translated by Peter D. Hertz as *On the Way to Language* (New York: Harper & Row, 1971).
Heidegger, Martin. *Kant und das Problem der Metaphysik*. Frankfurt: Klostermann, 1991. Translated by Richard Taft as *Kant and the Problem of Metaphysics* (Bloomington, IN: Indiana University Press, 1997).
Heidegger, Martin. *Phänomenologie des religiösen Lebens*. Frankfurt: Klostermann, 1995.
Heidegger, Martin. *Der Satz vom Grund*. Frankfurt: Klostermann, 1997.

Heidegger, Martin. *Grundbegriffe der aristotelischen Philosophie*. Frankfurt: Klostermann, 2002.
Heidegger, Martin. *Beiträge zur Philosophie (Vom Ereignis)*. Frankfurt: Klostermann, 2003. Translated by Richard Rojcewicz and Daniela Vallege-Neu as *Contributions to Philosophy (Of the Event)* (Bloomington, IN: Indiana University Press, 2012).
Heller-Roazen, Daniel. "Speaking in Tongues." *Paragraph* 25, no. 2 (2002): 92–115.
Heller-Roazen, Daniel. *Echolalias: On the Forgetting of Language*. New York: Zone Books, 2005.
Heller-Roazen, Daniel. *The Enemy of All: Piracy and the Law of Nations*. New York: Zone Books, 2009.
Homer. *Odyssey*. Translated by A. T. Murray. Loeb Classical Library, vol. 104. Cambridge, MA: Harvard University Press, 1919.
Howe, Thalia Phillies. "The Origin and Function of the Gorgon-Head." *American Journal of Archeology* 58, no. 3 (1954): 209–21.
Hume, David. *An Enquiry Concerning Human Understanding*. Edited by Peter Millican. Oxford: Oxford University Press, 2007.
Hume, David. *A Treatise of Human Nature*. Edited by David Fate Norton and Mary J. Norton. Oxford: Oxford University Press, 2009.
Hyginus. *Fabulae 150–199*. http://www.theoi.com/Text/HyginusFabulae4.html.
Jolly, Rosemary. "Witnessing Embodiment." *Australian Feminist Studies* 26, no. 69 (2011): 297–317.
Kafka, Franz. *Tagebücher*. Edited by Hans-Gerd Koch, Michael Müller, and Michael Paisley. Frankfurt: Fischer, 2002.
Kearney, Richard. *Dialogues with Contemporary Continental Thinkers: The Phenomenological Heritage*. Manchester: Manchester University Press, 1984.
Kermode, Frank. *The Genesis of Secrecy: On the Interpretation of Narrative*. Cambridge, MA: Harvard University Press, 1980.
Kierkegaard, Søren. *Fear and Trembling. Repetition*. Kierkegaard's Writings, vol. VI. Edited and translated by Howard V. Hong and Edna H. Hong. Princeton, NJ: Princeton University Press, 1983.
Kierkegaard, Søren. *The Moment and Late Writings*. Kierkegaard's Writings, vol. XXIII. Edited and translated by Howard V. Hong and Edna H. Hong. Princeton, NJ: Princeton University Press, 1998.
Kierkegaard, Søren. *Works of Love*. Kierkegaard's Writings, vol. XVI. Edited and translated by Howard V. Hong and Edna H. Hong. Princeton, NJ: Princeton University Press, 2013.
King, Peter, and Nathan Ballantyne. "Augustine on Testimony." *Canadian Journal of Philosophy* 39, no. 2 (2009): 195–214.
Kluge, Friedrich. *Etymologisches Wörterbuch der deutschen Sprache*. Berlin/New York: De Gruyter, 1989.

Krämer, Sybille. "Les ambivalences du témoignage." In *Témoignage et survivance*, edited by Emmanuel Alloa and Stefan Kristensen, 53–75. Geneva: Metis-Presses, 2014.

Krämer, Sybille, Sibylle Schmidt, and Johannes-Georg Schülein, eds. *Philosophie der Zeugenschaft: Eine Anthologie*. Münster: Mentis, 2017.

Lackey, Jennifer, and Ernest Sosa. *The Epistemology of Testimony*. Oxford: Oxford University Press, 2006.

Leibniz, G. W. *Die philosophische Schriften*. 7 vols. Edited by C. J. Gerhardt. Hildesheim/New York: Georg Olms, 1978.

Leibniz, G. W. *Philosophische Schriften*. Edited and translated by Wolf von Engelhardt, Hans Heinz Holz, and Herbert Herring. 4 vols. Darmstadt: Wissenschaftliche Buchgesellschaft, 1985.

Leibniz, G. W. *Philosophical Texts*. Translated and edited by R. S. Woolhouse and Richard Francks. Oxford: Oxford University Press, 1998.

Leibniz, G. W. *Discourse on Metaphysics & The Monadology*. Translated by George R. Montgomery. New York: Dover, 2005.

Leibniz, G. W. *The Shorter Leibniz Texts: A Collection of New Translations*. Edited by Lloyd Strickland. London: Continuum, 2006.

Leibniz, G. W. *Theodicy: Essays on the Goodness of God, the Freedom of Man and the Origin of Evil*. Edited by Austin M. Ferrar, translated by E. M. Huggard. New York: Cosimo Classics, 2009.

Levi, Primo. *Survival in Auschwitz and The Reawakening: Two Memoirs*. Translated by Stuart Woolf. New York: Summit Books, 1986.

Levi, Primo. *The Drowned and the Saved*. Translated by Raymond Rosenthal. New York: Random House, 1989.

Levinas, Emmanuel. *Autrement qu'être ou au-delà de l'essence*. Le Livre de Poche. Dordrecht: Nijhoff, 1978. Translated by Alphonso Lingis as *Otherwise than Being or Beyond Essence* (Dordrecht: Kluwer, 1991).

Levinas, Emmanuel. *Noms propres*. Montpellier: Fata Morgana, 1976.

Levinas, Emmanuel. *Humanisme de l'autre homme*. Paris: Presses Universitaires de France, 1994. Translated by Nidra Poller as *Humanism of the Other* (Urbana/Chicago, IL: University of Illinois Press, 2003).

Levinas, Emmanuel. *Existence and Existents*. Translated by Alphonso Lingis. Pittsburgh, PA: Duquesne University Press, 2001.

Levinas, Emmanuel. "Vérité du dévoilement et vérité du témoignage." In *Le témoignage: Actes du colloque, Rome 5–11 janvier 1972*, edited by Enrico Castelli, 101–10. Paris: Aubier, 1972. Translated as "Truth of Disclosure and Truth of Testimony," in *Truth: Engagements across Philosophical Traditions*, edited by José Medina and David Wood (Malden, MA: Blackwell, 2005), 261–70.

Librett, Jeffrey S. "From the Sacrifice of the Letter to the Voice of Testimony: Giorgio Agamben's Fulfillment of Metaphysics." *Diacritics* 37, nos. 2–3 (2007): 11–33.

Llewelyn, John. *Seeing through God: A Geophenomenology*. Bloomington, IN: Indiana University Press, 2004.

Locke, John. *An Essay Concerning Human Understanding*. SI: WLC Books, 2009.

Lyotard, Jean-François. *Le différend*. Paris: Minuit, 1983. Translated by George Van Den Abbeele as *The Differend: Phrases in Dispute* (Manchester: Manchester University Press, 1988).

Lyotard, Jean-François. *L'inhumain: Causeries sur le temps*. Paris: Galilée, 1988. Translated by Geoffrey Bennington and Rachel Bowlby as *The Inhuman: Reflections on Time* (Cambridge: Polity Press, 1991).

Lyotard, Jean-François. *Heidegger et "les juifs."* Paris: Galilée, 1988. Translated by Andreas Michel and Mark S. Roberts as *Heidegger and "the Jews"* (Minneapolis, MN: University of Minnesota Press, 1990).

Lyotard, Jean-François. *Lectures d'enfance*. Paris: Galilée, 1991.

Lyotard, Jean-François. *Toward the Postmodern*. Edited by Robert Harvey and Mark S. Roberts. New York: Humanity Books, 1999.

Lyotard, Jean-François. *Misère de la philosophie*. Paris: Galilée, 2000.

Lyotard, Jean-François. "La phrase-affect (D'un supplément au *Différend*)." In *Misère de la philosophie*, 43–54. Paris: Galilée, 2000. Translated as "The Phrase-Affect (From a Supplement to the *Differend*)," *Journal of the British Society for Phenomenology* 32, no. 3 (2001): 234–41.

Lyotard, Jean-François. "Les voix d'une voix." *Nouvelle Revue de Psychanalyse* 42 (1990): 199–215. Translated by Georges Van Den Abbeele as "Voices of a Voice," *Discourse* 14, no 1 (2007): 126–45.

McGushin, Edward F. *Foucault's Askēsis: An Introduction to the Philosophical Life*. Evanston, IL: Northwestern University Press, 2007.

McLennan, Matthew R. *Philosophy, Sophistry, Antiphilosophy: Badiou's Dispute with Lyotard*. London: Bloomsbury, 2015.

Meillassoux, Quentin. "Deuil à venir, dieu à venir." *Critique: Revue générale des publications françaises et étrangères* 704–5 (2006): 105–15.

Meillassoux, Quentin. *Après la finitude: Essai sur la nécessité de la contingence*. Paris: Seuil, 2006. Translated by Ray Bassier as *After Finitude: An Essay on the Necessity of Contingency* (London: Continuum, 2008).

Meindl, Dieter. *American Fiction and the Metaphysics of the Grotesque*. Columbia, MO: University of Missouri Press, 1996.

Melville, Herman. "Bartleby, the Scrivener." In *Melville's Short Novels*, edited by Dan McCall, 3–34. New York: Norton, 2002.

Melville, Herman. *Moby Dick or The White Whale*. Boston, MA: S.H. Simonds Company, 1922.

Michelfelder, Diane P., and Richard Palmer, eds. *Dialogue and Deconstruction: The Gadamer-Derrida Encounter*. Albany, NY: State University of New York Press, 1989.

Moran, Richard. "Getting Told and Being Believed." *Philosophers' Imprint* 5, no. 5 (2005): 1–29.

Mortier, Erwin. *Godenslaap*. Amsterdam: De Bezig Bij, 2009. Translated by Paul Vincent as *While The God Were Sleeping* (London: Pushkin Press, 2014).

Naas, Michael. *Miracle and Machine: Jacques Derrida and the Two Sources of Religion, Science and the Media*. New York: Fordham University Press, 2012.

Nancy, Jean-Luc. "Le ventriloque." In *Mimesis des articulations*, edited by Sylviane Agacinski, 271–338. Paris: Flammarion, 1975.

Nancy, Jean-Luc. *Le partage des voix*. Paris: Galilée, 1982. Translated as "Sharing Voices," in *Transforming the Hermeneutic Context: From Nietzsche to Nancy*, edited by Geyle Ormiston and Alan D. Schrift (Albany, NY: State University of New York Press, 1990), 211–59.

Nancy, Jean-Luc. *L'impératif catégorique*. Paris: Flammarion, 1983.

Nancy, Jean-Luc. *Le sens du monde*. Paris: Galilée, 1993. Translated by Jeffrey S. Librett as *The Sense of the World* (Minneapolis, MN: University of Minnesota Press, 1997).

Nonnus. *Dionysiaca: Books 1–15*. Translated by W. H. D. Rouse. Loeb Classical Library, vol. 344. Cambridge, MA: Harvard University Press, 1940.

Ojakangas, Mika. "Conscience, the Remnant and the Witness: Genealogical Remarks on Giorgio Agamben's Ethics." *Philosophy and Social Criticism* 36, no. 6 (2010): 697–717.

Oliver, Kelly. *Witnessing: Beyond Recognition*. Minneapolis, MN: University of Minnesota Press, 2001.

Parapuf, Andreea. *Hermeneutics and Relational Ontology: Hermeneutical Dimensions in Heidegger's Later Thinking of Being*. Nijmegen, s.n., 2015.

Plato. *Republic: Books 6–10*. Translated by Paul Shorey. Loeb Classical Library, vol. 276. Cambridge, MA: Harvard University Press, 2006.

Plato. *Theaetetus, Sophist*. Translated by Harold North Fowler. Loeb Classical Library, vol. 123. Cambridge, MA: Harvard University Press, 2006.

Plato. *Laws: Books VII–XII*. Translated by R. G. Bury. Loeb Classical Library, vol. 192. Cambridge, MA: Harvard University Press, 1926.

Plato. *Statesman, Philebus, Ion*. Translated by Harold North Fowler and W. R. M. Lamb. Loeb Classical Library, vol. 164. Cambridge, MA: Harvard University Press, 1925.

Plato. *Lysias, Symposium, Gorgias*. Translated by W. R. M. Lamb. Loeb Classical Library, vol. 166. Cambridge, MA: Harvard University Press, 1925.

Plato. *Laches, Protagoras, Meno, Euthydemus*. Translated by W. R. M. Lamb. Loeb Classical Library, vol. 165. Cambridge, MA: Harvard University Press, 1924.

Plotinus, *Enneads, Volume VI: 6–9*, Translated by A. H. Armstrong. Loeb Classical Library, vol. 468. Cambridge, MA: Harvard University Press, 1988.

Plutarch. *Lives: Pericles and Fabius Maximus. Nicias and Crassus*. Translated by Bernadotte Perrin. Loeb Classical Library, vol. 65. Cambridge, MA: Harvard University Press, 1916.

Pyper, Hugh. *The Joy of Kierkegaard: Essays on Kierkegaard as a Biblical Reader*. London/New York: Routledge, 2014.

Reid, Thomas. *An Inquiry into the Human Mind: On the Principles of Common Sense*. London: Thomas Tegg, 1823.
Ricoeur, Paul. *Philosophie de la volonté. Finitude et culpabilité. II. La symbolique du mal*. Paris: Montaigne, 1960.
Ricoeur, Paul. *De l'interprétation, essai sur Freud*. Paris: Seuil, 1965. Translated by Denis Savage as *Freud and Philosophy: An Essay on Interpretation* (New Haven, CT: Yale University Press, 1970).
Ricoeur, Paul. *Temps et récit. 3. Le temps raconté*. Points Essais. Paris: Seuil, 1985. Translated by Kathleen Blamey and David Pellauer as *Time and Narrative, vol. 3* (Chicago, IL: The University of Chicago Press, 1988).
Ricoeur, Paul. *Du texte à l'action. Essai d'herméneutique II*. Paris: Seuil, 1986.
Ricoeur, Paul. *Soi-même comme un autre*. Paris: Seuil, 1990. Translated by Kathleen Blamey as *Oneself as Another* (Chicago, IL: The University of Chicago Press, 1992).
Ricoeur, Paul. "Emmanuel Levinas: Thinker of Testimony." In *Figuring the Sacred*, edited by Mark I. Wallace, 108–26. Minneapolis, MN: Fortress Press, 1995.
Ricoeur, Paul. *La mémoire, l'histoire, l'oubli*. Paris: Seuil, 2000. Translated by Kathleen Blamey and David Pellauer as *Memory, History, Forgetting* (Chicago, IL: University of Chicago Press, 2004).
Sallis, John. *The Verge of Philosophy*. Chicago, IL: University of Chicago Press, 2008.
Schmidt, Dennis. *On Germans and Other Greeks: Tragedy and Ethical Life*. Bloomington IN: Indiana University Press, 2001.
Schmidt, Dennis. "The Garden of Letters: Plato's Phaedrus on the Nature of Texts." *International Yearbook for Hermeneutics* 12 (2003): 61–76.
Schumacher, Eckhard. *Die Ironie der Unverständlichkeit: Johann Georg Hamann, Friedrich Schlegel, Jacques Derrida, Paul de Man*. Frankfurt: Suhrkamp, 2000.
Sextus Empiricus. *Outlines of Pyrrhonism*. Loeb Classical Library, vol. 273. Translated by R. G. Bury. Cambridge MA: Harvard University Press, 2000.
Sheehan, Thomas. "*Hermeneia* and *Apophansis*: The early Heidegger on Aristotle." In *Heidegger et l'idée de la phénoménologie*, edited by Franco Volpi et al., 67–80. Dordrecht: Kluwer, 1988.
Sheehan, Thomas. *Making Sense of Heidegger: A Paradigm Shift*. London/New York: Rowman & Littlefield, 2015.
Sluiter, Ineke, and Ralph M. Rosen, eds. *Free Speech in Classical Antiquity*. Boston/Leiden: Brill, 2004.
Soucy, Gaétan. *La petite fille qui aimait trop les allumettes*. Montreal: Boréal, 2000. Translated by Sheila Fischman as *The Little Girl Who Was Too Fond of Matches* (Toronto: Anansi, 2000).
Stiegler, Bernard. *Prendre soin de la jeunesse et des générations*. Paris: Flammarion, 2008. Translated by Stephen Barker as *Taking Care of Youth and the Generations* (Stanford, CA: Stanford University Press, 2010).

Stiegler, Bernard. *Ce qui fait que la vie vaut la peine d'être vécue*. Paris: Flammarion, 2010. Translated by Daniel Ross as *What Makes Life Worth Living: On Pharmacology* (Cambridge/Malden, MA: Polity Press, 2013).

Stiegler, Bernard. *La technique et le temps, 1: La faute d'Épiméthée*. Paris: Galilée, 1994. Translated by Richard Beardsworth and George Collins as *Technics and Time, 1: The Fault of Epimetheus* (Stanford, CA: Stanford University Press, 1998).

Thaning, Morten Sørensen, Marius Gudmand-Høyer, and Sverre Raffnsøe. "Ungovernable: Reassessing Foucault's Ethics in Light of Agamben's Conception of Use." *International Journal of Philosophy and Theology* 77, no. 3 (2016): 191–218.

Trezise, Thomas. *Witnessing Witnessing: On the Reception of Holocaust Survivor Testimony*. New York: Fordham University Press, 2013.

Van der Heiden, Gert-Jan. "De onbestemde taal. Over *Het meisje dat teveel van lucifers hield* van Gaëtan Soucy." In *Sprekende werken. Over de ethische zeggingskracht van literatuur*, edited by Marcel Becker and Paul van Tongeren, 107–15. Budel: Damon, 2009.

Van der Heiden, Gert-Jan. *De stem van de doden. Hermeneutiek als spreken namens de ander*. Nijmegen: Vantilt, 2012.

Van der Heiden, Gert-Jan. *Ontology after Ontotheology: Plurality, Event, and Contingency in Contemporary Philosophy*. Pittsburgh, PA: Duquesne University Press, 2014.

Van der Heiden, Gert-Jan. "The Voice of the Past in the Present: On the Relation of Testimony and Dialogue." *Journal of the Philosophy of History* 8, no. 3 (2014): 426–44.

Van der Heiden, Gert-Jan. "On the Way to Attestation: Trust and Suspicion in Ricoeur's Hermeneutics," *International Journal of Philosophy and Theology* 75, no. 2 (2014): 129–41.

Van der Heiden, Gert-Jan. "The Letter and the Witness: Agamben, Heidegger, and Derrida." *Journal of the British Society for Phenomenology* 46, no. 4 (2015): 292–306.

Van der Heiden, Gert-Jan. "Vrienden van het verhaal." In *Rondom vriendschap. Filosofische beschouwingen. Opstellen aangeboden aan Paul van Tongeren*, edited by Marcel Becker, Edith Brugmans, and Janske Hermens, 18–32. Zoetermeer: Klement, 2015.

Van der Heiden, Gert-Jan. "Het literaire getuigenis in *Godenslaap*." *De Uil van Minerva* 29, no. 3 (2016): 192–205.

Van der Heiden, Gert-Jan. "The Dialectics of Paul: On Exception, Grace, and Use in Badiou and Agamben." *International Journal of Philosophy and Theology* 77, no. 3 (2016): 171–90.

Van der Heiden, Gert-Jan. "Technology and Childhood: On a Double Debt of the Human." *International Yearbook of Hermeneutics* 15 (2016): 16–34.

Van der Heiden, Gert-Jan. "A Hermeneutics of Attestation: The Death of God and his Messengers." In *Beyond Nihilism*, edited by Chris Bremmers, Andrew T. K. Smith, and Jean-Pierre Wils, 155–168. Nordhausen: Traugott Bautz, 2018.

Van der Heiden, Gert-Jan. "To Speak for the Speechless: On Erwin Mortier's *While the Gods Were Sleeping*." *International Yearbook of Hermeneutics* 17 (2018): 84–94.

Vandevelde, Pol. "The Challenge of the 'such as it was': Ricoeur's Theory of Narratives." In *Reading Ricoeur*, edited by David Kaplan, 141–62. Albany, NY: State University of New York Press, 2008.

Vila-Matas, Enrique. *Bartleby & Co*. Translated by Jonathan Dunne. New York: New Directions Books, 2014.

Visker, Rudi. *The Inhuman Condition: Looking for Difference after Levinas and Heidegger*. Dordrecht: Kluwer, 2004.

Vogt, Erik. "S/Citing the Camp." In *Politics, Metaphysics, and Death: Essays on Giorgio Agamben's* Homo Sacer, edited by Andrew Norris, 74–106. Durham, NC: Duke University Press, 2005.

Vries, Hent de. "Attestation du temps et de l'autre. De *Temps et récit* à *Soi-même comme un autre*." In *Paul Ricoeur*, edited by Jean Greisch, 21–42. Paris: Beauchesne, 1995.

Vries, Hent de. *Kleine filosofie van het wonder*. Amsterdam: Boom, 2015.

Watkin, William. *Agamben and Indifference: A Critical Overview*. London/New York: Rowman & Littlefield, 2014.

Woodward, Ashley. "Testimony and the Affect-Phrase." In *Rereading Jean-François Lyotard*, edited by Heidi Bickis and Rob Shields, 169–87. Farnham: Ashgate, 2013.

Zeillinger, Peter. "Zeugnishaftes Subjekt. Jacques Derrida und Alain Badiou." In *Tod des Subjekts? Poststrukturalismus und christliches Denken*, edited by Michael Zichy and Heinrich Schmidinger, 243–62. Innsbruck/Wien: Tyrolia-Verlag, 2005.

Index

abandonment, 49, 110
  of being (*Seinsverlassenheit*), 265
Abraham, 70–84, 87–90, 93, 95, 133, 179, 181, 197–98, 245, 255
abyss, 39, 76, 259
addressee, 43, 92, 94, 136, 139–40, 184–85, 206–7, 222–27, 241
addressor, 83, 139, 285
Adimantus, 111–12, 282
admiration, 78, 84, 90, 149, 181
advent, 88, 96, 161
affirmation, 21, 71, 129, 135, 159, 164–69, 197, 227, 230–32, 248, 267
afterlife, 8, 112, 114, 117, 120
Agamben, Giorgio, xiv, xv, 5, 7, 23, 26, 30, 35–36, 44–50, 53–54, 56, 59, 65–66, 69, 75, 80–81, 84, 101, 109–18, 120, 122, 128, 139, 151, 155–62, 170–72, 179, 182–83, 192–93, 196, 198–99, 205–13, 216, 229, 230–33, 237, 239, 241–43, 246–47, 250–52, 258, 260–61, 264, 267
Agathon, 97
aidōs, xiii
alētheia, 15, 24, 118, 120–21, 151, 155, 168, 174, 221
Alice, 13, 33, 38–47, 51, 55, 60, 70, 170, 172

alogos, xiii, xv, 35, 108, 154, 210, 213, 215, 219, 253
amelēs, 118–21
angel, 182, 299
animal, xiii, 10, 33–35, 48–49, 154, 157, 159, 161, 167, 214–17, 241
announcement, 142, 153–55, 157, 161–62, 175, 221–27, 235, 238–39, 249
  primordial, 222–23
  symbolic, 223–25
anonymity, 23, 46, 66
  anonymous, 22, 32, 56, 66, 87, 89–90, 93–94, 96, 100
answerability, 172
  answerable, 151, 164, 169, 172
anxiety, xiv, 38, 64, 79, 155–59, 162–64, 170–73, 180, 182, 214
Apel, Karl-Otto, 26, 30, 34
Apelles, 267–68
  cut of, 267
apodēmia, 110, 116
apologos, 11, 111, 113, 116–17, 184, 256
apophansis, 132, 153
apophasis, 132, 231, 237
aporia, 76, 182, 215, 268
appeal, 30, 32, 144, 149, 154–55, 184, 191, 221–22, 228, 252
  to faith, 143, 165, 168

appearance, 95–96, 109, 111–13, 120, 127, 141, 146, 226
arbiter, 191
archē, 3, 31, 92, 212, 270
archeology, 229, 231–32
Arendt, Hannah, 98, 146, 166, 196–97, 214, 233
Ariane, 44–47, 50, 70, 170, 172
Aristodemus, 97
Aristotle, 6–7, 26, 33–35, 48, 78, 84, 134, 145–48, 152–54, 161, 204, 208, 211–14, 221, 226, 230–33, 242
Arnauld, Antoine, 146, 286
articulation, 9–10, 36, 41, 50–51, 59, 97, 102, 140, 142, 154, 161, 171, 209, 213, 228, 230, 244, 247, 251
between being and language, 211
arts, xi, xiii, 97, 203, 215–17
assertion, 50, 250
attestation, xii–xiv, 6, 11 15, 21, 30, 36, 134, 151–75, 178, 185–89, 193, 199, 212–13, 224–27, 230, 240–41, 245, 250–54, 264
absence of, 12, 26, 84, 139, 142, 175, 250–53, 264
exceptional, 151, 160
attorney, 88–97, 100–4
attunement, xiv, 35, 39, 78, 84, 133, 135, 145, 149, 156–58, 163, 169–70, 187, 197, 205, 225–27
fundamental (*Grundstimmung*), 38, 156–62, 169
auctor, 190, 195, 198–200, 212, 216, 228, 250–51, 260, 263–64
audience, 3, 16, 84, 92–94, 126–28, 133, 143, 147–48, 166, 185, 245
Augustine of Hippo, 49, 129, 146
authenticity, 161, 165, 168, 170
authority (*auctoritas*), 198, 204, 209, 234, 263

awe, xiii, 90, 95, 103, 159

Badiou, Alain, 3, 70, 128, 134, 197, 233, 240, 243–48
ban, 34, 110
banishment, 49, 108, 180
barbarian, 80, 182
barbaric, 108, 182, 210
barbarous, 80–83, 93, 286
bareness, xii, 243, 246
Bartleby, 5, 13, 45, 87–109, 127–28, 133, 179, 206–8, 212–13, 245
battle, 22, 75, 77, 111, 196–97, 254
dialectical, 77
belief, 92–93, 133, 136–37, 141, 144–49, 221–27
believer, 46, 146–47, 227, 243
Benoist, Jocelyn, 203
Benveniste, Émile, 190–98
bifurcation, 133, 243
birth, xii–xiii, 34, 120, 160, 189, 214–16
Blanchot, Maurice, 65, 75, 84, 142, 248–52, 255, 264
blessing, 228–33, 237
body, xi–xii, 44, 66, 70, 79, 100–1, 109–11, 118, 195, 243, 252, 268
border, xi, 54
boundary, 47, 53–54, 76, 99, 102, 154, 266
breath, 66–67, 90–91, 159, 185–86, 189, 257–62, 265–66, 269
breathlessness, 159, 263
Büchner, Georg, 257, 259

call, xiv, 21, 30–32, 132–33, 153–59, 162–73, 177–80, 185–87, 210, 221, 225–28, 236, 254, 263. See also *Ruf*
of conscience, 155, 164, 168–69, 173, 180, 226
symbolic, 223

caller, 169–72
capacity to speak, 10, 23, 34, 44–47, 58, 70, 79, 80, 122, 127, 185, 197, 212–19, 243, 258, 261
care, xiii, 10, 19, 39, 84, 110, 113, 120–22, 171–73, 207, 241
  call of, 171
  call to, 171–72
  demand for, 120, 170–72
  of the self, 20. *See also* self-care
  of the soul, 117, 184
carelessness, 119–21, 173
catastrophe, 262–66
Celan, Paul, 62, 231–32, 257–70
child, 38, 43, 50, 58–60, 65, 70, 80, 116, 122, 182, 185, 214, 217. *See also* infant
childhood, 57, 61, 271
Christ, 46, 94, 129, 148, 243
Christianity, 71, 239, 243
Cicero, 192
clerk, 83, 85, 96, 98, 102–4
Code of Justinian, 91
commemorative place, 61, 120
commensurability, 78
commitment, 135, 239–40, 243, 248–49, 253–54
common measure, 77, 93–94, 99, 178
common sense, 77, 85, 93, 95, 99, 101–2, 133, 142
commonality, 92–93, 99, 101, 105
communicable, 77–78
communication, 16, 30–31, 69, 99, 101–3, 114, 179, 180, 185–87, 245, 255–56
  divine, 186
community, 80, 85, 108, 110, 114–17, 180–85, 256
concealment, 38–39, 111, 118–21, 131, 153, 226
conceptual persona, 107–9
conflict, 225
confusion, 181–82
conscience, 155, 159, 161–73, 177–80, 216, 226
constitution, 116–17, 145
  onto-theological, 188, 243
contamination, 112, 186, 225, 250
contingency, 59, 99, 215
contraction, 47, 189, 237
controversy, 19
convention, 34, 244
conversation, 17, 18, 21–24, 165
conversion, 239, 241, 244, 246–48, 269
conviction, 73, 96, 101–2, 146, 167–68, 194, 198, 223–26, 234, 236, 239–40, 242, 249, 256
court of law, 228, 249
credence, 109, 112, 126
credibility, 146, 163, 166, 221
credible, 148, 193, 227
credulity, 136, 144–48
cry
  of distress, 159
  of joy, 159
curse, 228–33, 236–37, 263
custom, 145–46, 148, 212
Cynicism, 237–47

danger, 11–12, 28, 228, 236
Dasein, xiv, 155–64, 168–73, 177–80, 203, 214, 241
De Man, Paul, 73
deactivation, 39, 74, 109, 140–41, 158, 209, 231
dead, the, xii, 22–24, 32, 36, 49, 50, 55–67, 82, 91, 107–17, 122, 127, 207, 212–13
  land of, xii, 107–16
  living, 94
death, xii, 22, 38, 41, 44–45, 50, 59, 64, 82, 94, 113, 117, 157, 188, 193–97, 207, 214, 243, 248–52, 262, 264

death *(continued)*
  second, 60–61
debate, 19–20, 25, 29, 32, 130, 136, 144, 151, 192, 194, 243
deceased, the, 24, 55–57, 61, 113
deception, 54, 64, 142, 165–69, 227
deconstruction, 75, 113, 232, 265
deformation, 109, 172, 218
Deleuze, Gilles, 87–91, 95, 97, 103, 107–10, 128, 139, 206
Delphic inscription (*Delphikon gramma*), 4, 6–10
demand, 7–12, 19, 26, 28, 36, 38, 47, 50–57, 60, 62, 65, 67, 69, 75, 79, 82, 93, 113, 117–22, 128–29, 132–39, 149, 151–55, 157, 159, 162, 167, 170–72, 175, 200, 204–16, 227, 236–37, 241–42, 259, 264–65. See also *esigenza*
demiurge, 208–9
Derrida, Jacques, xv, 3–4, 7–10, 22, 28, 42, 48, 54, 65, 71, 75, 79, 82–90, 97, 103, 113, 125, 128–29, 131, 139, 142–44, 147, 162, 167–68, 173–75, 179, 187–89, 192–93, 195–96, 206, 226–28, 231–32, 235, 237, 239, 248–55, 263–64, 266
descendant, 30, 55, 57, 67
despair, 44, 63, 196, 197, 254
destitution, 64, 246–47
desubjectification, 182, 184, 187–90, 196, 233, 237–38, 247, 251, 253
dialectics, 75, 77, 279
dialogicity, 15
dialogue, xi, xiii, 4, 8, 12, 15–32, 69, 109, 111, 121, 127, 183–84, 215, 269
  philosophical, 19–20, 28
  proper, 18–22
différance, 54

differend (*différend*), 34, 36, 128, 138–40, 142, 145, 204–6, 235
dikaiosunē, 33, 110–12, 117
dikē, xiii, 33
Diogenes of Sinope, 245–46
Dionysius Thrace, 49–50
disaster, 37, 56, 194
disbelief, 42, 92–93, 99, 105, 144, 227
  initial, 93, 144
disclosedness, 155–58, 162, 165, 168–69
  of the call, 165
disclosure, 38, 76, 119, 131, 151, 162, 165, 167, 169, 174, 225–26
discourse, xii, xiv, 34–35, 94, 99, 131–45, 151, 154, 162–66, 181–84, 200, 204–6, 212, 219, 221, 225–29, 235–36, 241, 245, 247, 251, 254
  argumentative, 8
  Christian, 46
  death-bringing, 262–65
  (*Rede*) general, 134, 151–52, 162–63, 166, 263
  genre of, 135–40, 145
  meaningful, xv, 97
  of the they, 163–68
  universal genre of, 204
disinterested, 7, 101–2, 194, 197
displacement, 140, 168
disposition, 33, 154, 156, 158, 161, 163, 167, 170–71
dissemination, 3, 9–10, 42
distance, 4, 84, 127–28, 197, 254–55
distortion, 4, 38, 54, 226, 228
distress, 8, 11–12, 79, 128, 159, 162, 170–73, 213, 218, 241
distrust, 30, 63, 140, 206, 225–27
divine power, 16, 185, 187–88
dolls of ash, 41–44, 47, 62
double, the, 44, 46, 174, 194, 196

doubt, 10, 37, 63, 142, 146, 168, 249–50
doxosophia, 10–11, 272
dualism, xii, 110, 243–44
duality, 9, 35, 47, 70, 172–73, 180–81, 198, 226
dumbness, 50, 62
dunamis, 75, 132, 211–13
dwelling place, 40–41, 58, 60–64, 171

embodiment, 104, 243–44, 253, 255–56
encounter, 258–70
  with reality, 206, 265
engagement, 21, 135, 181, 189, 195, 197–98, 206, 234–39, 265
enthusiasm, 178, 184–85
enthusiast, 184–88
epiphany, 146–49
epistemology, 203–4. *See also* testimony
  analytic, 130
  epistemological, xiv, 125–26, 129–31, 136–37, 143–44, 188, 203, 205, 222
  social, 129, 241
esigenza, 36, 56, 128, 152, 241. *See also* demand
ethics, 41, 135, 178, 206, 255
ēthopoiēsis, 6, 244
ethos, 109–10, 135–36, 206, 247
  of philosophical dialogue, 28
ēthos, 147, 242, 246, 256
euchē, 21, 132, 154, 221, 228, 232
Euclides, 22–23, 32
event, xii, xiii, 3, 4, 37, 45, 70, 92, 95, 126, 128–29, 155, 160–61, 169, 182, 193–99, 210, 233, 237, 244–45, 248–52, 255, 263. *See also* testimony
  extraordinary, 146–47

linguistic, 99, 134
marvelous, 148
normal, 144
of speech, 17, 23
traumatic, 248–51
everydayness, 157, 159, 163–65, 170–73, 178, 180
exception, 6, 77–78, 82, 114, 117, 128, 133, 139, 143, 161, 164, 166, 180, 224, 251
exceptionality, 143, 152, 156
exceptional phenomenon, xiv, 152–56
exigency, 56, 208
exile, 37, 107–11, 116–17, 128
existence, 6, 7, 10, 37–44, 58–62, 67, 69–72, 76, 78–85, 89, 93–95, 108, 112, 115, 128, 151, 157, 162–73, 178, 181, 196, 199–200, 208–19, 222–25, 240–49, 253–56, 259, 264, 266, 269
  bare, xi–xv, 178, 213–14, 253
  mode of, xiii, 5, 160, 163, 168–69, 216, 242–49
  mute, 85
  naked, 128, 169, 172–73, 254
expectation, 92–93, 146, 148, 164, 281
experience, xii–xv, 3, 6, 10, 12, 15, 37–39, 45, 47, 49, 55, 63–65, 69–72, 74, 78–85, 89–95, 99, 103–4, 111–16, 118, 120–21, 126–27, 136, 145–48, 155–56, 159, 162–63, 174–75, 178, 181–82, 194–97, 199–200, 205, 207, 213, 222, 228, 248–52, 254, 258–59
  lived, 89, 90
  self-, xiii
  traumatic, 70
experiment, xv, 7–8, 13–18, 33, 36, 38–39, 41, 45, 49, 51, 53–55, 64,

experiment *(continued)*
   69–70, 72, 90–91 107, 109, 115, 131–33, 142, 146, 160, 207, 266
   literary, 1, 3–6, 12, 37, 87, 89, 97, 112, 117, 125–26, 128, 149, 170, 183, 195, 206–7
   scientific, 5, 6
explication, 5, 15, 139, 153, 155, 164, 179, 190, 222–24
expression, 9, 16, 43–44, 48, 54, 58, 65, 71, 74, 80, 89–93, 99, 102–3, 115, 127, 134, 139, 154–55, 179, 214, 222, 225, 240, 244, 263–64, 268
eyewitness, 55, 190

faith, 70–78, 81–82, 93, 101, 135–37, 141, 143–47, 165–69, 174, 194, 197, 228–29, 245
   primordial, 167–68
falsehood, 53, 142, 221–22
falsity, 5, 37, 62, 134, 154, 191, 206, 222, 226, 228, 233
father, 22, 27, 31, 38–39, 44
   absent, 28
fatherland, 107, 109
Ferraris, Maurizio, 203
fiction, 3, 4, 37, 56, 66, 125, 131, 147, 227–28, 250
fidelity, 197, 239, 244, 246, 253
finitude, 41, 192–93, 205, 249
First World War, 55. *See also* Great War
fore-structure (*Vor-Struktur*), 155, 160
fore-understanding (*Vorverständnis*), 155–56, 160
forgetfulness, xiv, 118–22, 173, 228
   plain of, 39, 118
form of life, 109, 111, 218, 240, 242, 245, 247, 249, 253
formation, 88, 113, 217, 236, 238
   Bildung, 217, 291

formless, 88–91, 131, 214, 217–18, 238, 242, 253
formlessness, xii, 88–90, 93–95, 99–100, 104, 122, 172, 206, 212, 216
foster parent, 31
Foucault, Michel, 20, 128, 134, 232–47
fragility, 41–43, 228
fragment, 91, 93, 105, 118
Freud, Sigmund, 225
Fricker, Miranda, 126
friend, 7, 19, 21, 24–32, 55, 183–84
friendship, 21, 25–26

Gabriel, Markus, 203
Gadamer, Hans-Georg, 9, 16, 222, 257, 264, 266, 270
genre, 54, 133, 135–41, 145, 204
gesture, 3–4, 6, 8, 45, 61, 96–97, 100, 229
ghost, 31–32, 37, 65, 95, 253
gift, xiii, 33–34, 36, 45, 47, 155, 160–64, 215–16
   funereal, 60
Glaucon, 111–12, 122
glōssa, 179
glossolalia, 49, 80–81, 109, 133, 178–83. *See also* speaking in tongues
glossolalist, 81, 85, 88, 179–81, 184, 190, 254
God, 6, 16, 38, 53, 64, 71–72, 79–83, 85, 109–10, 116, 178, 180, 185, 187–88, 192, 198, 208–9, 224, 230–32, 247, 255, 263–64
   gods, xiii, 12, 15–17, 44, 53–55, 58–60, 84, 111–12, 184–92, 221, 230, 249, 263
Gorgon, 45, 260–63
governance, 237, 241–42, 251
grace, 43, 248, 268
gramma, 6, 9, 48, 51, 97, 161

Index

Great War, 55–56, 63–66. *See also* First World War
Gregory of Nazianzus, 240
guarantee, 29, 137, 142, 188, 191–94, 198, 229–34, 263
guard, xii, 32, 38, 51, 71, 132
guardian, 27, 183–84
guardianship, 29–30
Guattari, Félix, 107–10
guilt, 167, 169
guise, 12, 143, 146–49, 189
gumnos, xi–xii

habit, 58, 64, 97, 115–17, 145–46, 244–45
habitualness, 101
hardship, 70
Harman, Graham, 203
hearer, 130–37, 140–43, 147, 149, 154–55, 159–70, 173–75, 178, 199, 206, 225, 227–29, 236–37, 241, 247, 254, 266, 269. *See also* testimony
hearing, 7, 72, 81, 100, 134, 181, 189, 210, 223
  new possibilities of, 140–41, 163, 236
Hegel, G. W. F., 75, 77, 78
Heidegger, Martin, xiv, 9, 11, 15–16, 18, 21, 24, 35, 38–41, 63–64, 75, 78, 114–21, 128, 134, 140, 142, 145, 151–82, 185, 188, 197, 203–4, 206, 213–14, 216, 221–26, 241–45, 265
heir, 16, 27, 55, 61, 84, 89, 111, 245
Helena, 13, 53, 55–66, 131, 205, 207, 227
herald, 223
heritage, 27, 29–30, 95
hermēneia, 34, 153, 180, 222
hermeneutic, 9, 17, 72–76, 92–93, 100, 112, 154

hermeneutics, 3, 12, 15, 72, 91–92, 153, 222–26
  of the letter, 9–10
Hermes, xiii, 16, 53–55, 57, 61, 67, 84, 89, 111
hero
  tragic, 74, 76
hesitation, 8, 31, 102, 121, 146, 177, 189, 224, 231–32, 257, 260
heterogeneity, 103. *See also* otherness
heterogeneous, 103, 138
history, xi, xiv, 5, 129, 192
  anonymous, 66
Hölderlin, Friedrich, 40
homeland, 107–9
hope, 36–37, 85, 137–38, 189, 258, 260–61, 265–66, 269–70
horizon, 5, 16, 18, 130, 139, 160, 164, 197, 214, 219, 225, 245
  common, 102, 156
  of meaning, 9, 39, 100, 138, 140, 156–59, 168, 223–24
  of understanding, 102, 128, 131–36, 142–45, 156, 161, 163, 166, 174, 197, 224, 245
horror, 40, 261, 267
house
  of being, 40–41, 62–63, 265
  of horror, 40
Howe, Thalia, 261–62
humanity, 44–45, 47, 70, 90, 92, 98, 103–5, 196, 212
humankind, xii–xiii, 215, 256
Hume, David, 129–30, 136–37, 144–49
Hurbinek, 47, 50, 199, 260–61
Hyginus, 310
hypocrite (*hupokritēs*), 104

identity, 27, 46, 96, 103–4, 126, 242
idiolect, 83, 85, 133
idiom, 85, 90, 139–40, 231, 247

idle talk (*Gerede*), 163
illusion, 3, 10, 226–27
imagination, 184, 249–50
immediacy, 3–4, 147, 167
immemorial, 114
imperative, 3, 6, 8–9, 18, 31, 56, 62, 92, 178, 205
impersonation, 28–32
impossibility, 75, 91, 139, 142, 188, 211, 261, 263
improbability, 147
  improbable, 82, 147
in-between, 102
inaccessibility, 128
inadequacy, 9, 41, 43
inarticulate babble, 260
inauthenticity, 165, 168, 170
incapacity, 25–26, 47–48, 63–67, 74, 121, 198, 204–6, 211–12, 216, 228, 242, 246, 251–52, 260, 262, 264, 267–68
  incapacitated, 159, 186, 188, 263
  to speak, 66, 185–88, 199
incommensurability, 83, 94
incommunicable, 77, 96
incomprehensibility, 76, 98, 100
incomprehension, 42
indecisiveness, 12
individual, 5, 77, 80, 181–82, 269
infancy, xi, xiii, xiv, 35, 66, 67, 122, 128, 172, 199, 206, 216–19
infant, xiii, 81, 121–22, 171–72, 214, 216–18. See also child
inhabitability, 38
inhumanity, 93–94, 98, 100, 104, 262
injustice, 19, 27, 29, 57, 138, 171
innerworldly being, 156, 171
inoperative, 35, 74, 98
insignificance, 185–86
intention to signify, 34, 49–51, 81, 97, 100, 161–62, 179–82

interpretation, 7, 9, 25, 28, 30–31, 34, 46, 48, 65, 72–73, 94, 105, 108, 115, 120–21, 126, 128, 134, 153–55, 167, 171, 180–81, 185, 223–26, 261, 267
  conflicting, 225
interpreter, 9–18, 21, 23–32, 38, 42, 53–54, 62, 73, 80–81, 87–89, 104, 126–27, 179–87, 190, 223–24, 257
  -witness, 183
invention, 53, 69, 116, 247
involvement, 196–97, 234–35
inwardness, 95
irony, 79
  Socratic, 31, 247
irruption, 134, 160, 235–36
istōr, 190–94

Jeremiah, 177, 184–88, 213
Johannes de Silentio, 41, 70, 72, 74, 81, 90, 94, 245
judgment, 25, 58, 77, 113, 144, 146, 268
justice, xiii, 25–35, 67, 101, 111–16, 133, 143, 154, 175, 192, 205–6, 210, 237, 245, 260
  undeconstructibility of, 113

Kafka, Franz, 196–97, 254
Kant, Immanuel, 204
Kearney, Richard, 227
keeping silent, 26, 193. See also remaining silent
kenos, 120
Kermode, Frank, 72–73
kerygma, 222–25
  kerygmatic, 222–23
  symbolic, 224–25
Kierkegaard, Søren, 12, 41, 64, 69–80, 84–85, 95, 128, 179, 181–82, 207, 217, 227, 240, 245, 254–55

knight
  of faith, 74, 76, 82
  of resignation, 74, 76
knowledge, 4, 8, 11, 24, 27, 76, 125, 129, 144, 240, 249
  divine, 7

lament, 44–45, 62, 67, 159, 213
lamentation, 208–9, 213, 261
language
  capacity of, 62–63, 74, 231–32
  divine, 54, 80–85, 88, 178–83
  incapacity of, 63, 199, 260
  of the living, 61
  major, 90
  poetic, 59, 62, 69, 74–75, 85
  testimonial, 62, 152, 239
law, xi, 58, 94, 98–99, 112, 139, 148, 191, 228, 249, 253
legend, 6–8, 174
Leibniz, G.W., xiv, 207–12, 216
lēthē, 39, 118–21, 173
letter, 3–12, 15, 33, 48–51, 54, 81, 89, 97, 137, 161–62, 243–44
  dead, 50, 91, 206–8, 212–13
  exceptional, 8
Levi, Primo, 50, 251–55, 258, 260–61
Levinas, Emmanuel, 104, 151, 159, 269
lie, 63, 146, 227, 229, 233, 260
life, 5–8, 22, 35, 37, 39, 41–46, 53, 55–56, 59, 69, 73, 82, 84, 97, 99, 104–5, 107, 109–22, 127, 136, 141, 148, 172, 193–97, 207, 214, 217, 221, 233, 236, 239–57, 265
  bare, xi, xiv, 45, 128, 199, 254
  foreign, 94
  human, xii–xiv, 4, 11–12, 66, 70, 92, 93, 113, 212, 218, 242, 245–46
  nonhuman, 88, 91, 103

limbo, 58–62, 114, 127, 208
limit, 18, 34, 40, 54, 70, 74, 76, 91–93, 108, 157, 159, 183, 258
listener, 23, 30, 32, 127
literary, the, xv, 4–6, 10, 12, 90, 97, 116–17, 128, 149, 207, 257
literature, xi, xiii, xv, 6–8, 89–90, 97, 109, 140, 189, 203–6, 216
Locke, John, 136, 146
logos, xii–xv, 8–10, 15–16, 33–35, 45, 47–49, 53, 89–90, 109, 111–13, 117, 134, 147, 151–57, 161–62, 167, 182–84, 203, 209–10, 213, 219, 221–22, 226, 230, 232–33, 241, 246–47, 253, 256, 258
logos apophantikos, 153–54, 221, 226, 232
logos hermeneutikos, 152–53, 155, 157, 161, 222
loss, 64, 159, 187, 189, 248, 264
  irreplaceable, 26, 32
Lyotard, Jean-François, xi, xiii, xiv, 5, 33–38, 47–48, 54, 66, 83, 97, 128, 137–42, 172, 192–93, 199, 203–6, 210, 216–18, 235, 242–43, 251–52

machine, 94
  copying, 98
  writing, 98
machinery, 75, 99, 145, 186–88, 237, 244
  divine, 187–88
  of the law, 98
martus, 190, 194, 239, 247
martyr, 82, 193–94, 197–98, 239–40, 244–45, 247, 249, 253, 255–56
  -convert, 249
martyrdom, 82
Marx, Karl, 225
masters of suspicion, 225, 227

mediation, 16, 23, 70, 82, 187, 223, 255
  without, 23
mediator, 23, 188
medium, 23, 40, 74, 77–79, 114
Medusa, 259–62
Meillassoux, Quentin, 203
Meindl, Dieter, 91
melancholy, 104, 187, 200
Melville, Herman, 5, 13, 87–91, 104, 207
memory, xiii, 4, 56–57, 60–61, 107, 120, 129, 144, 228, 249, 252, 254
meridian, 257–58, 266–69
message, 11, 16, 53–54, 61, 84, 103, 185–88, 223
messenger, 13, 30, 53, 61, 83, 107, 113, 117–18, 122, 185, 189–90
  divine, 186
  of the gods, 15
messianic, 207, 246–47
Messianism, 232
militantism, 243–44
mind, 7, 30–31, 50, 59–60, 65, 83, 88, 96–97, 100–1, 131, 174, 179, 184–85, 187, 195, 214, 244, 258
minorization, 90
miracle, 125, 129–31, 137, 143–49, 169, 203, 205, 207, 210, 244
misery, xii, 4, 5, 11–12, 36–37, 41, 43–44, 46–47, 51, 70–72, 87, 104–5, 115, 117, 122, 127–28, 131–32, 141, 172, 190, 206–8, 212–13, 216, 218, 238, 243–47, 257, 259, 262, 264
mistrust, 63. *See also* distrust
mode of life, 5, 6, 240–47, 251, 256
mood, 35, 38–39, 78, 94, 99–100, 102, 105, 156
Mortier, Erwin, 12, 55–56, 60, 62, 66, 120, 195, 205, 227, 260, 263
mother, 36, 44, 57–60, 65–66

motionlessness, 56, 97
mouth, 57, 60, 80, 185–86, 261–62, 268
mouthpiece, 29, 32, 57, 186
muein, 38, 128, 132
murmuring, 38, 45, 47
muselmann, xiv, 252–54, 261, 263
muteness, 36, 38, 47, 143, 257–58
muthos, 8, 112, 116, 174, 184, 270
mystery, 33, 36, 38, 45, 47, 72, 88, 128, 258
  mysterious, 72, 94, 104, 113–14, 121, 253, 259
myth, xii–xiv, 3–4, 7, 10, 53, 128, 215, 217, 221–22
  of Er, xii, xiv, 8, 13, 39, 111–22, 173–74, 184
  lover of, 7. See also *philomuthos*
  Platonic, xii

nakedness, 64, 70, 141, 171, 206, 217, 245
Nancy, Jean-Luc, 15–18, 75, 101, 166, 222–24
narration, 41, 44, 55, 73, 90
narrative, 40, 44, 69, 72–73, 185
narrator, 38, 42, 45, 87–105, 127, 133, 135, 181, 207
  -witness, 55, 206, 248–55, 260, 264
negativity, 157, 161
negotiation, 98–99
Neo-Platonism, 95
Nietzsche, Friedrich, 38, 188, 225, 227, 243
noise, 262
  inarticulate, 34, 48
non-sense, 50
nonsense, 31, 93, 100
nothingness, xiv, 158, 169, 172–73, 178, 182, 214, 266–67
novel, 3–4, 12, 37–38, 40, 45–46, 55–66, 71, 75, 91

nuda vita, xi, xiv, 44, 128
nullity, 185–89

oath, 128, 134–35, 174, 190–93, 221, 228–33, 237, 239, 245–46, 256, 263
object, 6, 15, 38, 64, 87, 89, 141–44, 160, 170, 174, 181, 187, 191, 195, 197–98, 200, 205–6, 218, 221, 225–26, 231, 235, 245–48, 254, 269–70. *See also* testimony
   partial, 128
obligation, 58, 77, 115
   of friendship, 25
   of reason, 25
offspring, 28–32, 133, 184
Oliver, Kelly, 126
ontology, 203–4, 208–9, 211, 242
   ontological squandering, 56, 59, 207, 212, 252, 264
orphan, 27–31, 38
otherness, 75, 204, 206, 225–26, 243. *See also* heterogeneity
out of joint, 54, 59, 64, 140, 210

pain, 33–35, 46, 49, 155, 159, 167
Pan, 53
paradigm, 4, 6, 186, 232, 235, 237, 241
paralysis, 74–75
Parmenides of Elea, 107
parrēsia, 20, 128, 134, 232–37, 240–42, 245
parresiast. 233, 235–36, 238, 241–42
participation, 83, 223
Pascoli, Giovanni, 49
pathos, 33–35, 145–49, 156, 163, 170, 195
patriarch, 38, 70, 79, 179
Saint Paul, 49, 80–81, 179–83, 207, 213, 240, 243–46, 248, 257
perception, xiv, 27, 37, 129, 144, 228

perfection, 209–12, 216
perhaps, 247–70
peril, 6, 11–12, 69, 71
perjury, 3, 37, 191, 227–29, 252
persuasion, 25, 147, 167, 198
perversion, 77, 104
Phaedrus, 3–11, 28, 108, 117, 262
philomuthos, 7. *See also* myth, lover of
philopoiētēs, 183–84
phōnē sēmantikē, 216
phrase, 26, 34, 58, 62, 71, 83, 94, 101, 110, 145, 170, 200, 203–6, 231, 235, 263–64, 266
   -affect, 33–36, 142, 204
   articulated, 36
   linking of, 138–39
   regimen, 204
   theory of, 138–42, 203–4
phugē, 110
pheugein, 109
phusis, 39, 40, 118
pistis, 137, 229, 245
pistos, 147, 229–30, 242, 245
placeholder, 200, 264
Plato, xi, xii, 3, 8, 12–18, 21, 23–24, 28, 39, 69, 75, 97, 104, 107–16, 121, 174, 183–84, 192, 215, 221, 223, 241–44
pleasure, 33–34, 49, 155, 159, 208
Plotinus, 95
pneuma, 90, 258
poet, 13, 16–17, 40–41, 49, 53, 57–59, 62, 65, 69–75, 78–90, 133, 135, 174–75, 179–90, 198, 245, 254–55, 257, 263, 265, 268
poetics, 139, 257
poetry, 5, 60, 71, 160, 183, 257–63, 266–67, 270
poiēsis, 6, 74, 242, 265
polis, xii, 108, 110, 117, 183, 212
possibility
   discursive, 164

possibility *(continued)*
  not to, 188
  unforeseen, 164
potentiality, 122, 142, 160–61, 164, 169, 172, 204, 206, 208–18
  authentic, 160
  potentiality-of-being-one's-self (*Selbstseinkönnen*), 160
  to speak, 26, 217
poverty, xii, 4, 5, 35–36, 41, 70, 115, 132, 172, 200, 212–18, 246
  linguistic, 128
  phenomenological, 128
prayer, 132, 154
preparedness, 172–73
principle of sufficient reason, 209
privation, 46
probability, 145–48
Prometheus, xiii, 215
promise, 9, 12, 36, 42, 54, 62–63, 67, 72, 76, 82, 113, 117, 129, 133, 134, 138, 152, 154, 164, 189–91, 193, 200, 207, 218, 221, 227–29, 232, 253
  of language, 11, 43, 47, 51, 97, 135, 142, 157, 173, 175
  as *Zusage*, 129, 152, 173–74
propaganda, 63, 228, 260, 263, 265
prophet, 88–89, 179, 184–90, 254
prostates, 183–84
Protagoras, xiii, 11, 24–32, 36, 65, 121, 126, 133, 175, 183–84, 215–18, 251
pseudos, 192
psuchē, xii, 271
punishment, 191–92
  Fair, 44–45
pyramid of possible worlds, 208, 210

reader, 6, 9, 29, 37, 69, 75, 99, 120, 122, 153, 243, 269
realism, 140–41, 203

reality, 12, 35, 40–42, 54–55, 59, 94, 129, 131, 137, 141, 146, 149, 158, 173, 192, 198, 203–6, 209–12, 222, 225, 230, 256–62, 265–70
receiver, 136
redemption, 59
refusal, 18, 20, 21, 25–27, 29–30, 32, 65, 228
refutation, 25–26, 274
Reid, Thomas, 129, 136, 144–45
remainder, 34, 69, 109, 137, 194, 218, 231–32, 248
  singable remainder (*singbarer Rest*), 266–67
remaining silent, 24–25, 126, 245. *See also* keeping silent
remembrance, 84, 118, 158, 207
repetition, 23, 58, 65, 69, 77
representation, 23, 48
resemblance, 90, 145–46, 148, 179–81
  human, 92–93
reserve, 4, 26, 32, 34, 36, 45, 47, 69–71, 75–76, 79, 94–96, 99–105, 109, 127, 131–33, 135–37, 141–43, 152, 157, 161, 182, 200, 212, 219, 221, 237–38, 264–68. *See also* testimony
  austere, 95–96, 99, 104–5, 128
  of the perhaps, 266
  poetic, 266
  reserve/object, 127, 130–37, 140, 143, 149, 152, 155, 159, 162–64, 169–75, 190, 192, 195–99, 203, 206, 213, 216, 224–29, 236, 244, 250, 253–56
reservedness, 4, 95
residue, 26, 32, 274
resoluteness (*Entschlossenheit*), 164–68, 172–73
restraint, 4, 136
resurrection, 56–57, 82, 129, 148, 243
revelation, 146–49, 180
revocation, 158, 288

rhapsode, 16–17, 184–85
Ricoeur, Paul, 65, 92–93, 99, 146, 168, 200, 222–28, 230, 234–35
ridiculous (*geloios*), xii, 7–8, 11, 115, 272–73, 282. *See also* spectacle
righteousness, 8, 110–12, 116–17, 121–22
risk, 8, 10–12, 28–30, 54, 62–63, 84, 94, 111–12, 132, 182, 189–90, 227–28, 241
  unspecified, 235–36
ritornello, 107–9, 122
ruach, 258, 300
Ruf, 159, 162, 290. *See also* call

Sage, 173–74
Saint-Simon, Duc de, 41
salvation, 109, 207, 247
sayability, 133, 209–11, 219, 247
scandal, 245–47
Schmidt, Dennis, 113
scholar, 143
scholē, 7
secrecy, 72, 82, 132, 173, 190, 193
secret, 36–40, 44–45, 51, 64, 69–88, 132, 186, 250, 254–60, 268–69
  dark, 69, 72
  keeping the, 84
  telling the, 74
secretarious, 13, 33, 38, 40–45, 51, 70, 132
self, 8, 10, 20–21, 44, 110, 163, 165, 184, 237, 241, 248
  -attestation, 11, 128, 250
  -care, 25, 122, 241
  -expression, 49
  -governance, 237
  -identity, 248
  -knowledge, 3, 6, 8–9, 241
  -presence, 3
  -understanding, 25, 240
selfhood, 160

semantics, 49
semiotics, 12, 49–50, 161–62
separation, 92, 105, 110, 114, 117, 178, 266–67
Sextus Empiricus, 268, 301
shadow, 127, 131–32, 137, 141, 190, 264, 267–68
Shakespeare, William, 70
shock, 43–44, 47, 99, 162
signification, 9, 11–12, 49, 139, 161, 179, 188
signifier, 9, 12, 100, 103
silence, 25–26, 29, 30, 32, 45–46, 74, 78, 82–83, 99, 105, 135, 162, 173–75, 237, 253, 257–58, 262, 266
  empty, 158–59
slave, xi, 32, 87
  anonymous, 22, 32
Socrates, 3–15, 18–32, 53, 65, 97, 107–12, 116–22, 126, 133, 175, 183–86, 192, 222, 241, 251, 262
soldier, xii, 56, 63, 111
sōma, xii, 268
song, 16–17, 84, 185
Soucy, Gaétan, 12, 37, 38, 40, 46, 55, 60, 62, 64, 257
soul, 3, 7–8, 10–12, 107, 110–22, 127, 173, 184, 203, 241
  bare, xi–xiv
sovereignty, 246–47
  divine, 187–89
speaker, 16–20, 24, 26, 28–32, 43, 114, 116, 148, 182, 192, 227–29, 233, 235–36, 242, 252–53
  absent, 18
speaking
  in tongues, 80, 83, 179–80. *See also* glossolalia
  on behalf of, 26
spectacle, xii, 115–16, 122, 245
  ludicrous, 8, 241. *See also* ridiculous

330 INDEX

speech, 11, 17–23, 28–34, 45–47, 49, 53–54, 65–67, 79–81, 83, 42, 157–58, 161, 164, 166, 178–85, 188–89, 210, 212, 216–18, 221, 238, 253, 257–62, 265–66, 268
  decay of, 28
  human, xv, 33, 217, 232, 261, 270
  living, 15, 17–18, 21–22
  mode of, xv, 29–32, 65, 79, 132–33, 154, 179–82, 184, 210, 232–34, 241–43, 260
speechless, 138, 156, 197, 251, 262, 270
speechlessness, 70, 263
Spinoza, Baruch, 41
spirit, 19–20, 67, 80, 90, 180, 189, 196, 207
  living, 58, 213
steadfastness, 147
Stiegler, Bernard, xiii, 215
Stimmung, 35, 78, 84, 145, 155–58, 161, 171
story, xii, 3–8, 11–12, 22, 37, 38, 41, 44, 51, 55, 56, 71–73, 78, 83–84, 87–101, 104–5, 111–22, 127, 131, 184–85, 195, 206–7, 215–16, 218, 228, 248–52, 255–56, 268
  untold, 63, 65–66
strangeness, 108, 258–62, 265–66, 268
subject, 10, 32, 78, 80, 91, 129, 136–37, 141–44, 159, 170, 172, 182–83, 187–89, 231–45, 248, 255, 269. *See also* testimony
subjectification, 135, 182, 233–37, 240–42, 251
subjectivity, 182, 234, 240
substitute, 28, 119
sufferer, 194–200
suffering, 46, 65, 100, 194, 205, 260
superstes, 190, 193–99, 239, 247–51
supplement, xiii, 16, 22–23, 28, 48, 71–72, 83–85, 108, 142, 172, 197–98, 215–18, 250

  original, 16
  of writing, 23
survival, 122, 195, 215–16, 247–49
survivor, 55, 58, 60–61, 194–200, 239, 247–55, 263
suspension, 66, 69, 114, 209–10, 221–22, 230–31, 237, 250, 266
  of judgment, 268
suspicion, 37, 63, 128, 168, 205, 225–27, 230
swearing, 191, 229–31, 233
symbol, 222–26

tale, xii, 27, 84, 193, 194, 270
teacher, 18, 22, 82
technē, xiii, 49, 218, 242
technics, xiii, 215, 217
Terpsion, 22, 32
testimony
  absence of, 65–66, 175, 199, 263
  act of, 131–36, 140, 164, 174, 195, 236, 253
  affirmation of, 129, 168
  announcement of, 221, 239
  distinctive sense of, 123, 129, 136–37
  element of, xv, 125, 130, 134–39, 151, 159–60
  epistemology of, 125, 129–30
  ethics of, 135, 206
  event of, 130, 142
  exemplary, 137
  false, 226–27
  and fiction, 125, 131, 147, 250
  guarantee of, 191, 193
  hearer of, 130, 133–36, 141, 143, 187, 197, 252, 270
  impossibility of, 261
  incompleteness of, 253
  interruption of, 173
  limit of, 91
  of literature, 3, 12, 206

missing, 252
of miracles, 143–45
object of, 126–27, 130–34, 141–42, 195, 197, 219, 236–37
ontology of, 203
perhaps of, 137, 228
poetic, 65, 139, 259, 262, 264
possibility of, 142, 229
precarious nature of, 168
of reality, 230
reserve of, 132–35, 141–42, 221
reserve/object of, 127, 130–35, 140, 155, 169, 171, 192, 198, 206, 213, 227, 229, 244, 250, 254
subject of, 130, 133, 135, 178, 194–96, 234, 236, 242. *See also* witness
of the superstes, 197, 199
survivor's, 199–200, 252–53
symbolic, 230
task of, 247
theory of, xiv
true, 226, 255
trust in, 137
truth of, 151
untruth of, 221, 233
vulnerability of, 228
testis, 91, 190, 193–98, 239, 254
testis unus, testis nullus, 91
the They (*das Man*), 159–60, 163, 165–66, 168, 169
Theaetetus, 12, 15, 18, 21–32, 38, 47, 65, 87, 109–10, 133, 183–84, 251, 273–75, 281
theodicy, 208, 295
Theodorus, 18–32, 36, 126, 133, 175, 183, 251
thinking, xi, xiii, 5, 46, 75, 80, 97–98, 112, 127, 149, 160, 203, 216, 246–47
Thrasymachus, 111
threshold, xii, xiv–xv, 21, 40–41, 45, 48, 53–54, 65, 70, 83, 85, 96–97, 104–5, 108, 113–14, 122, 133, 135–36, 138–40, 142, 149, 151, 154, 157, 161, 163, 170, 172, 181, 183, 190, 194, 196, 201, 203–4, 209–10, 212, 219, 225–27, 231, 245, 253, 256, 266–67
of language, 45, 212
thrownness (*Geworfenheit*), 157, 214
tongue, 10, 36, 54, 57, 80–85, 88, 90, 95, 103, 179, 180–86, 245, 261–62
common, 83–85, 90
divine, 54, 81
human, 54
mother, 36
speaking in, 80, 83, 179–80
topos daimonios, 111, 113, 115–20, 122, 127, 173
trace, 61, 73, 79, 81, 94, 117, 127, 158, 210, 263
tradition, 39, 46, 92, 129, 148–49
transformation, 5, 54, 60, 88, 160, 205, 236, 244, 246
of the self, 20, 241
transgression, 51, 54, 62
translator-poet, 85
transubstantiation, 129
trauma, 70
traversal, 54
trenches, 56, 195
trial, xii, 183
tribunal, 36, 83, 85, 92, 183, 193, 205, 210
trip up, 19
trust, 26, 30, 37, 42, 63–64, 99, 136–37, 140, 147, 174, 175, 206, 224–27, 230–31
trustworthiness, 22, 37, 62, 126, 143, 147–48, 222, 230, 233–35, 242, 246, 249
trustworthy, 37, 62, 92–93, 134, 136, 166, 229–30, 235, 246

truth, 3–12, 15, 18, 20–21, 25, 32, 37, 40, 54, 58, 62, 66, 73, 77, 82, 89, 101, 117–18, 120, 134–35, 143, 146, 151, 154–55, 162, 166–69, 174, 191–92, 194, 197, 199, 217, 221, 226–55, 264, 299
  in the name of, 3–8, 10, 134
  to live, 4
  sworn to the, 4, 191, 221, 228, 233, 245
truthfulness, 168, 192, 194, 206, 221–22
turn of breath (*Atemwende*), 257–61, 265–66, 269
twin, 44–45, 70, 170
Tynnichus of Chalcis, 186
Typhon, 10, 241, 262, 301
tyrant, 235–36, 241

uncanniness, 8, 10–11, 44, 76, 155–58, 162–165, 169–72, 177, 214–15, 268
uncanny, xii, 40, 44, 47, 108–9, 114–15, 119, 157, 173, 178, 214, 230, 253, 259, 261, 263, 268–69
uncertainty, 129, 137, 228, 249, 259
undecidability, 12, 50, 149, 191, 227, 255
undecidable, 30, 54, 137
unexpected, 82, 98–99, 146, 237, 268
unforgettable, the, 56, 65–66, 118, 120, 131–32, 252
universal, 76–82, 85, 133, 145, 181–82, 195, 204, 209
unjust, 19–20, 113
unreliability, 192, 229, 233
untrustworthy, 135
untruth, 221, 226–27, 230, 233
upbuilding, 80, 180–84, 291
upright, 19–20, 218
urgency, 8, 64–65, 138, 265

vehicle, 63, 186, 188, 207
veridiction, 206, 232–42
victim, 63–64, 139, 151, 205, 228, 263, 277, 284, 287
vocalization, 154, 156, 161
vocation, 158, 288
voice
  absent, 17, 25–26, 30, 254
  alien, 170, 178, 183–84
  animal, 33–35, 49, 157, 217
  anonymous, 66
  articulate, 34–35, 38, 46–50, 67, 70, 83, 89–90, 151, 172, 190, 253
  of conscience, 155, 159–70, 177–79, 216
  dead, 24, 32, 49
  of the dead, 22, 24, 60
  divine, 16, 179, 186–90
  double, 17–18, 29, 32, 186, 189–90
  of the father, 22, 31
  give a, 1, 4, 12–13, 18, 23–24, 27–28, 31, 32, 44, 51, 55–56, 58, 90, 105, 126, 165, 183, 188, 236, 263, 270
  inarticulate, 33–36, 45–51, 66–67, 81, 83, 89, 152, 156, 159, 162, 167, 171, 173, 189, 199, 200, 204, 209, 216–17, 241, 251, 258
  lost, 29, 31, 126, 175
  meaningful, 33, 161, 216, 241
  mere, xv, 33, 154–55, 162, 171
  of misery, 11, 238
  mute, 36, 45, 47, 159, 173
  of the poet, 16, 83, 187
  poetic, 16, 70
  present, 17
  prophetic, 187–88
  sharing of, 16–17, 292
  silent, 25, 32, 133, 172, 228, 238, 251, 253
  of the survivors, 61

void, 26, 66, 119–20, 253–54
vow, 154, 174–75, 228–32, 239, 253
vulnerability, 63, 70, 214, 228

weakness, 28, 42, 63, 145–46, 192–93, 228–30, 246–47
what-can-perhaps-be, 147, 169, 218
what-is-borne-witness-to, 126–32, 141
wholly other, 223–26, 269–70
wisdom, 10–11, 215
  conceit of, 11, 272
  illusion of, 10
withdrawal, 78, 95, 112–13, 119–21, 174–75, 187
witness, 135–36, 190–200. *See also* testimony, subject of
  absolute, 127, 133, 190, 192–93, 199, 208–10, 221–22, 224, 226, 230–32, 251, 263–64 complete, 261
  involuntary, 103
  pseudo-, 84, 252
  single, 99
  split-, 133
  true, 32, 81, 84, 102, 191, 248–54, 263–64
  to the truth, 4, 89, 233, 239–40, 245, 251, 255
  for the witness, 231, 250
Wittgenstein, Ludwig, 46
wonder, 7, 31, 46, 50, 78–79, 129, 148–49, 170, 224
word
  power of the, 43, 47, 69
  sworn, 167, 231
world, xiv, 35, 38–41, 44, 55, 58–64, 72, 80, 89, 92–93, 103, 110, 113, 136, 156–58, 169–73, 178, 186, 204–5, 208–11, 214–15, 234, 239, 243–44, 246
writer, 43–44, 69
writing, xi, 8, 15, 22–23, 28, 42, 44, 65, 89, 97–98, 203, 216
  in the soul, 10–11
wrong, 33, 36, 116, 138–39, 141–42, 147, 204–5, 268–69

Yahweh, 185–87

Zeus, 6, 10
zōē, xiii
zōon logon echon, xiii, 34

www.ingramcontent.com/pod-product-compliance
Ingram Content Group UK Ltd.
Pitfield, Milton Keynes, MK11 3LW, UK
UKHW041915140426
5217IPUK00013B/168